WE LANDED BY MOON

WE LANDED
BY MOONLIGHT

Secret RAF Landings in France, 1940-1944

by

GROUPE CAPTAIN **Hugh Verity**

**DSO and bar, DFC,
Officier de la Légion d'Honneur,
Croix de Guerre avec palme**

Revised Edition

Crécy Publishing Limited

To the memory of those
who did not survive

Revised edition first published in 1995
by Airdata Publications Limited

This updated edition first published in 1998
by Crécy Publishing Limited

First published in 1978 by Ian Allan Limited

© Hugh Verity, 1995

Hugh Verity is hereby identified as author
of this work in accordance with Section 77
of the Copyright, Designs and Patents Act 1988

A CIP record for this book
is available from the British Library

Printed in England by Redwood Books, Trowbridge

ISBN 0 947554 75 0

Crécy Publishing Limited

1a Ringway Trading Estate, Shadowmoss Road, Manchester M22 5LH

Contents

Preface
by Monsieur Jacques Maillet

This book by Group Captain Verity is about the history of clandestine landings by the RAF in France during the occupation. It is astonishing and regrettable that this subject has up to now been mentioned only incidentally in some of the histories of secret warfare. Firstly, the history of these operations is an extraordinary adventure story. These operations involved clandestine radios; personal messages transmitted by the BBC; maquis volunteers keeping an armed guard; and, above all, the RAF pilots and aircrew who, at night, with no radio aids to navigation but only what they could see of the ground to fix their position, who, in spite of anti aircraft guns and German night fighters, had to land on a field lit by a few pocket torches. Each mission was an exploit whose success was only made possible by the extraordinary technical skill and high morale of the elite aviators who took part.

So this book is first of all an adventure story. But Group Captain Verity has also researched it with meticulous historical precision, using both the official RAF archives and also the evidence of very many British and French witnesses. So this book is also a useful contribution to History.

Here we are concerned with events which profoundly influenced the course of history. These operations were relatively few: some tens of aviators and some hundreds of travellers took part in them. But their historical importance was immense. Firstly for military operations, it was essential that those responsible for radio transmissions, for intelligence, for building up the secret army, should be able to visit London. When the time came for the battles for the liberation of France, the excellent co-operation of the French Forces of the Interior with the Allied armies owed much to these links.

But one must chiefly remember that these operations allowed those in France to group themselves into one fighting force with the Free French of General de Gaulle. On reflection, without them people like Jean Moulin, like Brossolette, like Morandat would not have been able to spin the webs, to build the structures, thanks to which the Resistance within France was organised under the orders of General de Gaulle. If France, in spite of the armistice in 1940 and the Vichy regime, was able at the liberation to re-establish itself as a great power, it was because General de Gaulle was able to speak in the name of France. And this was only possible because men could come from France to unite themselves around him.

Without clandestine air operations the Free French would have been a group of fighting men, no doubt a heroic and admirable group, but their Chief, General de Gaulle, would not have been able to speak in the name of France as a whole. In fact, thanks to the air operations described in this book, men and ideas could be exchanged between the French Resistance and first London and then Algiers. It was then that the Allies recognised that General de Gaulle spoke in the name of France.

It is not going too far to say that the clandestine air operations described in this book modified the course of the history of France. It would be justifiable to apply to the French and to the aircrew of RAF Tempsford the words of Winston Churchill on the subject of the British and their fighter pilots in the Battle of Britain: "Never in the field of human conflict was so much owed by so many to so few".

I have no doubt that the readers of this book will be grateful to Group Captain Verity for having written this history twice, once at the controls of his aeroplane and, thirty years later, with a pen in his hand for our pleasure and for our enlightenment.

Jacques Maillet
Compagnon de la Libération

Foreword

by Air Chief Marshal Sir Lewis Hodges KCB, CBE, DSO and bar, DFC and bar
Grand Officier de la Légion d'Honneur, Croix de Guerre

Almost every aspect of the many and varied roles of the Royal Air Force in the Second World War has been well documented in the many official histories, biographies and personal memoirs which have appeared during the last thirty years. The one omission amongst all these publications concerns the activities of the Special Duties Squadrons which carried out landings, mainly in France, ferrying agents to and from the Continent on their intelligence and sabotage tasks. The fact that the full and authoritative story of these special flying operations has not so far appeared is understandable as the official records have only recently been made fully available in the Public Record Office. Hugh Verity's account in this book fills a gap in the wartime history of the Royal Air Force which makes fascinating reading. I first met Hugh Verity in November 1942 when we both joined No 161 Squadron at Tempsford - he to fly the Lysanders and Hudsons while I joined the Halifax Flight to carry out parachute operations. My main recollection of those days was the tremendous spirit which permeated through the Squadron and everyone was completely dedicated to the job and proud to be associated with this special work. I remember particularly the importance of the moon. Operational flying was mainly confined to the moon period and was therefore very concentrated. Our lives were governed by the phases of the moon. We needed moonlight to map-read by; we needed moonlight to find our way to the dropping zones for parachuting and to the small fields that served as landing grounds; and we needed moonlight to be able to see the ground clearly enough to make a safe landing. This is a story of a remarkable group of young people - pilots and aircrew - engineers and mechanics and the supporting ground staff - all of whom in their separate and special ways contributed to the maximum to the important and demanding tasks that they were asked to undertake. This absorbing story certainly captures the spirit of the times and sets down for posterity the atmosphere, excitement and dangers of those days during World War Two.

Brunssum   L.M.H.
The Netherlands   1976

Author's Preface

In the Second World War the special duties air operations which created vital links with clandestine organisations in enemy held territories were developed to a remarkable extent in the Royal Air Force. They were flown by specialised squadrons into Europe from bases in Britain, North Africa and, later, Italy and Corsica. They were flown into territory held by the Japanese from bases in India and Ceylon and advanced bases in Burma. The United States air forces also joined in and quickly learned from the developed expertise of the RAF.

There have been references to these operations in books dealing primarily with secret operations on the ground and there have been other books of memoirs touching on some of these operations.

This is simply a subjective impression of one small part of the story - largely from the inside. It is about the clandestine air transport service which landed in occupied France to pick up agents and other important people who needed to come to England for the good of the allied war effort. It is written from the point of view of the flight commander of the pick-up flight of No 161 Squadron, Royal Air Force between November 1942 and November 1943. It also traces the history of RAF pick-ups in France from their origin in 1940 and covers the first half of 1944 when the author was organising clandestine air operations into Europe for the Special Operations Executive. It also quotes extensively from the recollections of a number of others who were involved.

At that time - and for some years afterwards - these operations were Top Secret. Although the German security services knew they were going on, they did not know the vital details: where? when? and who? (At least they did not generally know these details at the time). The effect of this secrecy was that we who were involved could only make oblique references to details in our log-books and we could not keep diaries. Although I have been through the relevant squadron and station operation records books in the Public Record Office this book has been written largely from memory - after over 30 years I am afraid memory fades on details. My apologies to any reader who can remember better than I can the details of the stories I tell. I would be grateful if any such reader would write to me. Since the first edition - and the editions in French - many readers have done so. Hence this extensively revised edition.   I hope that this book will illuminate the heroism of our passengers, the agents for all the various clandestine organisations, the resistance leaders, the political and military leaders. We were only vulnerable to the enemy on the ground for a few minutes at a time. They were at risk for months and years on end. It was they and their invaluable work that justified this unusual type of air taxi service.

Acknowledgements

My thanks are due to many published sources and to all those who put their memories at my disposal and lent me photographs. Most of these are listed in Appendix G. Drawings of people are by my daughter Charlotte.   It must be invidious to short-list here those who have made a specially substantial contribution to this book, but I cannot leave to the appendix my thanks to Moira McCairns, who lent me for a very long time the only copy of her husband's unpublished memoirs, which he had written after the war before he was killed in a flying accident. Air Chief Marshal Sir Lewis Hodges wrote not only the foreword, but also full accounts of several of his pick-ups specially to help me with this book and Sir Robin Hooper, whose detailed contemporary account of his time in France is quoted in full, also wrote extensive notes for my personal use. Peter Vaughan-Fowler went through my manuscript and greatly enriched it.

From the other side of the Channel I have had very full and detailed advice from Paul and Jannik Rivière, and from Michel Pichard. Between them they supplied very many detailed facts about particular pick-ups. Philip Schneidau too was an exceptionally helpful source, with a remarkable memory for details.

More references are made to Professor Michael Foot's *SOE in France* than to any other source. He has also been most helpful in advising me while I was working on the book. There are also many references to Marie Madeleine Fourcade's *Noah's Ark* and to Henri Noguère's *Histoire de la Résistance en France*.

I am also grateful to the publishers who have allowed me to quote passages from *The Big Network*, *The White Rabbit*, *Duel of Wits* and *Colonel Henri's Story*, and to Group Captain E.B. Haslam, Head of the Ministry of Defence Air Historical Branch, for invaluable advice.

Finally, there are three people without whom this book would not exist: Alan Hollingsworth, who asked me to write it; Beryl Walton, who voluntarily typed it all - much of it twice—in her spare time; and my wife, who has cheerfully accepted her part-time role as a 'book-widow' during holidays and most week-ends over three years.

Post Script for this revised edition

My warmest thanks to all the readers who have spoken or written to me to add to my story since the first English and French editions (*Nous Atterrissions de Nuit*, Editions France-Empire 1982, '88 and '89). I have acknowledged the help of most of them and of other sources in Appendix G. Some more recent sources are acknowledged in Appendix B.

I have had especially generous help in a variety of ways from: Colonel and Madame Louis Andlauer, Jacques Courtaud, Gervase Cowell, Sir Douglas Dodds-Parker, Sénateur Jean Fleury, Colonel Pierre Hentic, Air Chief Marshal Sir Lewis Hodges, Denis Johnson, Baron Fernand Lepage, Roger Lequin, Jacques Maillet, Air Commodore Henry Probert, Peter Procter, Pierre Raynaud, Marius Roche, Dr Michel Thoraval, Commandant Robert Wackherr, and Christopher Woods. I am most grateful to them all.

Finally, I must specially thank Barry Richards, Air Data's publisher, whose magnificent efforts achieved the recovery of the text from the corrected proofs when the former typesetter's computer was disposed of with this book in it - an original way of losing a book!

Hugh Verity 1995

PPS

The details in appendix B have been further revised and augmented thanks to recent research in France by Roger Lequin, General Lallart, Serge Blandin and Didier Fuentes. My warmest thanks to them and other correspondents including John Jammes for correcting the lack of accents on some French words.

Hugh Verity 1998

CHAPTER ONE

Pick-up Pilot

It was late summer in 1942 and approaching midnight. I was duty intruder controller in the intruder operations room at Headquarters Fighter Command, Bentley Priory, Stanmore. I was sitting with my assistant on a little platform in a bare room deep down below ground level. We had a sloping table below us, painted with an outline map and a reference grid. It was like the main map in the big air defence operations room next door, but ours was smaller, although it covered a wider area. This included the main bomber bases of the Luftwaffe in France and the Low Countries, as well as their probable targets in the UK. Two lively WAAF girls plotted any movements of either air force across the Channel and the North Sea.

Beside me sat my assistant, a Y-service officer (Y was short for Wireless Intelligence). He was told on the telephone any news we could pick up about the movements of the German bombers. My object was to 'scramble' (order off) long-range night fighters from bases in South-Eastern England to prowl round the German bomber bases at about the time they were taking off or - and this was easier to estimate - at about the time they returned to land after bombing England.

This was one of the nights when bad weather grounded both German and British bomber forces. On some of these nights I had noticed single RAF aircraft plotted as they crossed the Channel outwards and then, a few hours later, homeward-bound. These lonely singletons were called 'Specials' and I had not been told what they were. I wondered, but I gathered they were secret and not part of my private intruder battle.

I was contemplating just such a lonely single plot crawling south across the table when Dusty Miller came in for a chat. He had been the Senior Flying Controller at RAF Tangmere near Chichester. We had a cup of coffee and I asked him about the 'special'. He told me that it was a cloak-and-dagger Lysander. There were a few of them in a detached flight operating from Tangmere during moon periods to fetch agents from occupied France. They were commanded by a rather eccentric character called Squadron Leader Guy Lockhart. A previous flight commander called 'Sticky' Murphy had been ambushed in Belgium one night during the previous winter. I asked Dusty to tell me about it.

The agents, he said, were trained by the pilots to find suitable fields and describe them by wireless. They laid out miniature 'flarepaths' consisting of three pocket torches, tied to sticks, in the shape of an inverted 'L'. When the Lysander arrived they signalled a pre-arranged Morse letter with a fourth torch. If the pilot did not see the correct letter flashed his orders were to return to base.

On this trip to Belgium Sticky had found the field without difficulty. Not only was there a moon but there was also a little snow on the ground. He was put out to find that the signals flashed towards him did not give the right letter. He circled round, weighing up the situation. Should he just go home? Wasn't there a possibility that the agreed letter had been garbled in the messages by a primitive portable wireless? Perhaps the agent was in danger and needed to be rescued. He decided to land, acknowledging the flashing light by throttling back, momentarily, twice.

Because he was not quite sure what the reception committee might consist of - and as it was a clear night - he did not land on the 'flarepath' but well away from it. He taxied round and flashed his bright landing lamp towards the first torch. The beam lit up what seemed to be a company of German soldiers in their helmets. He turned through another 90° and took off without delay.

At this moment they started firing at him and, as he got airborne, he felt a bullet go through his neck. The Lysander was still in working order as far as he could see and he set course for Tangmere. He always carried with him as a lucky charm one of his wife's silk stockings which he managed to wind round his neck to reduce the bleeding. But when eventually he could call the tower on the radio telephone he sounded rather drowsy for he had lost a lot of blood.

Dusty said that they kept him awake by telling him rather blue limericks on the R/T and he made it eventually, though he had wandered off course on the way home. When he landed at Tangmere they found that the Lysander had been hit by 30 bullets.[1]

I was fascinated by the tale that Dusty Miller told me and I asked him a great deal more about it until he had to go. It was still a quiet night. There were no other movements plotted. Harris, the Y-service officer on watch, was reading a paperback by his little telephone switch-board. One of the girls was knitting. The strip lights over the table had been shaded to reduce the glare. The fan whirred quietly. I thought about what Dusty had told me.

Since I had started operational flying in 1940, I thought, I had not really achieved anything. I was already 24 years old and I had made no great contribution to the war. So what about these special operations? I had done a year's night flying on the Beaufighter, a much more difficult aeroplane to fly than the Lysander. I had read French and Spanish at Oxford and enjoyed various visits to France before the war. I would be able to train French agents in their own language.

There must be immense potential in the occupied countries of Western Europe - people who would be only too glad to do what they could to speed up the liberation of their countries. I thought that the rather specialised air transport service offered by these Lysanders could really do some good. It was four months since I had done any operational flying and this seemed long enough, so I decided to ask Dusty to arrange an introduction to Guy Lockhart, the flight commander.

On a subsequent evening I had another visitor to my intruder hole. This was Air Commodore Pearson. He startled me by talking in Spanish. I changed gear and replied in Spanish and we had a little chat. He then explained that there was a vacancy for an assistant air attaché for somewhere in South America. My papers said that I knew Spanish and he wanted to prove it. Would I like the job? It seemed a very odd idea in the middle of a war, but I asked him for time to think about it.

I thought about it for a day or two. I had a wife and son and another baby was on the way. I had been to South America and I knew I would enjoy it there if it were peace time. I well remember my debate with myself walking round the grounds of Bentley Priory under the stars. Against my responsibilities to my family I had to weigh the chance that we would lose the war. I found it quite impossible to accept the idea that I might survive to see my family (and millions of others) living under Nazi occupation, knowing that I might have done more to prevent it. Of course I did not imagine that my own contribution could be all that significant, but, whatever I could do had to be done.

Another, less worthy, idea influenced me. I was still suffering from a sense of private shame from my performance on the rugger fields of Cheltenham College. Here was an opportunity to demonstrate, at least to myself, that I need never again be worried by private recollections of physical cowardice.

Once I had calmly accepted what seemed to be the high probability of death, the problem solved itself. I went to RAF Tempsford near Sandy, in Bedfordshire, to see Guy Lockhart and Wing Commander Pickard to offer them my services as a Lysander pilot.

Guy was a striking looking, slim young man with good, rather thin features and wavy brown hair. He wore French military wings as well as his RAF wings, but on his right breast pocket. His shirt collar and cuffs, which were always showing, were well starched. He had a reputation as a successful card-player and keen gambler, who more than held his own in London bridge clubs.

Guy talked well, though he often said outrageous things. I gathered that he had already had to burn a Lysander that had been damaged on a field in France. Because of this, he did not particularly want to be on the run in France again.

He introduced me to the CO of 161 Squadron, Wing Commander P.C. Pickard. He was called 'F for Freddie' because of the part he had played in "Target for Tonight", one of those early war films, where he was the captain of a bomber called 'F for Freddie'. Pick, as he was called for short, was a big man, rather heavily built, with a pointed nose and very fair hair. He smoked a pipe. Whenever possible, on or off duty, he was accompanied by his Old English Sheepdog, Ming. He was still in his twenties but he seemed ten years older. One got the impression that he was driving himself hard and burning himself up. He had already earned a DSO and had led the Bruneval raid, when a company from the Parachute Regiment was dropped on a radar station. He had taken over 161 Squadron from 'Mouse' Fielden only very recently, on 1 October 1942.

161 Squadron had two flights: 'A' Flight had six Lysanders, plus one in reserve, for pick-up operations; 'B' Flight had five Halifaxes, two Wellingtons and one Hudson at that time, for parachute operations. The Halifaxes were large four-engined bombers converted for parachuting agents and packages through a hole in the floor of the rear fuselage and containers from the bomb-racks. Squadron Leader 'Bob' Hodges[2] was the CO of 'B' Flight.

Pick introduced me to the station commander, Group Captain E.H. Fielden[3], MVO, AFC. He had been the Prince of Wales' personal pilot and the Captain of the King's Flight, and had formed 161 Squadron. He looked more like a senior Army officer with his close-clipped moustache. I noticed a scarlet silk lining to his RAF uniform tunic. He could wear this because he had been Adjutant to an Auxiliary Air Force Squadron. After lunch they said they would like me to join 161 Squadron. It would take about a month to learn the job - if I could learn the job - then I would take over the Lysander flight from Guy Lockhart. He had done enough of these operations. I was - unworthily - rather pleased that I would be able to justify continuing as an acting squadron leader.

On 10 November 1942 I wrote to my wife - who was expecting our second baby at any moment - as much as I felt security would permit:

"...How I long to hear of your ops - It will be a great day...I have been offered several jobs lately.

"This Command is happy to offer me a night fighter flight with a strong recommendation for early promotion to wing commander.

"I am actually toying with the idea of another job which would mean very few operations and a lot of home life with you and co and which would be great fun. I hesitate to go back to the cushy and unprofitable life of a night fighter squadron, because I do not think the Hun will have much stomach for raiding this country after this North African show.[4]

"…How would you like to live with me for a fortnight each month?…It might be something like that…

"I am plainly relieved not to be going to South America at a time like this. It is far more suitable that an older non-operational type should do the job."

On 14 November I wrote to my parents:

"I am off to RAF Tempsford, near Bedford, tomorrow, to take up a new job which will give me a lot of fun and a real chance to make some personal contribution to the war as a whole. As the war swings from the defensive to the offensive, so do I go from Fighter to Bomber Command. My particular job will be an outstandingly important one that I am afraid I cannot describe to you. It will involve a little operational flying which will be very pleasant after four and a half months staff work and controlling.

"As I spent the first year of the war in Training Command, the second in Coastal and the third in Fighter, it seems fair that I should spend the fourth in Bomber. I have wangled my release from here with some difficulty, but my excuse is that Fighter have nothing much to do nowadays.

"I will be doing training only for a month and a half, after which I should be operational.

"I fear that this news may be unpleasant to you and Audrey. I am sorry. Personal fears and hopes must shrink before the importance to millions of people of shortening the war.

"I will come and look you up as soon as may be. Unfortunately, I am pressed to join my new squadron as soon as possible."

The next day I drove my old second-hand Morris 10 up to Tempsford. It was not much of an RAF station, I thought. It was a rush job quickly built in wartime like hundreds of others. Officers' mess, station headquarters, squadron offices and all the

RAF Tempsford in 1943.

rest were temporary huts. That winter of 1942-43 was cold and wet and there was a lot of mud.

There were two permanent buildings. One was the old Gibraltar Farm barn[5], discreetly situated away from the rest of the camp, where the containers were stored and the agents were strapped into their parachutes by their dispatchers with accompanying officers from SOE (Special Operations Executive) and other organisations. The other pre-war building, a few miles from the airfield, was the local manor house, Hazells Hall, which had been taken into military service as the sleeping quarters for the senior officers. I was glad to find that, if I had to share a bedroom, I was sharing it with Bob Hodges, the other newly arrived flight commander in 161 Squadron. This old house, which belonged to the Pym family, was lavishly decorated with glass cases full of stuffed birds. It stood in large gardens up a little hill near Sandy.

Now I could get to know the other pilots in the Lysander Flight. They were: Flight Lieutenant John Bridger, Peter Vaughan-Fowler[6], Jimmy McCairns ('Mac'), and Frank ('Bunny') Rymills, who had just been posted in from 138 Squadron, the other special squadron at Tempsford. They were as pleasant and amusing a little group of young pilots as I had met anywhere. All were different; all had strong personalities. Not all would be ideally suited to a conventional career in a peace-time service.

Peter was only 19 years old, 6 ft 2 in and remarkably good looking. His father had been one of the first naval aviators before World War One. I wondered if his good hands with an aeroplane had been inherited. He was a laconic young man. His main leisure pursuit was listening to the jazz of the day[7] in which he had a deep interest. Pilot Officer J.A. McCairns, MM (who survived the war but was sadly killed in a flying accident after it) had been a sergeant pilot in a day fighter squadron under Bader[8], whom he almost worshipped. He had been shot down behind the enemy lines, had evaded capture and was the first fighter pilot to return to fight on in World War Two.

Mac was a much smaller man with a thin face and a very bright twinkle in his eye. His hair, which was rather long on top for those days, was brushed straight back. He looked remarkably like the young King Peter of Yugoslavia. He always gave me the impression that he was highly charged with nervous energy. As I noted at the time, he was "frightfully polite, with an odd pseudo-Scots, half American accent".

Pilot Officer 'Bunny' Rymills DFM - who, like Peter, was very tall - had fair hair, a long nose and a rather casual manner. He was 21 or 22 years old and he had his honey-coloured cocker spaniel pup Henry with him whenever military discipline (or indiscipline) permitted. I gathered that one of his pastimes off-duty was keeping bees, but his favourite hobby was poaching and he was very good at it. Before the war he had been studying architecture. So far in the war he had done 50 operational sorties of which 26 were bombing raids and 24 were parachute dropping operations in No 138 Squadron.

Flight Lieutenant John Bridger was a rather older pilot. He looked exceedingly tough. Rather short, with curly black hair and a neatly trimmed moustache under a broken nose, he was less articulate than the others, even dour, but much more experienced. He had already completed something like 4,000 hours flying - an immense amount in those days.

By contrast, Peter had joined the flight in March, 1942 with only about 250 hours. A signal calling for experienced Lysander pilots to volunteer for special duties was intended to specify "at least 250 hours *night* flying experience". When this arrived at No 4 (Lysander) Squadron, the word 'night' was accidentally omitted. Peter was at the time six hours short of 250 hours *total* flying time, so he borrowed a Tiger Moth to add them on quickly before applying. It says something about the flexibility of mind of those in charge that he was accepted for the pick-up flight - in spite of his lack of experience - a decision which was rewarded by his outstandingly successful tour of duty in No 161 Squadron.

So this was the team of pilots I would be flying with and - very soon - commanding. I liked them all. I also got to know the 20 or so ground crew of 161 Squadron Lysander Flight, 'A' Flight. I specially remember young John ('Sam') Hollis, then a sergeant, who was to be such a tower of strength in making sure that all our Lysanders worked without fail.

My first flight in a Lysander was on 16 November 1942. That evening I was called to the telephone to hear the news that my second son had been born during the day in a nursing home in Cheltenham. Before I could get away to see my wife and little William, there were a few more days' hard training and when I did I told her that I was doing a different job but could not tell her what it was.

The training - which I was largely left to work out for myself - had to turn me into a competent special duties Lysander pilot in about a month. I had to be able to fly the aeroplane, to fly it by night, to land it short on a ridiculous little flarepath, and to navigate it by moonlight to any field in France.

I took stock of the situation. I had done about 850 hours, of which about 250 were by night. I had been trained as a navigator as well as a pilot, but I had not done very much pilot-navigation, and none of that had been at night. The others showed me how they prepared their route maps and worked out their flight plans, but I knew I needed a lot of practice.

First, however, I had to master the Lysander and learn the skill of landing it short on a patch of rough field no more than 20 yards from the light of a pocket torch.

The Lysander had been designed for daylight operations in close co-operation with the army, spotting for the gunners and lightly armed for ground attack. It had been built[9] for short landings on rough ground up near the front. For this reason the fixed undercarriage was basically an immensely strong alloy beam in the shape of a shallow inverted 'V'. The beam had been specially imported from Switzerland and was said to be virtually unbreakable.

It was a high-wing monoplane. The pilot had excellent views downwards on both sides but the Mercury engine in front somewhat obscured the forward view downward. The wings were equipped with automatic slats which lifted away from the leading edge as the speed decreased towards stalling speed. These slats controlled automatic flaps. Slow speed flight was therefore greatly simplified and it was possible to bring a Lysander down to land, if not like a lift, at least like an escalator.

Behind the pilot's cockpit was the 98 gallon inboard fuel tank and above it, behind the pilot's head, the oil tank. Behind these tanks was the air gunner's cockpit. During the fighting in 1940, the Lysander had been an easy prey for the Luftwaffe by daylight. Although it was very manoeuvrable at slow speeds, it was far too slow for Messerschmitt 109s.

When the first pick-up operations in France were laid on in 1940/41 it was ideal for conversion to this role. The little stub wings to which bombs or guns had been attached had been removed from the stream-lined spats round the wheels, as had the air gunner's gun mounting and other equipment. A fixed ladder had been added to the rear cockpit on the port side and a large torpedo shaped overload tank for 150 more gallons of petrol increased the radius of action very considerably. Peter Procter, at the time an Assistant Chief Designer at Westlands, was responsible for modifications to the special Lysanders. His note on them is at Appendix F.

The whole aeroplane had been painted matt black all over, in the mistaken belief that this would help to make it invisible at night. While this may have been true for searchlights, the night fighter's view from above on a moonlit night was a very different matter. We found that the silhouette against low cloud was far too positive. So I had the upper surfaces recamouflaged in dark green and pale grey.

The loose-leaf pilot's notes, reproduced from typescript in 1941, included about 10 pages of description with photographs and 10 pages of handling and flying notes. This was a very simple pilot's manual compared with others I have studied since. After sitting in the cockpit with these notes one could soon learn where every control, switch and gauge was and what it was for. One of the main controls in a Lysander was the tail plane adjusting handwheel, just below and behind the throttle on the port side. This was a very powerful control of the whole tail-plane's angle, and it was vital to get it right for landing and to adjust it for take-off. It was impossible to overcome it by pressure on the stick if one opened up to take-off power when the tail was adjusted for landing

The rest of the cockpit was reasonably typical of single-engined military aircraft of that generation. I sat in it (sitting on a parachute) and worked round it touching everything until I could find any switch or control blindfold. I learnt all the drills, checks and limits by heart.

On 17 November I did two hours flying, including a large number of circuits and landings on a daylight 'flarepath' with yellow flags instead of torches. We did this

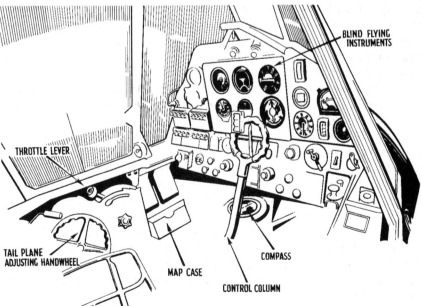

Lysander pilot's Instrument Panel.   HMSO

sort of training at Somersham. This was just a grass field not very far from Tempsford. As well as giving realistic practice for pilots, it was used for training the agents who would be finding fields for us in France and arranging our reception there. By 23 November I had flown the Lysander so much by day and night, once doing eight night landings in 40 minutes, that I was completely at ease with it as an aeroplane and perfectly happy with the short flarepath of three pocket torches in an inverted 'L' 150 yards long.

I was also practising my pilot navigation over England both by day and night. This I found much less easy, especially if the weather made long stretches of blind flying necessary. I found Tempsford to Exeter and back without landing - almost three hours - a reasonable practice route both by day and night.

During one of these practice cross-country flights at night, I got completely lost. I had made some mistake in map-reading over the blacked out towns and villages and felt a distinct urge to panic. How was I ever to lead this splendid team of young pilots if I got lost over Southern England? I reflected that I had been spoilt in the past. In Beaufighters in Coastal Command, I had always had a navigator to tell me where to go. In Beaufighters in No 29 Night Fighter Squadron, the ground controller was always in touch by radio telephone and watched one's blip on the radar screen. I resisted the temptation to call up for a homing bearing and sorted myself out. After a while I found a landmark on the ground that I could also find on the map, and I returned to base saying nothing about my little panic.

During the first half of December training at Somersham continued by day and night. The flight was running a short course for 'Joes', as we called the agents. They lived in one of the country houses nearby which had been taken over by their organisations. They were driven over to Tempsford for classes, or to Somersham for practical work. They were dressed up as Army officers and were driven by very attractive girls in the FANY uniform. We also went with them on drives round the countryside, when they were invited to pick fields that would match our specification, and taught how to draft descriptions of them for the wireless messages they would send back from France.

We taught them that the flarepath must be more or less into the wind. Lamp 'A' was near the command post for the agent in charge and waiting passengers. 150 metres into wind was lamp 'B'. 50 metres to the right of lamp 'B' was lamp 'C'. The flarepath needed to start 100 metres from the downwind hedge on a clear, firm, level strip of ground at least 600 metres long from hedge to hedge. Trees were not allowed in the funnel approaching this strip from either end, unless their tops were below a given angle. The strip had to be free of badly sunken cart tracks from 50 metres short of the first light 'A' to 100 metres after lights 'B' and 'C'. Grass cropped reasonably short by sheep or cattle was ideal. Stubble would do very well too, if the ground was firm. The serious hazard to avoid was soft mud. Then we taught them how to decide what direction any wind was blowing from without a wind sock.

We instructed them how to tie torches on to sticks, pointing downwind and slightly upward. The agent would stand by lamp 'A' to signal the agreed letter and his assistant, if he had one, would be ready to switch on lamps 'B' and 'C', when the letter was acknowledged by the Lysander. After the Lysander had landed and turned round ready to take off into wind, the load had to be changed over in under three minutes.

If there were passengers outbound, all but one would climb down the ladder, and the remaining passenger would then hand down the luggage and load the luggage for the homeward bound passengers before leaving the aircraft. When the new passengers were aboard and the cockpit roof had been slid shut, the agent in charge would give a thumbs up signal and shout "OK". All this was practised over and over again with each trainee agent, in a course lasting about a week. It became a very slick and efficient routine.

During intervals in the training we became very friendly with individual agents. Each of us was responsible for the training of one particular agent and felt responsible for his efficiency in operations over the months that followed.

During this first agents' training course that I took part in, I was particularly interested in Henri Déricourt. He appears in my log-book as "Lieut Henry D", and was unusual among the trainees because he was himself a professional aerobatic and airline pilot, and had been, briefly, in the French Air Force. He told me that he had escaped from occupied France and made his way across the Pyrenees making contact with the British in Spain or Gibraltar. His offer of his services had been accepted by the Special Operations Executive (SOE) French section. This meant that he was directly employed by the British, not by the French authorities under de Gaulle in London.

Henri was a pleasant fellow, 33 years old, with rather wavy hair and regular features. He spoke only a few words of English but my French gave him somebody to chat to. Not that he was very talkative, rather the reverse. I gathered that he was married and had a flat in Paris. He was also *maire* of a village somewhere in the country. Finding fields for us and laying on our operations was to be his main occupation when he got back to France. I liked him and he also made friends with Pick, the squadron commander.

Life was not all work and training, as the following extract from my letter home from Tangmere on 16 December 1942 will show:

"I went to a terrific party in London the other day. I remember standing on my hands on a beer barrel in the public bar of the Park Lane Hotel, and playing rugger with the same barrel in the hall. We later went to a squalid boîte known as the 'Bag o' Nails'…"

On 15 December, just a month after joining the squadron, I joined the others, now at Tangmere for the moon period's operations. RAF Tangmere, about four miles east of Chichester, was so much nearer to our target areas in France. My training was to be completed by a cross-country over France without passengers. What I did not realise at the time was how carefully new pilots were assessed by the mechanics who worked on the Lysanders. This is made clear in a snatch of conversation between airmen recalled for me by Les Dibdin, one of our electricians:

" "What's on tonight?"

"Two on ops, Bridger in 'G' and McCairns in 'E' - and Bunny Rymills in 'F' on cross-country." "Oh," said F's rigger, George Pears, "What's my skipper on cross-country for? I thought he would be doing that from Tempsford".

"He's on cross-country over France" said Sam Hollis.

"Ah, well", said George, "That figures. He needs a bit of practice because when we flew down here, if we hadn't come to the Channel, we shouldn't have known where we were."

"It's queer you should say that", said one of the wireless mechs. "I flew back with him to Tempsford last op period and we got to Barford Power Station before we turned back to Tempsford. He will never make the grade at this job if he can't find the target in the daylight. I am sure he will be hopeless at night."

"I'm afraid you're right" nodded George.
How wrong was the ground crew opinion over this pilot, who went on to become one of the top Lizzy pilots!"

For my own operational cross-country, I was carefully briefed except on one particular point. I was told how to make my way through a corridor free of flak (anti-aircraft guns) to a pin-point south of Saumur. This is what I tried to do, but I was shot at just inside the French coast, where I could see coloured tracer curving up towards me and then away. It was not a bad night and the navigation gave little trouble, but I was astonished that the pin-point I had been told to find was a brilliantly lit rectangle. I worked out that it must be a prison camp with flood-lit wire all round the perimeter. In 1988 Roger Lequin discovered that it had been a German prison camp for gypsies near Montreuil-Bellay. In a country otherwise blacked out for the war it stood out as an obvious landmark from many miles away. When I reported this on my return I was let into the secret. This was just to test new pilots to see if they had really been there. That was my qualifying test; I was now operational.

Guy Lockhart

CHAPTER TWO

First Lysander Operations

The cottage at Tangmere was just opposite the main gates of the Royal Air Force station. It was partly hidden by tall hedges and the car park was hidden behind overlapping screens of woven laths. There was little that the passer-by could see by looking through the gate.

It was a simple little house, made from an original seventeenth century cottage which had been considerably extended like many week-end cottages. The walls were thick, the ceilings low and the windows small. On the ground floor there was a kitchen (which also served as an informal guardroom) and two living rooms. One went in through the door at the back and through the kitchen. At least one went in if Booker or Blaber agreed. They doubled the roles of cook/batman with the role of security guard.

Flight Sergeants Steve Blaber and Bill Booker of the Royal Air Force Service Police were the main life support of the cottage, although we did not use that phrase in 1942. Whoever selected them for that job was touched with inspiration. For those who worked there, they combined the qualities of Jeeves with cheerful adaptability and delight in doing anything that would help. Their mixed grill operational suppers and breakfasts were perfect - at any time of the night.

If, on the other hand, one were hostile or unidentified, I would not at all like to try to get past either Blaber or Booker. Blaber was tall, slim, fair and strong; Booker was shorter and rather tubby, but he was very strong. Beneath their charming smiles and jokes both were very tough indeed.

Having got past the kitchen and Blaber or Booker the two living rooms were as follows: on the right the operations room/crew room and on the left the dining room with two long trestle tables. Robin Hooper, who was to join us later, discovered pencilled numbers I to XIV round the walls of this room. He thought that they had been used to locate the stations of the Cross in a private chapel. It had in fact been used as a chapel by the Roman Catholic chaplain to RAF Tangmere. The ops room had a big map of France with the flak defended areas marked in red. There was a table and a map chest. There was a mixed collection of chairs, some of them very comfortable and arranged round the coal fire. Black beams supported the ceiling. There was a normal black telephone and, later on, a green 'scrambler' telephone for confidential conversations.

When the scrambler was installed at the beginning of 1943 the old Post Office engineer sat on the floor smoking and connecting pieces of wire. He muttered: "Mr Churchill's got one of these; Mr Anthony Eden's got one of these. I don't know why you young buggers want one of these."

There is not much more to say about the geography of the cottage. Upstairs there were five or six bedrooms with as many beds in each as could be fitted in, rather like a cheap Turkish hotel. When I first slept there I shared a small room with Guy Lockhart who insisted on keeping the window shut and the electric fire burning all night. Later we had a hut added behind the cottage where there had been a vegetable garden; this gave more room for pilots and visitors to sleep.

Tangmere Cottage was to be my home from home for 13 moon periods. We - the Lysander Flight pilots - were normally there for about a week before and a week after each full moon. We walked across to the normal RAF officers' mess for meals at the usual times when we had no secret visitors. Our ground crew were lodged in the main station, but they came to the cottage for a party when operations for the night had been cancelled and we had a new 'gong' (decoration) to celebrate. On these occasions we always installed a pin of bitter. We all loved it there. I think it was partly because we were such a small unit away from our parent squadron and station. We were very free and relaxed - even casual- about anything that did not affect the success of our operations. We were wholly professional about anything that did.

My own first operational trip in No 161 Squadron was on 23 December 1942. The Air Transport Form had come in a couple of days earlier, duly approved by AI2(c), a special section of Air Intelligence in the Air Ministry. This gave me a lot of time to prepare my maps. I followed the technique that the older hands had developed and cut strips out of half-million maps (1:500,000) so that the track I meant to follow was in the middle and about 50 miles on each side was shown in each panel. I folded the map so that I could hold it in one hand and study two panels while flying the aeroplane with the other hand. Each panel was of a size which permitted one to stuff the whole folded map into the top of a flying boot or into the map-case fixed in the cockpit on the port side. The last two panels were on twice the scale (1:250,000) to give more detail round the target. For this trip the target was a field just to the east of the River Saône, north east of Mâcon.

I marked the maps with the latest intelligence on flak defences near my route and I marked distances along the track from the coast of France. I spent two hours learning the map. Then I made up my 'gen' cards with basic navigational data for each leg. This could only be completed an hour or two before take-off when we had the latest 'met' winds (forecast winds from the meteorological forecaster). The gen card also gave the Morse letters to be flashed that night by beacons in England, which might help if there was a failure in the radio telephone on one's return. We stuck the gen card on the route map, over the blank 'Channel', with scotch tape.

The briefing folder we had been sent for the operation included a recent vertical air photograph of the field and its immediate surroundings. This had been specially taken for us by the Photographic Reconnaissance Unit at RAF Benson. I studied it with admiration. The photograph showed a huge clear meadow with no trees near the landing area, nor tracks across it. It could not be easier to find alongside that great river. The Air Transport Form gave details of the agent's description of the field; his map reference on the local sheet of the Michelin map; the dates and times he should be ready for the landing; the planned number of passengers both ways and the name of the escorting officer who would visit Tangmere for the operation. We soon learned to tell an Air Transport Form from the Secret Intelligence Service. Theirs were typed in mauve, while those from the Special Operations Executive were typed in black.

Each morning of the moon period we would decide which trips - if any - would be possible that night in view of the weather forecast. We would then get agreement by scrambled telephone from Pick, the squadron commander, at Tempsford. The operations room at Tempsford then told the 'firm'. This was generally the Special Operations Executive (SOE), but sometimes the Secret Intelligence Service (SIS). That evening the BBC French language news programmes would end with a list of 'personal messages', including those for our trips. These messages were distinctive phrases like *'le lion a deux têtes'*, which were meaningless if you did not know that they applied to a particular field. They had to penetrate through heavy jamming to a portable wireless set in a barn or attic where the agent in charge was very carefully listening to hear if his operation was on that night.

On the morning of 23 December 1942 the general weather picture looked fine. A high pressure system would ensure clear skies over most of the route. There was, however, a slight chance of fog in low-lying ground in the target area. On balance Guy Lockhart and Tempsford agreed on the telephone that my trip should be on that night.

That evening at supper my passenger was not entirely relaxed. Nor may I say, was I. I was wearing a mixture of civilian clothes and uniform. If I had by any chance to abandon a bogged-down Lysander I wanted to be able to merge into the French countryside. I could burn my battledress top and would still have a dark blue roll-neck sweater to keep me warm. Shoes and beret would go in the starter handle locker with my escape kit - a standard sealed package containing a wad of French money, a map of France printed on silk, a compass, fishing hook and line and some concentrated food tablets. All my clothes were innocent of makers' names and laundry marks and I had passport photographs of myself to help if forged identity papers should be required.

Then we went out to the Lysander in a big American Ford station wagon driven by our army driver, Elston-Evans, who had been a 'cellist - another splendid member of our team. Here I showed the passenger where the luggage should be stowed under the hinged wooden seat and on the shelf in front of him as he faced the tail. I fitted his parachute harness, reminded him how to take it off and how to clip the observer type parachute on to his chest if it should be needed. I showed him how his flying helmet plugged in to the intercom and how to switch his microphone on and off.

Then I strapped myself into the little pilot's cockpit up front, slid the roof shut, did all my checks, primed the engine and started up. I let the engine tick over until the oil temperature was 5°C, meanwhile testing the flying controls and brake pressure. Then, against brakes and chocks, I opened up to 1,800 rpm, changed the propeller to coarse pitch, noted the large drop in rpm, and returned it to fine pitch. Then, at cruising throttle I checked the alternate magneto switches.

Happy that the aeroplane was 100% - it always was, thanks to its fitter and rigger - I waved away the chocks, waved to the little group who were standing by to see off my passenger and taxied out.

Before getting take-off clearance I muttered to myself "TMP fuel and gills", checking that the tail actuating wheel was set for TAKE-OFF, the mixture control in NORMAL and the pitch control pushed in for fine pitch. The fuel gauges were all reading full, because it was to be a seven-hour trip. The gills were open to increase the air flow over the engine. At 2020 hours, I turned on to the long flarepath, eased the throttle fully open and took off. When I was at the safety speed of 80 mph, I eased the stick back and climbed away, turning on to my first heading (or 'course' as we called it then).

It was a lovely clear winter night and the moon was already rising. I was soon across the coast near Bognor Regis, heading for Cabourg, near Caen. I would have no difficulty in seeing the coast-line of France from any height so I climbed to 8,000 feet, well above any light flak of the sort that had shot me when I did my training trip into France a few nights before. When I was about three quarters of the way across the sea I called Blackgang radar station who had a 10 cm scanner: "How now, "Handy"?" Their reply: "Steer 2 starboard" confirmed that I was just about on track. The course was good and the light met wind must be about right. Then the French coast came into view, a darker grey than the light grey of the sea. The inlet between Ouistreham and Cabourg is in a sort of funnel to which one is led by the coast-line on either side. At Cabourg itself a marine beacon was flashing red. To the left Le Havre was a heavily defended port to be avoided at all costs. To the right and a little inland is Caen, defended too, especially the airfield, though not heavily. I had a word or two with my passenger, drew attention to the coast, asked if he was warm enough and reminded him to keep watch for any German night fighter that might be prowling round.

When I crossed the coast, right over Cabourg, I was within a couple of minutes of my ETA (Estimated time of arrival) at the end of my first leg. I set course for the second leg to Beaugency between Orleans and Blois and put the nose down to lose height gently to 2,000 feet.[1] This was a good height for map-reading on a clear night. There was no colour, apart from an occasional yellow pinpoint of light. Everything was in various tones of bluish grey. I checked the landmarks coming up as I expected them from the map - woods, *routes nationales,* showing up as a straight line of trees, and railways. There was a suggestion of ground mist forming in a long pale line along a railway, following its curves where a train had passed by. There was more mist lying along the streams in little valleys. The little town of Nogent-le-Rotrou, completely blacked-out, slipped by underneath. I was dead on track.

After this the fog became continuous. I could not check my position crossing the Loire at either Beaugency or Nevers. I pressed on flying accurately on my compass and airspeed, according to my dead-reckoning flight plan. From Nogent-le-Rotrou the first time I saw the ground again was in a clear patch including Bourbon Lancy, near the Loire south-east of Nevers and about 60 miles west of my target.

Eventually, after flying for three hours and twenty minutes, I had flown over the high ground near Cluny and I knew I was approximately over my target. Below was a sea of thick white fog, reflecting the moonlight. I circled round in wide sweeps but there was no break in it. So I had to tell my passenger that I was defeated by fog and set course for home via the route I had come.

The whole December moon was most frustrating for us because of fog and cloud - and ice forming on the Lysander in the cloud. It must have been even more frustrating for small groups in hiding in France, waiting for our aircraft. Of the six sorties attempted only two were successful, and these were by the squadron commander and flight commander. But it was Guy Lockhart's trip on 17/18 December - his last successful pick-up - that I remember especially well.

Half an hour before he was due back a few of us who were waiting for him were telephoned by the tower. He had radioed to say that he had damaged his tail and could not control the Lysander properly. We jumped into Elston-Evans' station wagon and drove quickly to the tower. Guy's Lysander arrived overhead following a curious flight path in the vertical plane. He was either going up or down but never flying level. I was not at all sure that he would be able to land it safely. We made sure that the fire-engine and ambulance were warmed up and alert.

Guy did an approach in this saw-tooth vertical pattern and then climbed away, went round again and somehow brought it down in one piece, by intermittent use of the throttle.

He dragged his damaged tail into the flight's dispersal area where we met him. We found that the tail undercarriage had been bent right up into the tail plane, making it impossible to control the vertical attitude of the Lysander properly.

Guy told us that there had been a deeply rutted farm track across the landing strip (near Bourges) and that he had hit it with his tail as he landed. His stick could not be moved fore and aft and his rudder was jammed. He jumped out to inspect the damage, tried to free the elevator by kicking it, but without success. Nor did it move when he got six Frenchmen to stand on it. He did succeed though in breaking the bottom rudder struts and this freed the rudder, although he had some doubt about whether the Lysander could be flown safely or not. Remembering the last time he had escaped from France he decided that he did not want to try that again. He weighed up the risk that the Lysander could be uncontrollable and decided to try it on, advising his two homeward-bound passengers that he could not promise anything. But they decided to take the risk and come. After taking off he found, with great relief, that the Lysander would climb very steeply at full throttle and did not stall. However much he pushed the stick forward, he could not move it or make the Lysander fly level. So he climbed and climbed until it got too cold. Then he throttled back wondering what would happen; the Lysander behaved beautifully. It just sank, without spinning. And so he came home, alternately climbing and losing height. His knees were raw from pressing on the stick, but he was really very lucky.

Les Dibdin, who was an electrician in the Lysander Flight at the time, remembers[2] the next morning, which was nice and sunny, when Guy arrived and explained to his ground crew what had happened to his aircraft. A corporal from a fighter squadron, who was ignorant of the facts, said as he was passing, "You've got some good pilots on your squadron; can't even land a little old Lizzie!"

Everybody turned but nothing was said; the airmen just glared. The airmen still remember that Guy organised a free Christmas Dinner by the 'A' Flight pilots for the ground crews; yet, when Mrs Lockhart wanted him to make a speech he could not bring himself to do it.

After he left 161 Squadron to join Air Ministry Intelligence for a rest, we did not

Standing: F/O Bridger P/O Jenkins P/O Wotton F/O McBride P/O Fowler P/O Stevens P/O MacGuire P/O Russell
Sitting: F/O Atkins F/Lt Boxer S/Ld Gunn W/Cdr Fielden F/Lt Lockhart F/Lt Powell F/Lt Harcourt S/O Johnson

Whitley with Wing Commander Fielden and 161 Squadron officers, June, 1942.   *Crown Copyright*

see Guy again for several months. Then he came to see old friends and tell us what he was up to. He was planning to parachute into France to steal a German night fighter so that our boffins[3] could take its airborne radar to pieces. He had been flying a captured JU 88 and he was fitted out with a snappy suit (made by a French tailor in London) and false papers.

We never heard exactly what happened about this extraordinary enterprise. We thought it must have been cancelled. Those who needed the information about the German airborne radar probably found they could get it in some less dramatic way. We heard much later that Guy had commanded No 7 Pathfinder squadron and had been killed in a raid on Friedrichshaven. He had always impressed us as a dedicated pilot who would be intolerably restless in any job which was not aggressively operational.

We spent Christmas at Tangmere and, when operations were cancelled, would go for the evening to Arthur King's splendid pub in Chichester, the rounded red-brick 'Unicorn' which, alas, is no longer a pub. One evening Pick gave us a demonstration of pin-sticking, of the sort recorded by Mac.[4] He would roll back his coat and shirt sleeve, borrow any sort of pin or brooch, clean it by holding it in the flame of a match and then, after puckering the skin of his left forearm with his right hand, he would demand that some innocent spectator should take the pin and push it through the folded skin. Once Mac tried to force the pin of an American colonel's shoulder badge, and felt sick as the needle went in with a faint sound. After Pick had put about ten similar emblems on his arm, he demanded, as proof of the loyalty and courage of his followers that in turn they should suffer a like fate. And then, as Mac put it: "such was our allegiance to the Big White Chief that in the space of the next ten minutes some half a dozen pilots were walking round with a badge neatly pinned on the left forearm." On Boxing Day 1942, I wrote to my wife:

"...How I wish I could be with you this Christmas ! I am doing damn all really, because of the weather, but I cannot get away. It was so lovely to hear you on the blower...

"One of the best of my new friends is John Hunt, a pianist of great renown. I particularly want you to hear him play some time. I am told he is in the very first rank of European pianists and ranks with Moiseiwitsch and Co. Last night at a camp concert he played the 'Dante Fantasia' by Liszt. It was the most beautiful music and I felt the blood coursing through me. John is a most modest type and very clever and pleasant. He is much older than I am but I like him very well. He is cultured and interesting..."

Flight Lieutenant John Hunt was a German-speaking interrogator. He had lived in Germany, learning to play the piano, for many years before the war, where he had been a pupil of the great Artur Schnabel. When Luftwaffe aircrew were shot down and became prisoners-of war, he was one of the linguists who extracted intelligence from them, mainly by very civilised conversation, sometimes by tricks. The worst part of his job, he told me, was the search for information in the remains of crashed aircraft and crews. His main task at this time was to look after the administration and security of 'the Cottage.'

It was not until 14 January 1943 that I could try another operation. Meanwhile we had taken the Flight back to Tempsford for the non-moon fortnight. I had been home for a short but blissful leave and we had run another short course for agents. During this I flew Henri Déricourt twice and let him fly a Lysander. On 10 January 1943, I

Back of Tangmere Cottage in 1943.   Moira McCairns

find that I wrote to my wife:

"...I have a very good friend called Henry. I have given him your telephone number and told him that you would do whatever you could to help him, no matter when. Don't forget, Darling, even if he rings up after several years, to think of him as an old friend of mine. You will find him very nice."

I was not the only person to like Henri Déricourt. He was befriended by Pick and his wife Dorothy. In 1982 Dorothy revealed that Pick's Old English sheep dog Ming was very truculent towards Déricourt when he visited their home in Willington village. Ming would not remain in his presence and had to be confined to the kitchen when Déricourt was in the house. Ming was never belligerent to any other person or dog. Squadron Leader Wagland, station navigation officer, remembers him thus:

"Déricourt spent some days with us at Tempsford and I think he was with us one Christmas. Flight Lieutenant Macmillan (also a navigator, but subsequently squadron leader in charge of the Hudson Flight) and I found him pleasant company. He was in Army uniform."

For my second operational flight my target was a field near Loyettes, east of Lyons - a long way in a Lysander. My aircraft was 'D' for Dog. The large red squadron letters on the side of the black fuselage were 'MA'. Then came the RAF roundel, then the aircraft letter 'D'. I flight tested it during the morning for half an hour.

The weather forecast was reasonable, although there would be some cloud and rain to fly through over Northern or Central France. A mild warm front was said to be lying diagonally from SW to NE right across my track. At least the winds were sure to be enough to make the risk of fog negligible. After preparations much like the last time, I took off and set course along a planned route which was to be the same as before as far as Nevers. This time, as I approached the Loire the cloud was building up over Normandy and it was getting darker and darker. I turned up the cockpit lights. Eventually I found myself flying through freezing rain which built up a little ice on the leading edges of the wings. I checked that the pressure head heat was switched on. If the pitot tube was blocked with ice, I would have no air-speed indicator and my flying instruments were my only frame of reference in this black rain. I switched on the heat to the carburettor air intake and opened the throttle a little. I thought of the story I had heard about Nesbitt-Dufort's trip on 28 January 1942, just one year before. Clear ice forming fast on his aeroplane in a stormy cold front had forced him down to an emergency landing in France. The resistance people hid him until he could be picked up on 1 March by a twin-engined Anson flown by Sticky Murphy.[5] Meanwhile, they had managed to tow the Lysander to a level crossing just before a train arrived so that it was completely destroyed.

On this trip, however, there was no great drama. The ice was not building up fast, the Lysander was maintaining height and I pressed on. I thought it might be better to go down a bit into slightly warmer air but maintaining a safe height above the high ground ahead. All went well and I came out of the bad weather. My first fix was near Châteaudun. By the time I approached the River Saône, it was quite comfortable below the cloud and there was enough light to see rivers. I was intending to fix my position North of Lyons and South of Villefranche. When I was sure I was looking at the Saône, but not at all sure which part of it, I kept my head down studying the map for a few seconds too long. I looked up and found I was flying straight at a huge wireless mast, one of several in a group. I pulled round to the right in a savage bank and just missed it. The heavy 'g' loading as I pulled the stick back must have increased my apparent weight two or three times. I was badly frightened by this near miss and the sudden charge of adrenalin in my blood left me trembling.

I collected myself and figured out the lie of the river below me and found the place on my map. I flew along the river to the point where the track line on my map crossed it and then set off again towards my target. The lights of Lyons showed up very clearly. My field was now easy to find, lying as it did just between the rivers Rhône and Ain. And there was the agent's torch flashing the right letter in steady Morse. I flashed my own letter on the signalling key and saw the three other lights switched on. Their inverted 'L' shape looked so familiar - exactly as if I was circling round Somersham on a training course.

I flew parallel with the long leg of the 'L', noting the heading on my direction gyro. I turned through 180° on to the down-wind leg at about 500 feet above the ground, throttled back to reduce speed to 100 mph and wound the tail trim back. I checked that the mixture control was in normal and the pitch control pushed in for fine pitch. I had a good look at the field and its approaches. There were no trees to bother about. Then, about 400 feet above the field, I started a gentle descending turn to port through 180° to straighten out over the hedge at about 70 mph with my slats out, my flaps down and just a little throttle open; then straight down on to the ground after the minimum of flattening out and float, cutting the throttle. I put the brakes on, gently at first, as the Lysander was bumping along a bit. When the second lamp was passing my port wing, about 150 yards from my touch-down point, I was trundling along slowly enough to do a sharp U-turn to starboard, inside the third lamp, and taxi back to the reception committee at the first lamp. Meanwhile, I did my cockpit drill to be ready for take-off. As I drew up with my port wing tip over the reception committee, after another U-turn, I had my right hand on my Luger 9 mm automatic in its holster on the port cockpit coaming just behind and above the throttles.

When I saw the little group clearly I put the safety catch back on, waved to them, shouted my best wishes to the passengers and slid my roof open. The agent in charge jumped on the port undercarriage housing and shook me by the hand with a welcoming smile. His hair was caught by the slip-stream as my propeller continued to turn. He asked me if I was Flying Officer Lockhart.

After about four minutes, the luggage and the passengers had changed over, the agent shouted "OK", and with friendly waves I was off. The time was 0014 hours. Really it had been very easy, my first landing in occupied France. The field was good; the flare path and the whole reception drill were perfect.

This must have been the operation referred to by Christian Pineau[6] as the landing near Loyettes in the "last week" of January. The operation officer on the field was Pierre Delaye who had been flown in as a wireless operator for the 'Phalanx' network. The passengers I picked up were Christian Pineau and two young agents who were to be trained in Britain. Pineau remembers - though I had forgotten - that we were chased by a night fighter near the French coast on our way home and that I zig-zagged very low to shake him off.

I landed at Tangmere eight hours and forty minutes after I had left it, tired but very happy. I had broken my personal duck and brought the total of pick-up operations for the war up to about 28. We gave my three passengers breakfast, heard their hair-raising stories, which I cannot now remember, packed them off with their escorting officer and FANY driver and went to bed.

There were two other Lysanders out over France on that night of 14/15 January 1943, flown by Flight Lieutenant John Bridger, by then DFC, and Flying Officer Peter Vaughan-Fowler.

John's target was Thalamy, near Ussel (west of Clermont Ferrand). He landed at midnight and found the ground "extremely bumpy - not at all suitable in view of the growth of heather." In six minutes on the ground they unloaded the two packages he had brought and three passengers squashed in with their baggage. They were General de Gaulle's old comrade-in-arms Claude Hettier de Boislambert, whom he particularly wanted to see, Léon Faye, and Henry Leopold Dor, both of the Alliance intelligence organisation. John had brought with him a Belgian secret agent who had no connection with Alliance, but they sent him on his way. In September 1977, I met Monsieur de Boislambert, then Chancellor of the Order of Liberation, at Thalamy on the occasion of the unveiling of a fine granite monument which records Lysander pick-ups there. He told me that his Lysander had been unable to identify itself on the approach to the UK air defences because of a radio failure, so his pilot had followed closely behind a returning bomber. In spite of this, they were shot at as they crossed the British coast.

This completed 'Ajax', which both John and Mac had been unable to do a month before because of fog.[7]

Peter found such heavy cloud round the Mâcon area that he could not find the field. Little did he know that René Massigli was waiting there in the snow after trying since November to get a passage to England. There was no felucca available from Gibraltar, the Royal Navy could not spare a submarine, and several previous pick-ups had been frustrated by the weather.

Monsieur Massigli, who was then 55, was a professional diplomat. Before the war he had been the French ambassador in Turkey. However, he was picked up successfully by Pick twelve nights later on 26/27 January 1943 on operation 'Atala'. The field was near Issoudun. Pick, whose passenger was Pierre Brossolette[8], arrived over the field at 0130 and saw no lights. It was a very dark night and difficult to pin-point the actual field. He stayed in the area until 0315, when he saw a lamp flashing the signal. The passengers later said that they had heard an aircraft overhead from 0145 onwards, but they had understood that it was up to the aircraft to make the first move by flashing an identification letter.

As had sometimes happened to Guy Lockhart, Pick came out of France west of the Cotentin instead of east of it. He later attributed this to compass error caused by taking his stainless steel whisky flask out of his breast pocket and shoving it into the top of one of his flying boots, very near the compass, but Peter Procter attributes the deviation to a steel bayonet in one of his flying boots (See Appendix F). Major André Manuel[9], who was the other passenger, told André Gillois[10] that Pick was asking on the inter-com where they were. Later he told his passengers that he was running out of petrol. In fact, he managed to land his passengers at Predannock in Cornwall. When he landed, his petrol tanks were dry. It was 0630.

A sequel to this pick-up was the following letter from Monsieur Massigli to *The Times* of 2 November 1944. It refers also to operation 'Jericho', in which Pick was killed leading Mosquitos attacking the walls of the prison at Amiens to permit French Resistance prisoners to escape.

"As one of the many Frenchmen whom the RAF pilots helped to escape from France in the recent years of affliction, may I be allowed to pay to Group Captain Pickard my tribute of admiration, gratitude and regret?

The time has not yet come when it will be possible to reveal to the full what British airmen did in helping Resisting France. So much courage was demanded of them, so

much ability and endurance when, on a moonlit night, they had to discover, somewhere in the French countryside, the field or glade that was "target for tonight". Among these admirable men Group Captain Pickard was one of the greatest.

Yesterday, as I was reading the thrilling story of the flight to Amiens, where he had a rendezvous with death, I was vividly reminded of the steady bravery, of the indomitable energy, of the boundless devotion to duty of the pilot who, although petrol was running low, tried with so much dogged obstinacy on a certain night of January 1943, to

Wing Commander P.C. Pickard, DSO, DFC.

discover the field where he was briefed to drop a Frenchman and to pick up another. That night the homeward bound passenger was Pierre Brosselette, who a few months later was to fall into the hands of the Gestapo and commit suicide rather than let out any of the secrets in his possession. Among the brave country-folk who had escorted me to a field there was one, probably the best as well as the youngest, who was to lose his life last August on a maquis battlefield.

The men of the French Resistance will never forget that Group Captain Pickard, after giving them so much help in so many ways, at last gave up his life to rescue some of their fellow-fighters."

Monsieur Massigli joined de Gaulle in London. In September 1943, having been disowned by the Vichy administration, he was appointed by de Gaulle to be French Ambassador in London. It was in this capacity that he later pinned our French Decorations on a number of us at an investiture in London. I wondered how I would react to His Excellency's 'embrassade' when I received my Légion d'Honneur and Croix de Guerre. In the event, the chief surprise was the strength of the scent in his after-shave lotion.

It was not until that same night of 26 January that the weather forecast allowed me to have another trip. This was to be a double Lysander pick-up west of Lons-le-Saunier. We could not carry more than three passengers in the back of a Lysander, except in emergency. Even with three it was very uncomfortable for the third, who had to sit on the floor. On this operation, five or six passengers must have been expected for England. I decided to let two other pilots, Bunny Rymills and Jimmy McCairns, take on the trip, but, as I had not been able to do much that moon, I went myself as well, as a reserve aircraft in case one of the others failed to arrive for any reason. In the event, this proved to be an excess of zeal, because the party on the ground were only expecting one Lysander, and there were no passengers for me to collect after Bunny had done his pick-up. But there were at least 10 people on the field, standing there in the low-lying ground mist, including the Mayor of the village.

The mayor, who was about 80, owned the field and would only allow it to be used for pick-ups if he was invited to be present at the operations. His son was doing forced labour in Germany, so he was left looking after his grandchildren. Bunny Rymills remembers supplying toothpaste for them, since he was told that it was unobtainable. This involved dipping tubes of toothpaste in the flight's dope thinners to get the paint off the tubes. The manufacturer's name was then filed off the caps. Bunny arranged for these anonymous tubes of toothpaste to be posted to the old Mayor by the next agent he took to France.

The agent in charge was Paul Rivière. He was 30 years old, of medium height, with black framed spectacles and a strong chin. He always sparkled with good humour and high morale. His father had been a school-teacher in his native Montagny in the gentle country east of Roanne on the Loire. Paul had been a school-teacher in Lyons. I did not know then that Paul Rivière had been one of the three main Gaullist air operations organisers in the Zone-non-occupée during 1942, nor that, over the next 11 months, we would transport more passengers on successful landings with him than with any other agent in France. During 1943, he would be the Gaullist chief of air operations, both parachutings and landings, over about a quarter of France. Nor could I imagine, then, that in 1972 my family and I would be staying for a superb holiday with Paul and Jannik in their country house at Montagny. By then he would be a retired colonel (with an OBE and MM as well as his very distinguished French and Allied decorations), *Deputé* (member of Parliament) for la Loire and the *Maire* of Montagny. In fact, in January 1943, I doubt if either Paul or I felt at all sure that any plans based on the assumption that we would survive the war were worth making.

Paul told me (in 1975) that the BBC message was *"Le castor foulera la neige deux fois"*, indicating that two Lysanders were coming when they had been expecting only one. Bunny Rymills delivered two agents and picked up Colonel Manhes and Jean Fleury. Jean Fleury wrote to me that he "was surprised by the calm and relaxed behaviour of the reception committee. From the field they could see a *route nationale* in use by German vehicles, all with headlamps on, whose occupants, thank God, showed a complete indifference to the two aeroplanes which landed in the open country and took off a little later. Each of them was minding his own business and paid no attention to anything else."

Jean Moulin and General Delestraint arrived at Villevieux, hoping to fly to London, a few hours after we had taken off. The next day, 28 January, they received a signal to the effect that the next possible pick-up would not be before 14 February. They went back to Lyons and returned to the Château de Villevieux on 11 February.

Mac had had to abandon his flight because he heard a recall order on the radio which neither Bunny nor I picked up. They must have had a revision for the worse of the weather forecast. I remember part of the homeward trip vividly. It was necessary to fly through a bad cold front; there was no way round. In the cloud and rain, it was really filthy weather; there were towering cumulo-nimbus clouds hidden in the general bad weather, so that one could not see to fly round them. In the strong up-draughts and down-draughts, the four tons of my little Lysander were tossed around like a cork in a whirlpool. Flashes of lightning temporarily ruined my night vision and St. Elmo's fire (some sort of static electricity discharging itself) flickered with blue light round the tip of my propeller and off other parts of the aeroplane. My gyro horizon toppled, and I came to the conclusion that hell could hardly be worse. Then it got worse, because I felt air sick. I opened a sliding window, took off my oxygen mask and vomited, meanwhile doing my best to go on flying the Lysander through the storm. I wondered how much I should tip the airmen who would clean out the cockpit.

The storm had built up thick ice on the Lysander, and it began to lose height. I pressed on; it could not be worse ahead. After what seemed a long and very disagreeable time, I found the worst was over. Eventually I could see the ground again and, after some delay, establish my position. The rest of the flight home was routine.

There were two other uncompleted operations in that moon, both on 23/24 January. Bunny Rymills attempted his first pick-up (though it is not recorded in the RAF archives). He found no recognition signal flashed from the field near Issoudun. This was probably another attempt at 'Atala', whose reception-committee seems to have expected the Lysander to signal first. The other was operation 'Miner'.

McCairns flew over his target, the disused Périgueux aerodrome, four times between 2340 and 0030 on the night of 23/24 January. In bright moonlight he could see two small hangars and the wind sock. Peter Churchill - as he told us later in the year - had arrived on time and found the landing ground defended, when, earlier, it had seemed to be deserted. He hid in a ditch and waited to see what would happen. Nothing happened. The Germans were more interested in interrogating agents from England than in taking pot shots at Lysanders. In fact, Peter Churchill overheard them passing the word round: "Do not fire; wait until the pilot lands."

The January moon of 1943 had been reasonably successful, with five landings completed out of the nine attempted. Only in November '42 had there been more pick-ups completed - six out of nine. I was settling in happily to my new role, although still a beginner. In February I wrote to my parents:

"The work I am doing gives me more satisfaction than any I have done before. In a sense I feel a vocation to it, and that my former jobs were experience paving the way for me. I have met so far with a fair measure of success, both as a pilot and as a flight commander, but I must try to avoid a swollen head and plod along for a year or so. It is now quite clear that I might well be a wing commander, had I stuck to my old job, or rather, gone back to it after my rest. That has no meaning for me, as I would rather do my present job than be a group captain in another one."

Now that the reader has some idea of the detail of typical Lysander pick-ups from my memory of my first months with 161 Squadron, I should go back to the beginning of these operations in World War Two, basing the story on such scanty contemporary official records and other primary sources as remain, and filling in details here and there from published histories and memoirs, and from the memories, of some of those who were involved at the time.

Howard Coster

Hugh Verity when ALO (Air Liaison Operations), SOE, in early 1944.

CHAPTER THREE

How it had all Started

There had been many clandestine landings in enemy occupied territory in the First World War, though these are not the subject of this book. In 1943, for example, I remember reading a French book about the exploits of Jules Védrines, a great French ace of World War One. He had done many pick-ups, landing spies behind the lines in his little monoplane which he called *La Vache*. He later startled Paris by landing his Caudron 393 on the roof of the Galeries Lafayette. In 1972, the student airline pilots of Saint Yan commemorated Védrines in a project summarised in a lavish brochure. I was very greatly honoured when Philippe Badaire forwarded me a copy of this brochure signed by all the St Yan student pilots of '72. I also remember Professor Foligno, who lectured about Dante when I was up at Oxford in 1937-39. He told me that he had done pick-ups in the Italian Air Force in World War One. So it was not altogether novel when the need for pick-ups emerged in 1940 after the German occupation of much of Western Europe. Churchill had said "Set Europe ablaze". He had also told the French that "we will come back".

It was Flight Lieutenant W.J. Farley who was the first to come back. This he did in a Lysander on the night of 19/20 October 1940, landing near Montigny to pick up 'Felix' (Philip Schneidau), who had parachuted in on 9/10 October. The story of Philip's arrival in France is a digression in a book about pick-ups but I will tell it nonetheless as he told it to me.

As a sergeant in the RAF in 1940, he had been driver and interpreter to Air Marshal 'Ugly' Barratt, the AOC in C, British Air Forces in France (BAFF). After the fall of France, at the age of 37, he was commissioned as a Pilot Officer. He had been born in Paris and so was French according to French law, though his parents were both British. He had opted for British nationality when 21. Before that he had played international hockey for France.

The Secret Intelligence Service agreed that he should be one of the first agents to go back to occupied France. He knew Flight Lieutenant Holmes, who had been 'Ugly' Barratt's personal pilot, very well, and they concocted a scheme that Holmes should land a DH89 at a point well known to both of them, without a reception, and come back there a few nights later to pick him up. The Air Ministry decided that it was far too dangerous to risk a pilot and aircraft on "such a stupid arrangement". So Philip Schneidau had to accept that the only way he would arrive in France would be on the end of a parachute. The Whitley that took him there was flown by Jacky Oettle and navigated by Jacky Martin.

Because of bad visibility they failed five times. The captain of the aircraft, Jacky Oettle, was then instructed by a certain officer: "Take the bugger out and don't bring him back." Reporting this, Oettle said: "Philip - word of honour - if we don't find the place we won't let you go."

In preparation for this trip to France, Philip had, among other things, to do three things: change his appearance, learn about pigeons and arrange for his return journey. He changed his appearance by growing a modest beard and wearing spectacles. He was afraid that his clean-shaven face might be too well known from the days when he had been a hockey international. The pigeons were to be his only means of transmitting a message from France. In those days, portable wireless transmitters for agents were in their infancy. He would have to be able to send a message if there were any difficulty with the Lysander pick-up arranged before leaving England. The only alternatives would be a pick-up by a motor torpedo boat on the coast of Brittany or a long hike over the Pyrenees.

Squadron Leader Rayner explained to him how useful the pigeons would be if they were kept incommunicado from other pigeons, who could have given them other ideas. He advised Philip that the pigeons should be put into a pair of socks before they were carried in a ruck sack. As instructed, Philip purchased a special pair of socks and cut off the toes. Before embarking on the Whitley, he carefully threaded a pigeon into each sock so that their heads stuck out of the holes in the toes.

When he arrived in France, Philip boarded out the pigeons with an old friend in the country who had a pigeon loft. Ten days later, the Lysander failed to show up as arranged. Unknown to Philip, there was very bad weather over Tangmere. Philip encoded a message to the effect that he was still awaiting transport. He attached copies of this to the pigeons' legs and allowed them to fly away at 0800 on a Sunday morning, from the Fontainebleau area. At 1630 the same day they arrived at their owner's pigeon loft at East Grinstead. Fifteen minutes later, the owner telephoned for a despatch rider. The rider signed for the two little tubes taken off the pigeons' legs and tore off to the Air Ministry London on his high-powered motor-cycle. The messages were signed for by the duty clerk at 1830, just over 12 hours from the release of the pigeons in France. It took another 13 hours before there was anybody on duty empowered to open them and telephone their message through to the section concerned.

Meanwhile, on 19 October 1940, Flight Lieutenant Farley was at Tangmere, frustrated by the bad weather. Well aware of how impatiently Philip would be expecting him, he pleaded with the commanding officer at Tangmere to let him have a crack at the operation, in spite of the bad weather. It was finally agreed that he could, but that, if the weather was still bad over the French coast, he would turn back. He took off from Tangmere in pouring rain which soaked the radio set in the back. The sliding roof over the rear cockpit had been removed to make it easier for Philip to climb in.

The weather was better over France, and Farley found the field south of Fontainebleau. As arranged, Philip switched on the inverted 'L' shaped pattern of lights which he had designed with Farley on a tablecloth in Oddenino's restaurant - the basic flarepath design for a Lysander pick-up landing which never needed to be improved throughout the war. Farley landed at 0117, and taxied back to the first lamp. Philip climbed up the fixed exterior ladder, which he had designed, and Farley took off. After taking off, he remarked that there was something jamming the free movement of the elevator. He throttled back until he could clear it, losing a little height. At this moment Philip believes that a bullet went through the compass between Farley's knees. This must have been fired by the sentry outside the CO's villa in the neighbouring village of Marlotte. For some time Farley could see to map-read by moonlight, but then the cloud built up. Climbing to 16,000 feet, they were still in cloud with no navigation aid at all, not even a compass. The wireless was too wet to work and the rear cockpit, with no canopy, was bitterly cold. Over the French coast, the weather was just as foul as it had been when Farley had taken off from Tangmere. There was a south westerly gale blowing, and Farley was afraid that they might be drifting over Belgium or Holland. They were completely lost, but they plodded on and on. Farley told Philip to look out for any sight of land, especially if there was any field visible which offered the possibility of a forced landing.

At about 0630 Farley said that the petrol tanks had been indicating 'empty' for some time and that "JC must be doing His stuff" to keep them airborne. At 0650 Philip reported seeing some land along the top of some cliffs where a landing might be possible. "Good-oh! Then we'll go down", said Farley. Then he said that it might be the North German coast. Philip said that, "when a nipper", he had read a book called 'The Riddle of the Sands' and so this could not be the North German coast. With cliffs like that Philip guessed that it might be the West Irish coast. At this point the petrol finally ran dry. They glided down and, when about 50 feet up, they observed that the ground above the cliffs had been planted with pine posts to stop enemy aircraft landing there. Farley told Philip to lie down before the landing because there was a danger of a post folding back a wing in such a way that it would chop off his head if he sat up.

Farley also told Philip to take all his clothes off as he was dressed as a civilian and they might be in enemy occupied territory. Philip did this and - at 0655 - they hit the ground. The wings came off as predicted. Philip thrust all his clothes into a haversack with two bottles of brandy and, stark naked, jumped out of the wreck of the Lysander, clutching the haversack. He ran round to the front saying: "Wally, get out! This will catch fire." Farley replied: "If there's one thing this won't do it's catch fire. There's no f...ing petrol." Farley climbed out and set off, saying that he would look for help. If he came back with help he would raise his right arm. Otherwise Philip should throw everything into the sea. To be ready to do this he should now go to the top of the cliff.

Ten minutes later Farley reappeared with two enormous men. Philip was glad to see that their rifles were slung over their left shoulders. He hastily put on his underclothes and went to meet them. Farley said: "I can't understand a word they are saying, but it appears we are in Scotland." They were invited to a hastily prepared but substantial breakfast which neither of them could eat. RAF Oban, which was nearby, was telephoned and the RAF police soon arrived to collect two obvious spies.

They were brought before the station commander of this RAF Coastal Command Station. He quite reasonably asked them who they were and what they had been doing. Farley confined himself to giving his name and number. Philip said that they had been doing a special recce over the Atlantic, but that he was not allowed to give his name. This did not seem to humour the station commander. Faced with almost total lack of co-operation, he put them under armed guard in a bed-room - where they found the beds very much to their liking. Meanwhile, the officer in charge of this operation, a naval lieutenant, had arranged to borrow an aircraft from the Fleet Air Arm station at Ford to patrol the Channel to look for the wreckage of the Lysander. I suppose nobody had told him that a ditched Lysander sinks instantly. After an hour and a half, they were told that a Lysander had crashed six miles north of Oban. The first reaction was that it could not possibly be the Lysander they were looking for. When they later heard that the pilot's name was Farley, they incredulously called off the search[1]. So, on 20 October 1940, ended the first clandestine pick-up operation of World War Two.

At the time of this pick-up operation, Flight Lieutenant Farley was commanding No. 419 Flight, which he had formed in about September 1940. It consisted of two or three Lysanders and two Whitleys (twin-engined bombers adapted for parachuting agents). The flight had been bombed out of North Weald in Fighter Command and transferred to Stradishall in Bomber Command on 9 October 1940.

Wally Farley went on leave, leaving Flight Lieutenant Keast as acting flight commander. Farley borrowed a Hurricane from North Weald, while he was on leave, to take part in an air battle that was in progress. He was shot down and crashed. He could not fly for some time while one leg was in plaster. Some time later, he recruited John Nesbitt-Dufort to fly the Lysanders on pick-ups, though the first recorded landing that the latter carried out was not until September 1941. Farley's leg mended and by 20 April 1942, when he was missing (killed) on an operation, he was a wing commander with a DFC, and officer commanding No 138 Squadron. Flight Lieutenant Keast was shot down on a Whitley trip to Czechoslovakia and became a prisoner of war. This happened one week before his wife gave birth to triplets[2].

John Hollis (known as 'Sam') was Leading Aircraftman (LAC) in the flight at that time and told me about this period. He remembers 419 Flight using a small grass airfield at Stapleford Tawney and being operated direct from the Air Ministry, AI2(c) to the station commander. In March 1941, the Flight's number was changed to 1419 because it had been confused with 419 Squadron. It was now commanded by Squadron Leader E.V. Knowles, DFC.

Ron Hockey[2] remembers Teddy Knowles as "quite a character, a fighter boy and a chum of Victor Beamish." More than once he had to be carried home from the Craven club in Newmarket. He was "quite a solid chap to carry". Presenting him at his living-out billet in the early hours was hazardous; it meant being greeted by an outsize and growling Alsatian.

Sam Hollis recalls that 419/1419 Flight used Hurn as an advanced base. He was the fitter and 'Ox' Harckness was the rigger. They would both fly there in the back cockpit. 'Ox' was so strong that they did not bother to get hold of trestles to support the tail of the Lysander for a wheel-change. 'Ox' would just lift it on his back while Sam changed the wheel. The engineering support for the Lysanders was run on a

Philip Schneidau in France.   *And in England.*

shoe-string, but not inefficiently. Spares were scrounged, even direct from the manufacturers, regardless of official stores procedures, and everybody was most co-operative. Trips to the works were made by Lysander, by van, or, on occasion, by the old Rolls-Royce car that was attached to the Flight with its army driver from the RASC, the 'cellist Elston-Evans. The modifications to the Lysander to fit it for its new long-range special duties were done by Fairfield Aviation (See Appendix F).

The second pick-up was by Flying Officer F.M.G. Scotter. Gordon Scotter was not yet 22 years old. He had joined No 2 Army Co-operation Squadron in January 1939, and was therefore an experienced Lysander pilot. Early in 1941, when at RAF Sawbridgeworth, he was "detailed to volunteer" for special duties, replacing a New Zealand pilot, Flying Officer 'Granny' Baker, who had volunteered first, but was lost on a navigation exercise over Europe. Scotter then joined 1419 Flight at Stradishall.

On 11 April 1941, Scotter took off on what he thought was to be the first successful night pick-up. His Lysander was fitted with a long range tank, a step ladder and special modifications of his own, including blackout curtains and plywood fairing of the rear cockpit (because he was expecting to pick up Schneidau and his wife and family on his next trip). After evading night fighters fitted with searchlights, and getting lost by mistaking the shape of woods for cloud shadows, he found the pick-up field which was north of Châteauroux. As he circled, he received a flashed letter 'M' from the ground. He landed well, but the field was incredibly rough, and the crossing of three shallow 'ditches' or surface drains nearly broke the undercarriage and almost stalled the engine. The field seemed to be full of men running everywhere waving their arms. Lieut. 'Cartwright', the agent on this occasion, climbed up to his cockpit and shouted something about "getting to hell out of here quick" and "no time for taxying for a decent take-off run". 'Cartwright' climbed in and various suitcases were thrown in after him. Scotter used the extra emergency boost provided and got away without incident. He saw car headlights streaking towards the pick-up field and concluded that the Vichy police aided by Gestapo were after the men below, but never heard what happened.

He flew back to Tangmere, which was under attack, so he waited for a little and landed without lights, much to the consternation of some ground crews who thought for a time that it was some kind of German aircraft. For this trip Gordon Scotter was awarded an immediate Distinguished Flying Cross.

Philip Schneidau had been dropped by parachute on 10 March by Flight Lieutenant Oettle and crew 700 yards from his own house in a clearing at the edge of the Forest of Fontainebleau. The operation was principally to convey to Philip's intelligence network in Paris a wireless transmitter and codes. There was a roaring easterly wind and Philip's parachute was carried into the forest and hit a tree. It remained open and dragged Philip up the tree "like a monkey on a stick"[3]. Philip had swung hard against the tree, knocking out two molars and damaging one leg so that he walked with a slight limp. It took him one and a half hours to get everything down, including the wireless set which was between him and the parachute.

Philip took his damaged teeth to a politically reliable dentist for repairs. He discovered that this dentist in Paris had another 'patient' who was a German colonel. Under threats, the dentist had agreed to help this officer to smuggle gold back to Germany every time he went home on leave. A thick layer of gold, which he had obtained somehow, had to be attached to the backs of his front teeth. After this routine had been in progress for some time, the German colonel was so well disposed to the French dentist that he made him an honorary member of the officers' mess - a commandeered hotel where one could eat the best food available in Paris at that time. Subsequently, Philip was frequently invited to dine there as the dentist's guest and often fell into conversation with senior German officers.

While in France Philip started an intelligence réseau which was headed by his father-in-law Paul Shiffmacher, who financed all the expenses at the start. After he was denounced by 'La Chatte', he just survived the war in Buchenwald, but recovered enough to live until he was 93.

Scotter's second trip was on 10 May 1941, to pick up Schneidau from a field not far from his house. Special diversions by Hurricanes beating up airfields and small bomber raids were laid on in the area to keep German defences busy, but, in spite of this, the Lysander was closely followed by German night fighters mounting searchlights, which Scotter managed to avoid.

In a performance curve on which Scotter had plotted his own flight data in long-range Lysanders, I found the following information: with a top speed of 180 mph, maximum cruising speed was 164 mph and the range at that speed was 1,150 miles. Flying for maximum range at the slow speed of 120 mph, the range could be stretched to 1 640 miles. About a year later, in May 1942, Gordon Scotter was briefly attached to 161 Squadron for 'Briefing'. After a few weeks he was to start his work as a test pilot which led on to a post-war career with Rolls-Royce. In 1969, when he died at the age of 49, he was their sales manager for the Middle East.

On 25 August 1941, 1419 Flight, which had moved to Newmarket in May, turned into No 138 Squadron, still commanded by Knowles who was now a wing commander. In November 1941, Teddy Knowles was posted to command RAF Jurby in the Isle of Man - where he was later to kill himself stalling a visiting Whitley which he borrowed after lunch one day. 138 Squadron was then taken by Wing Commander W.J. Farley, DFC, who had done the first Lysander pick-up. The squadron now had seven Whitleys, two long range Lysanders and a Maryland[4] (an American twin-engined bomber).

Gordon Scotter.

John Nesbitt-Dufort, just promoted to squadron leader to command 'B' Flight of the new squadron, was known as 'Whippy' because he had once had to do a forced landing in among the wild animals in Whipsnade Zoo. He did the first 138 Squadron pick-up on the night of 4/5 September 1941. His Lysander had a large red question mark painted on the side of the fuselage. He used Tangmere as an advanced base and landed near La Champenoise between Châteauroux and Issoudun. His outbound passenger was Major Gerard ('Gerry') Morel and he picked up Major Jacques de Guélis. I later came to know these two splendid members of Buckmaster's French Section of SOE[5]. When Whippy arrived over the field, which he identified positively from the specially flown air photograph he had, there was no signal flashed. After circling for quarter of an hour, when he was just about to go home, he saw the correct letter - 'G' - being flashed from a field far over to his right. As he approached, he found a miniature flarepath in a field which was much too small and which ended in a row of trees. The take-off was a nightmare on a very rough field and too little distance to avoid the trees completely. Besides that, the Lysander went through telephone wires and - with a blinding flash - high tension cables.

On the way home, he flew just beneath two patrolling German night fighters but eluded them with a violent diving turn. Fog was forming at Tangmere as he returned, and his wireless was out of action after his encounter with high tension cables. The funnel lights on their poles were just above the fog level, and he dropped the Lysander in through the ground mist[6]. In the Cottage, de Guélis told them how he and his assistant had been held up by a routine police check of papers for over an hour just as they were about to bicycle the 15 kilometres to the field from Châteauroux. They pedalled furiously and, finding the Lysander already circling, picked the first handy field. It must have been the smallest ever used for a pick-up[6]. According to Georges Bégué, Bouguennec, de Guélis' assistant, had to get two hired bicycles back to Châteauroux because Morel took off and got away in the nearest wood.

Whippy Nesbitt-Dufort (now DSO) did operation 'Brick', which was equally successful, on 1/2 October 1941. He crossed the coast at le Tréport, was on the ground for three minutes on the airfield near Estrées-St-Denis, West of Compiègne, and came out of France near Dieppe. He brought back to England Captain Roman Czerniawski (known as 'Armand' or 'Valentin') of the Polish Air Force. He was one of the Poles who had missed the evacuation of the Polish army units in June 1940 and stayed behind to set up clandestine cells and networks. The story of Armand's Inter-allié intelligence network and his notorious assistant Mathilde Carré ('the Cat') has been told in several books[7] and is well worth reading.

In his book *The Big Network*[8], Wing Commander Garby-Czerniawski explains why he chose a disused aerodrome. It was, he thought, less likely to arouse suspicion than a noisy night landing in an ordinary field. He was assisted by 'Adam' (Lt. Mitchell)[9], a 'British' Agent, who had been trained to lay out a flarepath for Lysanders and 'Volta', one of his own agents, who was a French Air Force officer. He took with him a load of intelligence data concealed in a portable gramophone. (Lt. Mitchell was actually a French Gunner officer. His grandfather had been a Scottish immigrant and the family had kept English going as a second language. De Gaulle asked him to liaise with the Poles as an Englishman.)

The 1st October was a lovely day. His local agent told him that all was quiet on the airfield, but that soldiers from the infantry regiment in barracks one mile away passed the road alongside it. Armand did not worry as the soldiers would not walk along the road at midnight. The three of them travelled from Paris to Compiègne by train, having cheese sandwiches and coffee in a buffet compartment. The other customers were all German soldiers who seemed to be returning from leave in Paris. From the station they moved separately towards the aerodrome, followed the road on the south side and turned along an unused path which was covered on both sides by overgrown bushes. Armand said: "Let's sit here quietly in the bushes and wait till darkness comes, then we will move to the hangars. They are nearer to our proposed 'flarepath'. They are obviously abandoned. How nice of the Germans to leave them open for us, and unguarded!" When it was dark and before the moon rose they went to the hangars. In the dark hangar each word seemed to be echoed loudly. Volta unwrapped their sandwiches and opened the thermos flasks. They ate and drank in silence, looking towards the open door and the moonlit space beyond.

"Quarter-past eleven", said Adam in a low voice. "Let's move to the door and take a look."

The moon was full, and the sky was covered with myriads of twinkling stars. The field was bathed in a bright, misty-blue light. For half a mile all details could be seen clearly. It looked more like a fairy-tale scene than reality.

"How quiet; how beautiful!" murmured Volta.

"Eleven twenty-five", said Adam, looking at his wrist-watch. "Take positions. Remember, don't flash your torches until I start, and then keep a steady light until the 'plane touches the ground."

They moved into position, forming a long improvised flare-path in the shape of the letter 'L', the longer arm of which was pointing towards the down-wind end of the aerodrome, some 300 yards from its flat edge. There was Adam; Armand's place was some 150 yards upwind, and Volta's about 50 yards to his left. The Lysander was supposed to touch the ground at the light of Adam's lamp and finish its landing run between the other two.

Adam waited until they reached their proper positions and then gave the sign to lie down. They looked carefully all around, and especially towards the road which passed the aerodrome. No human soul in sight... they settled down to wait. The night was so quiet that Armand could hear his wrist-watch ticking. He felt warm, wearing a light mackintosh which was to protect him against the wind and cold during the flight. He was lying against his gramophone case. In his outstretched right hand the metal case of the torch reflected the cold light of the moon.

Time passed. Eleven thirty-five... forty. Eleven forty-five... Armand thought: "They are late; I hope nothing is wrong..." He looked around. Everything quiet. The road on the south side, clearly seen now, was empty. The barracks, which before were clearly lit, were now in nearly complete darkness with only a few lights in the windows. Five minutes to midnight; then out of the quietness of the night a distant sound. No... yes... now louder, louder, but still very distant. Now - there was no mistake now! It was a low-flying 'plane approaching.

Suddenly from Adam's torch there was a strong beam of light. Then the other two torches were switched on. The aeroplane, visible now some 300 feet up, was coming straight towards the aerodrome. Armand expected it to circle first but the pilot made a quarter turn, barely sufficient to bring it into the wind, throttled it back and then was bringing it in to land! "Amazing fellow, this pilot! What quick decision and execution", thought Armand.

The Lysander made a short landing, bumping strongly, stopped, braking briskly, turned sharp left and taxied quickly back to the take-off position near Adam. Running beside it, caught in the wind produced by the propeller, hearing the roar of the engine, Armand felt himself suddenly back in the Air Force - a pleasant feeling, temporarily suppressing any other sensation. Adam took the gramophone box and helped Armand to scramble upwards. Then he thrust the gramophone up into his out-stretched hand and shouted: "Good luck!"

Whippy turned around smiling, his white teeth shining in the moonlight. Armand could clearly see his lean face with dark eyes and a black moustache.

"OK!" Armand tried in his best English.

"*C'est la vie. C'est la guerre!*" Whippy replied grinning, in his best French. These were the only words either of them knew in these languages.

With a high-pitched roar, the Lysander moved only a short distance before the nose rose suddenly, and they were airborne, turning steeply north-west. Looking down Armand clearly saw a man walking along the road alongside the aerodrome. He wondered what he would have thought had he noticed the RAF markings. Would he have thought it an hallucination or a dream?

They were flying very low; and in the brilliant moonlight they could see fields and houses as clearly as in daylight. Armand suddenly remembered that they could be followed. The cabin was not armed; the parachute was lying on the floor - a type entirely unknown to him. Turning the harness in all possible directions in the semi darkness of the cabin, he could not make head nor tail of it, and finally gave up, dropping it back on the floor. His eyes caught something more interesting - a thermos, and a packet of biscuits and chocolate! "No machine gun, no parachute, so let's get busy with the chocolate", he thought. "Delicious, after all the restrictions in German-occupied territory!" Munching happily at biscuits and chocolate, he could carry on admiring the magnificent view. By now, still flying very low, they were approaching the Channel. A searchlight from very far left suddenly crossed the sky above them; another appeared from very far right. Whippy unexpectedly fired a red Verey light and - the searchlights disappeared.

For a moment Armand was completely puzzled. What sort of co-operation was this? Then he laughed. Of course! The RAF must have known the German flak-protection colour for this night, and used it for their own benefit.

Now they had left the Continent and were flying over the Channel. As far as the eye could see the water sparkled in thousands of reflections of the moonlight from the tops of the small waves. The Lysander gradually gained height and John started to speak: "One, two, three, four - " and then speaking at intervals in English, words and sentences which Armand could not understand. On the misty grey-blue horizon appeared a dark line, becoming thicker and thicker; England approaching. Suddenly, on the right, thousands of lights burst into the semi-darkness of the night, bringing the contours of an airfield into view, and an illuminated runway. The Lysander turned sharply and came into the corridor of lights.

When, after taxying for a while across a (by now) darkened aerodrome, they stopped, two shadowy figures approached the aircraft. With his precious gramophone in one hand Armand jumped down to the ground.

One of the two, Philip Schneidau, in RAF uniform, came up to Armand. He spoke in French:

"*Comment allez vous, Armand?* I am Flight Lieutenant Phillipson, RAF Liaison Officer, and this is the Station Commander. We are invited by him for a drink and then for dinner. It's rather an unusual time for it, but you must need it!"

"Thank you. Thank you very much. I will be only too pleased."

A car appeared and they rushed off at tremendous speed. It had been moonlight in France; here it was a dark, misty night with a hint of coming fog. Armand looked at the driver. Under the cap was the face of a lovely girl. They came to a road between houses and, on the first turn, suddenly another car appeared. Armand thought: "This is the end! We are on the wrong side of the road..." He closed his eyes, but - nothing happened. The girl was driving quietly, as though nothing unusual had occurred. Of course, Armand, realised, in England - left-hand driving. He could not help laughing. In all this interesting night the only thing which had made him afraid was English left-hand driving.

When, after dinner, he was picking up his mackintosh, a newspaper fell from its pocket on to the floor.

"Look - how funny - tonight's *Paris-Soir* from German - occupied France - and we are in England!"

"Wonderful!" exclaimed the Station Commander. "I will see that this newspaper is on the King's breakfast-table in the morning. I can imagine how surprised His Majesty will be!"

On this trip to London Armand was involved in high-level conferences with British intelligence and with the Polish General Staff. General Sikorski decorated him with the highest Polish gallantry award, the Order of Virtuti Militari, equivalent to the British VC. On 9/10 October he was parachuted back to occupied France by a Whitley. Whippy Nesbitt-Dufort's third and last successful pick-up was on the night of 7th November 1941. It is not recorded by the RAF but SIS records give it as operation 'Brick', taking one passenger to occupied France and bringing two back, 'Fitzroy' and 'Brick' himself.

This may have been the trip referred to in his book[10] as having taken place *before* the trip on which he picked up 'Armand'. They were both code-named 'Brick' and both seem to have been at Estrées St-Denis. 'Brick' must have been Lt. Mitchell - Armand's friend 'Adam'.

On one of his pick-ups, using Ford as an advanced base, John Dufort picked up an agent who had been on the run and was absolutely exhausted. His socks were soaked in blood. The escorting officer, 6 foot 5 inches Captain Douglas Dodds-Parker of the Grenadier Guards, agreed that he should rest at John's house in Middleton-on-Sea before going with him to London for debriefing. Mrs Nesbitt-Dufort, who now had to be told what her husband was doing, was astonished when the agent emptied "a positive arsenal" out of his pockets at 3 am[10].

On 8/9 December 1941 Flight Lieutenant A.M. Murphy (known as 'Sticky') flew the operation to Belgium on which he was shot. I have already told the story, as it was told to me in 1942, in Chapter One (pages 11-12). What follows is closely based on the 138 Squadron Operations Record Book. It is extraordinary that it makes no mention at all of Sticky's neck wound nor of the bullet holes in the Lysander. Sam Hollis remembers that there were many more than the 30 I had been told, and it was he who had had to supervise the repairing of the aeroplane.

The Squadron Record Book in the early days was deliberately vague. In 419 Flight, the adjutant was a part-time operational pilot; the security blanket was really tight - no base airfield names nor target names were allowed in log books. The intelligence officer at Newmarket did not know the real function, although he knew the area of each operation. Neither did the Station Commander at Stradishall know the operational function. There were a number of different clients, none of whom wanted any of the others to know about their operations. In fact SIS forbade any written matter. Their operations were "officially inadmissible"[11].

Bunny Rymills, who was flying Whitleys in 138 Squadron, knew Sticky and described him as having a "wispy moustache. He spoke in a limpid manner, rather like Leslie Howard. He was a bosom pal of Guy Lockhart". Bob Hodges remembers him at Cranwell as a cheerful, athletic extrovert.

Sticky was airborne at 2210 on operation 'Stoat'. He set course for Abbeville and from there to Neufchâteau where he pinpointed the aerodrome at 2350. Map-reading was easy because the snow on the ground made the woods stand out clearly. He circled the area until 0040 when he saw a light flashing south of the aerodrome and another light with a steady beam. To identify himself he closed the throttles twice. There was no sign of the agreed letter from the agent, Captain Jean Cassart of the Belgian Air Force. Cassart had chosen 'L' because it was his king's initial. Sticky "concluded agent was being chased so it was therefore decided to land". Twenty yards before the touch-down point he used his landing light and saw a sharp dip in the ground ahead so he took off again. He then decided to land on the eastern side of the aerodrome.

When the aircraft stopped moving he stayed where he was with his revolver ready. At 0055 there was an explosion "which I thought had been my revolver firing, but this was not the case and it was the enemy approaching and being belligerent". He took off at 0100 and landed at 0320. Meanwhile, on the ground, Jean Cassart was also shot by German soldiers but escaped. Ice on the roads had delayed his arrival at Neufchâteau until just before the agreed start of the rendezvous time, 2300 hours. With his wireless operator, Henri Verhaegen, he went to lay out the torches on the snow-covered field.

As they returned to the red lamp on the edge of the field Henri stopped him: "I hear voices." The moon was rising and they thought they could see shadows. Were they soldiers or peasants? After three more steps they realised that there were five dark shapes wearing helmets. Jean cocked his revolver. Suddenly the challenge: "*Wer da? Halt!*" Jean and Henri turned and ran. They were two against five. There were shouts in German and a fusillade. Jean realised that a bullet had wounded his left arm near his heart. He slid down a slope and rolled under some barbed wire fences, without a scratch. At the bottom of the slope he jumped a stream, slipped on ice, fell in and lost his revolver. Panting for breath he clambered up the steep slope towards a dark mass that he thought was a wood. Just as he was nearly at the top another cry, "*Halt!*" rang out. He dashed to his left and was greeted by two rifle shots. He dragged himself to some bushes by the wall of Neufchâteau cemetery. He thought he would climb a fence into a meadow but saw German soldiers there. Behind him others were closing in. He dropped down on to a pile of empty tins between the thin bushes and the wall.

Five soldiers were following his tracks in the snow with their torches. In his black coat against the snow he felt sure they would see him - especially when he was once in the direct beam of a torch. One of them said "I suppose it could be an old track" and they strolled off. Meanwhile his radio-operator Henri was captured but succeeded in escaping. His driver returned to their car, found it surrounded by soldiers and made off.

Then Jean started worrying about the Lysander pilot. He believed it would be Whippy Nesbitt-Dufort, who had trained him. Surely, nobody would find the torches and switch them on? They were in place but still in their boxes. He prayed that they would not be found. In any case, he was the only person in Belgium who knew the letter: 'L'. He heard the Lysander's engine. There was the aeroplane coming from the west, turning through 180° and flying low over the airstrip. There was the signal: throttling back twice. The torches must have been switched on. Surely, he would not land without the letter. Then he saw the Lysander come in again very low and switch on its brilliant landing lamp. Perhaps he would land, even though the signal had not been flashed, and become the victim of his own generosity.

From his grandstand view on the hill, Jean saw the Lysander do another circuit and land. Then German soldiers came out of the woods shouting and firing their rifles[12]. The Lysander immediately took off, turned sharply and flew low exactly over Jean. "How", thought Jean, "will I ever be able to thank that man for risking his life to save mine?" A few days later Captain Jean Cassart was captured and taken to Berlin for trial, but was able to make his escape and finally managed to return to England.

On 28/29 January, Whippy Nesbitt-Dufort took one passenger out to a field near

John Nesbitt-Dufort's Lysander in France.
Crown Copyright

Issoudun and picked up two. On the way home - as I have already mentioned - he was forced to turn back by heavy icing and force-landed near Issoudun. He tipped his Lysander on its nose and went into hiding. This was the last 138 Squadron pick up operation[13].

So it was that the early pioneers had started to establish pick-ups in World War Two. It was as if the forerunners of No 161 Squadron's 'A' Flight were tapping in the thin edge of a rather large wedge. Farley had done one, Scotter two and Nesbitt-Dufort three successful pick-ups. Before Murphy had finished, he would have done five.

'Sticky' Murphy

CHAPTER FOUR

161 Squadron Takes Off

Before Sticky Murphy could do another pick-up, the Special Duties Squadron strength was doubled. On 18 December 1941 No 138 Squadron moved to Stradishall. It had 12 Whitleys, 3 Halifaxes (four engined bombers adapted for parachuting agents) and 3 Lysanders.

On 14 February 1942, No 161 Squadron started to form at Newmarket under Wing Commander E.H. Fielden, MVO, AFC, who had been Captain of the King's Flight at Benson. Its establishment of aircraft was 7 Lysanders, 5 Whitley Vs, 2 Wellingtons and one Hudson (from the King's Flight). The initial complement of pilots included Flight Lieutenant A.M. Murphy, DFC, and Pilot Officer Guy Lockhart, both from 138 Squadron.

Before the war Guy Lockhart had been serving on a short service commission. One day he beat up the airfield flying so low that the Air Officer Commanding had to fall flat on his face. The ensuing court martial ended Guy Lockhart's service with the RAF in peace-time. When the war started he rejoined as a sergeant pilot.

The first 161 Squadron pick-up was successfully flown by Sticky Murphy on the night of 27/28 February. In preparation for this the Tangmere Station records show that: "Wing Commander E.H. Fielden, MVO (RAFO), Air Equerry to the King and Captain of the King's Flight (sic), arrived with Squadron Leader Murphy" on 26th February 1942. On the next day, Mouse Fielden and 12 men of 161 Squadron, who arrived that day, were billeted in Tangmere Cottage.

For operation 'Baccarat' Murphy took off at 2145 on 27 February. He found solid cloud cover over the French coast at 1,000 ft and only 3,000 yards visibility below. Failing to fix his position near Abbeville, he flew north-west until he could get a radio fix from base. Then he found Abbeville and set course for St. Saëns where, at midnight, he landed one passenger and picked up two, including Rémy.

The new arrival in France was an unknown young woman called 'Anatole'. Rémy reported: "She laughs, very happy to be back in France. I understand that she totally vanished"[1]. Rémy himself was one of de Gaulle's best intelligence agents[2]. His real name was Gilbert Renault-Roulier and he wrote many books after the war about his intelligence network, the *Confrérie de Notre Dame* (CND).

On 1 March 1942, 161 Squadron moved to Graveley and Murphy was promoted to Squadron Leader, commanding the Lysander Flight. That same night, 1/2 March, Sticky Murphy carried out a remarkable rescue operation in an Anson. It had been borrowed from 'B' Flight of the Bomber Command Operational Training Unit at Abingdon, where yellow Ansons were used for training. Curiously enough, the Flight Commander was John Corby who was later to be the Wing Commander Operations at RAF Tempsford. Although he knew what it was borrowed for, the rest of the unit never knew what it was used for on that sortie. All they knew was that when it was returned it had been sprayed black all over, including the windows. Ansons were very slow twin-engined aircraft used mainly for training navigators or patrolling round coastal convoys to keep submarines below the surface.

On this trip Murphy was accompanied by Pilot Officer Henry ('Tich') Cossar, a wireless operator. They set off from Tangmere at 2100, flew over Cabourg an hour later and set course for Tours. Then heavy cloud and rain made map-reading difficult and their fix on the Loire was delayed until 2315. From 2330 to 2355 they were lost. Then they could set course for Issoudun and they saw their reception committee's lights at 0010.

The four passengers, including Whippy Nesbitt-Dufort and the intelligence agents[3] that he had gone to collect, embarked "very rapidly" and the Anson then took off agonisingly slowly, according to Whippy's report[4]. They were airborne at 0015 and set course for Cabourg. For some unexplained reason they actually crossed the French coast at Dieppe and finally landed at 0240. This was the first pick-up by a twin-engined aircraft and the only one by an Anson. When the Anson was returned to Abingdon, the crew did not want to face its owner's fury that it had been painted black. They simply parked it and climbed into the back of the Lysander which had come with them and flew away.

On the same night of 1/2 March Flying Officer Guy Lockhart collected two passengers successfully on his first pick-up operation, 'Crème'. They were Stanislas Mangin and Louis Andlauer (later a French Air Force Colonel) who wrote the following account of this operation for this book:

"Just out of prison, I was hiding in a village in the Massif Central, waiting impatiently for my friends in the Ali-Tyr network to find a safe answer to the problem of what to do with a blown agent (me). At last a telephone message: "Tomorrow at 20 hours your sister will meet you at the Montluçon station." So, by gas producer coach and overcrowded train, 1 arrive at Montluçon station, which seems full of cops in uniform or in plain clothes. At the exit, after a baggage check, I hear "Follow me" and recognise the back of Descroizettes. He takes two tickets for the coach to Néris-les-Bains - a spa for curing rheumatism. Our hotel is full of old people there to take the waters. We find Gaston Tavian, Edgar Tupet and his radio operator. At dinner, the thin menu is reinforced by a tin of paté de foie (unrationed for those who can afford it).

Suddenly, the lights dim spasmodically. "It's nothing - just the radio transmitting." After dinner we go for a stroll, three young men of twenty, looking obvious among all the aged patients. I notice some uniformed airmen whose job is searching for clandestine transmissions. "Luckily, there's a metal grill between our aerial and theirs." Maybe, but my impression is that those lads are deaf and blind, even if voluntarily.

After a day or two, during dinner, when the lights have been flickering, the radio operator arrives, smiling from ear to ear. "It's in the bag!" The Lysander pick-up requested by Stanislas Mangin has been authorised by the RAF. The second seat has been allocated to the black sheep (me). Tavian went directly to the farm at Les Lagnys near Vatan to meet Monsieur Faillon; Tupet, Mangin and I went to Issoudun by gas producer coach and made our way separately to the Toulouse Hotel. Although we disappear separately during the day, in the evening we are three twenty-year-olds with meat, wine and all sorts of extras with unlimited (false) ration cards - but so discreetly.

We search for bicycles to hire but find only two. After a few days a discreet telephone call from Néris-les-Bains: it is on tonight. After dinner we three, with two bicycles, set off for Les Lagnys - twenty kilometres by little roads. In spite of these precautions, we come across some gendarmes who, luckily, let us pass by without asking questions. At the farm, we meet Tavian, eat a snack and at 2330 make our way to the field for the witching hour of midnight.

Monsieur Faillon had agreed with Edgar Tupet to put a field at our disposal throughout the year for parachute or landing operations. The demands of farming meant that three different fields were used, one of which belonged to an adjacent farm. Cultivation was planned so that one of the fields would always be available. The fields were camouflaged by growing different crops in the same field and carts and wagons were left in the field during daylight.

At midnight it is cold. We stamp our feet but dare not talk. After twenty minutes a distant hum. Is it an aeroplane? a train? a car? It is an aeroplane but the sound gets fainter. "The bastard! He's buggering off!" No, he is coming back. Morse letters are exchanged by torch. It was no easy matter to find torch batteries and transparent red paper, but somebody had succeeded in finding four torches and batteries. At last the flarepath torches can be switched on. An appalling roar as the aircraft flies over. "Good God, he will wake up all the gendarmes in Châteauroux and Issoudun!" OK a circuit and he lands. Damn! now we cannot see or hear him. A loud noise and he is back, ready to take off, and he throttles back.

Edgar Tupet runs to talk English to the pilot. I find a way to climb into the back cockpit. It is not easy by moonlight with an unknown aeroplane. I manage to open the cabin roof; I have no idea how. On the floor I find a packet. I throw it out with the free gift of my wallet with false papers, false ration cards, genuine cash and the obligatory photo of my fiancée. I help Mangin to climb in. I slide the roof shut. "Damn it, Edgar and the pilot are still talking. Will they hurry up?" At last, Edgar moves away, a great exchange of waves, full throttle and in a moment we are airborne.

On the floor of the cabin there is a shapeless heap. One could find a parachute, no, two, and a thingamajig which must be the harness. I try for several minutes to see how it works. No good; it is too complicated. Too bad. Forget it. We see a wide river ahead that we cross. It must be the Loire. Now we are over the occupied zone. OK if we don't hit a snag. The coast, the sea, an exchange of coloured rockets and we are over the English countryside. Phew! At last one can breathe freely. No more clink; no more continuous blue funk; no more need to watch everything, note everything; no more black fear as in a bottomless well.

We land. A car takes us to a very British meal. We have no opportunity to thank the pilot. For him, it is just his job. At last we can hit the hay with our mail under the pillow. The next morning, a delicious breakfast, egg, toast and tea. Mangin goes to London and I have three or four days rest at the "Patriotic School" as a Guest of His Gracious Majesty the King of England, to whom I owe, like so many others, the possibility of breathing again in freedom."

The field mentioned by Colonel Andlauer at the adjacent farm belonged to Monsieur Mouchet of Barillon. This and the fields at Les Lagnys were used for no fewer than five Lysander landings in 1942 alone, in spite of Jean Faillon's interrogation by the police after this one.

Guy Lockhart was successful again near Saumur on 26/27 March when he landed one passenger ('Rémy'), was stuck in mud on the field for 17 minutes and brought two people back. These were Christian Pineau of 'Libération' and François Faure of CND[5].

The tempo of successful Lysander pick-up landings was building up. In the whole of 1941, there had been five. In March and April, there would be six.

In the dark period between the March/April moon and the moon period at the end of April 1942, 161 Squadron moved yet again; this time from Graveley to Tempsford, near Sandy in Bedfordshire. This was to be the permanent base of the two Special

Duties Squadrons in the UK until the end of these operations. The Station Commander who opened up Tempsford was Group Captain A.H. MacDonald.

Meanwhile, in central France, the Gaullist SOE party 'Cod' was running into trouble. Its leader, Thomé, sent a telegram demanding a Lysander. Lockhart did the trip on 26/27 April. His outbound passenger was Pierre Beech ('Gazelle') on his way to join the Tyr network as a radio operator. The field, which was NNE of Châteauroux, must have been one of the fields on Les Lagnys farm. Guy reported:

"Unfortunately the landing ground was on a hill and I bumped my landing. The engine commenced to burn so I switched off. Meanwhile 'Gazelle' disembarked with luggage and disappeared. After six or seven minutes the flames died out so I started the engine and taxied to light 'A' where the two passengers embarked." The two passengers were Gaston Tavian and Lieutenant de Vaisseau Mariotti (Rousseau)[6].

Tavian, who had laid out the flarepath, "had no really urgent need to get out of France and no proper training in landing a Lysander"[7]. After this incident the RAF insisted on much tighter control of pick-up operations. The Air Ministry, on behalf of the squadron, refused to lay on any landings unless the agent in charge had been trained by 161 Squadron's own pilots. Anyhow, Tavian was trained to handle Lysanders properly while he was in England. He went back to France by Murphy's last Lysander operation on 29/30 May (operation 'Shrimp'), with a view to reinforcing 'Sol', a Gaullist organisation in St. Etienne.

On the following night, 27/28 April 1942, Murphy's target was a field near St. Saëns. Airborne from Tangmere at 2245 he tested his magneto switches over Beachy Head. The engine cut dead. He returned to base and was airborne again at 0045. He set course for Abbeville and struck the coast three miles north of le Tréport. Pressing on, he found it very dark under the cloud cover and difficult to pick out the shapes of the woods. Eventually he fixed his position on a wood 15 miles north of St. Saëns. At 0200 he saw the light flashing the correct letter and landed a minute later.

Christian Pineau and François Faure climbed out; a minute later the agent shouted "OK" and he took off. After setting course for the coast, he slid his side windows shut. "I immediately became conscious of a powerful smell of perfume, and I assumed that I had a female on board; it was with pleasurable anticipation that I flew back." His operation report gives no account of any sequel and this is not surprising. According to Noguères[8] his passengers were two very important male leaders of the Resistance, Pierre Brossolette[9] and Jacques Robert. Robert weighed about 16 stone; he had been one of the French tank commanders who put up a really stiff fight when the Germans broke through in 1940. The "powerful smell of perfume" must have been due to the stopper working loose in a bottle one of them was carrying.

April 1942 saw some changes in the cast. Squadron Leader John Nesbitt-Dufort, DSO, was posted to Headquarters Fighter Command and Flight Lieutenant A.H.C. Boxer, later to be the squadron commander, was posted in to the parachute dropping flight. Pilot Officers Peter Vaughan-Fowler and John Bridger were posted in to the pick-up flight. Guy Lockhart was promoted to Acting Flight Lieutenant.

On 28 May 1942 John Mott was forced to abandon his Lysander on the field in unoccupied France after trying without success to make it burn. The Germans exhibited the aircraft in their museum of captured enemy equipment at Nanterre, near Paris, until they destroyed the museum during their retreat in the Autumn of 1944.

Jimmy Langley[10] of MI9 had a young Belgian fighter pilot called Alex Nitelet who had been shot down over France losing an eye. Now that he could no longer fly, he volunteered to join the PAT escape organisation, which had helped him. He was to be a wireless operator working for Lieutenant-Commander 'Patrick O'Leary' (Albert Guérisse). Jimmy heard that a Lysander was scheduled for an operation in the May moon to pick up an agent on the run and managed to arrange for Alex Nitelet to fly to France with John Mott. When the Lysander was bogged and had to be abandoned, Alex escaped but John was arrested by the Vichy police and sent to a prison camp on the Riviera. He later escaped and returned to England, but not to 161 Squadron.

The agent in charge of the field, Claude Lamirault, was assisted by Pierre Hentic ('Trellu'). When the pilot had to abandon his Lysander, Hentic gave him his identity papers to help him on his way. Then, with no papers, Hentic was arrested and thought to be the pilot. He was thrown into the same police cell as André Simon, the son and successor of the wine expert. He had been due to receive Lockhart's Lysander on that same night of 28/29 May, not far away. No wonder Guy reported "No signal seen".

The only successful pick-up in May was Sticky Murphy's landing South of Vatan in the unoccupied zone of France, on 29/30, with two passengers each way. This was Sticky's sixth and last clandestine landing. Apart from the landing in Belgium, when he was shot by the Germans, every pick-up operation he had attempted had been successfully completed. His DSO had been awarded on 19 May.

He was posted to HQ 3 Group, and Guy Lockhart took over from him as OC 'A' Flight as an acting Squadron Leader. Even in the environment of rapid promotion to cope with the war-time expansion of RAF strength and to replace the casualties which were especially heavy in senior operational ranks, Guy's promotion record was phenomenal. He had been a Pilot Officer in February 1942 and in June of the same year he was already an acting Squadron Leader, having been promoted three times in four months.

Between the end of May and the end of August 1942 there is no RAF record of any pick-ups being laid on. After the defection of Mathilde Carré ('the Cat') and the consequent arrests, the French section of SOE had no properly organised circuits in occupied France at all[11]. It was necessary for the special duties squadrons to keep their hands in and to improve their skill at navigating over occupied France. The Lysanders joined the Whitleys in bombing targets in France, including the Oissel chemical works, the power station at Aure and railway targets. Lockhart, Bridger and Vaughan-Fowler were joined by Flight Lieutenant Huntley, Flying Officer McIndoe and Warrant Officer Kingham on these operations. They could drop two 250 lb bombs from the detachable stub-wings on the undercarriage fairings. These stub-wings also housed fixed machine guns and an air gunner was carried in the rear cockpit for these trips. Presumably the manoeuvrability gave the Lysanders extra accuracy to compensate for the small weight of bombs carried. Certainly they found their targets more often than the Whitleys.

After this long gap, one of the first pick-ups was almost disastrous. Guy set off on 31st August 1942, failed to return and was reported missing. But he was not away long: on 13th September, looking tanned and fit in tropical uniform, he hitch-hiked back to Tempsford from Gibraltar with Flt Lt Sutton of 138 Squadron.

It seems that the agent in charge of the landing was drunk and laid the flarepath over a ditch which broke the Lysander's undercarriage. There was no alternative to burning the aeroplane and setting off, with his intended homeward-bound passengers,

Christian Pineau and Cavaillès, to a maritime pick-up which, luckily, was planned on the Riviera. In a fit of alcoholic remorse, the agent gave Guy a wad of money to help him on his journey south. Guy already had three escape kits with him, his own and two that he had borrowed. Each contained 20,000 francs or about £100.

The Gendarmerie Nationale have in their archives a report of the crash at about 0300 hours on 1st September between Arbigny and the Uchizy bridge over the Saône NNW of Pont-de-Vaux. The aircraft was completely burnt, but they found nearby a parachute marked "LOCKHART". A 'nomad' who had been sleeping on the Uchizy bridge reported seeing two unidentified individuals crossing it.

Operation 'Léda II' took place on the beach at Narbonne-Plage. The passengers had to be ferried in a small boat to a felucca with a Polish crew from a peculiar part of the Royal Navy which was based at Gibraltar. The little boat had to make two trips. The first load (according to Noguères[12]) included 'Wing Commander Henry' as Guy was now calling himself, anticipating his next promotion. The boat was already on its way towards the felucca when some coast-guards (*douaniers*) intervened, firing their pistols, and carelessly wounding each other. (Other versions of this story have it that Guy shot one himself or, alternatively, butted him in his stomach with his head).

Guy Lockhart's burnt Lysander.

As the alert had been sounded Pineau and Cavaillès made off, but were picked up on the road by gendarmes in the small hours and imprisoned.

When Guy arrived in Gibraltar he found the local MI9 officer in desperate need of French bank notes for his agents running evasion routes across Europe. He was only too glad to buy 80,000 francs from Guy. So it was that Guy could afford to bring back enough sherry and cigarettes to keep 'A' Flight's mess bills down to negligible proportions for months. Another compensation for this alarming adventure was the immediate DSO which he was awarded on 27th September.

Although no other pick-up in August 1942 is listed in the Squadron Operation Record Book, there is the account by Marie-Madeleine Fourcade[13] of the first Lysander pick-up for her 'Alliance' intelligence organisation which took place during that August moon. This, she says, was their first use of Thalamy airfield in the mountainous country near Ussel in the Corrèze, West of Clermont-Ferrand.

Commandant (Air Force Major) Léon Faye was "whisked away as though by magic", on a mission to London. She had appointed a young Air Force pilot Pierre Dallas as head of her 'Avia' clandestine airmail service. He was 26, slim, and with a swarthy face that denoted gypsy blood. On the technicalities of meeting RAF requirements for landing strips and 'flarepath' lighting, he was assisted by "the British officer Crowley" (actually the bilingual Arthur-Louis Gachet) who had been parachuted in for the job the previous month, July 1942. He clearly remembered this pick-up when I met him at Thalamy in 1977. Baron Fernand Lepage sent out the

Belgian spy William Ugeux by this operation.

On 25/26 September Pilot Officers Bridger and Vaughan-Fowler attempted their first pick-ups. On operation 'Vesta', John Bridger landed in pelting rain near the junction of the rivers Ain and Rhône, but his flarepath was laid out in a field across the Rhône and 500 yards east of the field briefed. He found it covered with short stubble and very wet and soft. One wheel sank in axle deep and had to be dug out by four pairs of hands. To clear the mud from his wheels he used a screwdriver to remove the side panels of his undercarriage spats. He had great difficulty in taking off. But the worst thing was that Major Jean Boutron, the passenger he had come to fetch, had not arrived on the field because they all thought a landing on such a filthy night could not be attempted. All John brought back to England after a trip lasting nine and a quarter hours was one package of mail and the undercarriage panels he had removed. However, he had succeeded in bringing Léon Faye back to Marie-Madeleine's 'Alliance', and, with him, much needed cash and codes[14].

Another operation which had been planned for the last night of the September moon, operation 'Prune', was cancelled by Colonel Rémy[15]. Michel Pichard, who told me about it, was due to travel with him to a field of the *Confrérie de Notre-Dame* (CND) at Lyon-la-Forêt near Rouen. Waiting to be picked up were the Petit family, Max, his wife Fanny and their two children. "The Wing Commander" told Rémy that fog in Normandy made the chance of success only 25%. Rémy admits that "his" decision to cancel was in part due to the fact that he was "morally" tired at the time[15]. This story interests me as it is the only time I have ever heard it said that a passenger was involved in a decision to cancel a planned pick-up operation. If he was "morally" tired at that time, Rémy had good reasons. He had already completed two missions in France and his mother, five sisters and a brother had been arrested.

Rémy and Pichard were staying with Major and Mrs Bertram at the time. Tony Bertram was a good friend of ours as he often brought SIS passengers to the Cottage at Tangmere or picked them up. They lived in a delightful house not far away up on the Downs. We used to tease him mercilessly and he gave us good reasons to do so. For example, one night he came with us to see Terence Rattigan's play *Flare-path* on the stage of our camp cinema. As we walked out he remarked: "That's the sort of play I could have written but would not have wanted to."

On 1st October 1942 Mouse Fielden was promoted to Group Captain to command RAF Tempsford, replacing Group Captain A.H. MacDonald. He was replaced as OC 161 Squadron by Wing Commander Pickard.

The weather in the October moon was very bad. There was so much cloud in the target areas in France that four of the six operations attempted had to be abandoned. This was the fate of two attempts by Flg Off McIndoe and two by Pick. On the homeward flight from one of these attempts, Pick was shot at by a convoy as he crossed the Channel.

After climbing down from his Lysander cockpit following one of these flights, Pick was nearly run over on the perimeter track by a Halifax which had just landed. The captain of the Halifax was Bunny Rymills, who was just coming to the end of his tour of parachuting operations in 138 Squadron. When they were comfortably in the Cottage, Pick, who always wanted to play cards after a trip, asked Bunny to join him in a game. Pick told Bunny that any bloody fool could drop Joes over France and offered him a job as a Lysander pilot. This was agreed and Ron Hockey, CO of 138 Squadron, was furious with Pick for pinching one of his pilots.

Only on 26/27 October were there successful landings, by John Bridger and Peter Vaughan-Fowler. Peter landed south of Mâcon with two passengers, including Paimblanc for de Gaulle, and brought back Dubourdin with Cowburn. Cowburn had had to steal a boat to cross the Saône[16]. John Bridger, on operation 'Achilles'[17], landed at Thalamy airfield east of Ussel on a flarepath extemporised by Gachet with solid meta fuel. Pierre Dallas, who was supposed to be in charge, had the flashlamps with him and he had fallen asleep in the train, missing Ussel station. Mary Lindell, working for Jimmy Langley (MI9) arrived from England and went on her way. Aged 47, she had arrived in England during the summer and been trained by Airey Neave to run an escape and evasion line. From her base in Ruffec she set up the Marie-Claire line. Before boarding her Lysander she remembers her pilot saying how much he appreciated that she was going back to France to help aircrew in spite of the fact that she was already on the Gestapo's wanted list. She became the Comtesse de Milleville. The other passenger was the brilliant British wireless operator Ferdinand Rodriguez.

Just after John Bridger took off, Dallas and Marie-Madeleine's brother Jacques came sprinting on to the field. Jacques was supposed to have travelled on the return flight. For the second Lysander pick-up for the 'Alliance' organisation, John Bridger had flown home empty-handed. Marie-Madeleine was "utterly dismayed", but she said that she could not really blame Dallas. For months he had been perpetually on the move, "sleeping with one eye open".

While I was training myself at Tempsford the Operational Lysander pilots were at Tangmere for the two weeks operations of the November moon. I was of course very curious to know how it had gone, as soon as I could ask them - when they flew to Tempsford on 1st December.

On 18/19 November Guy had been defeated by the weather in the target area when attempting a double Lysander landing with Peter between Châteauroux and Vatan. By the time he crossed the French coast on the way home he was well off track and over St. Malo. There he was engaged by searchlights and flak. A little later on, flying near Jersey, he was, he said, attacked by seven Focke-Wulf 190s. (These were normally day fighters). They seemed to be coming at him from all directions so he evaded them by spinning his Lysander down to cloud level. They followed him and he finally threw them off by diving through the cloud and flying just above the sea. Eventually he landed at Warmwell near Weymouth, about two hours after Peter had landed at Tangmere. Guy then had only five gallons of fuel left of the 250 he had started with.

This was the first double operation ever attempted. If there were more passengers to pick up than one Lysander could carry it was obviously better for both Lysanders to land and take off as close together as possible. Every time a field was used there was a danger of alerting the security forces on the ground. The arrangement this time was that Peter would accompany Guy in formation, following his dim blue wing tip lights, which were fitted for formation flying at night in operations when normal red and green navigation lights would be dangerously bright. The experiment did not work. In the cloud which Guy had to go through on the way to Châteauroux, Peter found it impossible to follow him. After this it was always thought better for both Lysanders in a double operation to make their way separately to a rendezvous which was easy to find. This should be so near the target that they could easily go to it, but not so near that the first to arrive would alert the local defences if he had to wait because the other was delayed.

The other sorties of that November moon had no similar excitements to report. Of a total of nine, six were successful. John Bridger had successfully found his field ('Courgette') at Courlaoux near Lons-le-Saunier on 17/18 November after flying for long periods over cloud. He took with him: Henri Frenay, whose large organisation 'Combat' had been formed in 1941 by the fusion of 'Liberté' and 'Libération Nationale'; and Baron Emmanuel d'Astier de la Vigerie. They brought Moulin a letter from de Gaulle and 20 million francs. On the ground the operation was commanded by R.G. Fassin ('Sif') with the assistance of Paul Rivière ('Sif bis', 'Marquis', 'Yves Rolland', 'Galvani', 'Charles-Henri' etc). Fassin had spent the year setting up a body to direct air operations for de Gaulle throughout the unoccupied zone. This was called SAP (*service d'atterrissages et parachutages*)[18]. Paul Rivière had been in prison from June to October 1942.

John picked up General François d'Astier de la Vigerie and Yvon Morandat who was one of de Gaulle's finest political agents. Yvon had been dropped near Toulouse on 6/7 November 1941 on a mission to Christian trade unionists there and had spent the year achieving this and helping Jean Moulin. Now he was withdrawn for a rest by this pick-up. He was charged by Jean Moulin to confirm to General de Gaulle the immediate condemnation in the South Zone, of Darlan's manoeuvres, of Giraud's lack of character and of American diplomatic intrigues[19].

General D'Astier embraced his brother Emmanuel who had just arrived before taking his place. He had a damaged leg which was so stiff that he had very great difficulty climbing into the Lysander[20].

On 25/26 November, Peter and Mac were both successful in their separate operations[21]. This, Peter remembers, was the night when he had some trouble on his approach because the flarepath lights were dim and seemed to go off and on from time to time. When he landed he teased the agent in charge about this. The reason was that they had been on the run from the Germans a few days before and had lost their torches. They had been forced to use candles for the flarepath and it was difficult to keep them alight in the wind. Peter brought home three passengers which, at that time, was the biggest load ever. This was operation Apollo for the 'Alliance' intelligence organisation led by Marie-Madeleine Fourcade[22]. The three passengers - one of whom was hauled into the Lysander upside down - were Corsican police inspectors called Piani, Rutali and Reverbel. They had helped Marie-Madeleine escape from a Vichy prison just before the South of France was occupied. This was their first flight ever.

Before reading the story of Mac's first pick-up the reader may like to know more about him and how he became involved in special operations. In fact, since he completed no less than 25 successful Lysander pick-ups, he deserves a chapter to himself.

CHAPTER FIVE

James McCairns, DFC, MM

The son of an English engineer, James Atterby McCairns was born in September 1919 at Niagara Falls, USA. He came to England when he was 12 years old and completed his education at King Edward Vl Grammar School, Retford.

Six months before the war Mac enlisted as a volunteer pilot in the RAFVR. In 1940 he was a sergeant-pilot flying a Spitfire in Wing Commander Douglas Bader's famous 616 Squadron. On 8 July 1941 he was told to report to his station commander for an interview about his commission. A few hours later he was shot down, wounded and captured.

His first escape attempt was a failure. But on 22 January 1942 with a Belgian friend as chief plotter and guide he got away from Stalag IXc. Three days later, alone and exhausted, he crossed the Belgian frontier in the great blizzard of 1942. The Belgian underground sent him to Brussels and there he met an agent who had been parachuted into Belgium from a Whitley four months before. He was a brave and generous man but unfortunately he lacked experience; only a fortnight later he was captured by the Gestapo.

Meanwhile he had contacted London about Mac over the radio and had also told him about a special course he had taken in England. He amazed Mac by drawing a small diagram illustrating four lamps, explaining that on such a flarepath he could receive a Lysander and have him picked up.

As he described this jet-black Lysander with a long cylindrical tank, like a torpedo, hanging from the fuselage, Mac began to see daylight. In 1941 he had spent some six months down at Tangmere, where, set well apart from the warlike Spitfires, had been two modified black Lysanders. The curiosity they aroused was satisfied by the explanation that they did photographic reconnaissance by night using special flash flares. Once, when a Whitley crashed at night and five civilian bodies were fished out of the wreckage Mac had accepted the story that they were the more daring of our Press reporters who had been watching a raid. He now realised that they must have been a group of parachute agents who had been prevented from jumping by the weather.

After his friend's capture in Brussels and the breaking of the link with England, he spoke to several members of the underground about the air courier. Fields were inspected, signalling directions and flarepaths planned; all was ready for his return. Then he found that a passage to Gibraltar had been organised for him and it was at Gib that he made a lucky encounter. In May 1942, Lieut. James Langley of MI9 - the escape organisation - was on a duty visit to Gibraltar and Mac reported to him. After a long interview he asked what Mac expected to do in the future. Excitedly Mac told him of his scheme - the opening of an air-taxi service to occupied Belgium. "Splendid", he said, "You're just the man we're looking for."

Apparently, the Lysander pick-up scheme was only in its infancy, and pilots, preferably with experience of Resistance work and conscious of their debt to their Continental allies, were badly needed. But, because of the secrecy, it was impossible to make a public call for volunteers. Unfortunately, Mac had few of the qualifications demanded. He was not commissioned, his French was not fluent, nor had he 1,000 flying hours and, much more important, 500 by night. Worse still, the Air Ministry had clamped down and said that no prisoner of war would be allowed to do any more operational flying in the same theatre. North Africa or nothing, as they put it.

In view of these obstacles, it was largely due to the untiring efforts of Jimmy Langley that Mac did eventually become a Lysander pilot. In spite of his lack of qualifications Mouse Fielden conceded that, given a prolonged period of special training and, more important, the correct psychological adaptation, he might conceivably make the grade. Mouse impressed on him the fact that the job was purely voluntary: at any time, if he wished to withdraw, all that was necessary was to say the word. On such a flight as this there was room only for the keenest of the keen.

Mac completed his lecture tour on escape and evasion, joined 161 Squadron and was trained on the Lysander, which he found heavy in the hand after Spitfires. He also found that he disliked night flying. He believed the saying: "Only birds and fools fly by day; only bats and bloody fools by night."

On 22nd November 1942, while the other pilots were down at Tangmere, Mac was called into Pick's office at Tempsford and told the details of operation 'Skate/Squid'. This called for a pick-up operation in the Châteauroux area to pick up three passengers. At that time it was a rule that only two passengers should be carried in the back of the Lysander. To pick up the three agents Pick was sending two Lysanders. John Bridger would fly the first, and the second would be piloted by Pick himself after little more than a month's practice. If he did not arrive, Bridger was to try to take all three in his rear cockpit. Mac protested that it was his turn to become operational. Pick was adamant; but he suggested that Mac should fly in the back as his passenger and help with the navigation. They flew down to Tangmere, made their preparations and took off.

As usual, they planned to cross the French coast near Cabourg, just north of Caen. It meant 110 miles of Channel to cross. As they climbed up to 6,000 feet before the French coast, their speed was never more than 120 mph. This meant almost an hour for the Channel crossing. It was a great relief to Mac when Pick told him that the French coast was in sight and asked him to pinpoint as they crossed it. The passengers in our converted Lysanders had to sit looking rearwards over the tail - a most uncomfortable position which made map-reading difficult. Although the moon was bright in the cloudless sky, Mac was unable to pinpoint their place of entry. He was comforted by Pick saying that they were 12 miles to starboard of track. Once over the country they began to lose height fairly rapidly in a gentle weaving action and soon were down to 1,500 feet and able to study the detail of the country more thoroughly.

Just as they were settling down to the trip, a flak gun near the town of Falaise suddenly opened up. Exactly like a Roman candle, a string of golden balls of fire came drifting slowly up behind them. As soon as Pick saw the tracer he took evasive action and none succeeded in scorching the aircraft. They flew on for about another hour and Pick calmly announced that the river Loire was in sight. Sure enough, there was the huge silver snake glistening in the reflected light of the moon, stretching for miles on both sides. They had decided to make a rendezvous at Blois with John Bridger. Pick turned to port and flew along the river. In less than three minutes they saw the gleaming white town of Blois with its bridge and château. Pick called John to announce his arrival at the rendezvous, and back came John's reply that he was ready to go on to the target. Now Mac felt a little happier, as he crouched in the rear cockpit, with the map firmly clutched in one hand and the smothered rays from a hand torch as illumination, because he was able to pinpoint their progress and watch excitedly for the signal light to appear.

With about 15 miles to go, Pick decided that he would fly direct to the target instead of to a nearby town and then follow the main road up to the field. This unannounced change of direction had Mac completely foxed. He lost all sense of direction. Unfortunately, five minutes later, the same thing happened to Pick. At the moment when John called up to say he had found the field and was going in to land, Pick asked Mac if he knew where they were and Mac was forced to reply that he had not a clue.

Pick started cursing softly to himself in the microphone, when suddenly his oaths were turned to exclamations of delight for there, immediately below, was the three-torch flarepath, and the winking red and green lights of John's Lizzie attempting to attract their attention. Immediately Pick called to Bridger who took off. Without more delay Pick made a quick orbit and went in. The landing, loading and take-off were as smooth as a routine practice.

Tangmere's 'Drem' system, with its hundreds of lights marking outer boundaries, perimeter, funnel and actual flarepath, looked like Blackpool illuminations compared with the little strip in France. Soon they were down; the waiting crowd congratulated Pick on his first trip and the cars whipped them round to the Cottage, where the 'Joes'[1] received a complete British welcome with a mixture of tea alternating with Scotch.

Three nights later, after his operational cross country over France, Mac was given operation 'Pike/Carp', a new field south of Bourges, involving a trip of about six and a half hours, but presenting no major map-reading snags, as it was near to a main road. Mac worked out a very complicated track of approach which consisted of dodging from one major landmark to another, instead of the more conventional straight course method. When Guy examined his map and calculated the extra mileage involved, he threw it away with disgust.

"What is this dog-legged effort?" he asked.

Mac said that it had his complete confidence, but Guy replied that he would never find his way to the field on such a track, and offered to take a side bet of half a crown on it.

"And mark you, if you miss this chance tonight, you are out!"

Mac never realised whether he was joking or not, but took it seriously.

By 8 pm that night the Cottage was packed, not only with agents and escorting officers, but half the staff on the Air Ministry side had arrived as well.

Before take-off, each pilot collected his agent and briefed him. If the passenger had not already done a Lysander course, we showed him over the rear cockpit, how to open and fasten the tricky hood, where to sit, how to don Mae West and parachute, where to find a thermos of coffee, and how to speak to the pilot. This inter-communication often caused trouble. When we were talking to base, or to another aircraft, the passenger would suddenly butt in with:

"What you say, pilot? I no understand" and completely jam the answer from the station called. Eventually, we had to fit a cut-out switch. If the passenger did not behave, we would switch off his microphone and leave him speechless. But we preferred to be in constant communication, because as the pilot was completely blind to attack from the rear, it was the passenger's duty to keep his eyes open.

On this November night, Mac made sure that his passenger was certain of his drill, and then returned to the Cottage. As they had still an hour to take-off, he went up to his room, switched off the light, and relaxed on the bed, once again going through every detail of his flight, until he felt at last like a word-perfect actor. With 30 minutes to go, he rose and dressed: first of all thick underwear; and then, instead of a uniform, civilian clothes - the suit that he had been given in Brussels. Many people thought that it was asking for trouble if one were caught, but Mac felt that, as an ex-POW, uniform would make very little difference to the Boche - if he wanted to kill you, he would. He kept this blue Belgian suit purely as an escape outfit; it was lined with saw, maps and compasses, while in the pockets were all the usual escape aids as well as a little fountain pen which, when used, released tear-gas instead of ink.

Over his civilian clothes, to disguise his disobedience of orders, he wore a black overall which had a number of useful pockets, and, in the event of a forced landing, would provide excellent camouflage for night travel. He wore a pair of RAF escape boots - ordinary black fleece-lined flying boots, with a zipper front; but, when the uppers were detached, one was left with a fine sturdy pair of black civilian shoes. His final accessory was a .38 revolver, in a holster strapped round his waist. One could not be certain who would constitute the reception party at lamp 'A'.

Mac's dog-legged course worked like a charm, except that he nearly flew into a marine radio mast while flying low to pin-point a position. That incident upset him, with the result that he lost confidence in his position and, panic stricken, began to examine his map. However, dead on time, a town loomed up. After a quick orbit he realised it could be none other than Bourges. His field was 17 miles to the south. He checked his watch, set a new course and set off on the last leg. With three and a half minutes to go, he saw a pinpoint and realised that he was dead on track. Every minute some detail appeared to verify the carefully noted points in his mind. As the last 30 seconds were about to begin, he realised that the field must be in sight and it was time to circle slowly to search.

Just then, in answer to his wish, a lamp flashed, one mile away. He whipped the aircraft round as the light continued to flash - dash, dot, dash, dot - 'C' for Charlie. With a surge of delight, he flew over the field and flashed 'G' for George, at the same time yelling excitedly to his passenger: "We are here - undo your Mae West and parachute and be ready to land." The three lights of the flarepath appeared on the ground and Mac came in to land immediately without doing a circuit. He was so keen to get down, that he even forgot the last essential alteration to the trimming of the aircraft. The night was so clear that there was no need to use his landing light. 'A' went flashing by, there was a bump and he was down, still rolling fast. Just as he came between 'B' and 'C' there was a violent lurch and the Lysander was almost pitched on its nose, but, just in time, she regained balance and gradually drew up to a dignified stop.

As he turned to taxi back to 'A', the immense relief he felt at progress so far was somewhat neutralised by apprehension; as he had swept past 'A', he had seen a crowd of some eight people. This was contrary to orders - only the chief and passengers were supposed to be there. He wondered if it meant trouble, and thoughtfully loosened the revolver in his holster as he taxied back, making a careful note of the path with its rough edges near 'B' and 'C' which had thrown the Lysander into the air again. As he swung the Lysander round in the light of 'A', at least 10 people made a rush for the machine, and without hesitation out came his revolver. He waited a fraction of a second to make sure; but, as the leader, in his ragged clothes, came clambering up to his cockpit, he instinctively realised he was genuine, put the revolver back and grasped his hand. With a magnificent gesture, he presented Mac with a bottle of champagne and in return Mac offered a little box of coffee and cigarettes.

In the meantime, an exchange of luggage was taking place in the back and two men in the crowd were busy making their last adieux before taking their places in the back. Having checked his cockpit and tail trim, Mac waved at the passengers to hurry; he was anxious to go. He disliked aircraft engines ticking over for a long time as they tend to oil up, and he had already been on the ground eight minutes. Besides, he had no wish to wait until the Gestapo arrived. As soon as they were safely tucked inside and the hood fastened, the group yelled OK. He opened up the motor, keeping the brakes on. As soon as the tail began to lift, he released the brakes and, in no time at all, was batting down towards 'B'. Just as they were about to leave the ground, they struck the path. That jolt bumped them into the air and there they stayed. The first landing had been a colossal success and all that remained was to find the way home.

Once again he made for Bourges. This time, as he turned round the northern part, he noticed a small aerodrome. At the same time, that small aerodrome noticed him and immediately flak was coming up in all directions, but generally well behind his tail. Afterwards, he was told that it was fired mainly by French gunners who merely put on a show for their German superiors. As soon as he was 20 miles clear of France, Mac called up Tangmere. We used to have a little convention to announce success or failure to the waiting crowd at the Cottage. Usually, base would ask us what our colour was; sometimes an answer, red, would mean successful, and green not; on other nights the opposite would apply, so that only those with the night's code would appreciate the answer. In the excitement of the first operation, Mac had forgotten to arrange a convention, but he felt much too happy to keep the good news to himself. When he was asked for a homing transmission, he replied: "Here is a message for my boss - he owes me half a crown." It was a great night for Mac, for he had begun to repay his debt to the occupied countries of Europe. He swore that he would not rest until he had lifted out of France as many people as he had known there on his escape.

On 28/29 November 1942, Peter and Mac had a double, operation 'Perry'. It was not a long trip - the field was 20 miles to the East of Les Andelys on the Seine - but to be on the safe side they routed themselves in via Cabourg and then more or less parallel to the coast until they reached the Seine.

They were officially briefed that they should both land or neither: they were not to land independently. Peter, as the senior pilot, was to land first. Guy arranged a complete timetable of events, giving the hour for every pinpoint and a zero hour for landing. If they had not found the field by a certain time they were not to land but to return home. After dinner, they were advised by different people, all with varying ideas. Some seemed to suggest that they should act independently, although Air Ministry itself had stated that the operation must be done as a whole. In rather a haze when the time of take-off was near, they were driven out to the dispersal, looking apprehensively at the thick, low clouds.

By keeping radio contact, they managed to taxi in the pitch blackness to the flarepath and then take off together. Mac followed Peter's navigation lights until, as they crossed out from the English coast, he extinguished them, leaving only two minute blue lamps.

Cloud forced them to fly at a height of 500 feet. In gathering mists, Mac had to cling close to Peter to avoid losing sight of the two little lights, which seemed to dance up and down as he tried to follow.

For another 10 minutes, he kept it up. Then the lights disappeared and Peter said "Keep dead ahead for the coast." Mac immediately transferred his attention to his instruments. Eventually, he found that he was some 20 miles to the south of Les Andelys. As he flew up and down the river, Peter said that he was at their rendezvous, 3,000 feet over the bridge at Les Andelys. Five minutes later, Mac, too, verified his position, and asked Peter to go on to the target: he would follow in two minutes. The field was well chosen, on the eastern tip of the Forêt de Lyons. Mac saw the letter 'B' for beer flash from the ground, but he could not reply until Peter had landed. He checked over the radio and found that Peter had not seen the signal and was returning to Les Andelys for another run. Mac decided to return himself and, if possible, lead Peter in formation to the spot. But when he set course again for the field, from Les Andelys, he completely missed the target. That error disturbed his calm and he went haring after any possible light until he had succeeded in losing himself completely.

In the meantime, he gathered that Peter was having no better luck, when suddenly there was a complete R/T silence, and he heard no more. After 30 more minutes spent chasing round, and as it was well past the zero hour, Mac reluctantly set course for base. Ten minutes later, he heard a feeble message from Peter over the radio, but could not decipher it. Then he heard him say: "Mac, Peter just setting course for home."

He thought he must have been successful. When he chanced to look down, he recognised that he was directly over Les Andelys, so in a last attempt, just in case the operator had not left the field, for the third time he headed for the ground. As he approached, up came the letter 'B'. Immediately he gave them 'G' and without further thought came in to land. He was over-excited and dropped the aircraft the last five feet, which accounted for the broken tail wheel shock absorber which was discovered the next morning.

While the exchange of passengers took place, Mac asked the operator about the other aeroplane. In the roar of the engine it was difficult to understand his French, but he seemed to indicate that the other plane had not landed. The news infuriated Mac - apparently he had prevented Peter from landing, and then slipped in himself. In disgust, he told them to shut the hood, and off he went, taking an exceptionally long run on the soft ground. Without much trouble he found his way back to Tangmere and slapped the aircraft down on the runway, and then into dispersal. He felt no jubilation at a second successful operation.

The escorting officers were quite relaxed about it, and highly pleased with the catch he had produced: Max Petit, his wife and two lovely boys - four in a Lysander for the first time. Back in the Cottage, the whole story came out. Apparently, Peter had never found the field, but had persisted in circling the area in the murky weather until, in the end, he had been compelled to give in - it was this message which Mac had indistinctly heard. When Mac managed to calm down a little and talk to the passengers, he thought that after all, there was some justification for him. They were exceedingly charming, and Madame Petit presented him with some exquisite lipstick for his mother, and a little golden mascot for himself. Michel Pichard, who had done the round trip with Peter, was, however, appalled to find that Mac had landed. This meant that the field could not be used again that moon.

From the RAF point of view, it was quite a serious matter - a breach of discipline had been committed. The following morning, he was 'on the mat' in front of Guy, who insisted that he had tried to pull a fast one, with flagrant contempt for orders. Guy refused to deal with the case, and Mac was sent before Pick, who explained in great detail the rigid discipline required in the flight, and then suspended him from operations for an indefinite period. No punishment could have been more cruel - Mac would willing have done a month as Orderly Officer, rather than take this reprimand.

For years he remembered that flight as his black operation, and it was not until after the war, when he lunched with the Petit family in Paris and learnt how the very day after their escape the Gestapo had arrived to arrest them that at last he felt his crime was justified.

Another of Mac's early operations - his third as pilot - on 23 December 1942, did not go according to plan. This was operation 'Ajax', for the 'Alliance' intelligence organisation and for MI9, the organisation which arranged for the recovery of escapers and evaders. Captain James Langley MBE, MC, was a frequent - and most welcome - visitor to the cottage at Tangmere[2]. He had lost an arm earlier in the war and escaped himself. This is vividly and amusingly described in his book *Fight Another Day*.

Mac's passenger on this trip was a White Russian, Vladimir Bouryschkine, who had been brought up in Paris and the USA, and whose code-name was 'Val Williams'. He must have been the most frustrated 161 Squadron passenger, failing to arrive on no fewer than nine attempted parachute or landing operations.

The field, at Thalamy, had been used several times before as it was secreted away in the Massif Central. Perched high in the mountains, 400 miles from base, and with no landmarks near, it was recognised as our worst target. Moreover, to make matters worse, the operation was for Jimmy Langley, and Mac had trained 'Val', and liked him very much. The thought of letting Jimmy down was insupportable, so once again Mac talked himself into making a supreme effort. The weather report was worse than ever, with poor visibility and ground fog over most of France, but as the moon period was almost at an end, it was decided to fly a sortie. As soon as Mac had taken off, he realised how right were the Met. Below 500 feet there was a light drizzle, and above was solid cloud, through which, slowly and with many moments of anxiety, he climbed the over-burdened Lysander. Half an hour later, they emerged, but when the French coast should have appeared, there was nothing but cloud. He decided to dive down again, and at 1,500 feet came out of the cloud right over a large town, but whether Le Havre, Cabourg or Rouen, he did not know. After tussling with the Lysander in cloud, his courses had not been as good as expected. In no time at all, balls of fire came hurtling up from every quarter.

As Mac ducked into the cover of the friendly clouds, tracer still continued to chase them, tingeing the clouds with a bloody shade of crimson. For five minutes the Lysander went through every known and unknown contortion until at last, like a cork from a champagne bottle, it popped out of the cloud into a clear, star-lit sky. For the next hour, Mac steered a compass course, always hoping for a break in the fog. Not even when he estimated that he was over the Loire was there any change, so, with another alteration of course, he set off in the direction of Montluçon. Still the fog persisted, and it was not until 50 minutes later that it began to disperse, and in the distance the lights of a town were visible. By this time, he had no idea of their whereabouts, so he went to investigate this land-mark, and to his utter amazement it proved to be Montluçon itself.

The next leg was 40 miles due south, till he picked up a single tracked railway. As they approached this area, the fog started again, especially in the valleys. But luckily he managed to find the railway, and tried to fly along it and fix his position. He could scarcely believe that after such a nightmare of a trip he was only 20 miles from the field. But now a combination of deep valleys, heavily laden with fog, began to oppose him and a quick look at his watch and fuel gauges showed the position to be acute: they had been flying for more than four hours and had consumed just one half of the fuel. He told Val that they could devote only 10 minutes to a search for the field and that he should look out for the letter 'D'. Mac tried to do a square search, investigating every possible light which showed at 0330, but to no avail. The time limit expired, and as he climbed up before returning to base, he was forced to confess to Val that he had failed Jimmy[3].

In these early pick-ups, Mac had laid the foundations for his most successful tour of operations. Most of us were to find - as he already had - that it was not always easy.

James McCairns, MM.   Moira McCairns

CHAPTER SIX

It Was Not Always Easy

When I joined the Lysander flight there was an atmosphere of cinematic stunt-riding about the whole thing - among those who knew about it at all. There had been about 19 successful pick-up operations altogether in the past two years. Decorations had been generously awarded, quite properly, we thought, for the pioneering early operations when so much was unknown. Now that that early experience had been won, now that the underground networks in France were building up, now was the time to establish this service as a safe and sure methodical routine. We should study the various possible hazards and do all we could to eliminate them by perfecting techniques, and training ourselves and the agents, until each trip could be a guaranteed success, so far as it lay in our power to make it so.

In spite of this approach to our work, there were times when things did not go according to plan. An example of this was the long range sortie flown by John Bridger, which nearly ended in disaster during the landing. This was on the night of 16 April 1943, and his target was a small plateau west of Issoire in the hilly area south of Clermont-Ferrand. I remember him telling us about it when he returned.

The weather on parts of the route was bad, with a lot of cloud making the navigation difficult. Even so, he had had enough nerve -and enough confidence in his navigation- to let down through cloud on his dead reckoning ETA (Estimated Time of Arrival). But the main hazard was the landing strip, which was on a plateau on a mountain, between two valleys. There was quite a wind that night, and this created a down-draught over the escarpment on the approach to the plateau. To avoid undershooting, he had to give a burst of throttle during the last part of his approach to land.

He slightly overdid this, and touched down well past the first light, rather fast, and on a downward slope. He realised that he was rapidly rolling towards the valley on the far side of the little plateau and would probably not be able to stop in time. So he opened up the engine to go round again, but failed to build up flying speed before his Lysander rolled off the end of the plateau and virtually fell over the edge.

He put the nose down to build up flying speed as quickly as possible, diving into the valley. When he had done this, at maximum power, he climbed as steeply as possible towards the other side of the valley. Above him in the moonlight, he could see the crest. He very nearly cleared it, but not quite; in fact he bounced twice. His first bounce took him just over some buildings; his second was even more alarming, taking him through high tension cables between pylons. There was a dazzling flash which temporarily blinded him. But he had not crashed; he was now really airborne. He flew round quietly while his night vision repaired itself. Then he shone a pocket torch on to his undercarriage on both sides. All seemed to be reasonably well, though one tyre had been torn in one of the bounces.

He returned to the plateau and lined himself up for another approach. This time he made allowances for the down-draught and motored carefully down to make a short landing precisely by lamp 'A'. Expecting the torn tyre to cause a swing to port, he was ready to correct it with rudder and starboard brake. He taxied round, drew up by the agent in charge, Michel Thoraval, and the highly excited reception committee and climbed out of the cockpit to inspect the damage.

While the passengers were changing over the loads, he decided to flatten the good tyre, believing that the take-off would be easier to control on the rims of two wheels rather than on one good tyre and one flat one. Having failed with his Commando knife, he used his Smith and Wesson .38 service revolver to puncture it. It was not until he had fired five bullets into it that it finally subsided. It went down with a very slow hiss. In 1988 Docteur Thoraval told me that it took the heavy revolver of a policeman in his team to puncture the tyre.

The ground was dry and hard; the wheels did not dig in; and he took off with very little difficulty. According to some accounts he then flew through the high tension cables *again*[1]. I cannot remember him saying anything special about the homeward flight, but I do remember the metre and a half of thick copper wire that we found coiled round the boss of his propeller and the seven metres of it that his Lysander trailed behind it as he landed at Tangmere. Looking back on it, that landing of John Bridger's must have been about as near cinematic stunt-riding as any of us ever got.

My own landings in France never came near to competing with John's for excitement, but I very nearly killed myself - together with a *very* important passenger- on the night of 24/25 February 1943. This operation was 'Eclipse' and my Lysander was 'D for Dog'. I had just one passenger outbound. He was a Frenchman of some authority, I judged by his bearing although he wore a very ordinary suit and overcoat and a felt hat. His scarf did not entirely conceal scars on his neck, which I gathered had been caused when he attempted suicide while imprisoned by the Germans. I also gather that he had been Prefect of l'Eure-et-Loir at Chartres. I have since come to the conclusion that he must have been the great Jean Moulin, the main co-ordinator of de Gaulle's resistance networks in the Southern half of France at that time.

My target was a field near Issoudun, south of the Loire and near Bourges. It was not a long trip and should have been very easy if the weather held clear. The forecast indicated some risk of fog but a probability of a fine night.

By the time on my flight plan when, by dead reckoning, I should be over the Loire, I was flying over an interminable sea of solid fog. I had no visual reference to the ground at all. I set course on my final leg and flew that accurately, though I realised that there was virtually no hope of a clear patch over the target field. At the estimated time of arrival there was still no break in the solid fog and I sadly turned for home. After flying for about two hours over fog or low stratus cloud, I found that I was approaching the North coast of France in the wrong place. In fact I was near Cherbourg, where I attracted the unwelcome interest of a searchlight. Regardless of my passenger's comfort I turned and twisted in a violent dive until I shook off the beam of brilliant bluish light.

With the aid of a homing bearing I was eventually approaching Tangmere. This, too, was now covered with fog which had formed in the four hours since I had left. The top of the fog was 800 feet above the ground. I asked the tower what the landing conditions were. The reply was: "Let down to 300 feet and if you can't see the flares we'll think again. We're lighting Money flares for you." Money flares were very bright indeed. I asked them to put up two searchlights, one north and one south of the east/west runway that I would land on. There were half-a-dozen searchlights round the airfield as part of the ground defences against air attack. These two searchlights came on quickly, making large pools of light on the top of the fog and saving me the trouble of doing ZZ approaches by repeated voice transmissions to get bearings. They would give me a very accurate idea of what part of the fog to let down into.

Flying just above the fog I placed myself between the pools of light, over the airfield and flew an accurate race-track circuit (two straight parallel legs with a semi-circle at each end). After turning towards the point between the two pools of light I let down on instruments through the fog until I was at 300 feet. Then I saw the glare from one of the Money flares below me and to one side. Then there was another but I was not on the right line and I was too high. I told them that I had seen the flares from 300 feet and was going round again. Next time I came down lower but I was not properly lined up and I went round again. After repeating this manoeuvre eleven times I was beginning to tire of it. I decided that my twelfth approach would end in a landing.

I lined myself up as before on the gap between the pools of light and let down on the gyro instruments with a little power on. "All I have to do," I thought, "is just to motor steadily down and I'll know I'll be on the airfield, somewhere, if I see those Money flares. What does it matter if it is rather a bump?" Down I went, checking on speed, rate of descent and heading, while the artificial horizon helped me keep my wings level. Suddenly there was a tremendous glare in the fog. It was one of those flares. I got the impression that I was about to fly straight into the ground. Instinctively I pulled the stick back and cut the throttle. I must have done a three point landing about 30 feet up. The Lysander fell with a tremendous crack as the "unbreakable" undercarriage beam snapped off. The tail went up to an angle of 45° as the aircraft pitched forward and skidded along on three points: the engine housing and twisted propeller blades leading, followed by the broken stumps of the undercarriage legs.

I turned off the petrol and the ignition, threw off my helmet, safety harness and parachute straps and clambered out. I was concerned about my unfortunate passenger stuck up there in the rear cockpit with the little ladder unhelpfully far from the ground and at the wrong angle. I was very relieved that there was no fire. It amazes me to this day that that Lysander 'D' for Dog did not burst into flames after that 'prang'. There must have been some petrol left in the mangled extra petrol tank between the undercarriage legs.

My distinguished passenger managed to slide his roof back (and up) and climb out. I helped him to jump down. It had been a truly disastrous trip and I apologised profusely in my best French. He could not have been more charming and even went to the lengths of thanking me for "a very agreeable flight".

After a few minutes, with the aid of some shouting through the fog - visibility was 40 yards - I was delighted to see Elston's station wagon approaching. Sergeant Sam Hollis jumped out followed

'Sam' Hollis with the author at the RAF Museum, Hendon, in 1973.
Ministry of Defence

by Bunny Rymills. They said that the glare of the flares in the fog had made them think we were on fire, so by comparison the drastic damage I had done to the Lysander was quite a relief.

Thirty years later Sam Hollis reminded me that my main concern when he arrived was to retrieve my service hat from the starter handle locker near the tail. It was a specially smart Bates hat with a high front and almost new.

Mac's most dangerous landing was when he had trouble with a tree. This was on an operation with Henri Déricourt two miles N by E of Amboise on 14/15 April. It was a double with Peter (who avoided the tree) on a cloudy night with little moonlight penetrating to the target area.

When Peter took off Mac flew in, but came down too low when still a few hundred yards from 'A'. He continued to stay low, dragging the aircraft on with the nose up and full throttle. Something loomed up ahead. Mac tried to climb, but it was too late. There was a crash and he heard the sound of splintering and tearing above the roar of the engine. The aircraft rose for a moment and then, as he throttled back, it crashed to a landing just by lamp 'A'. The landing run was small, and as he taxied back it was difficult to tell what was wrong. He beckoned to Déricourt and asked what the devil had happened. He explained that there was a small poplar - about 12 feet high - which Mac had completely demolished.

Furious, Mac asked what damage had been done to the aircraft, and was told that just the aerial had been ripped away. Not bothering to climb down to check, Mac took off. The moment he was airborne he knew that something was radically wrong with the controls. The stick was shaking in his grasp and now and then there would be a violent snatch. Worse still, the oil temperature was creeping up until it was almost on the emergency figure. He decided to climb as high as possible and, as there was a fair amount of medium cloud, he started forcing up on instruments. Ten minutes in the cloud, and the engine spluttered, coughed, and died.

Jazzing the throttle had no effect. Mac was in the predicament of having to concentrate on his instruments, try to locate the error if possible, and in addition, to talk to his passenger and warn him. He glided down, still in cloud, and with no idea of what sort of ground was below. He realised that he must try a forced landing.

Three thousand feet to go, when suddenly he found out what was wrong. The carburettor hot air control had slipped out of position, allowing the carburettor to freeze up. Once this was put right, the engine picked up and they were able to continue their uneasy trip back to base.

When he landed, Mac hopped out to survey the damage. The whole of the spinner, that is the centre boss of the propeller, had been stove in; there was enough wood round the exhaust ring to kindle several fires; the supplementary petrol tank was gashed and only just hanging on; and, as for the most essential tail controls, the tail-plane was attached with only one bracket held by a single screw.

That night, just before take-off, Mac's rigger had slipped him a miniature Pop-eye the Sailor as a lucky mascot. The next day, in conference with his crew, he decided to adopt Pop-eye as the Patron Saint of 'E'. That afternoon, after a design had been approved, he was painted on the side, complete with four successful sortie stars under him.

One of the consequences of Mac hitting the tree was that we made it a rule to switch on our landing lights before landing.

I thought at the time that this incident was due to Déricourt's error of judgement. He must have placed the lights far too close to that tree and forgotten our training about the clear approach funnel. I was quite satisfied that Mac had done his usual impeccable approach and not come in at too shallow an angle. The difficulty I thought must be that Déricourt was getting over-confident after a number of successful pick-up operations. He was an experienced pilot and he may have thought he knew too much about it to bother to obey our rules. To make sure he did not take chances of that sort again I decided he should be 'torn off a strip', i.e. informally reprimanded. I informed SOE 'F' Section, through the usual channels, that we would not do any more landings with Déricourt (apart from one to pick him up) until he had been back with us for refresher training. I also thought that he might have been overdoing it in France and that a short rest in England would do him good.

This time we dressed up Henri as a flight lieutenant, with wings of course, and had him to stay in the officers' mess at Tempsford. He seemed contrite about the tree and promised to be more scrupulous in future about all our field specifications. After he had done a bit of flying in our Lysanders and really rested up he wanted to get back to work and opted for a blind parachute drop. This meant that he would have no reception committee. Bob Hodges would drop him over a bend in the Loire which would be unmistakable even by starlight. He knew that there was just soft farm land in that bend.

This operation was on the night of 5 May. It was before our moon period at Tangmere had started so I went along for the ride to keep him company. I waved him goodbye as he dropped through the circular hole in the rear fuselage of Bob's Halifax into the black night outside. We were in good time for him to catch the milk train up to Paris, his *appartement* and his wife. He told me some months later that he did an amazingly soft landing and did not even fall over; he just bent his knees and straightened them again. Then he collected up his parachute and took it with him until he could find a suitable place to bury it. Making his way towards the railway in the dark he fell into a ditch that he had not seen. He said that he had fallen about two metres and jarred his spine so badly that he had to rest for some time before he felt able to go on. As a result of this delay he missed the milk train.

Déricourt was soon laying on our landings again with his normal dependability. He found some excellent fields, mainly around the centre of France, often not far from the Loire.

On one occasion I was doing a landing on one of his operations. When I got there I could see the field in the moonlight without any doubt and there was a lamp flashing the correct letter followed by a series of dits or short flashes. I circled around a landmark some way away and came back over the field every now and then to see if there was a flarepath. As he kept me waiting for over an hour I was fairly testy when I landed. He jumped up on my port undercarriage and explained that *"les sales Boches"* had planted poles all over the field to stop Lysanders landing on it. He was sweating with the effort of putting his shoulder to these poles to clear a strip where I could land. I had not seen the poles and I was startled to discover that he had only cleared a very narrow strip, just along the line of the flarepath.

His comforting conclusion was that he would put the poles back after my take-off and that they would be much easier to get out next time. I later heard that Déricourt had designed and manufactured a special tool for extracting posts. It was like one of those corkscrews with levers that one presses down. This tool had two long arms; when these were pressed down by Déricourt and his assistant, up came the post.

Peter Vaughan-Fowler was, as I said, a very skilful pilot, with beautiful hands for an aeroplane. His trips were usually uneventful - as a result, no doubt, of his careful preparation and accurate pilot-navigation, combined with a fair share of luck. Even so he had an unusually alarming experience. On 17 March 1943 he was sharing a double Lysander pick-up with Bunny Rymills on a field near Poitiers. On landing he found the field a bit bumpy and after rolling over one of these bumps he was alarmed to see that flames were belching out of his engine exhaust. We had never thought of the possibility of this happening, nor had we worked out an emergency drill for dealing with it as part of our training. Peter immediately turned off the petrol, put the brakes on hard, and switched off the ignition.

As soon as the Lysander stopped rolling he leapt out of the cockpit, pulled the tapes fastening his Mae West life-jacket, tore it off his shoulders and rammed it through the flames into the exhaust. This effectively put out the engine fire. He started the engine again and taxied back towards lamp 'A'. Once again he rolled over a bump. This time he did not have an engine fire, but his engine cut. Once again he started it, hoping that his battery was not going to be exhausted. All was well and the rest of the trip was a proverbial 'piece of cake'.

This was not the only time that Peter had trouble with his engine. On another trip he was "fairly alarmed" to find flames at least six feet long from his exhaust, instead of the usual six inches. He had flight-tested the Lysander carefully after an engine change and checked all the instrument readings. In daylight these long flames had not shown up. In spite of feeling like an illuminated target he pressed on and completed the job, hiding in cloud for most of the time. The next day the engine was stripped and the timing was 10° out. It was a new engine which had been made in one of the "shadow" factories.

I have picked out a few examples of the difficulties we had in the early months of 1943 to illustrate my point that "it was not always easy", even with the most careful training and preparation by all concerned. Now I propose to take up again the chronological account of Lysander pick-ups during February and March, leaving the story of Hudson landings for later chapters. The weather during the February moon was generally bad and operations could only be authorised on four nights between 13-27 February. Of the five Lysander landings attempted only three were successful.

On 13/14 February two of the successful landings were in operation 'Porpoise, Prawn and Gurnard', the double pick-up by Peter Vaughan-Fowler and Jimmy McCairns near Ruffey, NW of Lons-le-Saunier. Between them they landed three passengers and picked up four. The only trouble they had was radio unserviceability. This much is clear from the RAF records written at the time. Noguères quotes[2] the operation officer Pierre Boutoule who was in charge of the field near Lons-le-Saunier called 'Léontine' in an interview long after the war. Pierre remembered this operation as being on the 12th or 13th February. He expected three passengers for the UK to turn up, but one of them, Kalb, did not arrive. The other two were most important in the history of the Resistance, General Delestraint and Moulin himself, General de Gaulle's top man in France. Boutoule only recalls mail being delivered by the first Lysander, which collected Delestraint. The second Lysander, he remembered, brought out Colonel Manhès, Moulin's assistant and took away Moulin[3]. This conflicts with the RAF record of the numbers of passengers but it fits in with Passy's recollection that Moulin and Delestraint arrived in London at the beginning of the February moon. So it was probably McCairns who had the honour of flying Moulin to England. It is sad that he did not survive to attend the inauguration of a roadside monument commemorating this pick-up, when Peter Vaughan-Fowler and I met Pierre Boutoule in 1986.

There are monuments to Jean Moulin in Béziers and elsewhere and he is generally recognised as one of the greatest heroes of the French Resistance. In November 1941, as 'Delegate-General', appointed by the Free French Committee in London to control and co-ordinate all their supporters in France, he had been given orders by General de Gaulle to develop resistance cells as a nucleus for a secret army to rise when the allies came, and ultimately to take over the civil power. Meanwhile the cells could be used for sabotage and assassination. These orders represented a conversion of de Gaulle by Moulin. Until then the General had been more in favour of propaganda[4].

Known as 'Rex' and later on as 'Max', his first tour of duty in France lasted for almost 14 months from 1 January 1942 until he was brought out by Lysander. In October 1942 de Gaulle had him preside over the new military co-ordinating committee in southern France to direct the work of the secret army-to-be whose Commander-in-Chief was General Delestraint.

Before I leave February there are extracts from two of my letters to my wife that I might quote to illustrate different aspects of time off in war-time England. The first was opened and re-sealed by the censor.

10 February 1943

"I had a very sticky flight this afternoon - not dangerous because I never take any risks, but binding because there was a lot of cloud and I had to do a blind approach. I quite enjoyed it - like the old days when I used to specialise in bad weather flying. Almost immediately afterwards we had a raider low over and he got a direct hit. I saw him very well[5]. Soon afterwards there was a loud crump-crack. We motored out to where he had gone in, in very small pieces. It was a big Dornier. Three bodies (dead) and three bombs (alive) were scattered among the many small fragments. A lot of the aeroplane was still burning. I told the police and RAF Regiment that no souvenirs were to be collected, as they would be valuable for information. There was nothing I wanted to do more than collect them myself. I had a loaded revolver and was very disappointed there weren't any live Germans to arrest."

26 February 1943

"I went out to a wizard dinner last night - partridges en casserole followed by a rum omelette with eight eggs for three of us"

This must have been at the Unicorn pub in Chichester. We often went there if there were no operations on for the night. Arthur King, the jolly fat landlord, always made a fuss of us and made sure we had an excellent meal, however harsh the rationing. He always had a good bottle of claret or burgundy for us too. His bar was decorated with photographs of RAF pilots from squadrons at Tangmere and their aeroplanes - fighters and fighter-bombers but not our secret Lysanders.

There was one more outing at the end of February. The Windmill Theatre put on two shows in the camp cinema at Tangmere on the 28th. Phyllis Dixie was the fan-dancer who caused the most awed gasps of astonished delight when, at the end of her dance, she held both fans out at arms length. I see from the Tangmere Station official records that the Duke of Norfolk and party, from neighbouring Arundel Castle, were the Station Commander's guests at the evening show.

The March moon was better. We were at Tangmere from 11th to 27th and the weather allowed us to lay on operations on four of the six nights between 17th and 24th. Of seven Lysander landings attempted, six were successful. The failure was in Bunny Rymills attempt on 19/20 to find the field near Villefranche for operation 'Hector'[6], but this was successfully completed the following night by Pick. He took out one and brought back three passengers, reporting "perfect ground organisation and landing ground".

Originally planned to take place at Thalamy, near Ussel, 'Hector' was changed to a field by the Saône near Villefranche when 'Alliance' discovered that the Germans had obstructed the Thalamy field with stakes. On the first attempt Commandant Faye - an aviator himself - was maddened by the lack of communication with the pilot. Bunny probably left the intercom switched off. With the petrol tank in between the cockpits there was no way in which the passenger could tell the pilot that he was far too far to the east. Bunny himself realised this when he noticed that his height above ground looked very much less than the height on his altimeter and he could see snowy mountains in the moonlight. Eventually, short of fuel, they had to return. The three passengers picked up by Pick on the following night were: Pierre Dallas, who was sent to England for training to receive Hudsons as well as Lysanders; Dr Zimmern; and a colonel who had invented a better type of parachute - a design he wanted to offer to the British.

On 17/18 March Bunny and Peter had done a double on Henri Déricourt's field near Poitiers. This was the landing when Peter had the engine fire, already described. He had also had some trouble finding his way and arrived at the target 20 minutes after Bunny had landed and taken off, leaving only one of the four homeward passengers for Peter to collect.

Between them they took to France John Goldsmith[7], Pierre Lejeune[8], Dowlen and Mrs Agazarian. They picked up Claude de Baissac, Antelme[9], Flower and one other. What sort of people were in this random sample of our passengers? Captain John Goldsmith, who later had a DSO and MC, was a bilingual race-horse trainer. He had arrived at Cannes by felucca the previous October. On behalf of General Giraud he had arranged the escape of General Chambe, helping him cross the Pyrenees at the end of 1942. He was eventually to return to England by another Déricourt Lysander on 17/18 September 1943.

Lejeune was a Giraudist who had little to do with SOE's F section, although he was travelling by one of their Lysander operations. He was to return to England by another, on 16/17 June 1943 - a double in which both the Agazarians also returned, Jack and his wife Francine. Dowlen, a scoutmaster, was a wireless operator who was to transmit messages for Déricourt. He was later caught at his set by German direction-finders and arrested on 31st July 1943.

Claude de Baissac (later DSO) was one of F section's exceptionally successful agents. A 35-year-old Mauritian, he had been parachuted to the Bordeaux area in 1942 and had built up the 'Scientist' circuit there. His later organisation near Chartres was to give German divisions a mauling as they attempted to reinforce their defences against the allied beachhead in Normandy in 1944.

France Antelme, another Mauritian, was a business man in his middle forties. He had parachuted near Poitiers in November 1942 to contact Monsieur Herriot, which he did, and also to check on a number of autonomous resistance groups that were believed to exist. After this Lysander flight in March to England he parachuted back again in May. His circuit was called 'Bricklayer'. He was one of Buckmaster's best agents and was eventually to be captured by a Gestapo-run reception committee to which he parachuted at his own request, knowing it to be suspect.

Raymond Flower was a 30-year old British subject, born in Paris and brought up in the French hotel business. He had parachuted blind in June 1942 and set up a small circuit near Tours called 'Monkeypuzzle'. After his return to England he spent the rest of the war on training and liaison duties.

This then, was the sort of variety of passengers we carried.

Most of them made immense individual contributions to the war. It was irreverent of us at the time to talk of them, as we did, as 'Joes' or 'bods'.

None of them was more famous than Jean Moulin, however, who flew back to France on 19/20 March 1943 with General Delestraint and Christian Pineau. Their pilot was John Bridger and they landed north of Roanne, near Melay, on a flarepath laid by Pierre Delaye assisted by Henri Morier. This operation is now commemorated by a handsome monument in red granite on which are carved the names of passengers, pilot and agent. It was unveiled in March 1990 in the presence of Christian Pineau, Henri Morier, the pilot's son John Bridger, the author and 2,000 other people. In his book[10] Pineau says that the German police arrived ten minutes after they left the field. The extension of Moulin's control over Northern France at the end of May 1943 was swiftly followed by the collapse of the new CNR (*Conseil National de la Résistance*). In June the Gestapo arrested General Delestraint and a week later the dozen leaders of the MUR (*Mouvements Unis de Résistance*) were all caught in Caluire, Lyons. Jean Moulin was so barbarously interrogated that he died, still silent, within three weeks.

I had taken over Lysander 'J' (official number: V 9673) to replace 'D' which I had written off in fog. It was the fashion in those days to paint some terrifying or sexy symbol in crude pop art colours on operational aircraft. In a rather debunking frame of mind, I painted a colourful Jiminy Cricket on Lysander 'J'. This was a cheerful and harmless Walt Disney character, dancing along doing a 'V' sign with his right hand and waving an ebony cane in his left. With his tall top hat, his white gloves and his tail coat he fitted in well with my own nickname - although I did not know it until much later. My 'A' Flight ground-crew had secretly labelled me 'The Duke'.

Bomber pilots painted a bomb on their fuselages for every successful raid, fighter pilots painted a swastika for every German aircraft claimed; what should a security conscious pick-up pilot paint on his Lysander? I decided that a victory 'V' would do no harm and had one painted on for each successful trip. The other pilots did the same sort of thing. McCairns, for example, used stars and Peter used *fleurs de lys*, as in the Scarlet Pimpernel story.

The last operation of the March moon was 'Jockey/Playwright' on 23/24 March, near Estrées-St-Denis, not far from Compiègne - another short trip for me. My outbound passengers were a former schoolmaster, Francis Cammaerts, and Georges Dubourdin[11]; I brought back Captain Peter Churchill ('Michel') and Henri Frager[12] ('Paul'). Francis remembers that we were chased by a night fighter and shot at with tracer. To escape this I did very violent steep turns. I made no note of this at the time, merely recording that I had been hopelessly lost for some time on the way to the target.

The field and flarepath were admirable. Peter Churchill's description[13] of the actual pick-up includes the following, slightly summarised:

After many German aircraft had flown over - and been signalled to - the time was

'J' for Jiminy Cricket, the author's Lysander in 1943.

1.58. Now there was a low-flying aircraft coming straight towards them. This was surely it.

As it came in low and fast 'Michel' (Peter Churchill) focused and held the well-known shape. Instantly his torch flickered on the ground signal. As quickly came the pilot's recognition signal from a small lamp below the fuselage which he operated with slow, well spaced dots and dashes as he rushed by.

"Here we go!" said Michel, "au revoir, mes amis!" - as they dashed to light their lamps.

Following the triangle that gave him his line of approach, the pilot circled down, throttling back his engine. His wheels touched down in a perfect landing not 20 feet from Michel and 'Paul' (Frager), and he pulled up by the second lamp. A quick turnabout and Michel saw Riquet duck below his wing as he revved back - a trifle close - to the controlling lamp. A quick flick and he was round again, facing the two end lamps.

Running up to the pilot who had already pushed back his sliding roof, Michel shouted:

"You can let her idle, there's no one around for miles."

Throttling down, he turned his head and said, in drawing-room tones:

"Congratulations on a perfect field. This is a piece of cake."

Michel and Paul now waited for 'Roger' to alight. He was followed by a second man who was handing down their luggage. He shook hands with 'Roger' (Francis Cammaerts). "Welcome, friend... There's a car laid on. Good luck!"

Climbing up the ladder, Paul and he waved to the two passengers on the field who were giving the 'Thumbs up' sign to show the pilot they were in.

Pulling the roof to and sliding on the safety catch to hold it shut, Michel felt the powerful motor surge them forward. In 60 yards they were airborne and below stood the waving men on the end lamps.

Marsac had helped with the flarepath. In an over-crowded car using producer gas, he took Francis back to Paris where he was to stay for the night in a lady doctor's flat; across the road from Marsac. A day later a small boy came to Cammaerts with a message that Marsac had been arrested. He had gone off to meet a "friend". This

"friend" was Sgt. Bleicher - a most successful German spy-catcher - who had passed himself off as Colonel Henri, an anti-Nazi who wanted Marsac's help to defect to England. When Marsac did not return Cammaerts made his way south on his own, realising how lucky he was not to be in prison almost as soon as he had arrived in France. On his journey he was equipped to cross the Zones with a Red Cross pass.

Francis Cammaerts was one of the few agents we carried that I came to know quite well. He was 27, very tall and good-looking with a little moustache - not the physique to be inconspicuous in Southern France. He was the son of the Belgian poet Emile Cammaerts and had achieved a hockey blue and a second in

Monument at Melay, unveiled in March, 1990.   L'ACALM

history at Cambridge. He had been a pacifist and a conscientious objector. Early in the war, instead of military service, he worked on a farming camp. The story I heard was that the girl who was cooking for this camp (and later married him) persuaded him that he ought to do more for the war than grow food. It is more probable that he changed his mind when his brother in the RAF was killed. In any case he joined SOE late in 1942, preferring to use his bilingual talents as an irregular, since he could not bear the idea of the regimentation of regular soldiering. He was to build up the most formidable and successful secret army in South Eastern France - an organisation with exemplary security.

Dubourdin, who had travelled with him from England, was very soon arrested and never reappeared. He had been at work for F Section in Lyons during 1942.

The two passengers homeward bound from Estrées St Denis, Peter Churchill ('Michel') and Henri Frager ('Paul') are both subjects for many pages in the various histories of the resistance. Churchill's main role in France in 1942 had been to act as liaison officer with 'Carte', the resistance organisation on the Riviera, run by the artist André Girard (also called 'Carte'). Churchill - an ice hockey international - had parachuted near Montpellier in August 1942 and had previously put a number of parties ashore by canoe from submarines off the Riviera coast. His courier Odette Sansom ('Lise'), who had left three small daughters in England, married him after the war. Their story was the subject of many books and a film. They were both to be arrested by Bleicher and some Italian troops in their hotel, soon after Peter Churchill parachuted back to South Eastern France on 14/ 15 April 1943.

Frager, who had been Girard's staff officer, had visited England in July 1942, travelling both ways by felucca based on Gibraltar. During this visit to London in March 1943 he was briefed to keep clear of 'Colonel Henri' (Bleicher) and of the remains of the 'Carte' circuit. He came back to France in mid-April by a Lysander received by Déricourt. Frager was eventually arrested by Bleicher in August 1944; he was sent to Buchenwald, where he was executed. As we all breakfasted together on the morning of 24 March 1943, I could have no idea of the shadows that were already reaching out towards my two light-hearted passengers.

That day I wrote to Sergeant Hollis:

Dear Sam,

So far this has been our most successful month.

I want to congratulate the Flight on the fine show you have all put up, and thank you all for your enthusiasm and initiative.

The aeroplanes have been very operational and smart as well.

Not one flight has been spoilt by bad maintenance, nor one take-off delayed.

While most of the congratulations go to the pilots, we all feel that they should be passed on to the boys.

Thank you, and keep it up!

Sincerely,

Hugh Verity, S/L

The author's Lysander, J (for Jiminy Cricket) at Tangmere in 1943. From the left: McCairns, the author, Gp Capt P.C. Pickard and Ming, Peter Vaughan-Fowler, 'Bunny' Rymills and Henry.

CHAPTER SEVEN

Hudsons and Philippe Livry-Level

I had been introduced to the Hudson by Pick on 29 January 1943. It was Hudson 'O' for Orange and I counted the trip as one hour passenger flying. Pick was demonstrating how one could land a Hudson short. He ignored the ultra-safe advice of the pilot's notes about the speed you should be doing during the last stages of an approach to land (75 knots with engine assistance). He had found out by experiment at a safe height what was the slowest speed you could fly at with a little power on without stalling or dropping a wing (55 knots). He came in across the hedge just a shade faster than that, cut the throttles just before the wheels touched, put the brakes on firmly as soon as the tail wheel was down and stopped the Hudson rolling only 350 yards from the touch-down point at the near end of the runway.

I was admiring this, somewhat nervously, from the right-hand seat in which the navigator normally sat. My apprehension about Pick's sensitive control of the throttles was increased by the fact that his right thumb and much of his right hand were encased in hard plaster with signatures and graffiti scribbled over it. Pick had been demonstrating his agility in a party in the Mess which was to celebrate the birth of his son. The metal structure supporting the roof of the Nissen hut had been boxed in to look like wooden beams. Pick had heaved himself up to hang by his knees from one of these beams. He had then fallen off and broken his thumb. When the day came for Pick's plaster cast to be cut off he had a party in the Mess to celebrate its removal, swung himself up to hang from a beam by his knees, fell off and broke the same thumb again. I cannot now remember whether the plaster he had on 29th January was the first or the second. Whichever it was, it did not stop him giving me a superb demonstration of total mastery of the Hudson at slow speeds.

The Hudson was a low-wing monoplane with two Cyclone radial engines. It had originally been a small airliner, built in the USA by Lockheed-Vega who then called it the 'A24'. It had been developed into a military 'reconnaissance bomber' by the addition of a bomb aimer's position with perspex windows in the nose and an air gunner's turret projecting from the top of the rear fuselage. Some 161 Squadron Hudsons had had their dome-shaped gun turrets removed to improve control at low speeds for landings and take-offs. The weight was then adjusted by the addition of some 300 lb of lead ballast. The long tail-plane had twin pear-shaped fins and rudders

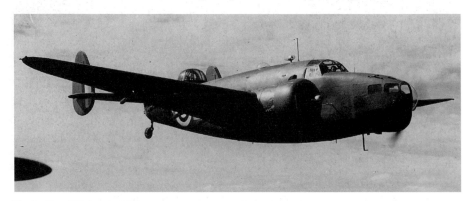

The Lockheed Hudson in Flight. *Imperial War Museum*

near its rounded ends. Hudsons were mainly used for escorting convoys crossing the Atlantic and protecting them from submarines. One of our 161 Sqn Hudsons had large and elegant lettering on its side: *Spirit of Lockheed - Vega employees*. It was a gift to the RAF by the workforce.

There was a door into the fuselage on the port side behind the wing. The interior was crude structural metal with no attempt at sound-proofing or comfortable seating for passengers. They had to sit on their luggage or on the floor, with their backs to the side walls of the fuselage. Every possible pound of weight had been saved. For our pick-up operations there was room for eight to ten passengers and their luggage. There was provision for small scale parachute operations through a chute through the floor. Moving forward through this egg-shaped compartment the pilot and navigator could reach their seats up front through a little door. The wireless operator/air gunner had two work stations: one for each of his functions.

After a couple of short flights to familiarise myself with Hudsons in the first week in February, I took the 'A' Flight Lysanders down to Tangmere for the moon period. At the beginning of March John Bridger and I went to the Coastal Command Operational Conversion Unit at RAF Silloth for a Hudson familiarisation course. I had been there before, just after my brief honeymoon at the end of August 1940, to learn to fly the ill-fated Botha.

After a concentrated few hours of ground school our flying training was packed into three days and nights. On 6th March I did no less than four daylight trips (including one when the main wiring circuit caught fire in the air filling the aeroplane with smoke) and two short night sorties. Our instructors (Flt Lt Thompson and Flg Off Holdsworth) were hard to persuade that we should practise landing Hudsons 20 knots slower over the hedge than everybody else. I had observed the burnt out hulk of a Hudson which one of the trainees had driven on to the runway at such a high speed that the undercarriage had been forced up into the engine.

Following this course, which had lasted less than a week, I stuck in my log-book a scruffy manuscript slip of paper certifying that I had "qualified as first pilot of Hudsons day and night". Writing this, I cannot help reflecting how long such a re-training course would last now and looking back with nostalgia at the pressures of war when we got things done at some speed.

After the March moon at Tangmere we went back to Tempsford in formation. I then flew Hudson 'O' (N 7263) by day and night, pounding round on circuits and landings. This was the King's aircraft. By 11th April I was practising short night landings on a 450 yard flarepath at Tempsford. I had 'Sophie' with me as a passenger that night. He was Wing Commander Sofiano, MBE, from 'ISLD'. I became very fond of 'Sophie'. He was much older than we all were and hard experiences had engraved deep lines in his pale face. He was a frequent visitor to both Tempsford and the Cottage at Tangmere when we were doing a trip for his 'firm'. He had a charming smile, infallibly good-humoured courtesy and a rather old fashioned elegance of speech and behaviour.

The April moon came and went without me having an opportunity to do a Hudson pick-up, though we had a busy and successful moon with the Lysanders. It was not until 19th May that I could do my first operational Hudson pick-up. This was to be in Hudson 'P' (N 7221). I was lent a crew from 'B' Flight and I was delighted to find that my navigator would be none other than Flight Lieutenant Philippe Livry of the French Air Force. At that time he already had several French decorations. He was a big man ("1m 86 et 95 kilos", he records in his book[1], *Missions dans la RAF*). His short but wavy black hair and black army-style moustache, his strong nose and chin, his voice like thunder; all these gave him a formidable and unique presence. He was twenty years older than me but he became one of my best friends.

Sergeant Shine was our wireless operator/air gunner. He was a not very tall, cheerful young Yorkshireman with wavy brown hair and pink cheeks. He was quiet, absolutely dependable at his work, with no sign of nerves. His long-term ambition was to run a pub. We three normally made up the crew for all the Hudson pick-ups I took part in.

The first time we flew together was on 18th May, when we worked up our co-operation as a crew on a short daylight cross-country. Then, on the morning of 19th May we flew Hudson 'P' from Tempsford to Tangmere to be in position for the trip that night. It was an uneventful flight lasting six hours and twenty minutes. We landed one and picked up eight passengers[2] at 'Orion', a magnificent field near Cosges, north west of Bletterans and Lons-le-Saunier that Paul Rivière was to show me after the war. It must have been two or three times as long as the 1,000 metres that we required for Hudsons. The agent in charge was Bruno Larat[3] and the whole conduct of the operation on the ground was impeccable. The flarepath was our standard Hudson lay-out of torches; 450 metres long with 150 metres between torches; one torch to the right at the end. The BBC message of agreement to this proposed operation was an accurate forecast of how it went: *"La route est belle"*. On

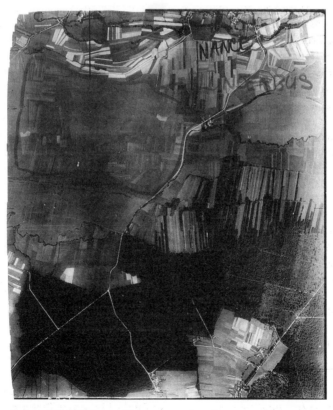

Hudson field 'Orion', near Bletterans.   *Crown Copyright*

this particular flight only one thing went wrong; the gyro-pilot, known as 'George', packed up - not that this mattered.

Comparing a Hudson trip with a Lysander trip, I came to the conclusion that the landing itself on the sketchy flarepath of small torches really was very much more difficult; the navigation was, obviously, very much easier. Not only was there a full-time navigator to concentrate on it, with both hands free; there was also a range of electronic navigation aids including Gee and a radio loop for getting bearings.

The landing called for a much larger circuit pattern. The Hudson weighed about three times as much as a Lysander and had to approach about 10 knots faster. It was not nearly so manoeuvrable at slow speeds. In these circumstances lining it up for the final approach was by no means easy, however accurately the race-track circuit pattern was flown. It was not unusual for these clandestine Hudson landings to be achieved after a missed approach. This meant opening up the motors to full throttle to go round again. What the party on the field must have thought of the noise, I shudder to imagine. They must have thought it a signal for any security forces within earshot to converge on the field as quickly as possible. This is perhaps one of the reasons why the *équipe de terrain* always included armed sentries on every approach road and track. They had weapons - mainly Sten guns - which had been dropped by parachute in large containers.

The pilot's drill before landing was more complicated than in the Lysander with its fixed undercarriage. One had to check that the carburettor air intake was COLD; that the brakes air pressure felt right and that they were OFF; that the speed was below 145 knots before the wheels were put DOWN; that the mixture controls were in AUTO RICH and propeller controls fully forward; that superchargers were in M ratio; that flaps were partly down at first and fully down over the hedge.

Of course I expected Philippe to help me double check vital actions in my cockpit drill before landing: two green lights (to indicate both main wheels locked down) and flaps down. The Hudson had huge flaps.

During the turn-round he would supervise the change over of loads. We often took out a considerable number - and weight - of packages with supplies for the resistance networks: arms, explosives, wireless sets and large wads of French currency from London banks' vaults. On this trip we landed 24 packages. Sometimes the agent in charge would find time to come up front where I stayed, strapped in; he squeezed me by the hand and gave me generous presents - scent for my wife, cognac or champagne for the crew. I did not realise at the time to what horrifying lengths the resistance networks would sometimes go to obtain champagne. It had all been confiscated by the Germans or secretly walled up in the *caves* by the French. By this time scent, too, was very hard to find in France, except at great prices on the black market.

The turn-round was quickly completed. I had done my take-off checks, including setting trimming tabs to ZERO, and we took off. As I opened up the throttles, adjusting them to check any tendency to swing, Philippe's hand would follow them forward and then hold them fully forward. The boost went up to 45 inches and rpm to 2,500 as we left the ground and then climbed away at 115 knots. This left me with two hands on the spectacle hand grips on the stick. Then, when I said the word, braking the spinning wheels, he retracted the undercarriage and the 15 degrees of flap that we used for take-off.

And so, early on 20th May 1943, eight passengers were excitedly eating their bacon and eggs for breakfast with us in the cottage at Tangmere. For the first time for ages they could really relax and the reminiscences bubbled out of them like champagne. To have brought back that load with Lysanders would have needed three aeroplanes instead of one.

Hudson flying and engine instruments.

Before we did another Hudson pick-up I had time to get to know Philippe better. I discovered after the war that 'Livry' was his *nom-de-guerre* (his family were still in France) and that his real name before the war had been Level. After the war he joined them together and was called Colonel Philippe Livry-Level.

In World War One[4] he was in the 61st Regiment of Artillery until he was wounded in 1918. He married Nicole, a most charming descendant of one of the grand old families of Normandy, the Percés, who were remotely connected with the English Percys (the family name of the Dukes of Northumberland). A famous ancestor had been William the Conqueror's cook. At the battle of Hastings he had rushed from his field kitchen brandishing a spit, with which he slew so many Englishmen that he was ennobled and given a large estate - at least this is what they told me.

Nicole and Philippe raised their five children living for part of the year in their comfortable flat at 77, Rue de Prony, Paris, but spending much of each summer and other holidays at their beautiful eighteenth century château at Audrieu, between Caen and Bayeux. During this period Philippe was a very successful business man and frequently flew across the Atlantic to complete important contracts for aluminium and other deals.

On 27th August 1939, on mobilisation, he rejoined the same gunner regiment at Metz. He spent the winter of 1939 and the spring of 1940 guarding the Maginot line. During this period he was wounded in the left knee and walked somewhat unevenly for the rest of his life. After the collapse of France he worked on secret service missions for some months, but he concluded that his great bulk and height made him too conspicuous. He decided to continue the war more openly and made his way to England via Lisbon, with false papers, early in 1941. Like so many thousands of others who arrived in England during the war he had to go through a thorough interrogation in the 'Patriotic School' to establish his credentials. He described it as a sort of prison, but they only kept him one night. He was determined to achieve an ambition he had failed to realise in the first war and again in 1939. He wanted to fight in the air. Besides, as he looked round the armed forces of the Western allies early in 1941, who else was really fighting the Germans at that time but the Royal Air Force?

He was, of course, far too old to join the RAF as aircrew. Anthony Eden listened to him politely and suggested that he should go back to France on a secret mission. General de Gaulle offered him a post on his Headquarters staff. (Philippe put three exclamation marks after this statement in his book. He did not believe sitting in an office was the way to fight a war). In spite of all his high-level string-pulling Philippe failed - until one day, with no recommendation, he walked into a recruiting booth on Euston station. He smilingly declared that he had been born on 16th June 1911 - when he had in fact been at least 13 years old - and was astonished and delighted to find that this declaration was accepted without question. He got through a stiff medical and joined the RAF (though formally a member of the French forces) to go to school to learn to be an air navigator.

I remember asking him in 1943 why he had been so determined to continue his personal contribution to the fighting in such an active way. He obviously thought it a silly question but he explained that France had been very good to him; he was much better off than most Frenchmen; he therefore owed France much more. It was an admirably simple, rather feudal, explanation - and perfectly genuine.

Now I feel I have had my revenge, because in his book he records a rather private conversation with me in which I confessed to being puzzled by the war; "weren't the Germans people like anyone else? Was it not sad to have to kill them?" He called this a "pacifist" declaration. In fact, I was rather pleased to find myself in a job where I could make an operational contribution to the war without killing people. It was also much more satisfying to carry people than bombs - especially when the people one carried were such outstanding personalities.

Philippe eventually prevailed on the authorities to post him to an operational squadron in May 1942 and found himself in No 52 Squadron, Coastal Command, escorting convoys and attacking submarines. During this tour Philippe's crew were detached for a while to an American base to hunt for submarines off their East Coast. He took advantage of time off to visit New York and call, unexpectedly, on his office there. His staff were thunderstruck. They had imagined that they would be free from his critical inspections until after the war was over.

On 2nd February 1943 Philippe arrived at RAF Tempsford to join No 161 Squadron. He had persuaded the security chiefs that he could be trusted but he had to exchange his dark blue French uniform for the lighter blue of the RAF. He said in his book - quite truthfully - that he spoke English with a deplorable accent and that anyone within 100 metres could tell at once that he was a foreigner, whatever the colour of his uniform.

Squadron Leader Philippe Livry-Level, DFC*.

His first special operations were in Halifaxes, parachuting men and supplies to triangles of light in France and Norway. His pilot on these trips was Dave Leggatt. On some of these trips he could fly over his château at Audrieu where Nicole and their children were asleep. He had not seen them - nor been able to exchange letters - for two years. He did not know what troubles they were having with shortages of everything and the occupation. At least, with their farms, they were unlikely to be really hungry. Nor did he know that, for a time, his wife Nicole was imprisoned by the Germans. On one of our landings with Paul Rivière, Philippe handed him a parcel with a pair of shoes and a few cakes of soap. This was subsequently delivered to Nicole at Audrieu with the simple message: "Your husband is well."

Thirty years after D-Day, in 1974, the French Resistance association *L'Amicale Action* invited more than a dozen of us old hands from Tempsford to join their Annual Congress which was, this time, in Normandy. While we were in Calvados, Philippe's son Gerard Livry-Level invited us all to the château at Audrieu which he was about to develop as a luxury hotel. We laid a wreath on Philippe's tomb and then had a splendid party. I met Jean Desollange who had taken the parcel to Audrieu in 1943 - a long and dangerous journey. He had delivered it personally to Nicole Level, even though German troops were billeted on the château at the time.

Now that I have given a detailed description of an uneventful Hudson pick-up operation, I should go back to the beginning of these larger scale pick-ups. The Station Commander, Group Captain Fielden, had been frustrated by the absence of correctly identified reception committees on the first two attempts at Hudson pick-ups. These were in the South of France in November and December of 1942. They are not recorded in the RAF archives but his widow, Lady Fielden, copied details from his private records for this book. (See Appendix B)

John Corby was in the cottage at Tangmere when Mouse came for his first Hudson pick-up attempt. He was in high dudgeon because the aircraft had not been serviceable. In the end, he took off for a landing in the South of France after the stand-by period had started, and only reached the field a quarter of an hour before close of standby. He thought the reception had given up and gone home early, but in fact, as John was later told, Peter Churchill had been prevented from going himself to control the operation and had sent a woman colleague in his place. She had (a) not been trained and (b) set up in a field two or three kilometres from the right one.

The first one successfully completed was on 13/14 February 1943 by Pick. His navigator was a Canadian Pilot Officer, Dicky Taylor and his Wireless Operator/Air Gunner was Flying Officer Henry Figg. The field was near St. Yan, north of Roanne and west of Charolles, and the route from Tangmere was via Cabourg, the islands in the Loire east of Blois, and Nevers. Henri Gorce-Franklin remembered that André Boyer stretched out on a blanket in the half-empty Hudson and fell asleep. When he woke up, he lit a cigarette. It must have been Henry Figg who pounced on him, reminding him that we were at war and that night fighters were everywhere. Apart from this the only break in the monotony of the flight was the arrival of sandwiches and coffee. The only other problem was one manufactured for some reason by Pick. When he saw the correct letter 'N' flashed from the field he "answered with an incorrect letter to see what would happen". All the lights went out. He then gave the correct letter and two red lights came on. Some time elapsed before the flarepath was laid out and fully lit. One can just imagine the consternation on the field when they must have thought that they had attracted the attention of a roaming German night fighter or bomber. They were on the ground for 10 minutes, landing five agents[5] and picking up only mail, since the passengers for England had not arrived.

When they landed and jumped out, Fernand Gane's hat blew off in the slipstream from the propellers and could not be found - until a German patrol found it the next day. They also found the Hudson's wheel marks. Less than a week later the field was ploughed up and useless to the Resistance[6].

One of the agents landed was Jean Fleury, who wrote to me in 1981:
"The reception committee was small and not well armed. In landing, the aeroplane had made a lot of noise and had swept the field with its powerful landing lamp. The passengers were many and bewildered. It was necessary to get away as quickly as possible. I suggested that, without separating, we should go straight to Roanne and get into whatever train arrived first.
"As we arrived, a train for Lyons came into the station. It was stuffed full of German soldiers. They very obligingly made room in the luggage rack for our suitcases which were full of Colts and radio transmitters. As for us, we slept until Lyons, lulled by the snores of our travelling companions."

The same crew were equally successful on the second Hudson pick up on 20/21 February, near Arles. They landed one passenger and picked up six[7].

The Hudson hat-trick for February was not so easy to complete, however, when the same crew were on their third pick-up - on the night of 24/25 February. Pick's target was Cuisery airfield, between Dijon and Lyons. He had reached the field at 0130 after much thick fog over the Loire as far as Le Creusot. He then

Hudson coming in to land.

had to wait around for patches of fog to clear and for his flarepath to be lit and eventually came down, rather heavily, and not really on the flarepath after his twentieth circuit. On each of these circuits Pick had done a complete approach and overshoot procedure, lowering and raising wheels and flaps. His right hand and wrist were still in plaster from his accident in the Mess and Henry Figg worked the throttles for him, as well as controlling the wheels and flaps. Each approach was helped by a church which showed up in the moonlight.

At the end of his landing run the Hudson rolled on to a patch of soft muddy ground and dug in when he tried to turn it. It was 0330.

By now there were quite a number of people on the field. There were the agent in charge, the flarepath team, the passengers, and the guards posted on the approaches to the field with Sten guns, to prevent any official interference from German or French security services. Many of these people rallied round to help dig away mud in front of the wheels and heave and shove. They were joined by more and more people from the village who had been woken by the noise of the Hudson's two engines.

Squadron Leader Wagland remembers[8] that: "In dear Pick's usual swashbuckling style his crew were armed to the teeth with revolvers, Sten-guns etc. but not so much as a teaspoon to dig themselves out. That they did get away was largely due to the air gunner, Flight Lieutenant (known as 'Colonel') Putt - an additional crew member from 138 Squadron. He was over 40 years old but dug away with his bare hands while everyone else was arguing with voluble Frenchmen."

Half an hour later Pick could taxi away and try to head back towards the point where lamp 'A' had been before all the excitement. After a quarter of a mile of firm ground, his Hudson sank into mud again and he could not move it with engine power. By now half the inhabitants of the village were on the field and they were organised as much as possible to help the crew dig out the Hudson again. Henry Figg's account of this reads: "Pick was at the controls and at every opportunity he opened the throttles to pull out, blowing everyone who was digging and pushing violently away from the aircraft. The problem was the tail wheel locking device. Either Pick was not locking it or the lock had broken. Every time Pick opened up the tail wheel castored and the opposite main wheel went deeper in the mud. Eventually, I obtained a long branch and used it as a steering arm. With the help of horses the aircraft was moved. (On subsequent trips we made sure of a tail arm being carried.) The most annoying and frightening part of the operation was the willing helpers running around the aircraft and I grabbed at least three, preventing them from going into the moving propellers. I must add that I think I suggested burning the aircraft at one stage when cars appeared before the horses arrived. Pick did not agree, thank God."

The aircraft was finally extricated at 0530. Pick tried to find out from them which way to point the nose to take off with the longest clear run. It was getting very late and he did not want to wait for a properly organised flarepath. He took off in the direction he had understood was best, but he struck trees with one wing tip and the leading edge as he got airborne. Luckily this damage was not serious - only 'George', the automatic pilot was put out of action. As they got airborne the crew thought they saw cars approaching the field. They were astonished that they had not been molested by the Germans after making all that noise for so long[9]. He flew across the French coast north of Le Havre just as dawn was breaking at 0703 - just as the German day fighter squadrons were taking off on their first patrols. Pick requested a fighter escort but it could not be arranged in time. So goes the official RAF story. Bunny Rymills remembers that local arrangements were in fact made at Tangmere with Wing Commander Scott whose Typhoons were based there. A flight was called to readiness before dawn and scrambled when Pick's Hudson showed up on the radar 30 miles inside France. When the Typhoons approached the Lockheed Hudson to escort it, Pick thought they were Focke-Wulf 190s and turned away.

As a sequel to the gallant help from the Typhoons from across the airfield at Tangmere, their CO, 'Scotty', was invited to a party in the Cottage one evening when there were no operations laid on. Elston-Evans picked him up in our old Rolls-Royce which had been blacked out inside for the occasion. We drove him round and round the aerodrome for half-an-hour and then into the Cottage yard. Late on in the night, when we had all had a lot to drink, he said good night. We said that Elston was in bed and so he would have to walk home. "Steady on", he said, "It must be at least 15 miles." We took him to the gate and showed him the main Officers' Mess, two minutes walk away[10].

There were no Hudson trips laid on in the March moon but Pick was successful in his last two, which he flew in April. For these he had a different crew: Flying Officer Broadley, navigator, and Flying Officer Cocker as wireless operator. On 15/16 April they landed north of Pont-de-Vaux with no trouble on an immense meadow near the Saône by the road from Arbigny to the Uchizy bridge. This field, code-named 'Junot', had been surveyed by Captain Claudius Four, assisted by 'Colette', a twenty-two year old graduate (now Mrs Marcelle Adamson). They were working for Paul Schmidt. As Schmidt and Four had recently been transferred to the North, 'Colette', who knew the field, took part in the operation as part of Bruno Larat's team. She and the radio operator went by train from Lyons to Fleurville and met for the first time at the railway station there. While waiting for Paul Rivière, Larat's assistant, to pick them up, they spent the time acting as lovers, canoodling in the bushes opposite the station. This was a security precaution which established unsuspected acting talent in the well behaved girl. Her feminine presence, sitting between two men with her arms round their shoulders, was also very helpful when Rivière's car was stopped by Germans on the bridge across the Saône as night was falling.

Pick's outbound load was two passengers (Closon and Fraval) and 12 suitcases. Then they found that they had a problem. Four passengers had been expected for the return flight and they found 11 waiting hopefully. They had brought along for the ride two passengers: Wing Commander Brooks and Wing Commander Lockhart who, according to the Squadron records, "made the journey unofficially." The maximum number of passengers that they could carry safely was 10 - so only eight of the eleven, and their luggage, could be picked up. This must have taken a few minutes to sort out because they were on the ground for a quarter of an hour.

Paul Rivière assisted Bruno Larat with this operation on the ground. He remembers: "On leaving the meadow where the aeroplane had landed at about 1 am, we happened to meet a patrol of French Gendarmes. They asked us what we were doing on a road so little used at this time of night and where we were coming from with two cars. I told them that they ought to know because they were there themselves. Their leader then told me that the Germans were guarding the bridge over the Saône at Fleurville and that we should on no account go that way. he added: "My son also is on the other side of the sea. If you are arrested, don't say that you met us." And so we reached Bourg without trouble at the stroke of 2 am."

This field is now marked by a stele which reads: "JUNOT, Terrain Atterrissage, Missions Spéciales R.A.F. Resistance, 1943-1944." It was unveiled in September 1988 by the Mayor of Arbigny, Monsieur Tricaud, the President of the Veterans of the Maquis of the Ain, Colonel Girousse, Paul Rivière and myself.

Pick's last Hudson pick-up was operation 'Zinnia' on 18/19 April on the *Causse Méjean* near Florac; the flarepath was laid out by Michel Thoraval who was working with 'Travaux Ruraux', a cover organisation for the French Army Secret Service (Counter-espionage) run by Paul Paillole. The weather was excellent. The load out was 200 lb of freight. After 20 minutes on the ground eight passengers were picked up. They were Petitjean, Koenig and his son, Colonel Guénin, Callot, Brohan, Michelin and Champion.

Before the May moon Pick was posted to RAF Lissett and promoted to Group Captain. Squadron Leader L. McD. Hodges, who had been awarded a bar to his DFC the day before, was promoted to Wing Commander to take over command of 161 Squadron (of which he had been 'B' Flight Commander, parachuting agents and supplies from Halifaxes). So the great maestro was no longer there to do Hudson pick-ups in May. Nevertheless the two that were laid on were both completed on 19/20 May: the first by the Station Commander and the second by the Flight Commander (already related above). Mouse Fielden and his crew (Squadron Leader Wagland, navigator, and Flying Officer Cocker) had failed in their first attempt at operation 'Tulip' on 15/16 May. There was a lot of fog in the area.

Mouse Fielden's second try at operation 'Tulip' on 19/20 May successfully landed Lheureux, Offroy and Bonnard and picked up the former Army chief of Staff General

Georges (5 star), Col. Duval, Capitaine de Peich ('Laprune'), Robert Masson, Capt. Hugo and Michel Thoraval[11]. The landing was not until 0215. If they had returned to England directly they would have risked crossing Northern France by daylight and their slow old Hudson - with its valuable passengers - would have been an easy target for German day fighters. So Mouse decided to return via North Africa and Gibraltar. They landed at Maison Blanche airfield near Algiers.

Philip Schneidau told me how operation 'Tulip' had been laid on. Winston Churchill sent SIS a note through Major Morton asking them to arrange for General Georges and half-a-dozen others to be picked up from the Massif Central and brought back to the UK. Philip went to see Mouse Fielden, the Station Commander at Tempsford. He explained that it was a "special op for the PM" and asked that it should be flown by the best qualified crew available. To Philip's dismay, the Group Captain said that he would do it himself. Philip explained that this was a particularly delicate matter. General Georges, as the senior French General, was two ranks senior to de Gaulle and might be able to influence him. Churchill wanted to win over General Georges before he saw de Gaulle and persuade him to act as go-between. He might even persuade Georges to give orders to de Gaulle.

"That's just what I'm here for", said Mouse Fielden. Philip Schneidau could not blurt out that a younger pilot in more active operational practice might be better for the job. So it caused no little dismay in the highest places when the Hudson went to Algiers instead of England. General Georges went straight to General Giraud. That, said Philip, was the end of the story.

Squadron Leader J.C.W. Wagland, who flew as navigator to Mouse, does not agree with Philip Schneidau's view that a younger pilot would have been a better choice. Although operationally inexperienced, there was no doubt, said 'Waggy', that Mouse was an outstanding aviator. Not only an outstanding pilot, he knew Europe very well from the air. Waggy's recollection[12] of that landing follows:

"That operation was my first landing in France since before the war. After landing we stopped the engines and must have waited ten minutes or so for General Georges' car convoy to turn up. During the interval I had my first 'pee' on French soil for many years.

The cars arrived with no lights. Passengers on board, Fielden started the engines. He drove, I held fully open the throttles and kept the mixture controls on 'RICH'. The wireless operator, Flying Officer Cocker, held the pitch control to 'FINE'. Evidently we were taking no chances. Fielden never braked the wheels before retracting the undercarriage. The smell of burning rubber as the rubber door seals scraped against the revolving wheels was alarming as well as unpleasant.

As we flew South we were "pooped at" by anti-aircraft guns on the Balearic Islands - a

Sir Edward Fielden, GCVO, CB, DFC, AFC, in the early 1960s.

85

gesture of neutrality as they were far away. Frankly, I did not realise the importance of our VIP until we got to Maison Blanche, when the crew tumbled out first. As the VIP left the aircraft, Fielden sprang smartly to attention and gave a magnificent salute - a courtesy I have only seen him extend otherwise to their Majesties the King and Queen on visiting Tempsford. I was quite shaken by the display."

When he returned to England, Mouse presented a bottle of French wine, which his passengers had given him, to the King. The King shared it with Winston Churchill, proudly showing him the label: "Vintage 1941". He knew that even the Prime Minister could not obtain such a bottle in London. The King refused Mr Churchill's insistent enquiries about how he had got hold of it and this infuriated the Prime Minister[13].

Although a complete digression, I must record another story Philip Schneidau told me about Mouse Fielden. Towards the end of 1943, Philip had to take two French agents to Gibraltar to put them on a felucca which would land them at Cassis, near Marseilles, complete with English-made French-type bicycles. Mouse decided to do the trip to Gibraltar - no doubt for shopping - and to dine in Cornwall during a refuelling stop. The air traffic signal to Gibraltar gave warning of the Hudson's arrival at 5 am, flown by Group Captain Fielden with two passengers whose names could not be given. When they landed at Gibraltar they were greeted by an enormous floodlit parade. Hundreds of troops had been up since 1 am polishing their buttons. Somebody in Gibraltar had realised that Mouse was the King's pilot and guessed that the two unnamed passengers indicated a royal visit wrapped in deepest secrecy. All Philip wanted was to unload his passengers unobserved in an unlit corner of the airfield.

Seven out of the first ten attempts at Hudson pick-ups had been successful in these months of November 1942 to May 1943 (five of them by Pick). This type of operation had definitely become established, in spite of its initial improbability. Now we should turn back to April to take up the story of the Lysander pick-ups.

'Pick'

CHAPTER EIGHT

Good Moons for the Lysanders

Over the moons of April to September 1943, we in the Lysander Flight had a remarkable run of good luck combined with a reasonable amount of good weather. An army friend of ours once told my wife and me that, on one evening on their honeymoon, he had looked out from the balcony of his hotel room admiring a beautiful moonlit view. "A wonderful moon for the infantry", he had said. Over the extended summer of 1943 there were, generally, wonderful moons for the Lysanders. In fact, with a few exceptions, some of which have already been described in Chapter Six, the Lysander operation became a routine job of work, stimulating and pleasant to do and only potentially dangerous. This was partly due to the fact that the small group of pilots involved were by now experienced and partly due to the excellent work done by the agents in the field who laid on our receptions. We did not realise at the time the degree to which the German security services were penetrating some of the resistance organisations on the ground, although we knew, of course, that the agents we worked with were in terrible danger all the time. In this Chapter I shall tell the story of Lysander pick-ups from April to July 1943.

In April 1943 we attempted 16 Lysander landings and completed 14. This was more than twice the number of successes in any month so far. Nine of the landings were on the five doubles we did. Apart from the dozen passengers landed and two dozen picked up by Pick's Hudsons, the Lysanders themselves took to France at least 16 passengers and brought back 28 or more in this moon period alone. Over the whole war so far up to the end of March 1943 only about 80 passengers are recorded as having been brought back to the UK by clandestine pick-ups. April's score of 44 (including Hudsons and Lysanders) indicates how the tempo was building up.

It was during April that Sir Archibald Sinclair, Secretary of State for Air, visited our main base at Tempsford. He was very enthusiastic about our work, but he arrived three hours late. This delayed some take-offs and the preparations for them.

We flew to Tangmere for the moon detachment on 10th April and our first operation was a double Lysander pick-up by Bunny Rymills and myself on 13/14. This was one week after my 25th birthday. Our field ('Marguerite') was north-east of Mâcon and our rendezvous to the south of it. We kept R/T silence until 0120; I landed

April, 1943. Sir Archibald Sinclair (Air Minister) talking to John Bridger. Group Captain Sir L. Greig chats to O.C. 161 Squadron, Wing Commander Pickard and O.C. 138 Squadron, Wing Commander Ken Batchelor.

Crown Copyright

87

at 0140, took off and called in Bunny who landed at 0150. We each took out one agent and six packages and brought back two passengers and a lot of luggage. There were no incidents. This seems to have been the operation in April when we carried some real VIPs.

Paul Rivière noted for me that he assisted Bruno Larat[1] who was in charge of the team on the field. They had both crossed the river Saône in a boat. He names only three passengers to England[2]: Henri Queuille, and E. d'Astier in my Lysander and J.P. Levy in Bunny's. According to André Gillois[3], the fourth passenger was Daniel Mayer. These were exceptionally distinguished passengers: Baron Emmanuel d'Astier de la Vigerie was de Gaulle's Minister for the Interior by the end of 1943; Henri Queuille, who was about 59 years old, had been a Minister from 1920 and was to be Prime Minister of France in 1948; Jean-Pierre Levy had created the *mouvement Franc-Tireur* in 1941 and was to be a member of the National Council of the Resistance; and Daniel Mayer was a distinguished French socialist resister and subsequently Secretary General of the SFIO (French Socialist party).

Gillois remembered Levy saying that on arrival, he thanked his pilot. "It's magnificent. You are splendid chaps (*des types épatants*)."
"No", protested the pilot, "It's you who are splendid. We only take risks for one hour. You take risks for 24 hours a day. You need not thank us."
"Such is the welcome of the English", commented Gillois - "and then the miraculous breakfast."

The next night was the Déricourt double near Amboise when Mac's approach took him through the tree (already described in Chapter Six). Between them Peter and Mac landed four and picked up one. The four were Frager; Dubois, an experienced radio operator; Liewer, a 32-year-old French journalist; and his assistant, a French Canadian called Gabriel Chartrand[4].

Philippe Liewer was to establish an excellent force of 350 effective saboteurs in the prohibited coastal zone round le Havre. Peter's homeward-bound passenger was Marcel Clech, a Breton taxi-driver, then a wireless operator, who had arrived on the Riviera a year before on one of Peter Churchill's submarine parties. After a month's rest in England he was to join Frager. After the operation Déricourt and Frager bicycled 20 miles to Tours, where Frager and Chartrand were left in a school. During breakfast they were almost arrested by a visiting Gestapo commission which was inspecting the history books[5].

The next night, 15/16 April, there were three operations attempted, one double and two single Lysanders. The visibility was excellent and all three were successful. The double, by Peter and Mac, landed three and picked up five in the Rouen area.

This operation is described in "The White Rabbit"[6] by Bruce Marshall as having happened on the night of 16 April. Yeo-Thomas's memory of it will illustrate an agent's view of a pick-up. Squadron Leader Forest ('Tommy') Yeo-Thomas of the RAF was Colonel Dismore's right hand man in the 'RF' country section of SOE, the section that arranged supplies and air operations for Géneral de Gaulle's clandestine operations. He was full of fun and bounce and was one of our most popular visitors at Tangmere Cottage. He was old enough to have seen active service in the First World War, though only through exaggerating his age. Between the wars he had, improbably, been a director of Molyneux' *"maison de haute couture"* in Paris. His story, as he told it to Bruce Marshall, includes the following:
"On 14th April word was sent from London to the three agents that they would be

picked up on the night of the 16th by a Lysander, from a field near Lyons-la-Forêt. They set out at once from the Gare St. Lazare, taking with them an American pilot called Ryan who had been shot down from a Flying Fortress and sheltered by a friend of Professeur Pasteur Valéry-Radot. Ryan had a fractured shoulder, which had been reset by the Professor, and could speak no French. He was told that if anybody spoke to him on the train his reply must be limited to 'oui' or 'non'.

They travelled in two groups to Pont-de-l'Arche, Brossolette and another agent in one compartment, and Yeo-Thomas, Ryan and Dutertre of the Lyons-la-Forêt reception committee in another. During the journey nobody attempted to speak to Ryan, who pretended to be reading a French newspaper. In the buffet at Pont-de-l'Arche, fumbling for, and at first failing to find, his wallet, Yeo-Thomas committed his only indiscretion. "Where the hell's my money?", he said in English. Fortunately there were a lot of people talking noisily in the buffet and his remark was not overheard.

From Pont-de-l'Arche they took a small local train to Fleury-sur -Andelle, whence they made another uncomfortable journey by bicycle to Lyons-la-Forêt. They reached the village after dark. Passy and Brossolette were sheltered by the Vinets and Yeo-Thomas and Ryan in a neighbouring farmhouse. All next day they remained indoors. Ryan, unaccustomed to clandestine life, kept talking loudly in his unmistakable American accent and on more than one occasion had to be silenced by the farmer's wife.

At 10.30 pm Yeo-Thomas and Ryan climbed into a van drawn up in the farmyard and hid behind sacks of potatoes. Dutertre sat in front with the driver. After an hour's bumpy journey the van stopped and they got out. They found themselves on a deserted country road beside a road-mender's hut, into which Tommy's suitcase was pushed. Beside the road a field shimmered like a silver lake in the moonlight. The stars twinkled brightly in the cold, thrown-up vault of the sky. They hurried across the magic field and lay down in a copse, where they were presently joined by Passy, Brossolette, Vinet and Jacot (Jacques Courtaud).

Soon there was a buzzing sound in the air. Dutertre, Jacot and Vinet rose and ran on to the field, where torches had been fixed to three sticks arranged in the form of an 'L'. Jacot flashed the recognition sign and the Lysander replied. The plane circled, landed, came down the longer branch of the 'L' against the wind, turned along the shorter and came to a standstill. In less than three minutes Passy, Brossolette, Yeo-Thomas, Ryan and their suitcases were in the gunner's cockpit and the Lysander was airborne again. An hour later they landed at Tangmere, back once more in the right sort of night.

Next evening the BBC French service sent out for the first time the message: *'Le petit lapin blanc est rentré au clapier.'* 'The little white rabbit has returned to his hutch.'"

According to Passy[7] the first Lysander picked up Yeo-Thomas, Captain Ryan and Jargon, a wireless operator. The second brought out Cavaillès and picked up 'Passy' and Brossolette. Cavaillès, formerly a *professeur* at the *Ecole Normale Supérieure*, was on his way to organise the intelligence network 'Cohors'. He was to be arrested (for the second time) on 28th August 1943. 'Passy' was Colonel A. Dewavrin, head of de Gaulle's *2e* and *3e Bureaux*, i.e. Head of Secret Intelligence and Operations from the beginning in July 1940. In 1942 these were merged under him into the *Bureau Central de Renseignements et d'Action* (BCRA). Pierre Brossolette had been in France since January 1943. He had been joined by 'Passy' and Yeo-Thomas a month later on mission 'Brumaire-Arquebuse' Their object was to develop in the northern Occupied Zone a military organisation like that in the South, under control from London.

Another of the pick-ups on 15/16 April, 'Antinea', was flown by John Bridger to Loyettes, east of Lyons, where he picked up Robert Wackherr, Henri Morier and Pineau's teenage son. After landing at Tangmere they were taken to Tony Bertram's house nearby. There, Robert Wackherr remembers, they met Brossolette and others who had arrived by Peter and Mac's double.

The flarepath for 'Antinea' had been laid by Pierre Delaye. He was the air operations officer and radio operator of Christian Pineau's intelligence network 'Phalanx'. Delaye had escaped from Germany via Russia and made his way to England. Here, aged 42, he volunteered for training as a radio operator to fight against Nazism. 'Antinea' was the fourth pick-up that he had laid on. He had also received many parachute operations.

Less than a month later, on 11th May 1943, Pierre Delaye was surprised by the Gestapo while transmitting and shot dead. His brother and sister continued their work for 'Phalanx'. He is commemorated on the bridge at Loyettes.

On 16/17 April I lent Bunny my Lysander J (for Jiminy Cricket) as the undercarriage on his own aeroplane had been damaged. He took three passengers each way, landing near Villefranche. There were no incidents, apart from an incautious error by the agent in charge: the flarepath was lit when Bunny arrived, before the recognition signals had been exchanged. Bunny prudently waited until he saw the correct letter flashed before he landed. We knew only too well that a number of agents had been captured and forced to talk by brutal tortures. There was always the possibility of our reception committee being manned by the Abwehr or the Sicherheitsdienst. We did not know at the time the extent to which the Germans' *Funkspiel* (radio-game) was beginning to succeed in deceiving SOE into thinking that some W/T sets were still under the control of our people who had, unknown to London, been captured.

However, this was not an SOE operation. It was operation 'Ulysses', for the 'Alliance' intelligence organisation. Bunny retrieved his reputation with them after failing to find Villefranche the month before by bright moonlight on a clear night. He brought back their chief of air landings, Lt. Pierre Dallas, who had been to England for a Hudson course. Since Gachet (their air adviser) was now in prison, the flarepath for 'Ulysses' was laid by an experienced pilot, Captain Henri Cormouls, a recent recruit to 'Alliance'. He had not been Tempsford trained, however, and this may have accounted for the flarepath being lit before the aircraft had identified itself.

The other two passengers from England included the poet Henry Leopold Dor. The three picked up included Commandant Cros[8] and the civilian pilot Pierre Berthomier, who had been involved in a plot - now leaked - to hi-jack an internal flight and make it land in England, thus kidnapping either Marshal Pétain or Pierre Laval, his evil genius. The third was Robert Rivat, a young radio operator who was sent to England for a training course[9].

On 19th April extracts from my letter to my wife were: "Lately I have been very busy really. In fact I have been having a grand time, but not really having much opportunity to get down to my private affairs, not even my log-book. I know this is no excuse for not writing you letters…

"The effect of Spring on my country walks has been magical. I came back yesterday from a long tramp with Bunny's dog, with an armful of cherry blossom. My leg was mercilessly pulled, coming into an RAF camp like that.

"My job has prospered fabulously. I am delighted. I am being restrained from personal effort by Pick, who thinks I have been hogging. I like that, coming from him, the biggest hog of the lot.

"For many nights now I have not slept long hours. I patch it with naps in the day but my eyes still feel heavy and tired. The weather has been so good that I have been sunbathing almost every day and it makes me feel very well."

That night, 19/20 April, the weather was not so good in France as it had been in England. The only Lysander operation laid on was the second attempt at 'Sabine'. Mac had another tough trip. The field was supposed to be two kilometres west of Luzillé in Touraine. The first problem was that the signal flashed was wrong — a clear morse 'K' (- · -) when the briefed recognition signal was 'O' (- - -). Secondly, it was flashed from the wrong field, according to the briefing folder we had been given. Mac must have attributed both these discrepancies to human error and, rightly - as it turned out - decided to land. But he must have been more highly charged than usual until he identified the reception committee as friendly.

On his last trip but one, five nights before, he had gone through that tree on the approach. This time he came in a little too high. It was not an easy night for one of those short landings; it was very dark under thick cloud and drizzling. So he overshot on landing and his Lysander hit a bump. His engine cut, he restarted it and taxied back to lamp 'A', still uncertain in his mind about the reception he would find when he got there. But all was well. His two passengers slid the roof back, unloaded nine packages and climbed out. Then *four* passengers climbed in. This was a rare overload. Although there were only seats for two - side by side, facing aft - Lysanders had often carried three, with one crouched under the sliding roof, sitting on the luggage shelf where the machine gun mounting had been removed. On this trip the fourth was crouching on the floor, under that luggage shelf, and between the legs of the two who were properly seated. As the French say, that Lysander was "full as an egg".

Mac took off and climbed away. Twenty minutes later, that is 25 minutes after his engine had cut on the ground, his engine cut again. He lost 1,000 feet while he changed the petrol cock to the fuselage tank and restarted the engine. He ploughed on through the dark drizzle, unable to do much map-reading. The estimated time of arrival at the French coast came up, but there was no sign of the coast. An hour later he found he was crossing the coast on the west side of the Cotentin, the Cherbourg peninsula. At last he could fix his position. He decided to fly between Cap de la Hague and Alderney. Then he was shot at both from the shore and from ships. So he dived from 8,000 feet to sea level to get out of the gunfire.

When he arrived at Tangmere we met him at the dispersal hardstanding. His four cramped passengers stiffly climbed down the ladder. One of them fell on his hands and knees and kissed the oily tarmac. I asked him if he was seized up with cramp and he answered in American English. He was an evading member of a United States aircrew which had been shot down. Remembering Christopher Columbus kissing the sand of the New World on his first arrival there, he was kissing the oily tarmac of the Free World.

On our return to Tangmere after the dark period we found a new Station Commander. Group Captain W.H. Crisham had taken over from Group Captain H.D. McGregor DSO. The May moon was not at all on the same scale as the April moon.

We only attempted five Lysander pick-ups (of which one was double). Of the six landings authorised two failed, one because of fog at the target and the other because there was no reception. The agent, who was in Paris, could not hear the BBC message because of jamming. On the field the passengers desperately burned newspapers.

On 14/15 the weather was good. Bunny and I did a double with Déricourt in Touraine near Azay-sur-Cher. We landed four: the newly trained Julienne Aisner (whom I had flown out a month before); Sidney Jones, an arms instructor; Marcel Clech, his wireless operator, both on their second missions; and Vera Leigh, a 40-year old dress designer who had been described during training as "about the best shot in the party" and "dead keen"[10]. We also took out between us no less than 14 packages or suitcases.

We must have brought back to England one of Buckmaster's best agents, Major Francis Suttill ('Prosper') later DSO, who had earlier been in charge of about 30 agents. His organisation now involved hundreds. Born of an English father and French mother in 1910 he had been a barrister before the war. In the first five months of 1943 his organisation, which included a number of Communists around the Paris area, had received 240 containers full of arms and explosives from England. He returned to France by parachute on 20/21 May 1943. The tragic story of the downfall of the Prosper organisation, its chief Suttill's own capture on 24th June and the capture of hundreds of his people in the summer of 1943 has already been told very fully in other books.

On 20/21 May John Bridger tried to land one kilometre north west of le Grand Maleray in the area of Issoudun, but found fog over the field. The next night he succeeded, delivering five packages and bringing back a French Air Force colonel and a police inspector on an uneventful trip. The passengers told him that he had flown overhead several times the night before. They blamed the fog and their weak signalling torch. This time they had replaced it by a car headlamp. This was operation 'Gauguin' for the 'Alliance' intelligence organisation. The group had been hit by a series of disastrous arrests, to say nothing of a car crash which put Pierre Dallas, their air landings chief, on the danger list. For 'Gauguin' he was replaced by Captain Henri Cormouls. The packages brought out by John contained arms, wireless transmitters, and a large sum of money. The sacks with arms and wireless sets were temporarily hidden in a confessional at the suggestion of a priest. The money and reports were stowed in the safe of a local "gentleman farmer" who later denied all knowledge of them and threatened to call the Gestapo. They had to be recovered by strong-arm action[11].

At the end of May Flight Lieutenant John Bridger was posted to Rufforth and went on to Halifaxes in No 4 Group Bomber Command. I believe he was killed years after the war, in a Tudor on the way to Australia when it crashed into Mount Ararat in Turkey. To replace him I had recruited Flight Lieutenant Jack Bartrum, who (like me) had been in the Oxford University Air Squadron before the war. Since then he had been a District Commissioner in the Sudan Civil Service. He joined 'A' Flight 161 Squadron on 6th May and started his Lysander training.

On 16th May I flew a Hudson from Tangmere to Tempsford. On board was Mouse Fielden, the Station Commander. His navigator 'Waggy' was in the nose and was the first to notice oil flowing from the port engine. I feathered the airscrew and carried on one motor, landing at Tempsford without trouble. Just after landing I saw a Lysander approaching for a landing. I knew it must be Jack Bartrum, so I watched to see how he was getting on. To my horror he stalled, crashed and burned. He must have been killed instantly, but it was horrible. I could not help remembering a dinner I had given him in a restaurant in Bedford a few weeks before. In a rather macabre way, Jack had pulled from his wallet a list of pre-war members of the Oxford University Air Squadron - on which he had crossed out what seemed like half the names.

The June moon period saw us detached to Tangmere from 10th to 25th. The Lysander flight was now very short of pilots - only Mac, Peter, Bunny and I. Pick had been replaced as CO of the squadron by Bob Hodges who had not yet trained himself to do pick-ups and John had left. Recruiting what seemed to be suitable new talent was one of my main preoccupations and it was not easy. We put the word round through official channels that we were looking for volunteers with above average assessments as pilots, plenty of night flying and navigational experience, and, preferably, fluent French.

During this moon we laid on 14 Lysander landings, including eight in four doubles. Three landings failed because there was no reception; one failed through generator trouble; ten were successful. Including my Hudson trip, each of us had four operations except Bunny, whose three were all successful at the first attempt.

Peter and Mac were on one of their many successful double operations - on 15/16 June near Estrées St. Denis. On this occasion Peter was over the target while Mac was having trouble finding it. Peter saw some tracer going up a few miles away. Mac's voice came through on the R/T:

"I'm being shot at. If you can see where I am tell me which way to go. Over."

Peter replied: "You seem to be about 20 miles south of the target. Over."

"Roger", said Mac, "With you in a few minutes. Out."

Mac had been trying to fix his position on the river Oise and had stumbled on Creil airfield. Some months before he had been given a silk scarf - a souvenir of a regatta at Cannes - as a memento for one of his operations. He had adopted this as a lucky mascot and would not have parted with it for the world — in spite of many offers from girls. As usual he was wearing it that night.

It was his habit to open his left window just before landing, stick out his left hand and wipe some of the oil from his windscreen so that he could see better. On this occasion, the wind must have loosened his scarf, for, just as he was about to touch down, he felt the wind tear the scarf from his neck. For the moment he forgot the business of landing, and letting go of the throttle he made a desperate effort to clutch the vanishing scarf. The next thing he knew was that in his excitement he had forgotten to hold off. The aircraft hit the ground hard, bounced and was airborne again. Next time he was able to concentrate on the landing. He then looked round the cockpit, but there was no sign of the missing souvenir. He taxied slowly back to the crowd waiting at 'A' - searching every inch of the ground. He beckoned to the agent and tried to make him understand the importance of this RAF mascot. He promised to find it and return it. Because the head of the group in London was a particular friend he even sent a telegram over to the operator in France urging him to find the scarf. Mac heard no more until nearly three years later, when at a grand re-union in Paris, up came the operator.

"Mac", he said, "here is the famous scarf - the farmer found it and kept it until after the war without saying a word."

This was Jacques Courtaud's fifth pick-up. On 28th June 1943, less than two weeks later, he was arrested by the Gestapo in Paris. After being a prisoner at Fresnes he was deported to Buchenwald. He came back to France in June 1945 and was still going strong at the age of 90 in 1995.

Bunny's trip on 16/17 June was a double with Mac in the area of Angers. Bunny told me about his passengers: "Cecily Lefort looked like a vicar's wife. Her French did not seem to me to be all that hot. Noor Inayat Khan was wearing a green oilskin coat." He also remembers that it was on this trip that he left his transmitter on and "broadcast to all and sundry. Black mark!"

Just after Mac had crossed into France, suddenly, loud and clear came the words, "Now, madame, we are approaching your beautiful country - isn't it lovely in the moonlight." Back came the answer in a soft accented voice: "Yes, I think it is heavenly. What is the town over there?" And so it went on for 30 minutes; step by step Bunny pointed out all the landmarks to his passengers. Mac wondered what the German listening-service, which intercepted all our broadcasts, thought of this running commentary, and how annoyed they must have been at their inability to stop the flights.

Mac landed first and, after taking off, circled the field while Bunny landed and took off. This was another Déricourt operation. He received Charles Skepper and three girls: Diana Rowden as well as Cecile Lefort and Noor Inayat Khan. Skepper and Mrs Lefort travelled south together[12]. He went on to Marseilles where he was to do useful sabotage until he was arrested in March 1944. Cecily Lefort was an Irish yachtswoman in the WAAF. She was on her way to join Francis Cammaerts as a courier. After three months she was caught and she did not return from Ravensbrück. Diana Rowden, a young WAAF officer, was also to serve as a courier and to earn an MBE. She was eventually executed at Natzweiler in July 1944. Noor Inayat Khan was a direct descendant of Tipu Sultan. She was almost bilingual in English and French and had been a corporal wireless operator in the WAAF. Her brief operational career as a wireless operator in France was exceptionally gallant and she was awarded a George Cross and MBE. She was arrested in Paris in October 1943, tried twice to escape and was executed at Dachau in September 1944. Looking back to the operational supper at Tangmere Cottage with our cheerful passengers just before take-off it was almost impossible to imagine that a group of four such as this would all have such terrible fates.

Vera Atkins of Colonel Buckmaster's French Section of SOE remembers seeing them off that night. When they were upstairs waiting for the bathroom, she spotted a paperback by a pilot's bed. It was called Remarkable Women. "That book will have to be re-written after these girls have done their stuff", she commented. She remembered the only trace of nerves was in a slightly trembling cigarette. She told me this while we were on our way to Natzweiler-Struthof concentration camp in 1975 for a ceremony which included the unveiling of the only plaque in the crematorium by the Prime Minister of France, Monsieur Chirac. Diana Rowden's was one of the names on this plaque.

Déricourt had brought to the field five passengers for England: Madame Pierre-Bloch, Flight Lieutenant Jack Agazarian and his wife Francine, Lejeune (a Giraudist) and Vic Gerson. Madame Pierre-Bloch remembers that they had all had a delicious *poularde à la crême* at a farm nearby belonging to a member of the reception committee.

Suttill had decided at short notice that his wireless operator Jack Agazarian should go to England for a rest after a chance encounter with two "Dutch agents"[13] in Paris. (They were actually Germans involved in counter-espionage). After this incident one of the agents due to fly to England was arrested. Agazarian replaced him.

On 20/21 June 1943 Bunny Rymills carried out operation 'Polyanthus' North of Blois, near Maves. He brought back one intelligence agent called 'Amiral' (Philip Keun). The operation was laid on by 'Trellu' (Pierre Hentic) who was later to be a Colonel in the French army and commander of parachute schools in French Indo-China and Algeria. By this time our operation reports on routine trips were laconic: Bunny's read:
"Operation Polyanthus completed, Lysander U, 47° 43 ' 50" N, 01° 19' 45" E via Cabourg and Blois. Reached target 0155 where landing was made - took on board one passenger and two packages and base reached at 0345 hours. Clouds were virtually on the deck."

The only remaining operation for the June moon was 'Curator/Acolyte' which I was to try three times before completing it. My outward-bound passengers were Robert Lyon and Colonel Bonoteaux. The field was one of Déricourt's at Pocé-sur-Cisse, three kilometres NNE of Amboise. On 20/21 there was no reception. On the 22nd I had to turn back after crossing the English coast outbound because of a generator failure and total loss of electrical services. We finally got there on the night of 23/24 June. The target was near the Loire and easy to find as the stars were bright and any water showed up luminously against the black land. It was such a fine night that I decided to land at 0140 before moon-rise. I thought the experiment might reveal whether or not we were right to confine our operations to the moon period. In the event I frightened myself so badly on that approach that I decided "never again". The worst thing was not being able to see if there were any trees. I think this must have been one of the only two clandestine pick-ups ever completed by a Lysander without at least some moonlight. Nevertheless, with the aid of a brief use of my landing light, all was well.

When I saw Robert Lyon in Paris in 1974 he told me that he had got to know Colonel Bonoteaux as a result of travelling with him three times, although in those days strange travelling companions were hardly ever indiscreet enough to say much about themselves. Chatting in the back of my Lysander on their third flight together, they discovered that they had served in the same artillery regiment in 1915/16. It emerged that Colonel Bonoteaux was not an SOE agent, but worked for the French army resistance organisation and had been to Algiers to contact General Giraud. After the landing Lyon and Bonoteaux were received by Déricourt and his assistant Rémy Clément. They were hidden in a little wood after some of the luggage had been hidden in a haystack on the field. In the morning they took a train from Amboise to Paris, travelling separately. Robert Lyon saw Déricourt walking up and down the train. At the Gare d'Austerlitz they all went their separate ways.

Robert Lyon (Captain 'Calvert') had been arrested by a Vichy police trap[14] in October 1941 when approaching an agent's house, whose address had been found on a captured parachutist. This address had also been given to a number of other agents and five of them were trapped in the same way, including Pierre-Bloch, the *Député*. After imprisonment in the degrading prison at Périgueux, Robert Lyon escaped with a group of others in July 1942 from the Vichyist concentration camp at Mauzac where they had been moved in the spring. They made their way to Spain. On this flight to

France with me, Lyon was to set up an organisation called 'Acolyte', arming and training a secret force in the country north west of Lyons.

My homeward-bound passengers were Richard Heslop ('Xavier'), and an evading airman. Heslop's tour in the field had lasted eleven months since his arrival from Gibraltar by felucca and had included a spell in a Vichyist prison. He is described[15] as "one of SOE's principal stars". Maurice Buckmaster told me that his reputation with the French was so great that about 4,000 of them attended the unveiling in 1973 of the monument near Echallon in the Ain, which contains his ashes.

One week of the dark period between the June and July moons was, as usual, spent in training agents. We also had two new pilots to train: Flight Lieutenants R.W.J. Hooper DFC and Stephen Hankey. I was very glad to have them both. They were a few years older than most of the pick-up pilots, very civilised in their own ways, and linguists. Robin Hooper had been at Tempsford for a full tour already as a Halifax pilot in No 138 Squadron, parachuting agents and containers. I had also been in contact with him years before when he had preceded me at Queen's College, Oxford. Since then he had been in the Diplomatic Service and, thanks to pre-war membership of the Oxford University Air Squadron, had managed to break loose to take an active part in the war - a trick not many of his contemporaries were able to achieve. (He became Sir Robin Hooper, KCMG, DSO, DFC and was, until September 1974, our Ambassador in Athens).

Stephen Hankey[16] had had a rather more colourful and varied career than most of us. He came of a distinguished Sussex county family, and had been brought up at a beautiful old house (Binderton) near Tangmere with associations with Nelson and Lady Hamilton, and which was used for most of the war by the then Mr Eden as his country residence. Stephen had for a while been a subaltern in his county regiment. Later, after a spell selling Delahaye sports cars to the gilded youth of London, he joined the RAF, and was in one of the Lysander army co-operation squadrons which was shot out of the sky in the Battle of France. His wife, who characteristically had refused to be separated from her husband more than was strictly necessary, and had installed herself in a flat in Paris, had an equally hairbreadth escape from France with her friend Hilary, who later married Peter Vaughan-Fowler. Later Stephen was in the Middle East on PR duties and training allied aircrew cadets. As a souvenir of this latter assignment, he used to wear a tunic whose every button came from a different Air Force.

Stephen would have been thoroughly at home in the Drones Club. But a somewhat Wodehousian exterior concealed an iron determination - it came as something of a surprise to his friends to learn that his broken nose - which often gave him agonising sinus pains while flying - had been acquired boxing for Sandhurst. He had had little night flying experience before coming to 161, and he found it difficult to catch up with colleagues who, by that stage of the war, mostly had more night hours than day in their log books. But by sheer guts he forced himself to learn and quickly became one of the flight's most competent pilots.

It is, however, chiefly for his personality that his comrades will remember him - the outrageously funny crack with which he would break up the tension which inevitably builds up in a small unit doing an exacting job; his endless resource; the philosophy he had learnt in the course of a fuller life than most of us had then known; the hospitality he and the enchanting Elizabeth gave us - for needless to say and in accordance with his adage of "any bloody fool can be uncomfortable", he had installed her in defiance of regulations in a delightful cottage near Tangmere.

Bunny Rymills reminded me that Stephen invited the Edens to tea in the Cottage to discuss something to do with Binderton. When he had been shown everything, Anthony Eden said that he did not know that all this was going on. As he was the Foreign Secretary we all roared with laughter. At this point, Bunny's dog, Henry, leapt through the open window on to Mrs Eden's lap with very muddy paws.

Our detachment to Tangmere was from 9th to 25th July. Out of twelve sorties attempted nine were successful. Two failed because of bad weather and for one there was no reception.

On 15/16 July, Bunny Rymills was fetching Guy Lenfant and his assistant Rapin from a field near Auxerre; it was very rough and appears not to have been properly approved by the Air Ministry. Their companion had been arrested in June and they had to bring to England what they called "a basket of cherries". Michel Pichard discovered in the Comité d'Histoire files that this "basket of cherries" was a detailed map of the defences built by the Germans along the coast of Morbihan in Brittany. It had been compiled by the gendarmerie under Commandant Guillandot - whose job it was to guard the forbidden zone all along the coast. In these circumstances it was not surprising that the arrangements for this pick-up were a bit impromptu and the field somewhat bumpy.

This was Bunny's last pick-up. He had added a tour of Lysander operations to his tour on Halifaxes without a rest in between. He had only failed twice, and one of his failures was certainly not his fault. His 11 other sorties had all been successful. But it was not until 1975 that he owned up to his bad habit of smoking in the air, which was, of course, forbidden. Always he took a box of 50 cigarettes with him and smoked one every 20 minutes, precisely. He also had trouble on every trip that he did not tell me about at the time as he used to feel airsick if he smelt rum. In spite of this, he put two thermos flasks of coffee in the back cockpit for his passengers, one of which he had laced with rum. When the fumes were sucked forward into his cockpit he had to slide a window open and put his nose out into the fresh air.

Another of his recollections was of an unidentified sergeant from the Oakington meteorological reconnaissance Flight who had been shot down on his way back from the Ruhr at about 4 pm. His parachute had landed him at the feet of an agent's wife and, three nights later, he was back in England. He could not believe this until Bunny walked him the few yards from the Cottage to the main gate where there was a large sign: "Royal Air Force, Tangmere".

The other pilots who were out on the night of 15/16 July were Peter, who had been promoted to Flight Lieutenant and Mac who were on a double some 20 miles west of Tours on a field called 'Gide' near Rivarennes. Paul Schmidt was the operations officer on the field for the pick-up and the head of the local team was Marcel Blée of Bréhémont.

On 17/18 July Peter and Mac took their Lysanders over different parts of France. Peter landed three and picked up three "on Betz-Bouillancy aerodrome" north-east of Paris noting in his log-book that it was "a perfect op".

This was operation 'Renoir' on which Marie-Madeleine Méric of 'Alliance' the great intelligence organisation, was, at last, to fly to London. She had refused for years many suggestions that she should have a break from her dangerous work. According to her book[17], the landing was on a newly-cut cornfield at Bouillancy which she reached by taking the train from Paris to Nanteuil-le-Haudouin. Among many other points covered in her briefing in Paris before she left were details of approaches from the anti-Hitler plotters in Germany who wanted to make contact with the British authorities.

After the welcome by Richards, her contact in London over three years, and the relaxed hospitality of Tangmere Cottage, they were taken to Major Anthony Bertram's house nearby and welcomed by his wife Barbara to spend what was left of the night.

Mac found no reception on his field in Touraine near Azay-sur-Cher. After waiting in the target area for 25 minutes he had to bring home his two outward-bound passengers. Déricourt had failed to show up for operation 'Athlete'.

Two nights later, on 19/20 July, Mac tried operation 'Athlete' again. This time the weather was very bad over the Channel which caused him "50 minutes strenuous flying", but he was successful. He landed Isodore Newman and one other and picked up Major Antelme and Jean Savy. Major France Antelme was the aristocratic, 43-year-old owner of large plantations in Mauritius. He brought with him to England his friend, the Paris barrister Jean Savy, for training as an agent[18]. A false rumour, started by Déricourt himself, that he came to London for one night on this flight was firmly denied by Jean Savy.

On 21/22 Peter and I did a double, 'Floride', near Châteauroux. The weather along the whole route was generally bad with very low cloud. The cloud base at Tangmere when we left was 200 feet and it was raining. We were the only two aircraft of any command to leave the UK on operations that night. We took out three and brought back seven passengers. My four[19] included two children and their mother Madame Jacques Robert. Their father was one of the most distinguished agents. The slightly blasphemous story which I heard later was this: the children were told that they would go to sleep and wake up in England. They asked how they were going to get to England. I suppose it was security at work, but they were told that *Le Saint Esprit* (the Holy Ghost) would transport them. On the field they were given pills to make them sleep, but the drug wore off and they woke up before we landed at about 0240 in the morning. As the children saw the Lysanders circling and flashing morse letters, they jumped up and down, clapping their little hands with excitement, and shouted "*Le Saint Esprit vient! Le Saint Esprit vient!*"

I told this story in the Observer colour magazine of 20th March 1977. An astonishing consequence was that I had a letter from Paris which started "Dear Holy Ghost". This was from Madame Fodor who, as Marianne Robert, aged three, had been one of these little girls. Her sister Chantal, who was six at the time, has this clear memory of her journey, which she wrote for me in excellent English:

"My family, that is my mother and sister and I, had been hiding at the time a few months from the Gestapo (who were after our father) in St Gervais near Chamonix.

My mother was then told that she had to leave either for Switzerland or for England. St Gervais, where we lived a quiet life going to school and skiing, was not safe enough any more. My mother decided to fly over to England.

We hid a few weeks in Lyon and then a few days in Châteauroux. I still remember the rather narrow street of Châteauroux and the house right on the street. On about the third day my mother told us we were leaving for England that night and that there would be no nasty Germans over there. I remember feeling very afraid, excited and happy to get out of the house.

We left that evening after dinner - it was pitch dark and we walked out of the town following a man pushing a bicycle. Having left the town, we went on walking behind the man for about twenty minutes. Then suddenly a car came up and we got into it. When we got out of the car we stumbled over a ditch, got into a field and hid near bushes or trees on the edge of the field. There were other people sitting there and everyone was whispering.

My mother had told my sister and I not to say a word because otherwise the Germans would come and cut off our heads.

It was a little chilly, very dark and I was very afraid. Time seemed endless. At last we heard at first a very faint noise coming from the sky and it got stronger. Torches lit up, then were switched off. We were told it was not the right plane. We waited again, I think not very long - until we heard the noise again; this time it was the right plane. We started getting up anxiously in case the plane did not land.

It landed about 20 or 30 metres from us and we rushed to the plane. I think there were two or three people with us, and two people or one person came towards us from the plane to help us and make us rush. Everything went very quickly, the plane took off and I do not remember the trip.

I remember arriving in England, people greeting us with large smiles - what a difference after those dull days we had spent hiding and after the fear a child feels even if she is not told much. I also remember people speaking English to us and how surprising, curious and how nice all this looked.

The next thing I can remember was the street we lived in - in London - being shaken by bombs and the windows blowing off. But that was probably a few weeks after our flight.

When I met my father in Passy's office, he was wearing a French Army Officer's uniform. The only uniforms I had seen for years were German. I thought my father had joined the Germans and I was most upset."

On 22/23 July, while Bob Hodges was doing his first pick-up in a Hudson, Mac tried operation 'Antirrhinum' for the first time. The target was near Fère-en-Tardenois near Soissons. There was thick low cloud all the way. Mac completed his flight plan on instruments but there was "nothing discernible in the target area". The second attempt at 'Antirrhinum' on 25/26 July was another round trip for Mac and his two passengers, but worse than the first as they were nearly shot down.

Again they were over low cloud for most of the way. Mac let down to about 300 feet above ground level when he was in the approximate area of the target. At this height he was below cloud but the visibility was only 1,000 yards. His report reads: "In searching around ran over aerodrome thought to be Creil and there received everything they had in the way of flak and searchlights - very lucky to get clear." So the July moon ended without 'Antirrhinum' being picked.

During the last nine nights Mac had flown five operations. As he put it: "We all worked very hard to make the Verity Service as sure as the Green Line." What he completely concealed from me at the time was how exhausted he had become. He found that after an operation he was almost completely deaf for 24 hours. So, unknown to me - his Flight Commander - he consulted a specialist, who explained to him that eardrums are the most sensitive part of the body and that his deafness was due to fatigue.

But Mac (then Flying Officer J.A. McCairns DFC, MM) had a consolation prize. In July he was awarded a bar to his Distinguished Flying Cross. Bunny (Flying Officer

F.E. Rymills DFC, DFM) was also awarded a bar to his DFC.

Pick had sent for Mac and Bunny and told them that he was recommending them for DSOs: "I think you're worth it. I don't know if you'll get it, but that's all I can do for you." They did not get their DSOs. Mouse Fielden, the Station Commander said that he had never heard of Flying Officers getting DSOs. They were only for people in command. Hence the bars to their DFCs.

We were all very sad that we had to lose Bunny, but that was his last Lysander moon. He had come to the end of his tour of operations. It would be almost 20 years before I chanced to meet him again, while we were both still serving as RAF officers.

Flying Officer 'Bunny' Rymills, DFC, DFM in 1943.

During the July moon, my wife's mother looked after our two little boys for a few days so that Audrey could be near me We - or rather she - stayed in the Ship Hotel Chichester, where the bill came to: inclusive terms, one guinea (£1.05) per person per day, including all meals. A three course lunch then cost 3/6d (or 17.5p), and that in a very comfortable and attractive old hotel. While she was there I was really very busy and did not have time to be with her much. I remember one night I came back to the Ship at about 3.30 am after a trip. It was all locked so I climbed up the iron fire-escape stairs round at the back and in at our bedroom window. I woke Audrey and emptied a shower of French lipsticks on to her bed. They had been in France earlier that night. She remembers that they were called *Le Rouge Baiser*.

I suppose we were under some strain during these moons, but sustained at concert pitch while we were hard at it. Sometimes reaction set in during the dark periods when we had no operations to keep up our motivation. To illustrate this I quote from a letter to my wife dated 30 July 1943:

"I am in a squelching sweat sopping and slopping and stewing. Work is most unattractive and I am tethered to a telephone and a desk. I lie in bed in the morning guiltily wondering if my night flying is enough excuse. The weather would be lovely by the sea but here it seems hotter and muggier, much muggier than where I was a day or two ago.

Since I last saw you I had quite a ticklish job to do and only just did it. I was very lucky with my weather.

The letter you wrote me a day and a half after we parted was very much more so than I thought. I mean you seemed terribly impressed and stirred and I am glad that it was so, but I do not understand it, nor did I expect it. It was so lovely for me to have you to come back to that I am looking forward enormously to repeating the experiment. It was unlucky that things worked out badly from our point of view. I cannot ever remember ten days when I was busier or had less spare time. This meant that I was necessarily tired and rushed much of the time I was with you, and I felt often that I was not coming up to scratch, not being sweet enough nor amusing enough. I was and am sorry that this was so, and it is lucky that you understood...

There are times when I get sick and tired of this bloody war. I am in a low state at the moment; largely sheer fatigue. I am not really cheered by all the optimistic news - I do not really appreciate my good fortune in my job. I sometimes feel I would like to go for a peace-time cruise in pleasant company, pleasant weather, utter security and with you. I know that if this were to happen I would be as bored as hell in two minutes with safety, itching again for the excitements of war. Nevertheless I think a few weeks *dolce far niente* would be fun. Mind you - I wouldn't swap my job for anything!"

Bunny Rymills

CHAPTER NINE

Home via Algeria

It was the Station Commander, Mouse Fielden, who had started the fashion for bringing Hudsons home via Algeria and Gibraltar after landing in South-eastern France on these short summer nights. I was to do the same on operation 'Knuckleduster' on 15/16 June 1943. Philippe Livry, Eddie Shine and I set off from Tangmere at 2359 in Hudson PN 7221 with two passengers and fourteen packages to deliver to Paul Rivière's people on his great meadow 'Marguerite' near Feillens a few miles up and across the river from Mâcon.

One of our passengers was probably Claude Bouchinet-Serreulles[1], who had been General de Gaulle's *'chef de cabinet'* for two and a half years, and was on his way to assist Jean Moulin (who would be arrested five days later).

The weather got worse as we flew across France from Cabourg, via Tours. Cloud became almost continuous. At last we could fix our position visually when we saw le Creusot, with the distinctive shaped lakes nearby. There was more high ground to fly over, in cloud, before we could be sure we were over the Saône valley. To make sure we allowed a few minutes extra and gently let down on instruments. At last we broke through the cloud-base and found the country-side below very dark. It was raining. We did a U-turn back towards the Saône and just distinguished it by its different shade of black. But we did not know whether our field was north or south of the point where we found the river. We turned starboard and flew north along the river for three minutes. Then we turned south and, after four minutes, there was Paul's torch flashing a morse 'C' very clearly through the rain. It was 0230 and very dark.

I found the next quarter of an hour about as difficult as any flying I have ever done. I tried to avoid going too near to Mâcon on the down-wind leg, misjudged my first approach and found I was overshooting. I opened up the motors, continuing to lose height until I built up enough speed to climb safely and go round again. The next time I was too far to one side of the line of four torches when they emerged from the black, rainy night. At slow speeds, particularly with some flap down, the aileron control on Hudsons was sluggish. Again I had to open up the engines to 2,500 rpm, making a terribly loud noise which I felt sure must have woken the German forces in Mâcon. I was too busy to think how appropriate the BBC message for this operation was to my situation in that dark downpour: *"Ecoute mon coeur qui pleure"* ("listen to my weeping heart").

On my third approach I was lined up and about right for height and speed (about 100 knots). Apart from the pin-pricks of the torches ahead everything was black. I switched on my landing lamps. In their bright beams the slanting rain was lit up like a bead curtain, almost obliterating my view of the flarepath torches. I checked once more that my wheels were locked down, checked my speed, now about 70 knots, and throttled back a little. I lowered the rest of the flap and levelled out, cutting the throttles. A moment of doubt, a bump and we were rolling on the meadow with the second torch going past the port wing-tip at about 50 knots. I did a U-turn just past the end of the 450 metre 'flarepath', and taxied along it rather wondering if our fat rubber tyres would sink into the rain-sodden meadow under the 11 ton weight of the Hudson. Another U-turn by lamp 'A', pre-takeoff checks, and I could relax until takeoff, leaving Philippe and Eddie to unload our packages and welcome our eight new passengers into the 'cabin'.

During this turn round Paul Rivière, who was one of our passengers this time, came up into the cockpit, where I was still strapped in, and shook me by the hand. Bruno Larat was in charge of events on the field, assisted by Jannik, who was to become Madame Paul Rivière. They welcomed our outward-bound passengers. Paul remembers among his companions on this flight: R.G. Fassin of 'Combat' and SAP (Air Operations Service); Henri Frenay, leader of 'Combat'; Marcus, Captain Robert; and "an old General". This was General Arnoult. Maurice de Cheveigné, a young radio operator who had miraculously escaped from Gestapo direction finders in 1942, clearly remembers the flight to England. He was carrying the mail including a report from Jean Moulin.

When I was given the thumbs up signal, we took off and climbed up. "Philippe", I said, "We must go to Algiers; it is far too late now to go north. The day fighters would get us; dawn will be breaking long before we get to the Channel." "OK", said Philippe. "But I have no maps or charts for the Mediterranean with me. All I have are the frequencies for the Allied radios near Algiers." He checked through the contents of his canvas covered navigator's chart-case. He was right. We had neither of us thought to make sure that we would have the right map-sheets on board in case they should be wanted. Still, I had flown a Beaufighter from Gibraltar to Malta and back two years before and I did not think we needed a map to find Algiers.

We did our best to remember the general shape of the Western Mediterranean and the relationship of Algiers to the French Riviera. We decided to go slightly West of South. Over Provence the cloud had cleared. Just before dawn we could see the Balearic islands on the starboard side. As we approached the coast of North Africa we called and called on the various Allied frequencies by R/T and Eddie Shine did the same by W/T, but we got no answer. Then there was the problem of which way to turn when we could see the Algerian coast. We planned to strike it to the east of Algiers and turn west. Our guesswork on the geography worked well and we landed at Maison Blanche airfield, near Algiers, at 0650 on 16th June.

We had been flying all night and we were all tired but I thought it best to go straight on to Gibraltar, as soon as we had filled up with petrol, had breakfast, signalled home and scrounged some maps. Otherwise it would be impossible to keep my eight passengers together and deliver them, in good order, to their authorities in England.

One of the eight, a grey-haired military looking Frenchman, courteously thanked me for the trip and said he was leaving now to go to Algiers. I, equally courteously, explained to him that my orders were to deliver our passengers to the right organisation in England and that no member of the party could leave it. He then said that General de Gaulle was a personal friend of his and that he wanted to report to him in Algiers as soon as possible to put himself under his orders. As that did not persuade me, he then told me that his ancient mother was in poor health and living in Algiers. If he did not see her now he might never see her again. Finally, in desperation, he asked if there wasn't anybody in authority that he could speak to. (I suppose I did not look specially authoritative, wearing a civilian blue shirt with short sleeves and an open neck.) Although I was Captain of the aircraft, I called on Philippe to back me up. He was 20 years older than I was. In his voice like thunder he put an end to the argument and we could go off to get some coffee.

In the unusual glare of the South Mediterranean sun, we took off from Maison Blanche at 0910. We all managed to keep awake until we landed at Gibraltar at 1200.

The Rock Hotel found rooms for us when invited to do so by the local military intelligence - who were, no doubt, experienced in dealing with a great variety of unexpected arrivals by various forms of transport.

We stayed the night and took off at 2210 on 17th June for a night flight back to England. By this time we had rested well and had spent some hours shopping. The profusion of fruit, wine, silk stockings and all those things which were unavailable or rationed in England was amazing to see. We loaded a 15 cwt Army truck with crates of bottles of sherry and sacks of fruit, such as lemons and bananas, which my family at home had not seen for years. My 5-year-old brother-in-law was totally baffled by one of these bananas and had no idea how to zip it open. The runway at Gibraltar was by now quite long and I judged that we would get airborne in spite of the extra weight. I can now admit that we cut a few corners on that flight home, flying over parts of Portugal and Spain without permission. It was most striking to see the towns lit up after years of flying over blacked-out towns and villages at home and in France. Maurice de Cheveigné, who had been put into the gun turret by Eddie Shine and told to look out for aircraft, was the only passenger who could enjoy the view.

When we arrived over the south coast of England Philippe was having some difficulty with the navigation. I cannot now remember what was out of order, possibly the Gee or the R/T. But I do remember that there was a blanket of low cloud over the coast and that we did not know exactly where we were. Then we saw a flock of tethered barrage balloons floating just above the cloud tops as if grazing on them. We thought it must be Portsmouth that their cables were protecting from low-level air attack. We were right and soon found our way back to Tangmere and breakfast. We landed at 0555 on 18th June - after quite a memorable trip.

I had no idea what a flap my decision to go via Algiers had caused in Whitehall until I got the following letter from Robin Brook. He was then the SOE chief to whom both country sections involved in France reported:

"Many congratulations and thanks for your latest exploit. I once saw Babe Ruth hit a 'home run', and he got more applause but deserved it less. Yours was certainly a more original rounder.

I was so sorry that the holiday side of the excursion was spoilt for you. I will try and arrange a better tour next time.

It might amuse you to know that in the unexpected limelight that flooded this op. four British cabinet ministers got involved and practically all the French equivalents. When I got back here on Monday evening, I had to bully the General into getting the Minister out of bed, and thus to lay on a lunch between the PM and Foreign Sec. the following day. However, all these high-level snags ironed out in time, much to everyone's surprise. I felt rather guilty at not warning you, but the only hope seemed to be to assume that it would go, and it did."

There were no other Hudson pick-ups in June, but there were two in July: 'Buckler' and 'Game-keeper'. Group Captain Fielden, with Squadron Leader Wagland as navigator and Eddie Shine as wireless operator, attempted 'Buckler' on the 16/17 July. With two passengers on board they made their way to the target area north east of Loyettes, to the east of Lyons.

On the way Waggy remembers that they were flying at about 5,000 feet in moonlight when they spotted another aircraft. It might have been a training aircraft, but it might have been a fighter. That Hudson's gun turret had been removed. Mouse

Fielden dived for the ground increasing speed. "This", comments Waggy, "did not help navigation. Nor was I, the navigator, amused when Fielden decided to test his fixed forward-firing guns - a most unkind act! The guns were, of course, in the roof of the navigator's compartment in the nose. What with the smoke and smell of cordite and the noise, I nearly died on the spot without German intervention. Subsequently we could see Lyons, but we did not make contact at the target."

They flew on to Maison Blanche, near Algiers. They left Hudson T 9465 in a dispersal and went off to breakfast. Waggy told me that they went off to Blida, the other airfield near Algiers, where there were some old friends who had been at Tempsford. He remembers that: "A pilot solo in a short-nosed Blenheim lost a prop and had a hell of a job getting down. On landing he skidded and wrote off the port wing of our Hudson. The pilot luckily escaped being smeared over his dashboard and finished up with a few stitches in his head."

"Lancasters", continued Waggy, "were operating on the Sicily landing from Blida. We thumbed a ride on a Lancaster returning via Gibraltar. The pilot was Flight Lieutenant Bunker, who was later Wing Commander Bunker with a DSO for the Warsaw epic. Fielden suggested the 'straight-up' route from Gib (cutting across neutral Spain and Portugal) but Bunker did not like the idea and we took the usual route. We landed at Fairwood Common and were kindly off-loaded at Tempsford afterwards. During this time we had our two 'Joes' with us, which seemed very curious to the Lancaster crew. Those 'Joes' did some travelling because, within three days, you flew them out again!"

The 'Joes', I am informed by Colonel Paul Rivière, were Baron Emmanuel d'Astier de la Vigerie, who was later to be in charge of de Gaulle's department of the interior, and Jean-Pierre Levy. Paul Rivière was in charge of the field when operation 'Buckler' was next attempted on 24/25 July. His team on the ground consisted of Barbachou, the farmer, and members of his family and M. Martin. Philippe Livry, by then a squadron leader, successfully navigated us to the field through very poor visibility on our route. We arrived at the target, where the visibility was better, at 0330.

On this particular field we had scrutinized the vertical air photograph taken for us by the Photographic Reconnaissance Unit at RAF Benson. I had noted a tree standing rather too close to the field and the best line of approach. We had accepted the field for a Hudson landing on condition that the tree was cut down first. I was enraged to find the tree still standing there in the moonlight, not far from my starboard wing-tip, on the last part of my approach to land.

After landing our two passengers and twenty-two packages, we took on board eight passengers[2] and their luggage. Among them was Georges Libert, an Air France pilot, who later became one of the two Frenchmen to fly Lysanders to Southern France on pick ups. The other, Bernard Cordier, had arrived a little earlier by Lysander. Others included Gérard Brault, a radio operator, who had been in prison since October 1942, and his 'assistant' Maurice Roschbach, his gaoler who had released him. This turn-round was quick for a Hudson - only ten minutes - but my take-off did not go so well. For some reason or other the port motor faltered as I was on my take-off run. It picked up again, but not before I had failed to check a swing to port which was enough to take me to the wrong side of the flarepath. Ahead I saw a hedge in the moonlight. I barely had flying speed by the time I got to the hedge and had to charge through it with my wheels only just off the ground. This did not seem to damage the aeroplane and we clambered into the air with no more trouble.

It was not until 1975 that I discovered[3] why that tree was still standing. Paul explained that he had only arrived a few days before in Saône-et-Loire by parachute from England. He had not had time to check the field carefully and, in particular, he had not succeeding in 'eliminating' a big tree near the end of the landing strip. He had been in England for training by the RAF and had been recalled urgently to take over from Bruno Larat as chief of the SAP (*Service d'Atterrissages et Parachutages*) as 'COPA' was now called[4].

This time our route home via Algeria took us to Blida, near Algiers, where we landed at 0750. Nearby was a seaside holiday camp which had been taken over by the Special Operations Executive (SOE) Headquarters in Algeria. We were met at the airport and given a comfortable night there. On 26th July we left Blida at 1135, by which time our Hudson was really too hot to touch. After seven hours at Gibraltar another night flight took us back to Tangmere, complete with our eight passengers, at 0455 on 27th July. I reported that the landing ground near Loyettes was not recommended for further Hudson landings because of its situation and lay-out. That same day Guy Lockhart wrote from Air Ministry (AI 2c):

"I have been meaning for some time to write and express my admiration for the way you and your pilots have carried out pick- up operations. The record of successes has been simply terrific, and is entirely a tribute to the great skill which has been shown in these operations.

Particularly may I congratulate you on BUCKLER, which is quite evidently a case where skill alone overcame every obstacle… Good luck, and keep up the good work."

This was the last I heard from Guy Lockhart. He was killed in action on the night of 27/28 April 1944 and his grave is in the beautiful Durnbach cemetery in Bavaria.

Air photograph of field 'Figue' for Operation 'Buckler', near St. Vulbas, annotated by the photo interpreter.   Crown Copyright

Meanwhile Wing Commander Hodges, our new Squadron Commander, did his first Hudson pick-up, 'Gamekeeper', on 22/23 July on a big meadow near Angers that Déricourt had found for *his* first Hudson pick-up. The weather was "none too good" and the visibility so poor that their first visual fix was at Saumur. Bob Hodges remembers being "greatly relieved to get down in one piece" and reported that the field "was most satisfactory" and the lights "excellent". Bob Hodges' navigator was Flight Lieutenant J.A. Broadley, who had been Pickard's navigator. His wireless operator/air gunner was Flight Lieutenant L.G.A. Reed, who was known as 'Lofty'. Their three outward-bound passengers were Major Nick Bodington, Jack Agazarian and Cdt Adelin Marissal, a Belgian in SOE. They brought home only three passengers, two Belgians and Mr Latimer[5]. One wonders why a Lysander had not been sent. There must have been more passengers planned for the Hudson's homeward flight, but there had recently been many arrests.

Bodington had persuaded Colonel Buckmaster to let him go to Paris for a brief reconnaissance to investigate the large-scale catastrophe that had overtaken Suttill's organisation 'Prosper'. As no newly trained wireless operator was available, Agazarian was recalled from leave. He had returned by Lysander from a very dangerous situation in France only a few weeks before. After one week in Paris on this second mission he investigated an address known to be suspect and was captured. He heroically resisted brutal torture under interrogation and was executed by firing squad six weeks from the end of the war[6].

It was a spun coin that had decided against Nick Bodington investigating that suspect flat. Now he was left without a wireless operator. Of those he might have used only Noor Inayat Khan was still at liberty. Through her, he arranged the Lysander pick-up for himself and the de Baissacs, which I did on 16/17 August, and no doubt some of the planning for the Hudson pick-up which Bob Hodges and crew did on 19/20 August.

This was in the same great meadow by the Loir NE of Angers which Déricourt had used for his first Hudson landing in July. Bob fixed his position on the river near Saumur and then flew to the target which was covered with ground mist. It gleamed white in the moonlight but it was only a thin layer because he could see the signalling lamp flashing through it. Then the other torches of the flarepath were switched on and he could see the long inverted 'L' of these lights. He decided to land in the mist. He had used the field on the last trip and knew that it was very much bigger than the Hudson would need, even if he failed to touch down by lamp 'A'.

Hodges set up his race-track circuit flying over the lights, noting their heading on his directional gyro. As he did so, though he could not see them, a herd of frightened bullocks stampeded past the group of agents waiting in the mist. Turning on to the downwind leg, Bob could still see the signalling torch with which Déricourt was following him round. Soon after it passed his port wing-tip, he began his turn "into wind" - not that there was any wind that night. As he straightened up for the approach he could see the flarepath lights ahead through the mist. He let down for the landing but, as he approached ground level the lights faded from view. Their beams could not penetrate the mist at that low angle. But they made pools of light on the top of the mist which was rather confusing. He went round again.

On his second approach, Bob decided to motor on down into the mist on instruments as he knew it could only be about 20 feet thick. He gently eased the Hudson down on its main wheels, cutting the throttles when they touched. He made no attempt to do a three-point landing. When he was down on the ground the mist was too thick for him to see the lights. He rolled to a halt in a straight line on his directional gyro. Then he turned through 180° but could not see where to go. One of Déricourt's team ran towards the sound of his motors waving a torch. Then he ran back towards the sound of shouts from lamp 'A', leading the Hudson, which taxied slowly after the waving torch.

Their one passenger ('Paul' Deman* of SOE's DF Section,) disembarked and they took on board their 10 passengers[7] for England. They included: Boiteux and his 'Spruce' team - Marchand, and Madame Le Chêne; Tony Brooks, Octave Simon, 'Vic' Gerson and Robert Benoist, the prosperous racing driver. His small circuit 'Chestnut' had collapsed since their wireless operator Dowlen had been caught at his set by a direction finding team on 31st July. On 4th August, a couple of days after his brother, wife and father had been arrested, Robert Benoist himself was arrested in the street. He was bundled into the back of a car between two Germans, but one door was not properly shut. As the car turned sharply, Benoist flung himself against his neighbour and they both rolled out into the street. The rest of this fantastic escape is well described by Foot[8].

Tony Brooks was one of Buckmaster's best men, and the youngest. His circuit 'Pimento' was one of the best equipped and most secure. It was in the areas around Lyons and Toulouse. By D-Day in 1944 'Pimento' was able to make a major contribution to stopping German troop movements in Southern France by railway sabotage. Brooks was an Englishman who had been brought up in Switzerland. In France until May 1941, he was locally recruited by Ian Garrow for the Pat escape line. He left to join SOE but spent six months in prison in Spain on his way to Gibraltar. He was parachuted blind into France in July 1942 when he was just 20 and spent the next three years there, apart from the three months in Great Britain which were just about to start. They were divided between refresher courses and a honeymoon.

Robert Boiteux had arrived in Lyons in June 1942 after a dangerous parachute descent. Aged 35, he had been a Bond Street hairdresser, a gold prospector and a colonial boxing champion. In October 1942 Dubourdin had handed over his circuit in Lyons to Boiteux before leaving by Cowburn's Lysander on 26th. In January 1943 Boiteux had moved 'Spruce' out of Lyons into the hills to the north-west. Now that he was going to England on this Hudson he had handed over part of 'Spruce' to Robert Lyon, who had arrived on my Lysander in June. Madame Le Chêne completed the 'Spruce' team on this Hudson. She had arrived in Southern France by Felucca to act as courier to her 50-year old husband.

Octave Simon's circuit 'Satirist', in South Normandy, had been a sub-circuit of Suttill's 'Prosper' and had received many arms drops for it. Like it, 'Satirist' had just collapsed with many arrests. Simon himself, a 29-year old sculptor, had been in resistance work in various ways since 1940. He had been lucky to get to this Hudson, after several hair's-breadth escapes from the Gestapo, while most of his colleagues were caught.

Victor Gerson was in a rather different role from the others. His country section in SOE was DF which organised escape lines across France, and his was said to be the best and biggest of them all. In building it he made six clandestine visits to France.

They had all settled rather uncomfortably into the Hudson's cabin, huddled together near the front to ensure that their weight was in the best place for take-off. Déricourt came up through the cabin to the front and through the little door into the cockpit,

*His real first name was Peter, formerly Erwin.

leaning over Bob's right shoulder. Pointing into the wall of fog he shouted: "Take off in that direction, but look out for the cattle!"

My own attempt at a Hudson pick-up in August failed on 22/23 when I saw Paul Rivière's lights on his field called 'Marguerite' near Mâcon through fog which I decided was too thick for a landing. In Paul's pocket was a most friendly letter to me which ended: *"Revenez me voir souvent, je ne demande que cela. Bien amicalement à vous, Yves Rolland."* ("Come and see me often; that's all I ask. Very kind regards, Yves Rolland").

The next day, Paul ('Galvani') sent the following telegram to General de Gaulle's BCRA in London:

"Galvani. My ops eight of twenty-third stayed on Marguerite last night until 0400 hours Aeroplane arrived at 0330 circled over field at least six times and could not land because of thick fog stop Did not reply to calls on S-phone If equipped we could have fixed something stop Made no reply in Morse to mine stop If arrived half hour earlier could have landed without difficulty no fog End"

Bob Hodges completed this operation ('Trojan Horse') the next night, 23/24 August. His navigator was Flt Lt J.A. Broadley and his wireless operator/air gunner Flt Lt L.G.A. Reed.

They had one passenger to France, Louis Franzini, and brought back eight[9], including Sgt Patterson who had survived a Tempsford Halifax crash on 23rd July. They also brought me Paul's letter. They reported that the landing ground felt rather soft and could not be recommended for use in wet weather.

In the early morning of 24th August, at about 0300, the Germans searched every nook and cranny of the village of Feillens near the field 'Marguerite', even emptying a pond thinking that arms or sabotage equipment might have been hidden in it. They found nothing because nobody there knew anything about what was going on. The team for the field had been recruited on the other side of the Saône. The only consequence (wrote Paul Rivière) was that the field was "blown" (*"brûlé"*).

In the September moon, when the Lysanders were very busy, there were only two Hudson pick-ups laid on. Both were completed at the first attempt. The first, operation 'Tank', was on 14/15 September on Paul's field 'Orion' 15 kilometres north-west of Lons-le-Saunier. Bob Hodges did this with Sqn Ldr Wagland as navigator. On their way, Louis Mangin remembered, "there was a small fire on board which was put out by the crew." They delivered eight passengers and picked up four[10]. More were expected on the trip home but they had not all arrived on the field. Bob's account[11] of this incident was:

"I got out of the aeroplane, leaving the engines running, to try and discover exactly what was going on. I was told that as all the passengers hadn't yet arrived it would be best if I turned off the engines and waited for their arrival. This was the last thing I intended to do and when I expressed surprise, the reception committee made it clear that I was in Maquis country and all approaches to the airfield were well guarded by armed men and there was not likely to be any danger.

However, having visions of failure to start the engines on internal batteries and finishing up with flat batteries, I had absolutely no intention of switching off. After about five or ten minutes wait I decided not to delay any longer. We had four passengers and I remember asking if there were any more volunteers for England and one young man decided to come with us. I never discovered who he was!"

While they were on the ground, one of the crew picked wild flowers and told Mangin that he always brought home French wild flowers on every trip to France.

Louis Mangin, who told me this in 1976, was the newly-appointed chief of the South Zone. Other arrivals by Bob's Hudson included, Maurice Bourgès-Maunoury, who was Regional Military Delegate (DMR) for Region 1 (Lyons); and Paul Leistenschneider ('Carré' for short), who was DMR for Regions 3 and 4 (Montpellier and Toulouse)[12]. In the 1970s the Carré and Verity families were to make friends and exchange daughters for a few weeks.

Squadron Leader Wagland remembers[13] an amusing little incident before take-off on this occasion:
"Since the famous occasion when Pick got stuck in the mud, Bob Hodges, who was and is a very practical man, decided that he would carry shovels. We never had to use them. On the above trip, however, after the sorting out, Bob clambered back to his seat and began to rev up the engines for take-off. The aircraft would not budge. "Oh my God ! ", he cried, "we're stuck. Wag, go and see what it's like". As I was moving out of the second pilot's seat to go to the rear exit, I luckily noticed that the parking brake was still on. Brake off and we were away."

On 21/22 September Philippe Livry, Eddie Shine and I set out for Paul Rivière's great meadow 'Junot' near the Saône, nine kilometres south of Tournus. We were carrying four people, including Richard Heslop ('Xavier') and Jean Rosenthal ('Cantinier'). They were an Allied mission to survey the potential of the maquis in the Jura and the Savoyard Alps[14]. After three weeks they returned to London for 48 hours to report and then got down to work, assembling a formidable secret army. Heslop's circuit was code-named 'Marksman' and this Hudson operation was wittily named 'Peashooter'.

The navigation on the way there and the landing were very difficult because of low-lying cloud. It was only on the third approach that I was able to land. We picked up eight passengers[15] and, after only eight minutes on the ground, took off again. We were flying in cloud almost all the way back to base.

To give examples of the curious phrases used by the BBC 'personal messages' after the French news, the message agreeing to this operation was: *"Moïse dormira sur les bords du Nil"* ("Moses will sleep on the banks of the Nile"). The message announcing that it was on that night was: *"L'ange rompera le sceau de cire rouge"* ("The angel will break the seal of red wax").

That completes the story of the Hudson pick-ups from June to September 1943. Out of nine sorties, seven had been successful. The only Hudson lost was destroyed by an RAF aircraft while peacefully parked at Maison Blanche. Now it is the turn of the Lysanders again and their story will be brought up to date in the next chapter.

Colonel Paul Rivière, OBE, MM, after the war.

Jannik Rivière after the war.

CHAPTER TEN

Harvest Moons

We took the Lysanders to Tangmere from 8th to 24th August. Flight Lieutenant Robin Hooper was now operational on Lysanders and replaced Bunny Rymills. Flight Lieutenant Stephen Hankey and a newly joined New Zealander, Flying Officer Bathgate, were still under training. This August moon brought a harvest of success for the Lysanders. Apart from one failure on the first operational night, we flew a sequence of 12 successful landings out of 12 sorties laid on.

Jimmy Bathgate, who was about 25, had come to 161 Squadron from Transport Command, where, by the sheer luck of the draw, he had just missed the Liberator trip on which General Sikorski was accidentally killed at Gibraltar. Jimmy was small, fair and moustached. He was a good pilot and a particularly methodical and careful navigator.

On 14/15 August Peter and Mac did a routine double operation south of Bourges after meeting at their rendezvous over the town of Châteaudun. They landed three and picked up five passengers, noting that the landing ground was excellent. While he was on the ground, Peter noticed Dorniers going overhead from the airfield of Châteaudun. That night Robin Hooper's first Lysander operation was defeated by bad weather which made it impossible for him to see pinpoints on the ground. His target for operation 'Aster' was in the area of Dreux. He succeeded on the following night.

On his way to the target Robin flew very nearly over a German airfield north of Dreux at St. André de l'Eure. Night flying was in progress and they flashed him permission to land with a green signalling lamp. He ignored this. Intruders (our long-range night fighters) must have been at work because he saw a crash flaming on the ground. He reached the target, not noticing a car moving towards it on a country road nearby. This was his first landing in enemy-held territory and, not surprisingly, he could not land off his first approach. ("First-night nerves" he called it). He landed off his second and taxied to lamp 'A'. There Pierre Hentic, the operator, pointed over Robin's right shoulder and shouted *"Allez! Allez!"* He saw two strong headlights approaching.

Robert Champion heaved his luggage out, replaced it with the homeward-bound luggage and climbed quickly down the ladder. Two other intelligence agents, Le Commandant Feyfant and Paul Fortier climbed quickly in. Robin was rolling on his take-off run before they had slid shut their sliding roof. As he lifted off he saw that the car had just reached the gate of the field. Meanwhile Hentic and Champion disappeared hurriedly into the night leaving in the grass a parcel which Hentic had not had time to hand over to Robin. It contained a bottle of champagne, a present for Robin and a little bottle of Chanel No 5, a present for his wife Constance.

After the war, Hentic met Robin in Paris and told him that he had seen the car approaching as the Lysander arrived. Robin had scared the daylights out of him by going round again, but reckoned that there would still be time to do the operation - which proved to be the case - if only just. He, Champion and their assistants kept their heads and very sensibly put as much plough between them and the car as they could. They escaped fairly easily. Robin thought that the car might have been out on the road looking for the crashed aircraft that he had seen burning.

On that night of 15/16 August, Peter Vaughan-Fowler went north-east of Paris to land on Betz-Bouillancy airfield, north of Meaux. He landed two and picked up three "without a hitch". This was another 'Alliance' pick-up: operation 'Durer'[1]. Again their Chief of-Staff, Léon Faye, left for London. This time he brought with him a detailed report of the top-secret V-weapon rocket development at Peenemunde.

Meanwhile Mac and I were doing operation 'Popgun' near Couture-sur-Loir to the north of Tours and west of Vendôme. When we arrived there was no sign of a torch flashing at us. We circled the area for a quarter of an hour before we saw it. When I landed the agent in charge climbed up on my port undercarriage to shout to me through the slip-stream that their car had had a puncture and to apologise for being late. When I took off I called in Mac. Between us we landed four and collected five people.

Michel Pichard told me that this field was called 'Rabelais' and that Paul Schmidt, 'Kim', was the operations officer in charge on the ground. Apart from the puncture, "almost everything went wrong". They had boat trouble crossing a river. Crossing by a bridge they ran into a German detachment. 'Kim' told his party to march in step and the Germans thought they were another German detachment. Then, when one of the Lysanders was on the ground, a suitcase full of forged ration cards opened accidentally and the slipstream blew the cards all over the field. Quite a number could not be found in the dark and the field was considered *"brûlé"* for a long time. The passengers who arrived by 'Popgun' are thought to have included Jacques Bingen[2], who was the Free French Committee's Delegate for the South Zone. He was captured on 13th May 1944 and killed himself.

The next night (16/17 August '43) I was on my way to Couture-sur-Loir again. Near Alençon at 2225 I had a sickening experience which was fortunately rather exceptional on our lonely routes over France. Just a mile or two ahead of me I saw an aircraft shot down in flames. It must have been done by a night fighter which I did not see. In the glare of the flames I hoped to see some parachutes but I saw none. I had one package to deliver to Déricourt after landing and he had three passengers for me. They were Major Nick Bodington and Claude and Lise de Baissac[3]. De Baissac's main circuit, 'Scientist' was near Bordeaux but he had supporters in Paris as well and was a friend of Suttil. His group of port saboteurs had produced invaluable intelligence about blockade runners between Europe and the Far East. Claude de Baissac was awarded a DSO and his sister Lise an MBE.

Peter Vaughan-Fowler had an uneventful, successful trip on 19/20 August to a field just north of Villefranche where he landed one and picked up two. The agent in charge was the jockey who, back in June, had given Peter an almost invisible flarepath of red lights. On that occasion Peter had "torn him off a strip" for the red lights and for not tipping the driver with the traditional bottle of scent. This time he produced white lights and no fewer than sixteen bottles of scent.

That night - at last - 'Antirrhinum' was successful. This was a double for the French Air Force Intelligence Service by Mac and Robin. Among the four they picked up was Georges Bourguignon, a Belgian who kept watch on Luftwaffe airfields in France.

It was really in September 1943 that we had our harvest moon.

Flight Lieutenant Stephen Hankey and Flying Officer Jimmy Bathgate were now operational and the Squadron Commander, Wing Commander L. McD. Hodges, DSO, DFC, was now joining in occasional Lysander pick-up operations as well as Hudsons. Between the seven of us we attempted 25 sorties of which 19 were completed successfully - by far the highest score for any one moon. There were also two Hudson pick-ups, both successful, by Bob Hodges and myself. Altogether we took at least 38 people to enemy occupied France and brought back 63 in that September moon - to say nothing of all those who travelled by parachute. Of the 21 successful landings four each were completed by the three experienced pick-up pilots - Peter, Mac and myself. For a beginner, Bathgate did very well to succeed on all three that he was given to do.

On 12/13 September Peter, Mac and I did our first treble Lysander operation. There were eight passengers in each direction and the field was too small for a Hudson, one of which could have carried them all. Operation 'Battering Ram' was near Rivarennes in Touraine. To minimise the danger to our friends on the ground we planned to complete this treble landing and turn round as quickly as possible. We carried it all out, as planned, in nine minutes from first landing to last take-off. Our rendezvous was just east of Montsoreau where the Vienne flows into the bend in the Loire between Saumur and Chinon, making a very clear landmark by moonlight. We met there at 2330 using very irregular call-signs which we had arranged privately for this one occasion: "Freeman, Hardy and Willis".

In the area of Tangmere and the Channel we had used - as usual - 'Scrapper', the call sign of the Mosquito night-fighter squadron based at Ford, near Tangmere. (We would ring up and borrow two digit numbers from their pilots who were not on duty at the time. I never knew whether this cunning device actually helped by baffling the German radio intelligence service).

At 2336 I landed and taxied to a position to the left of the flarepath and facing the first torch. Once I was clear of the landing strip on the right of the flarepath I called in 'Hardy'. Peter landed at 2337. My two passengers each way were still changing over when Peter drew up on the other side of light 'A'. As soon as he took off I called in 'Willis' and Mac landed, turned round and took off as soon as his three passengers had changed over. Then I took off at 2345. This must have been the most noisy and eventful nine minutes in the history of that peaceful meadow near Rivarennes.

The eight passengers we brought out from Tangmere included: André Boulloche, Military Delegate for Region P, who survived arrest in October '44 and was to be Minister of Education in 1958; Colonel Marchal, a National Military Delegate who was arrested 10 days later and took his cyanide pill; Valentin Abeille, Military Delegate of Region M (West), who was arrested and killed in May 1944; Colonel Rondenay who replaced Colonel Marchal until he too was arrested in July 1944 and shot without a trial a month later; Kammerer, Abeille's assistant, who was to die in Germany; Colonel Palaud, who was arrested in March 1944 and deported, but is still alive; and Henri d'Eyrame, head of radio transmissions for Region P.

We brought back to England Paul Schmidt and his wife Françoise, who was very pregnant. She remembers me comforting her by telling her that Lysanders were so safe that I did not wear a parachute. (Of course I had to sit on a parachute - even if one could not use it on return flights when the new passengers had not had their harness fitted.) Schmidt was replaced in the west by Clouet des Pesruches who had arrived in Burgundy in August by parachute. Together they laid on the ground part of operation 'Battering Ram'. Michel Pichard, who kindly gave me this information about passengers, replaced Schmidt as Chief Air Operations Officer while keeping responsibility for air operations in the East. The other passengers we picked up were Professor Rocard, a well known physicist who specialised in radar (whose son became a socialist prime minister); Gilbert Vedy, one of the leaders of Ceux de la Libération, and his wife; a member of the Secretariat-General; a delegate of the Communist Francs-Tireurs et Partisans who later became a Member of Parliament; and Subiel or Drouot.

When we were back at Tangmere after this trip Peter remembers Mac telling us about how he filled in time waiting for his turn to land. He amused himself low flying by moonlight along the river Loire. While doing this he heard a sharp little sound: "Phltt". The next morning the groundcrew showed him two holes in the sliding side windows of his pilot's cockpit. A bullet had gone right through from one side to the other within three inches of his nose.

On 13/14 September I was circling a field near Reims while a Possum MI9 party were running to it. When they arrived they were alarmed to find that it had all been ploughed except for a strip of grass with a haystack at the end of it. My passengers home included a New Zealand pilot, Flight Sergeant Herbert Pond, whose Halifax had actually flown into the ground while being chased by enemy fighters and Sergeant Fred Gardiner[4a] whose Lancaster had been shot down over Belgium on the way to Mannheim on 9/10 August. These evaders were conscious of the lack of parachutes.

Meanwhile Stephen Hankey picked up his passenger from Hentic's field near Dreux (operation 'Daisy'). He had complete failure of electrics, including R/T, over Cabourg on his way home, but found Tangmere without difficulty. On Stephen's return, he told us that he had made his first pinpoint on the river Seine, not very far from his target. He had started flying along the river in the wrong direction and, to quote his words[4b]:

"I did not know where I was until I looked and recognised my flat in the middle of Paris. My God, I soon got out of that." (This was 'shooting a line' in the authentic RAF tradition).

The next night Stephen had another engagement with Hentic, this time on operation 'Gladiola' at the Cottainville farm near Baudreville, north of Orleans. This he failed to keep, though he claimed that there was no reception. Perhaps he arrived over the field before Hentic had reached it. It was a double operation with Bathgate, who waited 50 minutes at their rendezvous on the Loire without making contact with Hankey. He then went to the field and picked up three intelligence agents known as 'Dix', 'Six' and 'Fernand'. He reported that the signalling and flarepath were very good.

There was only one Lysander required on 15/16 September. Robin took three and brought back two on his second attempt at operation 'Ingres' on Betz-Bouillancy airfield. It was so hazy there that he missed the flashing signal on his first run out from Compiègne. He returned there, tried again and was successful. On his return across the Channel he gave the success signal he had arranged: in reply to the question "What is your hobby?" he answered "Fiddling" (from the French expression "Violon d'Ingres"). He had successfully returned Léon Faye ('Eagle') and Ferdinand Rodriguez to 'Alliance' as he thought. In fact 'Eagle' - exactly in line with Marie-Madeleine's premonitions - was to be captured by the Gestapo on his train to Paris[5]. Robin brought back to Tangmere Maurice MacMahon, Duke of Magenta, who had escaped from prison, and Philippe Koenigswerther, who was in very poor shape. The Duke of Magenta had been in the French Air Force aerobatic team before the war and would be French Air Attaché to Canada after the war. His ancestor Maréchal McMahon had been a somewhat royalist President of the Republic. His wife, heavily pregnant, had crawled under the barbed wire into Switzerland.

On 17/18 September[6] Bob Hodges and Jimmy Bathgate were on a Lysander double pick-up on Déricourt's field near Vieux Briollay in the Angers area. They met at the rendezvous and Bob led Jimmy to the target by flashing his landing light on and off. Out of their Lysanders climbed four people: Peulevé, Yolande Beekman, Harry Despaigne and d'Erainger.

Harry Peulevé had been dropped too low in July 1942 and suffered multiple fractures in one leg. He had made it over the Pyrenees on crutches and escaped from his Spanish prison camp. Now he was on his way to set up and train a powerful maquis in the Corrèze and the Northern Dordogne ('Author'), in conjunction with the brothers André and Roland Malraux. Yolande Beekman was 32 and Swiss. She was on her way to be Gustave Bieler's wireless operator in 'Musician' around St. Quentin. Despaigne, who had first arrived in France by parachute in 1942, was another wireless operator. He was on his way to Sevenet's new circuit 'Detective' near Carcassonne[7]. D'Erainger was an RF (Gaullist) agent from Alsace, with a rather German-sounding Alsatian accent. ("Makes him sound like a dog", I commented on Robin Hooper's report on his training).

Into these Lysanders climbed six including Cowburn, Goldsmith and Rémy Clément, (Déricourt's assistant). Foot described Cowburn as "invulnerable" and "one of Buckmaster's best men". By the end of 1944 he would have done no less than four tours of duty in France. John Goldsmith[8] had arrived by Lysander on the 17/18 March for his second.

Cowburn wrote to me: "I seem to recall that I travelled with Goldsmith and a young RAF air gunner we had rescued from a bomber shot down near Troyes. It was not quite according to the rules, but we owed so much to the RAF. I was only too glad to spare one of your chaps a trip across the Pyrenees and a stay in Miranda!"

On 18/19 September three Lysanders were out and were successful. Stephen Hankey was received by Hentic near Artenay and Baigneaux. He landed Philip Keun ('Amiral') and picked up Félix Jonc and 18 parcels for the Ministry of Economic Warfare. This may have been one of the occasions when we flew back to England special watch hair-springs which had been made in Switzerland. There had been very little watch-making capacity in British industry before the war and hair-springs were needed for clockwork fuses as well as watches. In 1988 Pierre Hentic told me that the boxes contained chronometers smuggled in from Switzerland.

The other two Lysanders were flown by Peter and Mac, now on 'Bomb', the last of their very successful series of doubles together, because Peter was soon to be posted. The field was by the river Charente, north of Angoulême, between La Chapelle and Ambérac. Fog was beginning to creep in over it as they arrived. They had maintained constant R/T contact; there was no waiting at a rendezvous; they flew straight in. When Peter landed, the lamps on their sticks were just above the ground mist. While his load was being turned round, the fog rose above the lamps, the top of it flat smooth and shiny white in the moonlight like a field of smooth snow. When he took off, his cockpit canopy was just above this smooth white surface - a very strange experience.

Meanwhile Mac circled, watching the river mist rolling in. There was not a minute to waste. Peter called him: "For heaven's sake, watch the cliff!" Mac found that the approach was over a cliff some 100 feet high, with a sheer drop to the level of the field on the other side of the river. To avoid missing the trees on the approach meant a drop of over 100 feet once over the river in order to touch down by lamp 'A', which had been placed far too near the base of the cliff. Mac overshot and had to try again. This time he crawled over the top of the cliff and, once clear, cut his motor and dropped almost vertically. Twenty feet from the ground he gave a burst of throttle which eased his rate of descent. With rather more than the usual jar, he hit the ground between 'A' and 'B' but soon pulled up. The turn round went quickly and efficiently and as he took off he could see Peter circling above. Looking down, he could scarcely recognise the field: it was almost entirely a blanket of white mist. Full of the joys of life, they set course for base. Just over two hours later they made a secret rendezvous over Selsey Bill; switched on all their navigation and identification lights; and in tight formation with Peter leading, at 4 am in the morning, flew over the aerodrome and beat up the dispersal where the gathered crowd were waiting to receive their passengers.

They had picked up four passengers: Eugène Bornier, who parachuted back some months later as 'Curé', and his wireless operator Jacques Pain; Mercier, a Communist member of parliament from Paris, and le Trocquer, the Socialist leader who became President of the French Assembly after the war. He was an older man who had lost an arm in 1914-18.

Peter and Mac landed three or four passengers[9], including Yeo-Thomas and Brossolette, on mission 'Marie-Claire', which had been suggested by Dewavrin back in mid-July after the catastrophic arrest of Jean Moulin and most of the Southern leaders of the Resistance in June. They were to discover how much damage had been done and to rebuild as much of the command structure as they could. They found they were going into a landslide of arrests[10]. Forest ('Tommy') Yeo-Thomas had visited us several times at Tangmere Cottage, either as a passenger or as a staff officer from SOE concerned with our operations. His memories of this trip to France, as recorded by Bruce Marshall, will help to give the agent's view of this form of travel and to illustrate how much more difficult the rest of their journey could be.

"This time it was to be a Pullman operation: there was to be no parachuting. Yeo-Thomas and Brossolette, who had just returned from Algiers, were to be landed like a couple of company directors by Lysander near Angoulême.

They took off from Tangmere at 11.30 pm on 18th September and once again, huddled in the cockpit, they were afraid that their journey was going to be abortive. It was cloudy and foggy over the Channel and the sea was invisible. Then the flash of German anti-aircraft fire lit up the clouds and made them look like monster pink powder puffs. The excitement, however, was brief. The Lysander rocked, shot up, swerved, twisted and turned and then went steadily on.

Soon the pilot told them on the 'inter-com' that they were over Poitiers. About 1.25 am, flying low, they caught sight of the three lights of their reception committee. When the regulation signals had been exchanged the aircraft began to circle. Below them lay the landing ground, bordered on either side by a stream shining with inconsequent loveliness in the moonlight. As soon as the aircraft came to a standstill Yeo-Thomas and Brossolette threw out the packages and then climbed out themselves. A leading French Communist called Mercier climbed in, and within five minutes of landing the Lysander was airborne again. Almost immediately a second Lysander appeared and landed. Two more agents got out after they had thrown out more packages. The packages created a problem for the members of the reception committee, who had not been expecting so many and had only one car at their disposal. The agents, after sorting out their own suitcases, had to wait behind bushes and were guarded by two men with Sten guns, while the packages were driven to a ruined and unoccupied house 15 miles away and concealed there. About 3 am the car returned. The car was a front-wheel drive Citroën, into which nine passengers had to be crammed. Once again they had to run the risk of being caught out after curfew, which was at midnight, and as they were in a car they could not quickly take cover. They resolved that if they met a German patrol they would fight their way through it. The possibility of such an encounter was considerable, as they had 40 miles to go.

Three-quarters of an hour after they had started their near rear tyre burst while they were driving through a village, and they all had to get out. Changing the wheel was, in spite of their precautions, a noisy operation and it was necessary to keep a sharp look out. The two men with Sten guns guarded the car, one in front and one behind. Brossolette and Yeo-Thomas hid in the shadow of a big farm door and the other two agents on the opposite side of the street. Those who were changing the wheel worked speedily, but in the silence of the night the noise seemed deafening. They had to fear not only the arrival of a German patrol but also discovery by unfriendly villagers. Anxious and impatient, Yeo-Thomas suddenly saw pink lines of light from one of the shutters in a house opposite. The shutters opened slowly and a man's head appeared. Yeo-Thomas stepped out of the shadow and pointed his Colt threateningly. The shutters slammed shut at once and the light went out. Yeo-Thomas could only hope that if the man were a collaborator there was no telephone in the house. Even when the wheel had been changed and the jack removed their troubles weren't over. The spare tyre turned out to be soft and a frantic search failed to reveal a pump among the tools. There was nothing to do but to climb into the car again and hope that the tyre would hold out under their heavy weight. They chose the lesser danger of driving quickly because they were afraid of being stranded far from their destination. The tyre had a slow puncture and as the miles went reeling past the bumps became heavier and heavier. By the time they reached the safe house they were riding almost on the rim of the wheel."

On 20/21 September, Jimmy Bathgate brought back four passengers from the general area of Châteauroux in spite of bad weather. Gaston Defferre, future Minister of the Interior and Maire of Marseilles, remembered smuggling on board a fourth passenger, though this was strictly forbidden. (Although he was picked up at Dun-sur-Auron, which is near Bourges rather than Châteauroux, this was probably his flight to England that autumn[11].) He was with Boyer who later died in Germany and a Colonel of the Army Resistance. Gaston Defferre returned to France a few weeks later by a Double Lysander operation, probably flown by Jim McBride and myself to the area of Bourges on 8/9 November, the night before the King and Queen visited us at Tempsford.

This had really been a harvest moon to remember. We had been able to send Lysanders to France on 11 nights running. (With my Hudson trip on 21/22 this meant for me 12 consecutive nights without proper sleep). Only on one of these nights, 19/20, had we not scored at least one success. During September we heard that Pilot Officer J.R. Affleck of 'B' Flight 161 Squadron was awarded the DFC for his parachuting operations. He was to join in our Hudson pick-ups in the next few months. Peter Vaughan-Fowler, now an acting flight lieutenant, had been awarded a bar to his Distinguished Flying Cross.

This was the end of Peter's long tour of duty with 'A' Flight 161 Squadron. During the preparation of this book he helped me a great deal with his memories of those days, reinforced by entries in his log-book. But there were three incidents he remembered which he could not date precisely.

One was the occasion when he brought back two American aviators. They had left

Flight Lieutenant Peter Vaughan-Fowler, DFC*, in 1943.

their base in East Anglia only three days before, and been shot down over Northern France. This must have been a record for quick recovery of evading aircrew[12]. The second was when carrying a heavy load in the back, with a full fuel load, he had to keep constant pressure on the stick, because it was impossible to trim the aircraft to fly hands off. The other incident was when Peter was flying through an electric storm and his VHF radio aerial was struck by lightning. On landing it was found to be flush with the perspex of the canopy - horizontal instead of vertical.

Peter was posted, at his request, not to a rest from operations but to fly Mosquitos under Group Captain Pickard ('Pick'). Here he was delighted when Philippe Livry also joined them and became Peter's navigator. These two were successful in continuing to fly operationally without 'rests' until the end of the war. At the end of each tour of operations they fixed postings to a new command.

Of course we could not have had such a run of luck and success if we had not been most fortunate in our ground staff, NCOs and airmen. I have already mentioned our young Flight Sergeant John Hollis (known as 'Sam'). The names of some of the others are given in the movement order quoted at Appendix 'E'. They were fiercely proud of their Lysanders and the serviceability they achieved was unsurpassed. Stephen Hankey's electricity failure was exceptional. Not that the airmen were grimly determined at all times; they had their stories to tell too. I am grateful to Les Dibdin, who was one of our electricians in 'A' Flight in 1942-43, for the following samples that he remembers and wrote down for me for this book:

Fred Ferris on Air Test with Peter Fowler

Rigger LAC Fred Ferris, sitting in the rear cockpit of Lysander 'B', Bertie, was flying around Tangmere on air test with his skipper Peter Fowler, when, over the intercom, his skipper requested permission to "Pancake".

"My Lord", said Fred, "We are going to crash land." He had a quick look round to see if he could see anything wrong, but all appeared all right and the engine was still running smoothly.

Coming up to the 'drome they were approaching over the hangar when the aircraft slipped sideways, righted itself, then slipped the other way. "We are going to crash on top of the hangar", thought Fred. With his heart in his mouth he looked out to see the hangar just below him and the aircraft flying nice and level just missed the top of the hangar and landed safely on the grass just near the perry track.

After taxying back to dispersal the aircraft stopped and Fred got out, white as a ghost, and said to his skipper: "What was wrong then?" "Wrong?" said Peter. "Nothing, everything was bang on." "What was the idea asking permission to crash land then?" Peter smiled. The old RT code had been altered from "permission to land" to "permission to pancake". "Oh", said Fred, "I thought we were in trouble when we were side-slipping." "No", said Peter. "I thought I would lose height to see if I could make a short landing; that's why we came in low over the hangar."

Fred's mates, who were listening to the story, chimed in: "Here Fred, have a cup of char; it seems you have nearly frightened yourself to death!"

On Patrol

The Lysanders of 'A' Flight 161 Squadron were parked at the side of a bombed hangar which had been damaged during the Battle of Britain. When the wind blew through the hangar it gave an eerie sensation, especially on moonlight evenings.

It was moonlight when LAC Les Dibdin was doing his patrol around the Lizzies. He noticed somebody walking round the back of 'G' for George. With thoughts of sabotage in mind, he had better find out what he was up to.

Walking towards the aircraft he noticed the figure had now stopped as his legs could be seen underneath the aircraft. Getting nearer the Lysander, the intruder moved round again quickly then stopped. As Les got to the aircraft the intruder jumped out from behind and met him face to face and shouted: "Sieg Heil Deutschland!" After seconds of silence, Paddy White, a fitter with a deep voice, said: "Alright Dib, it's only your relief. Who did you think it was? Jerry?"

Officer for a moment

Two 'A' Flight pilots drove up to the dispersal point in a Rolls Royce saloon, which was used as a pilots' crew-waggon among other duties, to do an air test on their aircraft.

When the two Lysanders taxied out, the conversation among the ground crews turned to the Rolls. The driver, an Army Signals Corporal, was saying about the servicing of the Rolls and how things were sealed by the makers. After lifting the bonnet to show us he started the engine to show us how quietly the engine was running.

"How about a quick trip on the perimeter track?" said LAC Jack Lingley and his mate Bob Seaman. "We would like a ride in a Rolls." "OK", said the corporal. "Jump in. We have just got time before the kites get back."

Whilst they sat in the back seat like lords, Jack noticed the officers had left their peak caps behind. So, with no more ado, Jack put one on and said "I wonder if anybody will sling us one up (salute)." Sure enough, the first airman they passed gave a smart salute. "Silly b...", said Jack. "I bet he thought I was the CO." "Take that damn thing off", said Bob. "We will get court martialled if we get caught."

The Rolls was back at dispersal before the aircraft and there stood Bob and Jack quite innocent with just a half smile on their faces. "Any snags, sir?"

Paul Schmidt

CHAPTER ELEVEN

Great Names

The trouble-free successes of the harvest moons of 1943 could not be expected to continue throughout the autumn and winter months. We always had enemies on these pick-ups - German flak from the ground, night fighters in the air and covert penetration of our customers' 'firms' and their radio traffic. Our targets - unlike main force bomber targets - were not in flak defended areas and we could, if we tried hard enough, navigate ourselves through corridors free of flak on the way to our target areas. German night fighters were increasingly concentrated well to the north of our routes to defend Germany itself; we had very little trouble with them. Besides that we flew too low over France, once we had overflown the light flak on the coast, to be easy prey to radar controlled interceptions. The German Abwehr and Sicherheitsdienst (Gestapo) activities were totally concealed from our direct experience at the time, though it is now known that several of our landings were discreetly observed from a distance by German agents who wished to follow the passengers we brought to France.

So it seemed to us that our really potent enemies were fog and mud. We could generally battle through other forms of bad weather - even icing cloud. It had mainly been fog that frustrated us and mud that endangered our aircraft on French meadows. We had not had too much trouble with either since the previous winter of 1942/43, but we were prepared for these problems to develop in the last quarter of the year. We could not have expected that we should be hit as hard as we were in December.

In the next two chapters I shall combine the story of the Hudson and the Lysander pick-ups during October and November 1943, that is up to the end of my time as OC 'A' Flight No 161 Squadron.

The first three pick-ups attempted in October failed through bad weather. On 8/9 Wing Commander Hodges and his Hudson crew (Sqn Ldr Wagland and Flg Off Bradbury) took Plt Off Affleck with them as second pilot, under training. Their operation, 'Shield', was across the river Saône north of Mâcon. Navigation was extremely difficult as there were only a few breaks in the cloud, but they luckily found the target and saw the lights of the reception through one of these breaks. However, it was impossible for them to keep the flarepath in view on the circuit and Bob decided that the visibility was so bad that it would not be safe to land. Little did they know what an important passenger was waiting there for a flight from hiding into the main stream of the war.

On 15/16 and 16/17 October Robin Hooper made two attempts to find Perriers-sur-Andelle near Rouen for operation 'Entracte'. On both he was defeated by haze so heavy that he found it impossible to identify particular bends in the river Seine. However, Stephen Hankey had better luck on 16/17 with Déricourt's field near Amboise. Here he landed Arthur Watt and Rémy Clément and picked up Maurice Southgate and two others. Arthur Watt was Déricourt's little radio-operator. Rémy Clément had been Déricourt's assistant since the beginning of 1943 and had just been in England for training so that he would have a licence to lay on operations in his own right.

While at Tangmere Cottage before this trip, he had flattered us with the following jingle:

Discrétion, célerité
Voyagez chez Vérité

This might (or might not) be translated:

For speed and care
Fly Verity-air

Or even (Robin Hooper's version):

If you're looking for discretion and
the maximum celerity,
Be wise, and take an aeroplane
of Squadron Leader Verity!

When I met Clément in Paris in 1974 he was 75 years old but hardly looked 60. He had been flying as an air-line pilot in Vietnam and Laos until he was 67, by which time he had done 18,000 hours. He told me about his early contacts with Henri Déricourt before the war. At that time they had met occasionally when they were both aero-club pilots - instructors - and had taken part in flying circuses. Clément had given three-minute 'baptisms of the air' in a six-seater and had dropped parachutists. Déricourt then worked for *Air Bleu*, the first air-post company. In 1939 the aircrew of Air France were mobilised separately to their different units. Déricourt and Clément were mobilised together to fly the Air France aircraft as military transports, backing up fighter squadrons on their forward bases. When there overnight they slept in their aircraft as there was no other accommodation. One night Clément happened to be in a village, finding billets for others. When he got back to his aeroplane he found that it had been destroyed by a bomb at 4 am.

After the 1940 armistice Clément found himself a good job as a director in a maritime firm in Marseilles. Déricourt, now with Air France, was withdrawn to Marseilles. Towards the end of 1942 Clement realised that Déricourt had disappeared. As soon as he returned to France after his training in England, Déricourt went straight to Clément, told him what he was doing, and asked if he would like to help. Rémy Clément told me that at the time he had a good job but his life was like a night-light - a very dim flame. Déricourt's proposition made it flare up into a bright flame. He agreed to work with the 'Farrier' mission, finding fields for us. As soon as he had collected his year-end bonus from his company, he gave in his month's notice and left.

Clément's job for Déricourt was to find suitable fields and to assist passengers to get to them or away from them (generally by bicycles between railway stations and the fields). He was happy to leave all contacts with radio operators to Déricourt. He thought all that end of it in Paris was far too dangerous. His first actual pick-up was near Amboise on 14/15 April 1943 (when McCairns flew through that tree).

There were two other Lysanders out that Saturday night of 16/17 October; both were in the general area of Compiègne and both were given faulty back bearings by radio - a most exceptional problem. Bathgate arrived over the French coast well away from his intended track and was quite unable to identify any pinpoints. This was the first unsuccessful attempt at operation 'Magdalen'. McCairns, who had the same baffling error from the ground station in his radio direction finding, later estimated that he had arrived over the French coast 20 miles off track. He spent one hour in a fruitless search for his position and then went back to the coast for a fresh pin-point. Having been airborne since 2120, he finally found his target near Estrées St. Denis at 0058, landed two, picked up three[1] and returned to Tangmere at 0220. One of his passengers to France, Colonel 'Vernon' from Algiers, was later to be General Henri Ziegler, the head of both Aerospatiale and Air France and thus virtually 'Monsieur Concorde'. Back in London in 1944 he would be Chief of Staff to the French Forces of the Interior under General Koenig. Among his passengers to England were Abbot Vorage, (who had been on the Germans' black list since 1916!) and René Gervais, Head of *S.R. Air* in France.

The fifth pick-up sortie laid on for the night of 16/17 October 1943 was a Hudson - second attempt at 'Shield', on the huge meadow called 'Aigle' near Manziat, nine kilometres NNE of Mâcon. Philippe Livry and I had with us Flying Officer Bradbury instead of Eddie Shine, our usual wireless operator/air gunner. Pilot Officer Affleck came as second pilot; he was completing his training as a Hudson pick-up pilot. John Affleck, later a senior training captain in British Airways European Division, well remembers this trip. During it he was standing behind Philippe's folding canvas seat, which was beside the pilot's seat, when Philippe stretched and broke the metal frame of his seat. His great weight fell backwards on top of John, who damaged his back.

This was otherwise a very uneventful trip for us. The operations record book simply gives the field, the code-name, the times and numbers of passengers (landed five at 2340; 2346 took off with "eight agents"). There seemed to be nothing else to record. John Affleck remembers my landing better than I do. He reminded me that the grass on this meadow was very long. Before touching down, I floated over it, dropped into it, and then had a very short landing run. I have since discovered that my passengers[2] from Tangmere included Jacques Maillet, a *Polytechnicien* and aero-engineer who had earlier been in the resistance in occupied France as a member of 'Combat'. In 1974 he was to be President of the French aerospace industries, President of the Intertechnique company and President of the *Amicale Action*, the main old comrades association of the French Resistance. In September 1943, Maillet was put in charge of the Economic Section of the Delegation of the Free French Committee. His role would be to organise food and industrial supplies for the population after D-day in 1944. In February 1944 he had a narrow escape when the fishing boat in which he was leaving Brittany for England was shipwrecked and his companions Bollaert and Pierre Brossolette were captured by the Germans. In the Spring of 1944, when Bingen was arrested by the Germans, Maillet replaced him as the Algiers Provisional Government's Civil Delegate for the South Zone of France.

I will never forget one little incident. After taking off from Paul Rivière's magnificent field 'Aigle', and settling down on our first leg towards Tangmere, I handed over the Hudson to John Affleck. I took a thermos of coffee into the dark cabin, shining a pocket torch on the pale green metal structure above me to diffuse a glow of reflected light. Eight[3] smiling faces welcomed me in the gloom. One of them came forward saying: *"Monsieur le pilote,* I have the great honour to present you to General de Lattre de Tassigny"*. I found myself shaking hands with a man in a cloth cap with a great black beard. From his clothes he might have been a rather self-respecting tramp.

He was rather an exceptional passenger in two ways: Firstly, he was one of the most senior that we carried; secondly, he kept in touch. He invited my wife and me to a small party in a private room in his hotel (was it Claridges?) some weeks after his flight with me. Even by January 1950, when so much had happened to him, he still remembered and sent me a generously autographed copy of his book *Histoire de la Première Armée Française - Rhin et Danube*[4]. The first three paragraphs of the first chapter of this book may be translated as follows:

"On 18 (sic) October 1943, before day-break, an RAF aircraft landed at Tangmere, to the east of Portsmouth. Three hours earlier it had landed clandestinely in the plains of the Saône, near Mâcon, and had picked up seven Frenchmen - to take them to freedom.

I was among these privileged men and it was in this way that I completed the last act of my escape. On 3rd September, with only the help of my wife, my son and several faithful assistants, I had succeeded in escaping from the prison at Riom, my fourth prison in ten months, where the national tribunal had condemned me to ten years imprisonment for having tried to save the honour of troops under my command on 11th November 1942 at Montpellier.

It is easy to imagine my emotions at this moment when a veritable miracle permitted me to take my place in the struggle for liberation."

General de Lattre had, in fact, been the only one of Pétain's commanders to attempt to resist the German occupation of the unoccupied zone in November 1942. Now he was to be the Commander of the French First Army. With seven divisions, he was to play a major role in the rapid thrust to the north from the Riviera in operation 'Dragoon', which landed on 15th August 1944. De Lattre was one of the four allied commanders to take the surrender of Germany, with Eisenhower, Zhukov, and Montgomery.

James Buchanan, whom we all called 'Jock', has reminded me of a silly incident at Tangmere in this Hudson after this trip. Philippe Livry had left his .38 revolver lying about in the aircraft. An airman picked it up and squeezed the trigger so that a bullet went through the internal overload petrol tank. When flying some of them back to Tempsford, Buchanan remembers my order: "No smoking, chaps!"

In 1973 I was invited (through Paul Rivière) to take part in a French TV documentary film production about de Lattre's escape. This film, called *Charles Dequenne Instituteur*, was made by Michel Duvernay. The field 'Aigle', where we had picked him up, is now marked by a small stone obelisk recording his departure by Hudson. It would not be suitable for another such operation today. Power cables and their pylons now march across it.

One of the Lysander pick-ups on 18/19 October was the first by our new pilot, Flying Officer J.M. McBride, who had only been with us since 4th October when he was posted in from No 85 (night fighter) Squadron. He was a large, strong young man, rather dark and clean shaven with prominent cheek-bones. He was rather quiet and shy. Born in Port of Spain, Trinidad, and educated in Strathallan School, Scotland, where he was Captain of the School, he had left St. Catherine College, Cambridge to join the RAF in 1940. In 1941 Jim McBride had flown Wellingtons over most of Europe[5]. He was known as 'McB' to distinguish him from McCairns, who was called 'Mac'. His target was near Baudreville, north of Orleans, and it took a little time to find because of "pin-pointing difficulty". This operation was called 'Primrose'. The agent in charge was Pierre Hentic. He received 'Victor' and despatched to England Colonel Brosse, Captain Louis and one American aviator.

Of the latter, Michel Pichard told me:

"Though this information is entirely miscellaneous, you will perhaps be amused to hear that the "US Airman" picked up by 'Primrose' (18- 19 Oct '43) was called Joseph Cornwall, and he had been hidden for some time in the dome of la Chapelle des Invalides, in Paris.

I got that story from the widow of the 'Gardien des Invalides', Monsieur Morin. Madame Morin and her daughter who came back from a concentration camp still live in Les Invalides where they did hide about 60 airmen, not at the same time. They rightly claim that searching the dome is an impossible task, as established by the fact that, even though they were arrested, they still have their files...and the pictures of their 'guests', because they kept all their papers in the dome. They even have some rather funny pictures taken on top of the dome, but complain that the airmen had the deplorable habit of throwing gravel or stones on the heads of the Germans who came in large numbers to visit Napoleon's grave.

Madame Morin's best story, I think, is about an American who "escaped" from Les Invalides after he discovered where M Morin kept the key to the main gate. When the family woke up, they were disturbed to discover that the guest had disappeared. A little later, he showed up with a patriotic "fille de joie" who explained "As he was leaving this morning, I realised that he was lost, and though he does not speak French, I gathered that he lived with Napoleon. So I brought him back from Montparnasse, and here he is."

A 'dirty story' not fit for printing, but I hope you will agree it's quite funny".

Meanwhile extraordinary things were happening near Lons-le-Saunier. Paul Rivière had no less than 18 passengers for England assembled on the vast meadow near Bletterans that he called 'Orion'. Two Hudsons were on their way to pick them up: 'O' for Orange, flown and captained by Wing Commander Hodges[6], with Squadron Leader Wagland, Flight Lieutenant 'Lofty' Reed and Flying Officer McDonald as crew; and 'M' for Mother, skippered by Pilot Officer John Affleck with Flying Officers Richards, Bradbury and Goldfinch.

The flight plan was to fly from Tempsford rather than Tangmere - as there was plenty of range with the Hudsons - and then to land back at Tangmere where we had the necessary organisation laid on to meet the passengers and speed them on their way to London by car. The Met briefing had been favourable with good visibility and little cloud in the target area. Moon rise was just after midnight and with about half moon they were confident that there would be enough light to see the details on the ground and make a safe landing.

They set course to the south climbing to 2,000 feet and crossed the English coast at Selsey Bill heading for the small seaside resort of Cabourg on the Normandy coast, our normal route into France as it was fairly clear of German Flak batteries and well to the west of their fighter defence zone. About half way across the Channel they reduced height to a few hundred feet above the water to avoid detection by enemy radar, and swept in over the coast gaining height only to get a better view of the French coast to be sure of their landfall. They then turned south-east into France keeping as low as possible consistent with the need to be able to navigate and map read accurately. Their next major landmark was the River Loire - a small island in the river near the town of Blois. This was a very prominent feature which was easy to identify and gave an accurate 'fix' of their position. And then from Blois they turned and set course for the target - the most difficult part of the navigation.

In this case there was a small winding river with many loops which helped and Bob had arranged to rendezvous with the second Hudson before going to the landing field so that they would arrive over the landing ground at the same time to cut down the total time of the operation to the minimum to reduce the danger to the people on the ground. Bob had arranged to circle at a prearranged spot and to flash his landing lights on and off to signal his position. They were also in radio contact and he very quickly had confirmation from Affleck in the second Hudson that he had seen the lights and was close at hand. Having established that they were both together they set course for the landing field.

By this time the moon was well up and there was enough light to see details on the ground as they peered ahead for a light signal from the 'Reception Committee'. The navigator had given a course and distance to fly from their last accurate pin-point, and in due course they saw light signals ahead. They flashed their code signal and got the correct response. The torch flarepath was quickly switched on and Bob told John Affleck over the radio that he was going into land while he circled overhead. The landing was always the most tricky part of the operation as we never knew quite what to expect. Bob can remember some high trees near the edge of the field which were illuminated by his landing lights but he was able to clear them comfortably. He touched down by the first torch and, with a fairly firm application of the toe brakes, came to a stop in a short distance.

He taxied back to the first light and turned into wind ready for take off again. The engines were of course kept running. The door was opened and they took on nine passengers. The Hudson was stripped right down for lightness and had no seats in the fuselage - conditions were certainly uncomfortable but no one minded that. They took off again after two or three minutes only on the ground and Bob called in John's Hudson while he circled overhead.

Leaves from Afflect's tree.

There was a strong cross wind and John misjudged his first approach, coming in too high. He went round again. On his second approach he went through the top of the poplars on his way down to the flarepath. Bits of poplar were removed from his air intakes when he returned to Tempsford. John told me that the angle of drift in the cross wind made it look as if he would land on the left of the lights. Paul Rivière, who was standing there with his signalling torch, pipe between his teeth, must have moved across to the other side of the lamp 'A' to be out of harm's way - as he thought. Then John says, he kicked off the drift to land on the right of the lights. Now Paul saw this large aeroplane coming straight at him blinding him with its landing lights. He fell flat on his face in the grass and one heavy wheel touched on each side of him. The tail wheel - luckily - had not yet touched ground. Paul says[7] that John actually landed on the left of the lights and this version is corroborated by another eye witness. The next morning the local Gendarmes from Bletterans were inspecting the scene of the crime with the Germans. A little later one of the Gendarmes surreptitiously returned to Paul his pipe, his torch and his spectacles.

John took on nine passengers and was soon airborne. He was well on his way home before he remembered to tell his Squadron Commander that he was OK. They landed at Tangmere three hours later and their passengers were handed over and whisked away in waiting cars; they had no chance to meet them.

Granite stele on 'Orion', near Bletterans, unveiled in May 1993, with Raymond and Lucie Aubrac, Paul Rivière and former members of the reception committee.   *Audrey Verity*

This operation took to France the Allied team that was to have dramatic results in arming the Maquis of the Ain, the Jura and Haute Savoie. They were Jean Rosenthal (French, 'Cantinier'), Richard Heslop (British, 'Marksman') and two Americans: Captain Denis Johnson ('Paul', radio operator) and Elizabeth Reynolds (courier).

The sequel to this story was that in 1948 the President of France, Vincent Auriol, came to London on a State visit - the first state visit of a French President since the end of the war. He asked the authorities if it would be possible to trace the name of the pilot who brought him out of France five years earlier. The records were checked and it transpired that he was one of the passengers[8] in Bob's aircraft in that double Hudson operation on 18/19 October 1943. In 1950 Bob and Waggy were summoned to the French Embassy to receive the *Légion d'Honneur* from the hands of M.

Massigli, the French Ambassador in London - who had himself been brought out of France by Lysander.

The fourth Hudson landing in the October moon was Affleck's again, two nights later, with the same crew. It was with Déricourt near Angers. There were four passengers each way, including: Albert Browne-Bartroli (later DSO), who was on his way to establish the 'Ditcher' circuit in Burgundy; Marchand, to do the same for 'Newsagent' to the south of 'Ditcher', and Robert Benoist[9] to found 'Clergyman' at Nantes.

The four picked up were Paul Frager, Nearne, Leprince and, perhaps, Alexandre Lévy. Monsieur Lévy had been in the administration of public services in Paris - a useful vantage point for someone with a moonlighting job in the Resistance. However, as a Jew, he was now forced to wear the large star sewn on his clothes which the occupying Germans required, so that Jews should be easily identified as such at a distance.

There was a quarrel between Déricourt and Frager before this pick up over breakfast in a café opposite the Angers railway station. The quarrel was partly because Frager had brought his friend and deputy Roger Bardet to see him off (which Déricourt forbade) and partly because Frager thought Déricourt was an agent of the Gestapo and Déricourt suspected that he did[10]. The security of this pick-up was even more fragile because Sgt. Bleicher of the Abwehr had released Bardet from prison in exchange for a promise to keep him supplied with information - a promise which Bardet appears to have kept[11]. But, as far as Affleck and his crew could know at the time it was a very straightforward operation.

The last operation of the October moon, which I did not find in the RAF archives, is recorded in the French archives and remembered by Michel Pichard. I quote from his letter to me of 19th April 1977:

> Looking through the cards of *Comité d'Histoire de la Deuxième Guerre Mondiale*, I recently found two notes which I quote:
> *21/22 Oct 43 – à Fontaines Fourches – atterrissage d'un avion anglais – Courrier et agent de renseignement – source groupe 'Vengeance' de Bray-sur-Seine*, and *Oct 21/22 1943 sur terrain 'Bouche', arrivée de 'Voltigeur' terrain détrempé. Avion décolle sans difficulté – second avion venu – balisage sans résultat"* – source: archives BCRA.
> According to your chart, the last 'October moon' landings took place the night before...and I believe that this one has been forgotten. Can it be traced?"

What happened at our end was this: 'Ampère' (Jacques Guérin, air operations officer for Region P) had been arrested on 10th October near Sens. We naturally wired London to cancel all operations in Region P. Nevertheless, around the 18th, the BBC announced a landing on that field near Nogent-sur-Seine. We wired again but decided (with 'Galilée' - that's Clouët des Pesruches) to get to the spot... and think it over if the BCRA continued to ignore our warnings. Neither of us knew the field... and we did not like it very much, rather bumpy and damp. Since 'Ampère', who knew the field, was in German hands we reinforced *l'équipe de protection*. Galilée, who was a French Air Force pilot, advised me to go ahead despite the poor conditions of the field...and the message came on the BBC, much to our dismay.

One Lysander landed…and got stranded at the end of the run, but it took a couple of minutes to lift the tail and turn it around. There were two 'Home' passengers - I only recall that one of them was 'Sénateur Azaïs' (Monsieur Godet, the uncle of Lenormand of 'Ceux de la Libération'). One passenger out, according to the files, was 'Voltigeur' (André Shock), Délégué Militaire Région C.

'Azaïs' was exceedingly attached to an umbrella with an ivory handle. As a joke, we told him that umbrellas were prohibited in Lysanders as a result of a crash caused by one of them - and when 'Azaïs' took this instrument to the field, we confiscated it… and Toubas broke it by sitting on it while waiting for the plane. After take-off, we discovered that in the commotion 'Azaïs' had managed to sneak the umbrella into the plane. I was told long afterwards that actually 'Azaïs' had concealed some documents in the handle of the umbrella.

The local team on the ground was led by Pierre Delahayes, who helped Pichard with the operation. Delahayes was arrested three weeks later, in connection with arms drops. He died in Germany.

Mac's unpublished memoirs give an account of a sortie which must have been this one. The weather forecast was so bad that his Lysander was the only aircraft that night on the Fighter Command plotting table.

He found that the weather was not as bad as the forecast. There was a certain amount of dodging round violent thunderstorms, and at each flash of lightning he instinctively flinched and heaved the Lysander over in violent evasive action. Flying low on the approach to the coast with the clouds causing Stygian blackness, he was thankful for one streak of lightning which lit up the shore in front of him as if by day, and showed the estuary near Cabourg, confirming that he was dead on track. But the rest of the route, except for a few rainstorms, was not too hazardous.

As he went in to land over the Route Nationale he noticed that there was not a bordering row of trees as he had expected. He landed close to 'A', and before he had reached 'B' he was at a standstill. When he started to taxi, he needed almost full engine to keep rolling on the gluey surface. Slowly and laboriously he made his way back to 'A' and, as he tried to swing the Lysander round into take-off position, he bogged, completed immobile. Without switching off, he unstrapped the harness and jumped down, sinking into the soft clayey ground. He called to the agent and told him that this sort of ground was quite impossible. The agent explained that a week ago it had been hard, cultivated ground, which had been harrowed quite flat and without bumps. But for the last 48 hours the rain had been persistent: hence the quagmire. Mac told him he considered take-off irmpossible.

"Oh, oui. Ça va", was his only reply.

They emptied the aircraft and Mac instructed the ground party on how he wanted them to push. After checking that he had another 500 yards before the first fence, he picked up a ball of clay for a Tangmere exhibit and climbed back into his cockpit. With the French pushing on the side of the Lysander, he opened the throttle fully and they slewed the Lizzie round until it was facing 'B' and 'C'. The passengers climbed up the ladder and, at full bore, he started to take off.

At first they scarcely seemed to move, and then bit by bit they gained speed. As they passed 'B' they must have been doing about 20 mph instead of the required 70 plus. Gradually the needle crept up. Mac became nervous and switched on his landing light, ready to cut the engine before they hit the fence, when, after about 400 yards run 'E' gave a last groan and bump, and they were airborne, happily skimming over the far boundary. Once back at base, all Mac could do was to walk into the Cottage, looking like a bedraggled scarecrow, and throw the mud ball at an Air Ministry type with the caustic comment: "Is that what we are supposed to land on?"

Later, carefully checking the Air Ministry plot of the field they had approved, Mac saw that it bore no relation to the one in which he had landed.

That ball of mud caked hard and was fixed into the Lysander Flight Line Book with Scotch tape. It has now disappeared but the line book is still bulging to accommodate its shape.

During October, fifteen Lysander sorties had been attempted but only eight of them landed successfully. This serious reduction in our rate of success was mainly - but not altogether - due to poor weather in target areas. DSOs were awarded during October to Wing Commander Hodges and to Flight Lieutenant Broadley who had navigated both him and his predecessor, Wing Commander Pickard, on Hudson pick-ups. Squadron Leader Wagland, who had navigated both 'Mouse' Fielden and Bob Hodges on Hudson pick-ups, won a bar to the DFC awarded to him for bombing operations in Whitleys in 1940/41. These awards for gallantry were not, of course, solely in recognition of the pick-ups. Bob and Waggy, for example, had that moon broken the ice again in Halifax drops to Holland - a very heavily defended area - from which two out of four Halifaxes failed to return.

On 24th October 1943, I wrote to my wife at Dell Cottage, Crocker Hill, near Chichester:

"I have decided that it is time you had a break and consequently I am not presing to stay on ops, although I would if I were not married.

"I must thank you for being so sweet and understanding and so damn cheerful and good for my morale, almost all the time over the last moon. By comparison with the way other people's wives behave, I must say you are a miracle. I shoot no end of a line about you, Darling".

The first three nights of operations in the November moon each saw one Lysander operation and all three were successful. On 7/8 November, Mac landed the Belgian Count Georges d'Oultremont of MI9 near Compiègne and brought home the exceptional load of four. This was the third time lucky on operation 'Magdalen' which had been laid on twice in the October moon. He flew via Cayeux, west of Abbeville, and was lost for some time in thick haze. He flew back towards base until he could radio for a bearing and then managed to find the field, though the lamps were weak and one was missing. This made it impossible to know which line to land on. He found that the agent had put paper covers over his torches ("to avoid dazzling him") and that lamp 'B' had failed. His four passengers turned out to be hefty American sergeants.

On 9th November the King and Queen visited Tempsford. I was lined up in front of a Hudson with Philippe Livry and Eddie Shine. I will never forget how charmingly the Queen chatted to Philippe in French. By the time she finished the King had shaken many more hands with an occasional slight stammer in his words of encouragement. The Queen had some way to go to catch up with him.

When I wrote to my parents the next day I reported:

"I was presented to the King and Queen yesterday. It was colossal fun and I was most

Their Majesties the King and Queen visit RAF Tempsford, November, 1943.

impressed. I liked them very well, especially the Queen who really impressed me for her sympathetic charm. She seemed very well aware of the work we are doing. She was beautifully made up. The King had rather fine bags under his eyes.
I would do anything for them, even if they were not the ultimate boss".

That night there was a treble Lysander operation - 'Oriel' - laid on south east of Châtellerault. Wing Commander Hodges found persistent bad weather which made pin-pointing impossible in the target area. He ordered Flight Lieutenants Hooper and Hankey to return to base and returned himself. Each of the three had two passengers on board for the five-hour round trip.

The next attempt at Oriel was two nights later, on 11/12 November, this time with Robin Hooper and Flying Officers McCairns and Bathgate. Robin landed first and found the surface of the field extremely soft. His two passengers jumped out but he cancelled the rest of the operation and had great difficulty in extricating his Lysander from the mud and taking off.
Robin remembers the sequel: "When we got back, both Mac and Jimmy Langley, for whom we were working, were furious with me for cancelling the second two landings. Mac was not in the least mollified by my saying to him that I didn't want to be responsible for his being put in the bag a second time. As for Jimmy, I think this was the occasion on which he made his classic remark - "What do you expect? Concrete runways?"

However, I was justified next morning when Sam, Jimmy Sweet & Co. opened up the spats of 'D for Dog' and dug about a wheelbarrow load of sticky yellow French clay out of each. We dumped it on a flower bed in the Cottage garden, chanting "There's some corner of an English field...That is for ever foreign..."

On that same night of 11/12 November, McBride found his field near Vendôme but there was no welcoming signal flashed from it. We heard later from the agent that they had been prevented from arriving there by the enemy.

The only completely successful operation that night was the double which Stephen Hankey did with me north-east of Paris, operation 'Salvia'. (SIS were beginning to find it difficult to think of any more names of flowers). The agent in charge, Pierre Hentic, was one of the six passengers to England, with Fortier, Captain Bertin and 'Simorre'. The other two were Monsieur et Madame Potelette. She was eight months pregnant. He was a senior railway engineer who intended to arrange for trains to be destroyed more by sabotage than by bombing. I did not notice it myself, but Stephen told me afterwards that he saw a Dornier 217 circling the field during the operation. It must have been unarmed - possibly a pupil pilot and crew on night flying practice. They were probably describing our activities to their base and getting a radio fix of the location of our field.

This must have been the field called 'Marot' by the Gaullist resistance, who had registered it and resented it being used by another organisation. They suspected Buckmaster's F Section of trespassing, but it was actually the Secret Intelligence Service who used it, no doubt in ignorance of the fact that it was already on the list of another organisation. It is located about 10 kilometres west of Reims. The passengers we picked up included Bertin who was head of *'Ceux de la Résistance'* in Reims and, no doubt, a guest of SIS for this flight.

On 12/13 November Bathgate and I did a double for the French Air Force Intelligence Service on their field at Estrées St. Denis. We landed René Gervais, head of their network *S.R. Air*, who had been in England and Algiers for less than a month. As he got out of the train at Vichy, he found Louis Jourdan waiting to warn him that his flat had been raided by the Gestapo a few hours before. Most of his people in the South had been arrested[12].

In April 1943 I had started a 'line book' in Tangmere Cottage. Authentic RAF 'line-shooting' of that time was a form of jocular boasting which nobody was expected to believe, e.g.,
"There I was, upside bloody down, with damn all on the clock
and the tail going bonk bonk bonk on the deck".

I have selected some of the more printable 'lines' for an appendix but the following series reached a level of poetic quality which justifies their inclusion here.
From the Cottage Line Book October/November 1943
As an answer to Patience Strong's "Quiet Corner" on "First Quarter" which started:
"The new moon sails into the sky..." Robin Hooper wrote:

    "LAST QUARTER"
    by Chastity Weeke
    The moon is sinking in the sky,
    We know we've damn well got to fly
    Or get into a fearful mess
    With SOE or SIS.
    The messages come thick and fast,
    "We've got a field for you at last,
    So come tonight and try your luck",
    "The farmer wants to spread his muck".
    With compass courses all to cock,
    With nothing showing on the clock,
    With Joes announcing near and far,
    "Des projecteurs! La DCA!!
    We dice through twenty-tenths of shit
    And no one seems to care a bit.

When he saw that Jimmy Langley retorted as follows (misquoted from memory in his book *Fight Another Day*):

"THE LAST QUARTER"

The moon is dying in the sky
And still you b...s will not fly.
Messages of dire despair,
Are pouring in from everywhere.
Zou-Zou wants 'un nouveau poste'
Without two million 'Coco's lost'.
Pierre says: "I'm on the run
Followed by a dozen Hun".
To the eternal question: "Why
Can't you fellows make one try?"
Comes the answer: "Do not fret,
It all depends upon the Met".
I'd like to see you tell a Joe
(In French) why you would not go.
(Signed) J.R. Langley
11/XI/43

The third poetic 'line' - again by Robin Hooper - reads:

"AS OTHERS SEE US"

"I'm the skipper of a Lizzie
And I'm feeling pretty swell
For the bottom tank's full of Chanel Cinq
And the back, of best Martell.
"I'm the skipper of a Lizzie
My Joes roll up in cars
And with glee they shout, as I hand them out
Their coffee and cigars.
"So Vive la France, and Up Free Trade
And long may it last, I hopes!
For watches (Swiss) are a piece of cake (?)
For a chap who knows the ropes".
Chastity Weeke

Bob Hodges

CHAPTER TWELVE

Robin Hooper in France

On 15th November Francis Cammaerts, travelling alone, took the train to Angers. He was met outside the station by a tall dark man whom he had met with Déricourt in Paris when making arrangements for his flight to England[1]. This was Rémy Clément. With one other passenger and three more of Déricourt's *équipe du terrain* the six of them bicycled the dozen or so kilometres to the field. Here he discovered that there were at least eight more passengers, who had all approached the vast meadow in small parties and were now spread out round it. Among them was François Mitterrand, future President of France. He was the leader of the National Movement of Prisoners of War.

Cammaerts had met Henri Déricourt in Paris while arranging this rendezvous, and had said something about arrangements for sending documents to London. Déricourt looked him straight in the eye and said: "After this operation you must never meet me again".

Bob Hodges, navigated by Wagland, was flying a Hudson towards them with five or six passengers on board including Jean Manesson, Paul Pardi and Maugenet[2].

The only comment on this operation in the 161 Squadron official records - apart from the number of passengers each way and its code-name and location - was: "Reception Committee excellent. Field reasonably hard". Francis Cammaerts remembers that: "The Déricourt operation was very smooth, although cattle had to be chased off. The Hudson was overloaded and we had to move up forward for take off."

According to Cookridge[3], 'Maugenet' was captured on arrival on the night of 15/16 November. The Germans knew about his arrival in advance because they were successfully working Frank Pickersgill's set, since Baker Street did not yet know of his capture. Cookridge refers to 'Maugenet's' arrival "by Lysander" but other evidence seems conclusive that he was on this Hudson. This would be one possible explanation of the reported fact that Kieffer (the Sicherheitsdienst leader) was watching this pick-up from a discreet distance. According to Cookridge it was 'Maugenet's' capture and substitution by an English-speaking French agent working for the Germans that led to the capture of Diana Rowden, who had arrived by Lysander on 16/17 June, and John Young and their eventual executions.

On 15/16 November, in spite of very poor visibility, Bathgate and McBride pulled off 'Water Pistol' near Vibrac in the Angoulême area. They landed four and brought back eight - yet another overload. Charles Franc was in charge of the team and the operation officer was Guy Chaumet. The passengers landed included: Claude Bonnier who was Military Delegate of Region B, and who was to take his lethal cyanide pill after his arrest on 9th February 1944; and André Charlot, an air operations officer.

The homeward bound passengers included Léon Nautin, who had been assistant to Eugène Bornier and half-a-dozen British and Canadian aircrews who had been on the run. They had been sheltered since the first attempt at 'Water Pistol', a month before, by Charles Franc at this farm near Malaville. One of them had a lung infection and was cleared for the flight by a doctor the day before. He was brought to the Lysander on a stretcher and did not reach the United Kingdom alive[4].

McCairns' operation 'Tommy-Gun' on 15/16 November was a short trip, only 2 hours 40 minutes away from base, to Canettemont near Frévent in the Arras/Abbeville area. He had two passengers to deliver and three to collect. The operation officer on the ground was Pierre Deshayes, of the *Voix du Nord* Newspaper in Lille. 'Tommy-Gun' was a 'Crossbow' top priority operation. 'Crossbow' referred to the rocket preparations made by the Germans and particularly to the concrete rocket sites on the French coast. Any agent who could supply information on this subject was urgently in demand. So when Mac was awarded a five-star 'Crossbow' operation he knew he was going for something big.

Air Ministry explained that an operator who had been trained over 18 months before, but had not yet done an operation, had what seemed to be an excellent field near Fécamp. It was only about 20 miles inland of the flak-covered French coast, less than five miles from the well-protected rocket sites, and three miles from the barracks of some 2,000 Huns. Squadron Leader Forest ('Tommy') Yeo-Thomas, GC, had now sufficient detailed information about these sites to make his withdrawal highly advantageous. Mac's last briefing was that on no account was he to take off from the field with information only; conscious or otherwise, Yeo-Thomas was to be brought out in the back.

The weather was not considered practical for such a sortie, and at 8 pm, after Mac had been in acute suspense for hours, the Wing Commander cancelled the operation. Mac now felt so disappointed that he pleaded to be allowed to go and do a weather reconnaissance. One chance in a hundred might be open and base was going to remain clear all night. After some hesitation this was agreed and we hurriedly remounted the operation.

Mac felt nervous and shaky as he climbed into his Lysander that night. The black, cloud-covered sky looked ominous and he knew that once again his aircraft would be on her own in the night skies. At least he had the satisfaction of knowing that he had nothing to fear from German night fighters. As he nosed his way slowly across the Channel, the clouds came lower and lower, until they were only about 500 feet above the water.

On the well defended coast of the Pas de Calais, Mac had to go in exactly on the dot; he could not afford to be even one mile out. After an hour of suspense, the sands of the French coast showed up in front, but Mac had no idea where he was. Praying that there were no E-boats lying off the coast, he turned sharply to port and flew parallel to the beach, waiting for signs of an estuary. In time it appeared, but, as there were several round this part of the coast, he flew on until he struck the main promontory, when he knew that his first guess had been correct. He returned to the original point of entry and went in over the coast defences at the ridiculous height of 500 feet. Not a gun opened up, and within 10 minutes he had struck the little town which was his last landmark.

The field should be three minutes away, and in less than two minutes a powerful beam flashed the letter 'X'. Pierre Deshayes definitely had the right ideas about torches; his was like a miniature searchlight. The weather had improved in the last 10 miles, and Mac was able to see the outlines of the field, which looked remarkably small.

Once the lamps were turned on, he went down and touched at 'A'. Then, almost as soon as he had passed 'B', he noticed that the colour of the ground ahead changed considerably. Instinct told him that this meant rough ploughed land, and he squeezed the brake lever as hard as possible, making the Lysander almost stand up on its nose. He skidded to a halt not more than five yards from the end of the grassland, went back to the waiting reception, and Tommy came up to speak to him.

"Nice work", he said in English. "It was pouring with rain here thirty minutes ago. You have about 300 yards in front of you for take-off. I am returning with you".

"Yeo-Thomas?" Mac asked.

"That's me" was the reply.

After take-off Mac was able to talk to Tommy over the inter-communication and give a running commentary on their progress. Tommy told him how he and the reception party had arrived with a hearse as part of a funeral procession[5]. In any case, he added, they had nothing to fear on the field: over 50 of the Maquis were guarding the approaches.

It was useless to try to climb through the black, icy cloud, so, trusting to luck and map-reading as he had never done before, Mac managed to guide the Lysander out of France on the exact route he had used coming in with no sign of opposition. Less than an hour later, they were back at Tangmere[6]. Yeo-Thomas's dramatic appearance was welcomed by everyone. For all his light-hearted and apparently care-free manner, he was privately determined to obtain an interview with the Prime Minister himself. He had to tell Winston Churchill exactly why the French resistance should have more aircraft to deliver arms and supplies. This interview took some weeks to arrange[7].

Michel Pichard wrote for me the following note about this operation.

"Yeo-Thomas was to be picked up with Claude Bouchinet-Serreulles ('Sophie') and myself. I got to Arras around the 11th, with my secretary Bel-A (actually my sister Cécile, whom we called Jacqueline, now Jacqueline de Marcilly as she kept that Christian name) in case there would be room for her; she had worked with me since January and was 'blown'.

On November 12th or 13th I rushed back to Paris after hearing that eight BOA (*Bureau d'Opérations Aériennes*) agents had been arrested at café Dupont, Versailles. Six of them belonged to BOA 'P', one to BOA 'M' (Fanette) and one to BOA National which I had been running since Kim had left in September. Hence, the situation was quite alarming and I decided to stay.

Serreulles, disregarding London's instructions, did not show up: so, this left two 'seats' available, and Yeo-Thomas flew back with Mademoiselle Virolle (his *agent de liaison*) and Mademoiselle Pichard".

On the following night, 16/17 November 1943, our astonishing run of luck, which had been unbroken for 15 months, was suddenly interrupted. During this time - although many operations had not been completed - we had not lost a single aircraft or pilot. Robin Hooper, who was earmarked to take over A Flight from me at the end of the moon period, failed to return. We heard later that his Lysander was so badly bogged in mud that it had to be destroyed but that he was in good hands. I am grateful to Sir Robin Hooper for permission to tell his story in his own words:

"On the night of the 16/17 November 1943 I took off from Tangmere on operation 'Scenery'. The weather was very much better than it had been the night before, when we had attempted the operation in low cloud and had been forced to turn back by icing conditions down to the deck. The outward trip was completely uneventful. We were on track the entire way from Cabourg down to Montsoreau on the Loire, every landmark on that fairly familiar 'milk-run' showing up at the expected time. The sky cleared and the moon came right out, south of the Loire, and Châtellerault and Parthenay showed up beautifully. I turned east just south of Parthenay and saw the reception signalling at me from at least two miles away. There were drifts of ground-mist lying over the field. Although the lights were intermittently visible, the mist was surprisingly thick, white and milky when one descended into it. However, I had had what I looked on as rather a succession of unsuccessful ops: the photograph had shown at least 1,000 metres run in the direction in which the flarepath was laid; and the agents had assured us that the ground was "very hard" - anyway I decided to go in. After two unsuccessful attempts I got down off a very tight low circuit (even for a Lizzie!) dropping in rather fast and rather late through the mist. I soon realised that the ground was very soft indeed - softer than it had been on 'Oriel' a few nights before when I had landed and - to their great disgust - ordered the others not to do so. At first, when I braked, the wheels just locked and slid; but very soon it was a question of using quite a lot of throttle to keep moving at all - and it seemed best to keep moving at all costs. Turning was all but impossible since the wheels dug into deep grooves. Finally we managed to turn 90° to port and there stuck. The aircraft was immovable even with +6 boost so I told the passengers to get out and got down myself to inspect. We were bogged to spat-level; the ground appeared to be wet, soggy water meadow. The reception committee came running up: I organised them to push and we attempted some more + 6 boost without the slightest effect except perhaps to settle the wheels a little more firmly in their ruts. 'Georges', the operator (a Belgian agent, Jean Depraetere) was in a great state of nerves and it was Albert, his second-in-command, (who had been failed on the Lizzie course for over-impetuosity), who really took charge.

At this point someone suggested getting some bullocks from the nearest farm; after a certain amount of fuss this was agreed to and a small well-armed party set off to collect bullocks, spades and some planks or brushwood - (my idea, as far as I remember). The rest of us continued to dig trenches in front of the wheels with the idea of making a kind of inclined plane up which they could be pulled. About 20 minutes later an odd procession loomed up out of the mist; two very large bullocks, trailing clanking chains, the farmer, Monsieur Fournier, his wife, his two daughters and the three chaps from the reception committee. The farmer shook me warmly by the hand, asked me when the British were going to land in France, and got to work. He hitched the bullocks (Fridolin and Julot by name) to the legs of the undercarriage, and we all heaved. Nothing whatever happened. Two more (anonymous) bullocks were fetched; we continued to dig; but the best result we ever got was to pivot one wheel round the other. This of course had no effect beyond making a large hole round the stationary wheel which stuck even more firmly. This must have gone on for about two hours. Why we weren't arrested ten times over I have no idea, except that the nearest Boche was at least ten miles away and the local gendarmerie had more sense than to poke their nose into things which were no concern of theirs. Finally, we realised that it was getting late and that we had not a hope of digging the aircraft out. We decided to abandon the struggle.

'Georges' burst into tears on my shoulder. I patted him on the back, said "there, there." "Allons, voyons mon vieux" and generally tried to convey the impression that mucking around in several inches of mud, some hundreds of miles inside enemy territory, with a bogged Lysander, four bullocks and thirteen excited Belgians and Frenchmen was an experience that any officer of the Royal Air Force would take in his stride. I got out my parachute, pulled it, piled all my secret papers on top, and then, with the greatest reluctance, started hacking holes in the petrol and oil tanks of poor

'D for Dog' - in which I had done all my trips and which no one else had ever flown on ops. The petrol spurted out of the bottom tank and soaked my trousers, so I thought it prudent to get Victor to apply the match. The aircraft burnt well, but as the fog was really thick by now the fire can only have been visible from any distance as a diffused glow. We ran (in my case at a very steady beagling pace indeed) to the car and piled in - nine people encumbered with suitcases, sten-guns, pigeons, pistols and what-not in a small Citroën designed to hold at the most five. This car, the property of the Ponts et Chaussées, played a great part in our lives. It was explained to me on the way that the party had meant to "borrow" the Préfet's car, but that it had run into a level-crossing barrier on another illegal expedition.

We drove rather slowly home - at one point past a German aerodrome, which shook me a little. Gradually we shed most of the party at their various homes or hide-outs, and at last it was our turn. As we relieved nature in a ditch beside the road, Albert explained that he was taking me and the agent who should have left with me to stay in the farmhouse where he himself lived. This was in the village of Chauray, near Niort. We picked up our various burdens, walking as quietly as we could to avoid waking the village watch-dogs.

The family were surprised to see Jean Weber (the would-be passenger to England) again, and amazed to see me; but they took it very well, made up an extra bed in the spare room, and gave us an enormous, oddly assorted meal which included red wine, pig's liver pâté, cheese and cake. In spite of this I went to bed and slept almost continuously for 36 hours, waking only to eat and drink. Meanwhile (I have been told since) the flap on both sides of the Channel was considerable, as well it might be, seeing that the flight had not had a casualty for eighteen months. Tangmere even laid on a dawn fighter patrol, in case I had been delayed and was coming out in daylight.

After the war: the Ponts et Chaussées Citroën which had transported Robin during the war, with his wife, Constance.

'Georges' sent off a very penitent signal, saying that we were safe, and ending *"Ne me considère plus de votre confiance"*. This relieved the strain at home a bit. My pigeon, which we despatched in the course of the morning, never made it - a pity, as I had rather enjoyed composing the message.

The Germans took the whole affair most seriously. They clamped pretty thoroughly over a radius of about 100 miles, putting extra Gestapo and uniformed police in all the major stations, and patrolling all main roads. They searched the landing-ground for me or my remains, prodding with Prussian thoroughness behind every bush. They brought a lorry to fetch away the burnt wreckage of 'D for Dog'. To the delight of the village of Périgné, the lorry got bogged as well. They grilled the farmer who had helped us, but he stuck stubbornly to the story we had told him to tell - that those "terrorists" had forced him at pistol point to bring out his bullocks. In the end, they let him go. After four or five days the excitement died down and Jean was able to go back to the North where his work was.

Wonderful stories ran round the countryside. The baker told us that an English aeroplane had landed and bogged, and that the crew had got out, mounted motor-bicycles which they had brought with them, and ridden away. The butcher's version was that we had wirelessed for another aircraft. This had arrived within a quarter of an hour - at, one can only presume, a cruising speed of about 800 mph - landed, and taken us home. But the best story of all was that of the two gendarmes. They came to the house, to everyone's dismay, the day after I arrived. After a glass of eau-de-vie the larger gendarme began to ask questions. Any trouble round here lately? No, André Bellot hastened to assure them; it had never been so quiet. Monsieur Bellot was quite sure? But of course - Funny - everyone else had been complaining about their rabbits being stolen... The smaller gendarme looked at his watch. A quarter past twelve. Someone in the town had been saying that Marshal Pétain had resigned: what about listening to the BBC and finding out whether it was true? The BBC was turned on: another round went its way, and the gendarmes departed in an atmosphere of amity and alcohol.

I am now settled down to a curious, suspended-animation existence. The intention was originally to lay on another operation on the organisation's other ground in Normandy. This fell through, as the ground was found to be unusable through rain, cold feet on the part of the farmer, ploughing, and a new line of telegraph poles. London signalled us the pinpoints of two other grounds some distance away, but both proved to be too wet. All this was moderately depressing. Time crept on, and we still hadn't got a ground: but materially speaking, life could hardly have been better, apart from the lack of fresh air and exercise. I was generally called at about 10 am with a large bowl of (ersatz) café-au-lait, several slices of excellent brioche and lashings of honey. Lunch was at about 1.30, after the family had finished. It generally consisted of some form of pâté, always one kind of meat and often two, fruit, cheese, red wine and more ersatz coffee - black this time. Practically everything we ate was produced on the farm - including the "coffee", which was grilled wheat and barley mixed with a little "mélange national". "Mélange national", which was heavily rationed, was alleged on the label to contain 10% of genuine coffee - the rest being chicory, cereals and various anonymous substitutes - perhaps acorns: so the pound tin of the real stuff I had brought with me went down very well. Meals were sometimes a bit of an effort, as Madame Bellot insisted on giving me huge quantities of the best of everything, and made no allowances for the fact that I practically never moved from the house. If

I left anything, "*Ah, c'est que vous ne le trouvez pas bon*", she would say. If, on the other hand, I ate a lot, I got twice as much the next time. A tricky situation, calling for much diplomacy. Supper, the only meal I could take downstairs with the family, was on a similar scale.

Life was complicated by the fact that the farmhouse was in a village. The village had accepted Albert as an evacuee from Paris, or possibly as a dodger of the "relève", ie conscription for work in Germany. It had also made up its mind that he was Jacqueline Bellot's fiancé. Since he had a wife and two children in Belgium this used to cause a good deal of good clean fun in the household. Casual visitors like Jean passed without much comment, but a new resident would have been noticed at once. I therefore didn't go out before dark on week-days and only showed myself on Sundays, when I might reasonably be presumed to be on a visit. Not that anyone was likely to give me away intentionally: but sooner or later, someone would inevitably have talked and my hosts would have been "for it". We got quite a laugh one day out of an announcement in the local paper that several people had been shot for having sheltered Allied airmen, "in hopes of a reward which they did not receive". Nor did I appear downstairs by day. The Bellots employed as a general labourer a small boy who had his meals with the family, and it was thought unwise to overstrain his discretion. Any move outside the front door thus became a party, and the complete absence of any sanitary arrangements at all - even the conventional privy- was almost compensated for by the fact that the alternative was a walk at least as far as the nearest haystack.

One night we went out poaching for partridges. The technique is, one hopes, peculiar to France. All you need is an acetylene lamp, a large net on the end of a pole, and a game-bag. You light the lamp and beat up and down a large field. When you come to a sleeping covey of partridges, you keep the lamp on them, thus dazzling them and preventing them from taking off, and bang down the net. Monsieur Bellot operated the net, his son René held the lamp, and I had the game-bag. Albert hovered uneasily in the background with an automatic, in case the gendarmes were out for poachers. We later heard that they were, and had caught Madame Bellot's nephew doing exactly the same thing a few miles away. Our bag was eight and a half brace.

Another minor excitement was a bicycle ride in search of a ground. The ground was a dud, but the ride was fun. We didn't see a single Boche - in fact the only representatives of authority we saw in 10 miles were two elderly "*gardes-champêtres*" to whom we politely raised our berets. I was then less used to moving round France than I became later, and I am sorry to say that when a complete stranger asked us to lend him a bicycle pump, I pushed on, leaving Albert and René Bellot to cope.

A few days later 'Georges', Albert and Louis Michaud came in in high spirits. They thought they had really got something in the way of a ground. Louis (Petit-Louis) was an altogether remarkable person. The garage foreman of the Ponts et Chaussées, he knew the department - in which he had been born and bred - inside out: he knew exactly where to go for forged papers, ration-cards or a hide-out for an agent. Best of all, his job gave him the use of a car (the famous Citroën) and a cast iron excuse for going almost anywhere. He probably ran more risks than any of us. As a local boy he was working under his own name, and was known to everyone. His boss, who was the complete "attentiste", had a very good idea of what he was doing. The dangerous position of a "contact man" between an organisation and the uninitiated public needs no explanation. He had a mother and a sister in the neighbourhood, and lived with his wife and two children. Yet I never saw him other than cheerful - in fact he was one of the most consistently entertaining people I have ever met.

The car arrived next day to pick me up and take me to see this ground. As we drove through the town, 'Georges' nudged me. "Those are your first, aren't they?", he said. They were. Two large resplendent German officers, walking along the opposite pavement. It was a curious thought that these were the first Germans I had seen in the flesh in over three years' of fairly active service. We drove through the village where the prang had taken place. We thought of visiting the field, but to my mind it savoured rather of the murderer who hangs around the scene of the crime. Besides, time was short and we had a long way to go. The fields, when we got to them, were completely hopeless. Approaches obstructed, dimensions too small, and surfaces doubtful to say the least of it. I began to realise that although there was no lack of good will, it was amazing that 'Georges' had had only one accident. It was a delicate matter to turn the grounds down without showing that I thought I had been driven a 100 miles for no good reason at all. It was a bitter disappointment all round. We got home tired out, soaked to the skin, and thoroughly depressed. In the evening we discussed the possibilities of a sea operation, which they thought would take two or three months to lay on.

All this time the moon was getting nearer and nearer, and we still hadn't a ground. SOE offered to give me a seat on an op near Lyons, but it seemed a long and risky journey across the demarcation line, which was still operative, and after much consideration we refused. Time got shorter, but in the end Petit-Louis and one of his colleagues told us that this time they really were on to a good thing. I didn't dare to believe them, but rather sceptically prepared for another outing in the Citroën. We drove off and arrived at our destination with only one puncture in 40 miles. To my amazement, it really was a practicable ground; rather short, but with perfect approaches and a good surface. We measured it out, making great play with a theodolite and various coloured poles, the property of the French state, and returned to town.

The occasion was celebrated by an enormous black market lunch at an hotel. The menu in the front room was vegetable soup and boiled swedes; we boys in the back room were given oysters, partridge, beefsteak, chocolate cream and three kinds of cheese - all excellent. The drinks were a Chablis for our oysters - burgundy, a very good brandy. Afterwards, 'Georges' and I went shopping. In a bookshop I bought a supply of books, of which I was getting rather short, and a diary. I also had a little quiet fun and made 'Georges' giggle by ostentatiously reading a volume entitled in huge letters "LES ANGLAIS SONT-ILS NOS AMIS?" Walking round the town, l was most impressed by the deterioration in the physique, bearing, and clothing of the German troops. It was obviously very much of a back area; but even so, their scruffiness was remarkable. Three soldiers came out of the 'Monoprix' as we passed it. They looked 16, and may have been an under-nourished 18. Their overcoats, far too big for them, were faded and frayed, with threads dangling down from the hems. An encouraging declension for the 'supermen' of 1940. There were a lot of fairly old gentlemen about, too, though I must admit that there was also a sprinkling of obviously A1 men, perhaps from the field army or units resting after a spell in Russia. We went back to coffee with Petit-Louis and his family - the two small daughters showed me their toys and picture-books, while Petit-Louis and 'Georges' typed out lists of troops and train movements to put in the next 'courier'. It was an odd little party: three agents: Petit-Louis' sister, whose husband had escaped from a German prison-camp, had made his way home, and now had to live in hiding, without papers or ration-cards, and unable to do anything for his wife and child: Petit-Louis' mother and myself. Every now and then a heavy step would go by outside, and someone would perhaps say, quite unemotionally, "*C'est un Boche*". Still there was a noticeable tenseness when anyone knocked on the door downstairs. Albert and I cycled home. The moon was getting quite high. I was silly enough to fiddle with the 10-speed gear on my very French, very sporting bike, which caused a certain amount of trouble.

Life became a good deal more hopeful from then on, though it was still not without its excitements. We had a long-distance wrangle with the Air Ministry, who thought the description of our ground not all it might be - as indeed it wasn't at first. The weather was consistently bad either in England or with us, and we were terrified that our ground would be too soft. Day after day we received the "not coming" signal, and Jean, who had returned by this time and whose third moon of waiting this was, began to get rather low. One night Albert came home very late, pale, garrulous from delayed shock, and thoroughly shaken. He had been bicycling out to a farm to make a wireless contact when he suddenly saw all traffic stopped in front of him - two German Feldgendarms were examining everything on the road. Turning back would have excited their suspicions at once. There was nothing for it but to go through and hope for the best. The Feldgendarms looked at his papers: then one of them tapped the panniers over the back wheel in which he had his wireless set. "What have you got in there?" - "Milk for my children", said Albert. "OK - move on". "*Il a loupé sa Croix de Fer, celui-là*", was Albert's comment. A minor excitement was the discovery, another day, that he had quite unintentionally won 600 francs in the Loterie Nationale. (He couldn't claim them, as his papers were not in order)"

The rest of Robin Hooper's story is quoted in Chapter 13.

In her book[8] *Résistance,* Françoise Bruneau refers to the bogged Lysander having to be burnt. She says that the reception was by a Franco-Belgian intelligence network called Delbo-Phénix and that Marcel Pairault hid the pilot at his home at Celle-sur-Belle, near Melle, ESE of Niort. Delbo-Phénix worked closely with a similar réseau called Zero-France.

On that same night of 16/17 November 1943 three other Lysanders were out over France. Stephen Hankey attempted 'Gitane' near Vierzon, but abandoned the operation when he found the cloud base "down to the ground" when 15 miles inland over France. The other two were flown by McCairns and myself in a double pick-up 'Magdalen II', east of Compiègne. We landed two Canadians, Ray Labrosse and Lucien Dumais, who had themselves escaped from France and were now to set up the Shelburne escape line from Paris to a beach near Plouha in Brittany. We picked up three USAF and two RAF aircrew. Our sixth passenger home was Capitaine Commandant Aviateur

Jean Depraetere, or 'Georges', or 'Taylor'.

Dominique Potier of the 'Possum' organisation. Working for MI 9, he had laid the flarepath with Count Georges d'Oultremont. A month later Potier was to parachute back, only to be betrayed and arrested by the Germans at the end of December 1943. During his ferocious interrogation he was terribly tortured without saying anything. After they had gouged out one of his eyes, he killed himself by jumping from the second floor of Fresnes prison[9].

Both Mac and I had come to the end of our last moon-period. Our operational tours were ended. Mac went off to the Air Ministry, AI 2c, the department in Air Intelligence which supervised all clandestine air operations on behalf of the Royal Air Force.

Mac's story of our last operation is as follows:

"I had sent in a damning report of an operator whose poor lights had nearly caused me to crash. His section, who were dealing mainly with evaders and POWs, took this very much to heart and requested that we should mount another operation to bring five escapees and the chief out. He could then be given a refresher course and be sent back to continue his job.

"I was against working with him again, but as the moon was nearly over, it represented my last chance of attaining the 25 mark; so, reluctantly, I agreed to go out with Hugh on a double. Once again the weather was bad, and we scudded into France almost at deck level.

"Both of us reached the vicinity of the field at the same time, but there was no sign of a signal. Eventually, after we had wasted some ten minutes searching the neighbourhood, Hugh spotted the faint glimmer of the signal torch and went in to land.

"As he took off again he flashed his navigation lights and with their aid I was able to locate the still dimly-lit flarepath. Fortunately the landing presented no difficulty, and with the erring operator in the back, I hurried home.

"With 25 landings to my credit, (concluded Mac) my tour as a special mission pilot was over. Now I was to sit in London and only come down to Tangmere to watch others as they went out to baffle the Gestapo."

Audrey and I had rented a small furnished cottage in Crocker Hill, a village near Tangmere, for a few weeks - in spite of all the arguments against wives being too close to their husbands' operational base. It belonged to a naval officer who had blackened the low beams with shiny pitch. The wooden surround to the fire-place was similarly treated and became tacky with the heat of the fire. One had to be careful not to lean against it. I had not had much time to be in this cottage but I was to spend a few days in it after the end of the moon period.

The end of my tour of operations released the tension on the spring which I had kept more tightly wound up than I had realised. I suddenly collapsed and was good for nothing but staying in bed for the best part of a week. A medical check-up revealed that I was totally exhausted. Bob Hodges' decision that I needed a rest was more true than I had believed possible. From 6th to 16th November we had laid on operations on eight nights out of eleven. I had myself flown on five of these nights and been responsible until pilots were safely landed and debriefed on all eight. Apart from the nervous tension - which one did not notice at the time - this routine left us all very short of ordinary sleep.

I soon recovered and went to my new job in Baker Street at the Headquarters of SOE

(Special Operations Executive). I was to be ALO (Air Liaison - Operations), in charge of the laying on of all SOE air operations from Great Britain to Western Europe and Scandinavia, both parachuting and pick-ups. As an acting Wing Commander, at the age of 25, I was rather pleased with myself — far too pleased with myself, no doubt. However, I often think how sad it is that peace time does not often offer young people opportunities to do responsible jobs which war proved they could do perfectly well.

CHAPTER THIRTEEN

A Bad Winter

The luck of 'A' Flight 161 Squadron ran right out in December 1943. Of seven Lysander sorties attempted only one was a success. Of four operational Lysander pilots (excluding Wg Cdr Hodges, the Squadron Commander) three were killed. No Hudson pick-ups were attempted. There was one bit of good news: Flight Lieutenant Robin Hooper, the new Flight Commander, returned safely from France on 17th December, exactly one month after being stuck there in the mud. On the 21st he was promoted to acting squadron leader.

On the night of 10/11 December, in weather which proved to be bad and getting worse, three Lysanders were out. Stephen Hankey tried to find the field in the Compiègne area for operation 'Snowdrop', got well off track and was shot at over Creil airfield. He found the weather impossible and came home. The other two were Flying Officers Bathgate and McBride on a double called 'Sten' near Vervins in the area of Laon. McBride found the weather getting worse and pin-points increasingly difficult to find. He could not make any radio contact with Bathgate and had to abandon the operation and return. Bathgate did not return and there was no news of him until June 1944. Then the Air Ministry were informed that NZ Flg Off J.R.G. Bathgate had been shot down on the 11th December 1943 and buried in the World War One British Cemetery at Berry-au-Bac, near the German night-fighter base at Juvincourt and on the N44 between Laon and Reims. One of his passengers, 'Moreau', was buried with Bathgate. His real name may have been Emile Cossoneau, a Communist Député. The other passenger killed with Bathgate was Captain Claudius Four ('Berrier') who had been Schmidt's assistant.

The party on the ground had a bad night too. I have the following note from Michel Pichard ('Oyster'), quoted verbatim in his own excellent English:
"The operation officer was Pierre (Deshayes). Home passengers were Brossolette, myself, Christian Longetti (from *Bureau d'Opérations Aériennes Est*) and (hopefully) six allied crew men. The field name was 'Farman'.
We all stayed for a couple of days in Vervins. Our hosts were M. and Madame Brimboeuf. This was a rough night for us too. We left Vervins around 10.30 pm, and around midnight Dr Mairesse arrived on the field to announce that the Germans had started raiding numerous homes in Vervins, including that of M. Brimboeuf. The guard around the field was immediately reinforced and we waited all night in rather bad weather.
At dawn, as the team members could not go back to Vervins, most of us headed for Laon (where we left a lot of machine guns in a friendly home).
I then drove to St Quentin with Brossolette and we took a train back to Paris. We heard two days later that one of the planes had been shot down at Berry-au-Bac - (Aisne) - the pilot and two passengers (including 'Berrier', coming back as 'Duc', operation officer) had been killed.
The raids in Vervins were not actually aimed at operation 'Sten'. They were part of 1,000 raids conducted that same night through the five northern *départements* as a result of the 'Farjon' case. Roland Farjon (of OCM), arrested a few days earlier, was accused after the war of having been "turned over" by the Gestapo and of having given them an enormous list of names. Farjon (who escaped from jail in the spring) is

said to have committed suicide after being indicted after the war. The story was that he blew up a hand grenade in his face and fell into the Seine. (I believe it was from Pont Mirabeau.) People from the north still insist that the body found in the Seine was one inch too short, while the face could not be identified, of course."

Pierre Deshayes told me part of the tragic sequel. When the Brimboeuf's house was raided they were caught red-handed. His wife had laid the table for about 12 people as they were also expecting parachutists and all the signalling lamps were there. Both the Brimboeufs were tortured until they died without releasing any information.

"After this", continued Michel Pichard, "Brossolette decided to go and join Bollaert who was expecting a pick-up in Saône and Loire. I chose to join Clouet - who was expecting a pick-up on the 'Gide' field at Rivarennes. Both operations did not go on.
In January, we all got back to Rivarennes and waited for over ten days. Weather was good in France, but bad in England. Nothing happened.
Through my father (André Pichard, alias 'Amphitrite' of CND) I had arranged to leave by sea at the end of January. But more trouble developed in BOA Est, and I decided to stay in France. Brossolette then asked me to give him that contact and this is how Brossolette and Bollaert got to Loctudy (Britanny) on January 28th, embarked on 'Jouet des Flots' and were captured the next day when this fishing boat ran aground on Ras-de-Sein."

Jacques Maillet who was with them, told me that this shipwreck was on 4/5 February 1944. He managed to escape. The French had paid a high price for our inability to do any pick-ups during the January moon.

On 15/16 December Bob Hodges attempted operation 'Scenery II' in a Lysander which had been fitted with an experimental Gee installation. Gee was a radio navigation aid which had proved invaluable in bigger aircraft normally navigated by a separate navigator. It depended on overlapping lattices of curves from chains of ground stations. The story is best told in Bob's own words, which he wrote in 1975.
"Robin Hooper came to grief in November 1943, having got bogged in landing his Lysander.
This was Operation 'Scenery I'. Through the ground organisation we got messages back and he went into hiding. He was down in the South West.
By the time we had all the details it was too late in the moon period to mount a rescue operation and we had to wait until the following month to lay on 'Scenery II' to pick him up.
I decided to do this job myself and had the idea of fitting a Gee set in the Lysander (radar navigational aid) and taking a navigator with us to give us the maximum chance of success. Flying at low altitude, the Gee would give us cover at least to the Loire and this could be very valuable in bad weather and success was most important. I can remember Mouse Fielden saying: "be careful, we don't want to have to lay on a 'Scenery III'."

We used the period before the next moon to perfect the modifications to the Lysander installing the Gee set and to carry out trials. Wagland my navigator flew with me. All went well and we were ready for the next moon.

Our first attempt was on 15/16 December 1943. We took off from Tangmere and followed our usual route but soon found that the Gee set was giving us large compass fluctuations which had not been apparent during trials, and then between the Normandy coast and the Loire we ran into foul weather and very low cloud and were forced to return to base.

This was a great disappointment but the necessary messages were sent out via the BBC Messages to France for the following night and we made another attempt. I note from my log book that I was flying a different aircraft this time, so we clearly abandoned the Gee set but nevertheless had Squadron Leader Wagland with me to help with the map-reading and give us the maximum chance.

The weather forecast was good over the continent; the only worry was the possibility of fog forming over Southern England on return. We therefore took off as early as possible, bearing in mind the moon, which I seem to remember was just about full at that time, so that we could be back around midnight and beat the fog. The time for the round flight recorded in my log book was 4.45. There were two other Lysanders out that night - Hankey and McBride.

To resume my story, we took off around 8 pm and all went well this time. We crossed the French coast with the usual amount of flak which didn't worry us and was some distance away. We crossed the Loire near Saumur and headed south to Poitiers. The field was further to the south, between Poitiers and Angoulême and we were able to find a small town we had selected as our last geographical pinpoint before setting course on a timed run to the position of the field.

The night was perfect - excellent visibility and bright moon and all seemed quiet on the ground. We set off on our run to the target and at the appointed time I started flashing the morse signal letters on my downward identification light but got no response and saw nothing although details on the grounds were very clear and we could see individual fields outlined in the bright moon.

I circled for a few moments and then I spotted the headlights of a car approaching down the road beneath us. The car suddenly turned off into a field and I could see people running in all directions. Within a few seconds the recognition signals were being flashed and the landing torches were switched on and I got ready to land. I was circling at about 200 feet at the time and in a minute or so I was on the ground in a good smooth stubble field.

I turned and taxied back to No 1 torch and turned again into the wind. Wagland told me over the intercom that Robin Hooper was aboard plus one other passenger and we were airborne again in a minute or so. Everything went like clockwork and it transpired that we were not expected so early - hence the last minute arrival of the ground party.

Now for the return flight to Tangmere. All was well over France. A trouble-free flight until we approached the English coast and I could see a bank of low cloud ahead. Tangmere advised us over the radio that visibility was deteriorating and the cloud base was 500 feet. On arrival overhead Tangmere we were flying in bright moon with a marvellous horizon and visibility above the cloud bank but the landing was going to be tricky.

Tangmere advised that they would bring me down through the cloud for a ZZ landing, which was the instrument approach system in those days for airfields not equipped with SBA (standard beam approach). In any case, we had no SBA in the Lysander - just a VHF radio-telephone set.

The cloud top was about 1,500 feet and we were directed by the controller on the outbound heading and eventually turned onto the direction of the runway for landing at about five miles from the airfield.

We entered cloud and descended on instruments maintaining a rate of descent and height as directed. At about 300 feet we came out beneath the cloud and I saw the runway lights immediately ahead and we were able to carry out a visual landing in very misty conditions. We were indeed fortunate to have returned in time.

We were all highly elated to have pulled off the rescue operation and I was most relieved to have got back when we did as fog was descending rapidly.

I went to the control tower to check on the other two Lysanders and they were already in R/T contact on their return flight over the Channel. Visibility was going down every minute and fog was imminent. Met reported similar conditions all over the South of England and the nearest diversion with any hope of an improvement was Woodbridge in Suffolk where a FIDO was available. Our Lysanders, however, simply hadn't got the fuel and they would have to attempt a landing at Tangmere or nearby.

Under normal circumstances in a situation such as this, I would have had no hesitation in ordering the pilots to bale out, but in this situation it was out of the question as they had passengers on board - agents they had picked up in France - and they didn't have parachutes.

There was no alternative but for them both to attempt a landing albeit in conditions of very low visibility. Both aircraft were due overhead at about the same time and therefore I decided to take one at Tangmere (McBride) and the other (Hankey) at Ford, the neighbouring Naval airfield. I waited in the control tower alongside the controller to render any assistance I could, and McBride was "talked down" onto a ZZ approach and landing.

By this time the visibility was down to 500 yards in fog and conditions were extremely difficult. McBride was brought down and turned onto the final approach on instruments but the cloud bank and visibility had lowered, making things much more difficult. He came in splendidly on a very good heading for the runway and over the end of the runway was given the code 'ZZ' which meant land straight ahead.

However at this point he saw the red light on top of the runway controllers' caravan and mistook it for hangar obstruction lights. He called out on the R/T "You are flying me into the hangars", and he opened up and went round again.

The controller assured him he was on the correct flight path for a landing and took him round for another attempt. He was in good R/T contact and came in once more on the final approach and seemed set for a successful landing. However, on the final run in the R/T suddenly went dead and nothing more was heard from him, and I realised at once that he must have crashed on the run into the airfield.

By this time the fog was getting really thick and it was clear that the rescue services were going to have a hard time finding him.

I then decided that the most practical way to find the crash would be to go to the end of the runway and work back along the approach path. This we did and after battling our way across fields and ditches for a mile or so we found the Lysander on its nose and burning fiercely. It was clear that McBride had no chance and he perished in the cockpit. Miraculously, the two agents in the back had escaped unhurt and although considerably shaken were none the worse for their traumatic experience, and we took them back to the "Cottage" by car - transport having arrived on the scene by that time. Who the passengers were I have no idea and the records give no clue.

Stephen Hankey, who attempted to land at Ford, also lost his life. I believe he lost control in cloud and crashed - his two passengers also being killed[1].

This was one of the most ghastly and disastrous nights I can remember. One was faced with an impossible situation - wide spread fog, no diversion airfields and impossible to order the pilots to bale out as one would normally have done in such circumstances. The odd thing which has always struck me is that in terms of lives saved the end result was the same in that two lives were saved - two agents. If the pilots had used their parachutes, two people again would have survived.

The night was also disastrous for Bomber Command as a whole - many aircraft returning from Germany were diverted to Woodbridge to make use of FIDO but many didn't make it and a number of Tempsford Halifaxes were also lost".

The story of operation 'Scenery II' and of the tragic sequel is worth telling again in Robin Hooper's words:

"At last we got the signal that they were coming. After many farewells and much touching of wood we got under way in the faithful Citroën which never let us down in a crisis in spite of its age, the fragility of its tyres, gross overloading and filthy wartime 'petrol' made of acetone, sugar-beet alcohol, and a little benzol. (One could only get up a hill by pulling the choke out.) We stopped by the roadside. Albert got out the wireless, connected it to the car battery, hung our clothes-line aerial in a tree and waited for the confirming signal. It came: we went on to the ground, laid out the flare-path and waited. It was a cloudless night and with brilliant moonlight, and how it froze! Between us, we drank a bottle of M. Bellot's home-made *eau de vie*, and felt neither warmer nor tighter. We hung on until after 3 am, the last ETA, then packed up and drove home very depressed. I was as disappointed as anyone but felt bound in loyalty to find excuses for the Squadron. I heard afterwards that they had started out, but had had appalling difficulties with weather and a Gee installation which deflected the compass thirty degrees every time it was switched on. Our return chez Bellot was rather an anti-climax but we were too tired to mind.

The signal came through again the next day, though to us the weather seemed none too good. This time we were determined not to tempt providence with too fervent farewells, so firmly said a mere "Au revoir" to the Bellots. We drove down to Petit-Louis's house, where we waited a little and said "au revoir" to Madame Michaud, who, not unnaturally, looked a little worried. We stopped as before to get the confirmation. It came, though it looked pretty dark and a few spots of rain were falling. While we were waiting Petit-Louis gave us an account, far funnier than anything in Chic Sale's masterpiece, of the plumbing in the digs he had occupied as a student in Paris. We got on to the ground a bit late. We had found ourselves behind a lorry, obviously black market. Thinking that ours was a Government car, as indeed in a sense it was, the driver had refused to let us pass. As soon as we arrived on the ground, a multi-engined aircraft passed over, and we hadn't nearly finished unpacking the car when we heard the unmistakable sound of a Lizzie. I told 'Georges' to send the "delay" signal while I laid out the flarepath.

It was just as well that I knew from the night before exactly where to put the lights. We stuck them in in record time. Hodges made a dummy-run over the top of them, and then landed and taxied back. The arriving agent got out and shook hands with me. The courtesies of life are seldom neglected in France. I climbed up, followed by 'Jean' (Joseph Dubar). At the top of the ladder I was greeted with a broad grin by the Station Navigation Officer, Squadron Leader Wagland, who had come along to map-read. I crawled down to the bottom of the fuselage, and we took off.

I was sitting right at the bottom of the aircraft and was not on intercom, so did not realise until we got out of the aircraft that Hodges had done an admirable ZZ landing with the cloudbase at not more than 230 feet. We went back to the Cottage. All was set for a celebration: the other two aircraft (Stephen Hankey and McBride) were on their way back, successful. Stephen Hankey had with him a very good friend of ours, an astonishing old White Russian of whom we had always been particularly fond, and whom he had specially asked to bring home. The weather got steadily thicker, and the nightmare began.

Both aircraft arrived over Tangmere within half an hour of one another. The visibility was down by then to 500 yards, if that. Stephen was sent off to Ford, to try to get in there, and McB attempted a ZZ at Tangmere. We heard him overhead once or twice, then he began his approach. He seemed to be coming in all right: then the sound of his engine suddenly stopped. It was much too thick to see any sign of a fire. Sofi (Group Captain Sofiano) and I got into his car and started off for where we reckoned the crash to be. The driver drove us slap into a five foot trench, a relic of the 1940 station defences, luckily without any serious consequences to her, us or the car, though the car had turned on its side and the door was where the roof should be. I climbed out and drove on with the Flying Control Officer.

We drove out along the line of approach and saw the crash two fields away. We ran to it across the plough. McB's two passengers - a man and a woman - were wandering about a little dazed, among the fire tender party. They had tried to pull McB out, but without success. It seems that he was pinned by the legs. I got them into a van and drove them back to the Cottage to be seen to by the doctor. When we got there we heard that Stephen had crashed into a hill near Ford. He had been killed, and so had our old friend; the other passenger died during the night.

There didn't seem much point in going to bed. I had a bath, shaved, ate some breakfast, and telephoned to Stephen's mother-in-law. Then Mac(Cairns) and I went down to see Stephen's wife. It was a harrowing business, but I felt I couldn't go home until it had been done. Then John Golding[2] drove me and a girl agent called 'little Ben' back to London.

The emotional shock of returning from German-occupied France to the relative normality of wartime England was considerable. One had, of course, always realised the physical dangers of an agent's life; but this experience gave one a faint idea of the psychological and emotional strains to which they were subjected. Air Ministry bureaucracy did its best to remind me that I was indeed back home. The morning after my return to London, my wife and I were woken up by the front door bell. Downstairs, I found a telegraph boy with a Priority telegram for my wife. We opened it. It read: GLAD TO ADVISE YOU THAT YOUR HUSBAND ... PREVIOUSLY REPORTED MISSING ARRIVED IN THE UNITED KINGDOM TODAY. Well, they'd done their best...As the Air Ministry's interest in me seemed to have revived, I thought it wise to go along and make my number. I accordingly reported myself to Alan Boxer, who gave me the only bad advice I had had from him in nearly 40 years - namely, to go and clock in at the centre for returning escapers and evaders in the Grand Central Station, Marylebone. I went to that vast and dingy building and eventually found myself with a selection of returning heroes who had forced their ways out of German prison camps, walked across France and the Pyrenees, suffered under Spanish internment, and, in general, performed feats of courage and endurance in comparison with which my de luxe return from Hitler's New Order began to feel rather shaming. After a long wait, I was taken into a very scruffy office occupied by a very scruffy Intelligence Corps captain. This gentleman (only doing his job, as I am the first to admit) started to ask me a whole series of questions, the answers to which I was strictly forbidden to give him. We soon reached an impasse, and I realised to my horror that he seemed to have every intention of keeping the suspicious character he had caught for the night, and perhaps indefinitely, in Marylebone Station. In near desperation, I asked if I might ring up Major Neave at M19. A rather dirty look from Sherlock on the other side of the desk; but he said yes. A dirtier look still when the call came through and I said, "Airey, for Christ's sake get me out of this f...ing dump. I've got to get back to work." Just to show there was no deception, I handed the receiver to Sherlock. It is a tribute to the personality which got Airey out of Colditz, and has since taken him to the heights in politics, that Sherlock actually rose to his feet and stood to attention. If he had had a cap on, he would have saluted. I was out of that office in seconds, and home before anyone had time to change their minds. But it has always seemed ironical that the only time in the whole episode when I stood in any danger of arrest was after it was all over, and in my own country!

So far as the home front was concerned, everyone seems to have got along very well without me — a salutary reminder that no-one is indispensable. My disappearance revealed a chink in our security armour, in that as soon as I was reported missing, the squadron adjutant - or, more likely, the orderly room clerk - set the ponderous machine in motion, and my wife and parents were notified before we in France had managed to signal that we were safe - which we did within 24 hours or so. This caused some distress, but - more important - might have led to a leak. All this was subsequently put right, and the squadron were marvellous to my wife - within hours, she had had a visit from Len Ratcliff and a letter from Bob Hodges. She was also visited by Peter Loxley - a friend in the Foreign Office who was then in charge of liaison between the Foreign Office and the intelligence services. She remembers that poor Peter was so distressed at his errand that she ended up by comforting him - plying him with the remains of her last bottle of gin!

Once clear of the security jungle, I went for a medical check-up, where the doctors obviously found it difficult to believe that I had been in enemy territory, returned to Tempsford - with, by this time, another half-ring on my sleeve - and took over 'A' Flight. Casualties and postings had resulted in my having become the only remaining pilot with operational experience, and I had been ordered to command the flight strictly as a "non-playing captain". This was not very satisfactory, though I understood the reasons for it and was glad, later, to have had the chance of helping to train pilots who gave very distinguished service. Anyway, it did not last long. Alan Boxer was itching to get back to operations and take over command of 161 Squadron. I was told off to take his place in Whitehall, and after a short time I did so."

That night of 16/17 December 1943 I happened to be visiting Tangmere Cottage in my new role as 'ALO' (Air Liaison - Operations). It was strange to be there without any responsibility for what was going on. In fact I was now drawing my salary from the Secret Vote, not from the RAF, and it would have been quite wrong for me to interfere in any way. After the Lysanders took off I dossed down in a hut temporarily built over part of the vegetable garden behind the Cottage, asking Booker or Blaber to call me a few hours later - so that I could welcome the returning Lysanders. I slept soundly until the morning - in all the flap over the fog I am not surprised that they forgot to call me. When I heard the news of the night's tragedy my sense of shock and horror is easy to imagine.

On 17th December, my letter to my wife includes:

"I must just say how much I thank you for giving me such wonderful weeks at Crocker Hill. I know it was the damnedest sweat for you. This gives me much pain,

but you were so marvellous and sweet that it had no effect on you from my angle.
Last night I spent at my last outfit. Stephen and McB were killed nearby. Robin saw
Con today. Jimmy was missing some time ago. You can imagine my feelings. If you
can write a line to Elizabeth Hankey it would be awfully good of you Darling. Tell her
that I feel his loss.

I cannot get over my good fortune while I was there. I tried to get back to help out
but Hodges would not play. Feeling pretty miserable and living on phoney good
humour and cheerfulness for a day or so."

I notice from the unpublished McCairns memoirs that Mac too tried to get back to
help out, since the Lysander Flight was now so short of operational pilots. He records
that Bomber Command would not agree to a break in his "rest" from operations and
that he would have to carry on at the Air Ministry.

When the fog unexpectedly formed there were also three 161 Squadron Halifaxes
out. On their return one crew baled out. At about 0500 two tried to land at RAF
Woodbridge, where a very long runway was equipped with paraffin-burning fog-
dispersal heaters. Both these Halifaxes crashed and four members of their crews were
killed. Many were badly injured, including Pilot Officer H.E. Shine, DFC, who, as a
sergeant, had been my wireless operator/air gunner on most of the Hudson pick-ups
we had done with Philippe Livry.

Eddie Shine was never fit enough to fly again during the war, but he became a
Flight Lieutenant on the administrative staff of the rehabilitation unit where he
recovered his strength. He satisfied his ambition of running his own pub after the war
and seemed in excellent health and spirits when I met him in Yorkshire in 1974, and,
in 1995, he still is.

From these badly wrecked Halifaxes it is amazing to think that two passengers,
whose dropping zones had not been found, walked out and were fit enough to travel to
London that same day.

161 Squadron's paper work for December 1943 records the posting of Squadron
Leader Livry and Flight Lieutenant
Broadley to No 21 Squadron at RAF
Sculthorpe. Pick had arranged for my old
navigator and his to join his Mosquito
Squadron. Their pinpoint daylight
bombing - eg operation 'Jericho', Amiens
prison wall, was to become famous. Both
Pick and Broadley lost their lives on
operation 'Jericho'. Decorations notified
that month included a DFC for Flying
Officer Bathgate, a bar to McCairns' DFC,
and an immediate DSO for Robin Hooper.

There is one last word to say about
December 1943. The Hudson crews,
including Flying Officer Affleck and his
crew, were not idle, even though they did
no pick-up landings. There was a third job
that the Special Duties Squadrons had
been doing all the time although I have not
mentioned it yet: 'Ascension' operations.

Squadron Leader Robin Hooper, DSO, DFC.

These consisted of flying Havocs up and down patrol lines off the French and Belgian coasts to permit conversations with intelligence agents by radio telephone. During December these were completed with agents code-named 'Bullet' and 'Player'.

CHAPTER FOURTEEN
Déricourt Picked Up

In January 1944 there was bad weather and no pick-ups were attempted. There were a number of new pilots to train, including two experienced pilot/navigators whom I had selected on a visit to the Photographic Reconnaissance Unit at RAF Benson: Flight Lieutenant Leslie Whitaker and his Scottish friend, Flight Lieutenant Murray Anderson. This pair were to become the successors to Vaughan-Fowler and McCairns as the aces of the Lysander doubles. They had been good at pilot navigation in pale blue Spitfires, taking photographs from a great height at a high speed by bright sunlight. They would become masters of the art of pilot navigation in grey, green and black Lysanders flying at low speeds by pale moonlight.

Sir Robin Hooper remembers them as follows:
"Leslie had at one point been shot down, or had forced-landed, in a PRU Spitfire in Sweden and has spent some months in internment before being returned to the UK by clandestine means. During his internment, he had grown a vast "PO Prune" moustache. This very soon disappeared, either because his very attractive girl-friend, a WAAF officer in the Tangmere ops room, objected, or because he had trouble stuffing it into his oxygen mask.

Leslie had been a junior reporter on a paper in Yorkshire before the war, and had absorbed a lot of rather simplistic, Left Book Club socialist ideals which so many of us had in those days. This used to cause endless arguments which I used to drop on the traditional grounds that officers did not discuss politics, religion or women in the Mess - though, God knows, the Cottage was no ordinary Mess.

Andy had been an Army officer - I think regular and in the Tank Corps. He was a fierce individualist and very reluctant to accept *idées reçues* or kow-tow to authority until he had satisfied himself that the authority in question knew its job. Brave as a lion and very good at his work, he was of middle height, darkish and clean-shaven. His light blue eyes looked at you very straight."

Other new pilots to be trained included Flying Officer Bell, the Australian Flying Officer McDonald and Flight Lieutenant Milsted. Bell was known as 'Duggie' or 'Dinger'. "Tall, fair, good-looking and very young" is how he is remembered by Sir Robin Hooper, who described Eric Milstead as "looking like what in those days was known as a spiv - dark, close-set eyes, a little Adolphe Menjou moustache. All this crowned by a cap with a ridiculously exaggerated "bow wave".

On the first night of the February moon when pick-ups were laid on, 4/5 February 1944, there were two Hudsons and three Lysanders out. Flying Officer Affleck and crew found no reception on his field for operation 'Bludgeon'. It was later discovered that, through somebody's mistake, the reception committee had been sent to one field while the Hudson had been sent to another. (I may add that the mistake did not occur in the SOE air operations room for which I was now responsible.) The other Hudson pick-up that night, was cruelly code-named 'Knacker'. The Hudsons in No 161 Squadron were now formed into a third flight, alongside the Halifax parachuting flight and the Lysander flight.

Apart from 'Ascension' operations for intelligence conversations and pick-up operations the Hudson crews were also to carry out small scale parachute operations through the chute. Len Ratcliff was the first Hudson Flight Commander.

Sir Robin Hooper wrote the following note on Len Ratcliff in 1975 to help me with this book:

"I first met Len at No 2 School of Air Navigation, Cranage, Cheshire. We were both destined for Hampdens, and - since the second pilot on these aircraft was also the navigator (and, in his spare moments, beam gunner) - aspiring members of Hampden squadrons had to go through a fairly rigorous navigation course. This was to stand us in good stead later on when we came to 161. We later went on together to OTU at Upper Heyford (now a USAF station). While there, we practised, among other things, changing pilots in mid-air. This was a perilous manoeuvre. The man in possession had to let down the hinged back of the pilot's seat. He then lay flat on his back, retaining a precarious control of the rudder pedals, while the second detail grabbed hold of the stick and, trampling over the prostrate body, eased himself into the cockpit. Meanwhile, the prostrate body extricated itself as best it could. With some foresight, I managed to get myself paired with the smallest man on the course (Len had, with equal intelligence, selected me as the thinnest), and we achieved our objective with the loss of only 5,000 feet.

Subsequently, we were sent on to squadrons on the same station (Scampton), he to 49, where Bob Hodges was a flight commander, and I to 83. He came to Tempsford (Bob had no doubt asked for him) from the Whitley OTU at Honeybourne, where they both went for their 'rest' after their tour at Scampton. You know his brilliant operational record from that point on. He took over AI 2c from me when I went to the Paris Embassy in 1944, and commanded 161 in the closing stages of the war in Europe. DSO, DFC and Bar, AFC, Legion of Honour, *Croix de Guerre* (plus, I think, a Dutch and a Polish one)."

As part of the background to operation 'Knacker', I remember a conversation in Baker Street with Colonel Maurice Buckmaster, who commanded 'F' Section in SOE. This was the country section responsible for those agents in France who were directly controlled by the British. Another country section ('RF') dealt with de Gaulle's Secret Service agency, the BCRA *Bureau Central de Renseignements et d'Action*. It must have been early in December 1943 that Maurice invited me to discuss a telegram from another network. This accused Henri Déricourt of liaison with the German counter-espionage people in Paris. I was shocked and incredulous. Henri was a good friend of mine and his 'Farrier' mission one of the most consistently successful at laying on good fields for pick-ups and efficient receptions. Nevertheless we agreed that - however hard to believe - we could not ignore the risk that there might be some truth in this accusation.

We agreed that we had to get Déricourt back to London for interrogation and meanwhile should not risk the lives of any more passengers by sending them out to his receptions. Maurice Buckmaster called in F Section's operations officer, Major Gerry Morel. Gerry's pale thin face looked even paler than usual when he was told. He also had counted Déricourt among his friends. He volunteered to kidnap him personally, at pistol point if necessary.

So we laid on operation 'Knacker' but it was delayed by bad weather until February 1944. Gerry was the only passengers in Len Ratcliff's Hudson when it landed on the huge meadow near Soucelle north-east of Angers. There were eight passengers[1] waiting for a lift to England.

Gerry, who was dressed for the occasion in RAF uniform, jumped down from the Hudson to have a word with Déricourt and to order him to return to England in the

Hudson. As he left the door of the aircraft, Gerry's new hat blew off in the slipstream. This of course, had to be retrieved. This loss of dignity and waste of time took some of the edge off Gerry Morel's approach to Déricourt.

When Déricourt was told that he had to come to England on the Hudson he asked why. According to Clément, Gerry replied that he thought Colonel Buckmaster wanted to give him a pleasant surprise by telling him that he had been awarded a DSO. (It was true that a draft citation for a DSO for him had been recommended some months before by Brigadier Mockler-Ferryman, Buckmaster's boss in SOE, but it never was gazetted.)

The next question Déricourt asked could not be answered satisfactorily. It was; Why weren't there any passengers out to France? He had been led to expect 10. What could be done with 11 surplus bicycles? Rémy Clément, and his other assistant could not dispose of them all before dawn. He consulted Clément who confirmed this. If the bicycles were left there the most valuable field he had would be 'blown' for good. In his book *SOE in France*, Professor Foot suggests (p297) that the 11 surplus bicycles could have been loaded into the Hudson. I asked Rémy Clément about this in 1974. "Quite impossible," he said. "They were hidden in bushes a long walk from the flarepath. It would have meant the Hudson staying on the ground far too long to have fetched them."

Gerry Morel accepted Déricourt's promise that he would return to England by Lysander a few days later. This was actually arranged inside the Hudson when Déricourt could easily have been arrested. In the event the promise was honoured and Gerry's decision vindicated.

In any case, whatever the validity of the bicycles argument, Déricourt had two real reasons for preferring to return to England a few days later. He had to wind up his affairs in France in case he did not come back. He had to make arrangements with the Germans which could protect his assistants[2] and he had to rescue his wife. That very evening of 5th February he, Boemelburg and Goetz dined together (according to Goetz[3]) to agree that brief for Déricourt while he was in England.

The final pick-up laid on by Henri Déricourt was on 8/9 February 1944[4]. This operation ('Grower') was flown by Leslie Whitaker. The field was east of Tours. There were - rather surprisingly - two passengers to France: Lesage and the Canadian wireless operator Beauregard, who were under orders to establish a circuit in Burgundy called 'Lackey'. Beauregard was to be caught by direction-finding in July and executed by the Germans.

Madame Déricourt was an unexpected second homeward-bound passenger, travelling in an expensive looking fur coat. She was short and plump and had brassy hair. She had come "on a shopping trip to London", Déricourt explained to me, when he arrived in London at breakfast time on 9th February. He expected to return to France in about a week - or so he said - and his wife would parachute with him (though she had so far had no training, nor taken any known part in the war).

Maurice Buckmaster and I received Déricourt that morning in the F Section flat at Orchard Court with the famous black-tiled bathroom. Once we were all sitting comfortably in huge armchairs, Maurice told Déricourt that he had been accused of co-operating with the Germans in Paris. Déricourt's face showed absolutely no trace of emotion of any sort and, at first, he made no reply. He later explained that he had a number of German friends from his prewar days as an international airline pilot. He kept up with them in Paris during the war and supplied them with black-market oranges as part of his cover. It was only by this method that he could ensure his safety to continue the good work he was secretly doing for us. So he said.

I came to agree with the decision that was eventually taken at a very high level: that the Déricourts should not return to France during the war. There was clearly too much doubt about his integrity, but I still felt that he was a friend and a great partner in our operations. As a gesture to cheer him up a little, my wife and I arranged a small party for them. About eight of us, including the Déricourts and a very pleasant fair-haired young Belgian agent (who had been one of my passengers), went off to the Savoy Hotel for dinner and dancing. Déricourt was dressed in a very new looking RAF uniform with wings and Flight Lieutenant's stripes on the shoulder. He was wearing the solitary ribbon of a DSO. (I did not know at that time that it had not been gazetted.) He had no shoulder flash indicating an allied origin. This omission combined with his almost total lack of English, would have struck an interested observer as very odd. As his stocky figure danced around the crowded floor at the Savoy - rather silent and expressionless - I thought what an astonishing situation he was really in. It seemed rather incredible to my wife too. She was shocked to overhear a girl we did not know say in a loud voice: "The last time I heard that tune I was in Paris." That made at least four people in the conventionally secure and familiar luxury of the Savoy Hotel who had recently been living in enemy occupied Europe. To a civilian like Audrey it had, for three and a half years, seemed as remote as the other side of the moon.

It has only very recently occurred to me that Déricourt may have bought his wife's expensive fur coat with some of the money paid to him by the Germans for information which led to the arrest and death of four patriotic Frenchmen.

When Déricourt was court-martialled in France after the war, Robert Lyon, who had shared the back of my Lysander with Colonel Bonoteaux in June 1943, wrote to the Court giving evidence that he had been well received by him. But in 1953 Lyon was a member of the commission for the Déportés. He saw Bonoteaux's file which revealed to him that his travelling companion in my Lysander had been arrested in Paris on the day of his arrival. He had later died in a concentration camp. Lyon told me that he was sure that Déricourt had pointed Bonoteaux out to the Germans to let them have something. He believed Déricourt had not betrayed him as well because they had known each other in London.

Bob Hodges' Hudson flight of 15/16 November took to France three who seem to have been betrayed by Déricourt: Jean Manesson, Paul Pardi and Maugenet. Jean Overton-Fuller talked to Déricourt after he had been acquitted at his court martial and he admitted betraying four people - these three and Colonel Bonoteaux.

She told me that Déricourt's eyes had filled with tears as he told her and that he had said "You must think I am a monster. I am no monster." Whether he was a monster or not, there is an ugly rumour[5] that the Germans had paid Déricourt four million francs (about £20,000) for information about this pick-up on 16th November - and that this was rather more than the sum of money he needed for a chicken-farm in Provence that he was trying to buy. The Germans must have had ample cash for this sort of payment. For example, Colonel Bonoteaux was carrying four million francs when he was arrested. This money, from Algiers, was intended for the ORA (the Army Resistance Organisation[6]).

It is interesting to see a glimpse of Déricourt through German eyes and, incidentally, to have fresh light thrown on the incident with Frager before the Hudson pick-up on 20/21 October 1943.

In his book[7], Hugo Bleicher describes how he recruited Roger Bardet as a V-mann (informer) and how he ingratiated himself with 'Paul' (Henri Frager) by warning him that 'Gilbert' (Déricourt) was a double agent, who worked with Kieffer. There was no sympathy and little co-operation between Bleicher of the Abwehr (Counter Intelligence) and Kieffer of the Sicherheitsdienst (Security Service).

In November 1943, Bleicher relates: "Paul flew once more to London. He hoped to be back in a fortnight. His visit had been facilitated by Gilbert who still enjoyed the confidence of the British and had recently become chief of all ground personnel for secret flights and landings of the French Section of SOE. It could not have been easy for Paul to accept Gilbert as the organiser of his visit. On this occasion there was an open dispute between them, as Roger related to me.

Roger had accompanied Paul to the secret airfield. They had hardly arrived there when Gilbert rushed up and said that Roger was to accompany Paul to London and that this was an order from the French Section in London. If he resisted this order he was to be forced to board the plane.

As Paul knew nothing of such an order he at once felt suspicious. I suppose that Gilbert, who was a daily visitor to Kieffer's office and knew the officers of the SD well, had been told by them of Roger's real role and therefore wished to dispose of him by betraying him in London. If Gilbert succeeded in that, the position of Paul would be shaken. There was a serious altercation at the airfield between Paul and Gilbert. It was only the determination of Paul, who threatened to use his pistol, that prevented Roger from being kidnapped and flown to London against his will."

Jean Overton Fuller's book *Double Agent?* (Pan 1961) and Professor Foot's SOE *in France*, Chapter X, cover a great deal of the extraordinary story of Henri Déricourt which I will not repeat here. But the problem remains: "What made him tick?" This is a problem which has puzzled me for most of my life[8].

I was lunching with Michael Foot in Soho just before *SOE in France* was published. We discussed Déricourt at length and he told me about all the references to him and his operations in the German archives. I asked him where he thought Déricourt's loyalties had really been. Foot said: "I think that, at heart, he was a *Déricourtiste*."

Many years later I was lunching with Rémy Clément in Paris, discussing Déricourt. He had, after all, known him better than anyone alive (except for his widow). I told Clément about Foot's remark. "That's excellent", he said, "A *Déricourtiste* - a perfect description. I had not thought of it that way." He went on to tell me that the rumour that Henri Déricourt came from a good French family was false. He had indeed spent his childhood in a luxurious chateau - but in the basement. His father was a gardener and his mother an indoor servant. Clément suggested that what really drove Déricourt on was a life-long ambition to achieve the wealth which would enable him to afford the life-style of his parents' employers[9].

For the first edition of this book I consulted Colonel Buckmaster who had been his employer during the war. I am most grateful to him for reading the typescript of this book and for his considered views about the Déricourt affair:

"I have read particularly carefully Chapter 14 regarding Déricourt. My recollections, and the assessment of this episode which I have made subsequently, coincide almost precisely with yours.

Insofar as it is possible to analyse Déricourt's motivation, I subscribe entirely to the view you and Clément express - that he was a "Déricourtiste" first and last - that he was ambitious for money and position - that he was unscrupulous enough and arrogant enough to think that he could outsmart anybody - but that he was by nature a man who would not stab his friends in the back. To the British he felt he needed to parade the "stiff upper lip" and he was sufficiently fair-minded to return trust with trust - at least until such action interfered with his basic ambition."

It now seems that Déricourt had done a deal with Boemelburg, the head of the counter-espionage section of the *Sicherheitsdienst* in Paris. He would give advance notice of where and when his pick-ups would take place in exchange for immunity for his team, the aircraft and the passengers. This was to maintain his credibility in the eyes of SOE. Boemelburg's reward would be the opportunity to photograph the mail that would be carried to England on these aircraft and to have the arriving passengers trailed. He may also have hoped for early warning of the Allied landings in France. With a few exceptions on both sides, this deal seems to have been honoured. Little did we realise at the time that a safe conduct had been arranged for most of the pick-ups that we did with Déricourt through the Luftwaffe and flak commands, at least from May 1943. However, the operation taking Bodington to safety (according to Jean Overton Fuller) was not revealed.

Since this book was written, Anthony Cave Brown advanced another explanation of Déricourt's co-operation with the Germans. In Chapter 8 of his *Bodyguard of Lies* (W.H. Allen & Co., 1976), he suggested that Déricourt played an important role in feeding false information to the enemy as part of an Allied deception plan about the date and place of the invasion of northern France. In 1987, Robert Marshall developed a similar notion, claiming that Déricourt was planted in SOE by the Secret Intelligence Service, making him not a double but a *triple* agent. (*All the King's Men*, Collins 1988). Professor M.R.D. Foot demolished this theory in his review in the Sunday Times of 24th January 1988, labelling it "too bad to be true". A much more reliable account of the Déricourt story appeared in 1989 (*Déricourt, The Chequered Spy*, Michael Russell 1989) by his post-war friend, Jean Overton Fuller. She concludes that it was "a loyal treason" but confirms my own view that Henri Déricourt was the most convincing con man that I have ever known.

Now I return to the story of pick-ups in 1944. On the same night as Déricourt's last operation, 8/9 February, Affleck completed 'Bludgeon' at his second attempt. They landed at their target at 2330. The field, which had been hard with frost, had thawed. It was water logged and the Hudson was bogged while taxying back to the take off point. Affleck had to stop the engines and call for assistance from the team on the ground and the passengers. They all manhandled the heavy aeroplane back to the take-off point and turned it into wind. It was trying to snow.

Once the loads were turned round Affleck started the engines but the Hudson would not move as the tail wheel had sunk in. They manhandled it again to clear the tail wheel. When this was done they found that the main wheels had sunk in up to the hubs so the engines had to be switched off again. A crowd of villagers arrived to help with the digging and pushing. The only French words the crew could muster was the navigator's "Allez-hop!"

Some oxen and horses were then brought to the scene and hitched to the Hudson to drag it forward out of the mud, but they could not move it. At one point all work ceased as a German aircraft flew overhead. Affleck worked out that the latest safe time to take off would be 0300. If not airborne by then the aircraft would have to be destroyed. He said to Paul Rivière, who was in charge on the ground: "If we have to burn the aircraft we'll stick to you and run like hell for the Spanish frontier."

He also decided that channels should be dug out in front of the main wheels so that he could taxi forward on the engines. This was eventually achieved. Meanwhile he had to stop the men from the Maquis removing all the guns and ammunition from the Hudson. Affleck attempted a take-off but could not build up enough speed and had to throttle back. While taxying back to line up for another attempt they were bogged once more, but this time managed to extricate the aeroplane quite quickly. He decided to take the minimum load and confined his passenger list to an RAF evader, Raymond Aubrac, his wife Lucie and their young son. He was a very senior resistance leader who, under the sentence of death, had been rescued from a police van by his wife and friends. His wife had attacked the Gestapo in the van, tommy-gun in hand, when eight months pregnant. He seemed to be a nervous wreck. His wife was now within hours of giving birth. She just sat there in the mud.

At 0205, after they had been on the ground two and a half hours longer than intended, a final attempt at taking off succeeded - but only just. When very near the boundary of the field the Hudson hit a bump and bounced into the air at about 50 knots. Affleck just managed to keep it airborne, build up a safe speed and climb away. He had taken off with rather more than 15° of flap. He was cold, wet and covered with mud from head to foot. After half an hour he realised that the Hudson was going very slowly, wondered why and realised that he had forgotten to put his flaps up.

He had no aerials left - they had all been broken off in the struggle on the ground. They found their way home without being able to identify themselves to the air defences of Great Britain. Eventually they landed at base at 0640. The Hudson, covered with mud and "looking like a tank", was greeted by the Station Commander, Group Captain 'Mouse' Fielden[10]. A few days later Flying Officer J.R. Affleck was promoted to acting flight lieutenant and awarded an immediate DSO.

When he was describing this incident to me in 1975, John Affleck had two thoughts to add. Firstly, that, had he thought about it, he should really have flown all the way home with his wheels down. In the wisdom of hindsight, towards the end of his career as a professional airline pilot, he realised that there was a great danger of that mud-covered undercarriage becoming stuck or frozen up so that he would not be able to lower it for the landing at Tempsford. The other afterthought, looking back, was that he could have almost died of laughing at the struggles of the crew to communicate with the crowd of French helpers without any common language and that his main pre-occupation during this time was to stop these helpers damaging the Hudson.

The evader whom he brought back was Flight Lieutenant J.F.Q. Brough, of Carlisle, who had been with the Resistance since he crashed in France, in a 138 Squadron Halifax on 3/4 November 1943. In his letter to the author, Brough wrote:
"As well as myself, we also carried Mr and Mrs Aubrac[11], two top members of the Resistance, and their young son. Mr Aubrac had been elected to the French Consultative Assembly in Algiers; Mrs Aubrac was nine months pregnant and gave birth to a baby girl in Queen Charlotte's Hospital in London the day we landed at Tempsford."

Jacques Maillet was one of those hoping to fly to England by that Hudson. He remembers leaving the field with an equally disappointed Monsieur Aboulker, a great brain surgeon. After the Hudson had gone, a patrol of Germans were shot at by the sentries round the field. Before taking the train for Paris they thought they had better tidy themselves and opened their little suitcases. Aboulker had picked up one, identical with his own, which had arrived by the Hudson. It contained nothing but a portable wireless transmitter.

On 10/11 February, Flying Officer McDonald and another new pilot, Flying Officer D.S. Bell, set off on a Lysander double called 'Serbie'. In spite of poor visibility, they made their rendezvous at Vierzon at 2315. Bell had been waiting there for four minutes when McDonald arrived. The latter had been ordered to land first on the field south east of Bourges. Bell watched him make two unsuccessful approaches, overshooting, after which he went round again. On his third attempt at landing McDonald seemed to touch down and run along the field very fast. Bell saw him tip over and burst into flames, well beyond the flarepath. All the lights went out. Bell decided that he could do nothing by waiting and returned to base. The squadron was later informed "through certain sources" that McDonald had been killed. It was believed that his two passengers were rescued. McDonald was buried in the churchyard of Farge-en-Septaine, very far from his native Australia. In the spring Frenchmen put wild flowers on his grave[12]. It was later thought that a possible cause of this accident could have been forgetting one of the "vital actions" before landing: putting the mixture control from 'weak' to 'normal'. If left in 'weak', it is not possible to throttle back completely.

On 15/16 February 1944 Wing Commander L.McD. Hodges, DSO, DFC (and bar), attempted his last Hudson operation ('Corpus'), which failed through bad weather. This was for him the end of this most successful tour of operations. In March he was posted to the RAF Staff College. Bob and I were to meet again in 1945 when I was in Ceylon as the Staff Officer in Air Command South East Asia responsible for "cloak and dagger" air operations and he came out to take command of No 357, our main special duties squadron, at RAF Jessore, near Calcutta.

Meanwhile No 161 Squadron at Tempsford was to carry on under entirely new management.

Sir Lewis Hodges
Wing Commander L. McD. ('Bob') Hodges, DSO*, DFC*.

CHAPTER FIFTEEN

Under Entirely New Management

In March 1944, Wing Commander A.H.C. Boxer[1] was posted to command No 161 (Special Duties) Squadron. He had taken over AI2(c) from Guy Lockhart and had made it immensely efficient and smooth-running. AI2(c) was the branch of Air Ministry's Air Intelligence organisation which controlled special duties air operations for the clandestine organisations. It came under the Director of Intelligence (Research), who was Air Commodore J.A. Easton (later Air Vice-Marshal Sir James), and the Deputy Director who was the Australian Group Captain John Palmer - a future CO of RAF Tempsford. Alan Boxer had previously commanded 'A' Flight of No 138 Squadron which was also engaged on special duties in enemy occupied areas ranging from inside the Arctic Circle to the Mediterranean and as far east as Poland and Czechoslovakia. His earlier experience as a flying instructor no doubt contributed to his successful completion of a number of pick-up operations in France.

When Alan came back to Tempsford he was replaced (on 13th March 1944) at AI2(c) by Robin Hooper who went to Air Ministry as an Acting Wing Commander. Robin was to find the top brass of D of I (R) fully occupied with operation 'Crossbow' (VIs and V2s - the German 'vengeance' weapons). They left him a free hand with special duties air operations, including the immense problem of the Warsaw rising and siege.

Tempsford had been transferred from Bomber Command to come under No 38 Group, which was building up to give air transport support, particularly to airborne forces. The Air Officer Commanding, Air Vice-Marshal Sir Leslie Hollinghurst, selected Bunny Rymills to take over the Lysander Flight from Robin Hooper. In February 1944, he sent Bunny to report to the Station Commander, Mouse Fielden. Mouse told Bunny that he had already given the job to Squadron Leader Sells. Bunny went back to his AOC who was furious with Mouse. He "tore him off a strip" on the telephone while Bunny was in his office. He then gave Bunny a flight in No 644 Squadron, where Bunny was to make another successful tour, including Arnhem. By the end of the war he had done no fewer than 85 operations.

Squadron Leader G. de G. Sells had been attached to 161 Squadron from RAF Feltwell. In 1941, he and Robin had served together on Hampdens in No 83 (Bomber) Squadron. He had later done a second tour of operations in the Pathfinder Force and earned a DSO and DFC. A Wykehamist and former schoolmaster teaching modern languages, he had a good knowledge of French. He was of middle height, stocky, with sandy hair and a close-cropped moustache.

Two new pilots had arrived in the Lysander Flight in February: Flight Lieutenants Bill Taylor and George Turner. They both came from a night-fighter squadron. Robin[2] remembers 'Willie' Taylor as "small, darkish and rather wizened-looking - probably not so old as he looked". George Turner had been a Metropolitan policeman.

The third newcomer to pick-up operations was already very experienced in Special Duties air operations and an old hand at Tempsford: Lt Hysing-Dahl of the Royal Norwegian Air Force had completed a full tour of 30 operations on Halifaxes parachuting agents and supplies all over Western Europe from Norway to France. Not only was the pick-up flight under entirely new management, it also had no pilots who had been operating on pick-ups for more than one month when the March moon period started.

It started well with two successful Lysander pick-ups on 2/3 March. One - not recorded in the RAF archives - was the SIS operation 'Laburnum' on 'Pierrot's' field west of Baudreville. 'Pierrot' was Pierre Tissier, who had taken over from 'Trellu' (Pierre Hentic). On his first successful pick-up, Douglas Bell landed two SOE agents, Robert Benoist and his radio operator Denise Bloch, both of whom would die in concentration camps. The agent picked up was Polish.

The other was operation 'Gitane' by Andy Anderson, who carried two people each way. The field for 'Gitane' was unusable and the lights were set out on a substitute field nearby which was bumpy with snow. This was "third time lucky" for 'Gitane' which had been frustrated twice by bad weather in the February moon period.

The passengers who arrived on this operation near Châteauroux were S.J. Savy and Eileen Nearne (Jacqueline's sister. They both received MBEs for their work). Savy, a friend of France Antelme, was to organise an F Section circuit in Paris called 'Wizard'. Eileen Nearne was his wireless operator. They were received off the Lysander by 'Greyhound', an SOE escape line run for DF section by a Belgian business man, Georges Lovinfosse, from a country house near Châteauroux[3].

Georges de Lovinfosse (as he was called after the war) told me that he organised this flarepath himself and that he returned to England by Andy's Lysander. His travelling companion in the back was Maurice Durieux who had only one leg. The other had been amputated after a parachuting accident. Getting him through the snow to the field was an arduous struggle for them both.

Anderson was a remarkable pilot/navigator. In his book[4] Per Hysing-Dahl tells of a double operation when the other pilot told Anderson on the R/T that he was lost. "Describe exactly what you can see" said Anderson. The other pilot did this. Anderson found the place on the map which fitted the description and told the lost pilot where he was, and what course to set for his target.

161 Squadron 'A' Flight at Tempsford in 1944   *Peter Arkell*

On 3/4 March, Per Hysing-Dahl set off on a double called 'Framboise' near Issoudun. He quite failed to contact the other Lysander flown by Flying Officer D.S. Bell, DFC. He landed, picked up two passengers and brought them back to Tangmere, where there was still no news of 'Dinger' Bell.

Meanwhile Bell had crossed the coast of Normandy. Near Lisieux his engine began to fail. He turned back but when he was six miles out to sea his engine was giving so much trouble that he could no longer maintain height. He decided that he must turn south again to make a forced landing — if he could reach the French coast — rather than risk a night ditching in the Channel. He was losing height all the time but he just made it, recrossing the coast at about 600 feet. Luckily, he could see by the moonlight that there was a stretch of flat treeless land. He crash landed there, north of Caen and just east of Plumetot, at 2250.

Bell's face and leg were "only scratched", but the Lysander was badly damaged. He discarded his flying kit and left it by the wrecked aircraft. This much is recorded in the 161 Squadron Operations Book. Then the story dries up. To protect those who helped him, all that Bell reported after that was: "My journey to the UK was arranged for me."

Luckily the story, as recounted to Marie-Madeleine by one of Bell's passengers, is recorded in *Noah's* Ark[5]. The passengers were Count Elie de Dampierre ('Berger') and his team-mate Commandant Robert Lorilleaux ('Icarus'). 'Berger', who was small and fair with blue eyes, had been Tempsford trained to lay on landings in France. He was to replace Pierre Dallas, the 'Avia' team leader who had been captured. 'Icarus' was to re-establish contact with Deuxième Bureau agents in Lyons They took with them a 'monster' consignment of equipment, mail and cash (which they referred to as "gin"). This load was important to help revive the 'Alliance' intelligence organisation which had been suffering crippling losses to the Germans.

'Berger' reported that he was the only person unhurt in the crash landing. 'Icarus' was flung out and suffered multiple bruises. The pilot, in addition to the "scratches" he reported, was cut "very deeply" in the leg and his uniform was soaked with blood. He was tall and red-headed which was difficult to camouflage. 'Berger' gave him his raincoat to conceal the RAF battledress.

They had crashed in a zone fortified by the Germans, actually in a minefield. Burning the Lysander would only draw attention to it. They had to abandon the cases containing money and equipment. Bell just detonated the IFF identification equipment and 'Berger' took the mail. After two miles walking they found a woman farmer, Madame Lechevalier, who gave them some clothing, and they set off on foot to cover the seven painful miles to Caen by dawn. They rested a few hours in a hotel used by the Gestapo while they waited for a train. 'Berger' thought that this was the last place that anyone would think of looking for them.

There was still such a shortage of operational pick-up pilots that Bell's return was swiftly organised. Anderson brought him home only 10 nights later, on operation 'Lautrec' according to the RAF records. Marie-Madeleine's account suggests that he returned on operation 'Rubens' two days later. This was on a field near Angers; it brought back three to the UK in addition to Dinger Bell. These three were: Count Elie de Dampierre ('Berger'), who had been scrupulous in looking after his wounded pilot; Jean Sainteny, who brought back a 55-foot long map showing details of all the Cotentin's defences and a mass of facts about secret weapon sites, and Micheline Grimprel, the secretary of Alliance's Intelligence Section. She was a "society woman", tall, dark and with naturally curly hair.

While Dinger Bell was crashing in Normandy on 3/4 March, Anderson and Whitaker completed their third successful double together: operation 'Fantôme', south of Bourges. There were four passengers out and six home. Hysing-Dahl remembered how their passengers stamped their feet - they were so stiff and cold - as they climbed down the ladders from their Lysanders. He also remembered how Anderson and Whitaker stuck together on the ground as they did in the air. After all they had both come together from the Photographic Reconnaissance Unit. 'Andy' used to play endless gramophone records of sentimental French songs in Tangmere Cottage but, on great occasions, he would perform very adequately on his bag-pipes.

The same team successfully completed their fourth double Lysander pick-up on the night of 6/7 March, near Estrées St Denis. This was for the French Air Force Intelligence Service (Le SR Air). Among the six passengers collected was René Gervais, the Chief of SR Air. Roger Camous, their air operations officer, had laid on the operation on the ground, assisted by his radio-operator, Robert Geneix.

The last operation attempted in March was 'Alexandre', described by Per Hysing-Dahl as very unpleasant. It was quite dark and there was a lot of light flak. The field was just inside the coast of Normandy, but Hysing-Dahl said he much preferred the longer routes deep into France. This trip was abandoned because of heavy cloud and thick haze.

In spite of their inexperience on Lysander pick-ups the new team had been successful on seven out of the nine sorties laid on in that March moon of 1944. Of the seven successes, four were Anderson's. Meanwhile the Hudson flight were parachuting but not doing pick-ups.

Again the April moon saw no Hudson pick-ups and more changes in the team. Len Ratcliff, who had been commanding 'C' Flight Hudsons, replaced Squadron Leader Sells as CO of 'A' Flight, the Lysanders. Dinger Bell was posted as "tour-expired". But Bill Taylor and George Turner were now operational and Flight Lieutenant 'Bob' Large and Flying Officer J.P. Alcock (who had been a guardsman) soon would be. In all, eight pilots would take part in Lysander pick-ups during April 1944. The Flight was, once more, up to strength.

Operation 'Rubens'[6] on 9/10 April was unusual at this stage of the war in having only one passenger each way. Bob Large remembers carrying Vicomte Elie de Dampierre ('Berger') on it. He landed on a huge field, near Angers, which could have been used for Hudson pick-ups. (It was about 10 km south of the field that Déricourt had used the year before.) The returning passenger must have been Jean Godet - "a captain in the reserve and the proprietor of an excellent brand of cognac". He brought back terrible news of widespread arrests, including 20 people who had contributed to the intelligence on the fantastic 55-foot map of the Cotentin defences, which Sainteny had brought back on Andy's Lysander a month before. All these 20 were to be executed on 7th June, the day after D-Day.

It helps to put our pick-ups into a proper sense of proportion to think that the cost of this one map in human lives was much greater than the cost in aircrew lives of all the RAF pick-up operations in France from 1940 to 1944. Of course these 20 executions were only a very small part of the losses sustained by 'Alliance' in 1944 alone, and 'Alliance' was only one among very many organisations operating underground in France. (It is also interesting to speculate how many hundreds or thousands of Allied lives may have been saved by the information on the 55-foot map when American troops took the Cotentin.)

Bob Large, whose first pick-up this was, was remembered by Per Hysing-Dahl as a "fantastic character. Not the most disciplined man (in a military sense) I have met, but an extremely good fellow, with unusual ability as a pilot".

On one of his early trips Bob Large was given a bottle of champagne with the following words written on the label: *"A votre écarlate bonne santé* - and next time bring English cigarettes." It seems that he was working for the *'Réseau Ecarlate'*. In his previous job he had been personal assistant to Air Vice-Marshal Hollinghurst, Air Officer Commanding No 38 Group. The AOC had said to him: "Bob, you are not only the worst PA I have ever had; you are the worst I've ever heard of." At the first opportunity he flew to Netheravon to present a bottle of champagne from France to his former AOC. He also remembers going into the officer's mess at Tangmere where there were still people who remembered him well from his days there as a Spitfire pilot with Douglas Bader's wing. When asked what he was doing now with these ancient Lysanders, he humbly replied: "Searchlight Co-op"[7].

It must have been Bill Taylor on operation 'Chauffeur' who brought back to France the old stalwart from the early days, Philippe de Vomécourt, and two other SOE officers, one of whom was a girl. Major de Vomécourt, who had a wife and seven children, would have arrived by parachute if he had not torn a leg muscle a few days before he was due to jump. He was to command five teams of agents in the Loire valley. In his account[8] they landed near Châteauroux. On the side of their Lysander was chalked the words: "Jacqueline MUST come"[9]. Buckmaster had tried before to get Jacqueline Nearne to come home when he had summoned her Chief, Squadron Leader Maurice Southgate ('Hector') for consultations. She had been in the field for 12 months and had heard of the capture of her sister Eileen by the Gestapo. In spite of all this she had surrendered her seat on that Lysander to a French political refugee. This time she came with Savy who had arrived by Anderson's Lysander on 2/3 March and found his plans disrupted by Antelme's arrest. Instead he had stumbled on a piece of intelligence so important that he came back to England on this flight to report it. He had details of a large secret ammunition dump in quarries near Creil. It contained 2,000 Vl rockets, ready to fire at London. Bomber Command stove it in early in July[10]. The third passenger to England was Mrs Josette Southgate, whose husband, Squadron Leader Maurice, was the agent in charge. She understood that the male passenger was Monsieur Régis.

Jean-Bernard Badaire was a young member of the reception team that met de Vomécourt. He told me in 1976 that our landings had an important effect on the morale of those involved on the ground. For them it was a lonely war. They had to live on faith, and their morale could easily be broken by the loss of friends. Then an RAF aeroplane, that they could touch, arrived with reinforcements and their morale and faith was immediately re-established.

On 11/12 April George Turner and Per Hysing-Dahl successfully completed operation 'Hollyhock' for SIS, landing one kilometre north of Outarville. Their approach to the target made sure that they used the unrivalled visual aid of the Loire and avoided the flak near Orléans. From Cabourg they followed the traditional Lysander milk run to the Loire near Mer, where an island and a nearby bend in the river give an excellent 'fix'. They then cut across, south of Orléans to Châteauneuf-sur-Loire, followed the D11 road north to Toury and then went to the field.

George Turner wrote:

"I shall always remember the inequity of the mutual presentations at lamp 'A'! Coffee beans and a bar or two of Bourneville versus Chanel No 5 or a bottle of Moët et Chandon. In my day we had a barrel of bags of Dutch coffee beans at Tempsford"[11].

This reminds me that I was astonished to find a senior officer at Tempsford - when I visited my former base in the spring of 1944 - who was really concerned about these "mutual presentations". "After all, Hugh," he said, "they are infringing the Customs regulations, aren't they?"

On 30th April/1st May, Flt Lt Large and Flg Off Alcock were successful on operation 'Organist' in the area of Châteauroux but only delivered three passengers and picked up two between them. The agent in charge was 'Shaw', remembered by Pierre Raynaud (who knew him in London) as Alexander Schwatscho or Shokolowsky of Romanian origin.

One of George Turner's operational maps.   Tony Bugbird

The two homeward-bound passengers were considerable figures in the history of the Resistance: Violette Szabo and Philippe Liewer ('Charles Staunton'). Bob Large remembers this trip for several reasons that he told me about later. He found ridges on the field and his landing run was very bumpy, making the Lysander vibrate as he put the brakes on. The engine stopped as fuel was thrown up. When over-rich, a hot Mercury engine was very difficult to restart and there was a danger of running the battery flat. Bob pulled the slow-running cut-out to restart the engine - a control which was there to stop the engine. (George Turner had the same trouble on one of his trips.)

On his way home they were shot at by flak near Châteaudun. "The lady in the back squeaked, so I switched off the intercom" Bob told me. He forgot to switch it on again. When they landed at Tempsford the Lysander did a ground-loop; one tyre was flat because it had been hit by flak. He threw off his helmet and jumped out. He solicitously approached his passenger and was received with great hostility and a brandished umbrella. She thought they had pranged in hostile territory and that he was a German. "The lady" must have been Violette Szabo.

Violette's father had met her French mother in the First World War when he had been a British soldier. She was brought up in a working class district in South London and had married a Free French Sergeant Szabo in 1940. A Czech, he had been in the French Foreign Legion. A few months after their daughter was born he was killed at El Alamein. She met Liewer during parachute training at Ringway early in 1944 and, at his request, accompanied him to France by parachute early in April[12].

Philippe Liewer, a 30-year-old French journalist, had fought in the French Army in

1940. He was recruited by SOE for work in the South of France in 1941, escaped from a Vichy prison and reached Britain via Spain. On 14/15 April 1943 he arrived back in France by Lysander[13] to set up 'Salesman', a Buckmaster circuit covering Le Havre and Rouen. He was withdrawn on Déricourt's last Hudson for his own safety and a rest in London, with his young assistant Bob (Robert Maloubier). Bob had been wounded by three German bullets and only just survived[14].

On this flight back to England with Violette Szabo on 30th April 1944 Liewer had found Rouen too dangerous. His portrait as a wanted man was on posters on the walls. They were to jump back into France together in June just after D-day. Violette was captured in a shoot-up with Germans three days later.

On 3/4 May Flight Lieutenant Affleck pulled off the first successful Hudson pick-up there had been for three months: Operation 'Halberd', with eight passengers each way. His second pilot was Flg Off H.B. Ibbott, who would fly his own Hudson on a pick-up in August. The rest of the crew were Flt Lt McMillan, Flg Off Jarman and Flt Lt Corner.

Among the passengers he picked up were Maurice Bourgès-Maunoury (later Minister) and Madame Fleury with her baby daughter, who was to celebrate her first birthday on 10th May in the Patriotic School. Jean Fleury, her father, was already an experienced traveller by Lysander.

He wrote to me:

"No doubt the presence in London of my wife and daughter embellished my stay there. But that was not the main reason for their journey. My wife had been arrested by the Gestapo a few days after my second departure from France and was imprisoned at Fresnes. She had taken part in my activities which were in the field of clandestine radio so that the sort of revelations she could possibly make were such that they could lead to catastrophes.

"The Germans threatened physical ill-treatment of our baby during her interrogations. They also put a stool pigeon in her cell who said she was another prisoner but whose task was to drug her and make her talk. My wife managed to overcome all these trials and the Gestapo let her go after four months without having been able to extract any information from her.

"This is why the British and French services decided to bring her and the baby out of France. This is how one was able to see a strange sight on their arrival in England: a tall pilot in operational uniform getting out of the aeroplane and, confronted with a tiny baby, asking her: "Are you a terrorist?" But the reply would have been too long to give him."

Another pick-up operation mounted on 3/4 May, operation 'Forsythia' ended in disaster and the loss of the pilot, Flight Lieutenant Leslie Whitaker, DFC. The squadron records give no details, but Philip Schneidau remembered that there was an RAF bombing raid within 50 miles of the SIS field which the Lysander pilot was not expecting. "He had to move out of his target area in a hurry and unfortunately flew low over a German Air Force airfield, with the result that he was shot down by flak and killed[15]. He crashed over Mon Désir airfield, 10 km south of Etampes and was buried in the cemetery at Guillerval, l'Essonne. Philip learned later that French bank notes in their thousands were found on the airfield after this had happened. Actually watching this was Major 'Bud' Mahurin, an American fighter pilot who was waiting to be picked up. He remembers a heavy bomber raid on Châteaudun and seeing German fighters everywhere in brilliant moonlight.

In April 1989 I had a letter from Docteur A. Perpezat, who had also been waiting to be picked up:

"On a visit to the Jean Moulin museum at Bordeaux the *Conservatrice* offered me your book *'Nous Atterrissions de Nuit'*. I read with great emotion and passion these pages which reminded me of a slice of my youth. May I give you some details about operations which you mention in which I took part?

I was on the field, I believe near Ouarville, with Major Budd (sic) and Fanfouet on the night of 3/4 May 1944 (operation Forsythia)...We were comfortably settled on the edge of a ditch with our protection team headed by Philip Keun and Pierrot, eating bread and *charcuterie* washed down by a good Loire wine.

At about 0030, by magnificent moonlight, we saw wave after wave of RAF bombers...on their way to their target at Châteaudun. When they appeared an Me 110 took off from the Etampes-Mondésir aerodrome, located about 15 miles ENE of our position. He made each attack from under the belly of the bomber, passing each time several hundred feet above our heads. So, with great sadness, we saw five or six bombers shot down in flames. The moon was so bright that we were afraid that the German night fighter would see us. So, when Leslie arrived at about 0100, at about 1,000 feet, vertically above our landing field (which was easily identified by a corrugated iron roof shining in the moonlight) we could not make ourselves known by flashing the recognition letter. Then it seemed that Leslie, thinking he was mistaken, set course to the East to check his position on the Paris-Orleans railway line which was easy to see that night. By great misfortune, he went off exactly in the direction of the Etampes-Mondésir airfield. We saw a burst of tracer bullets go up from that base and the Lysander shot down.

On Saturday morning we went to make enquiries at the Quatres-Vents restaurant just near the aerodrome. So we were able to attend Leslie's funeral at the Guilleral cemetery. He was buried next to two other RAF airmen. He had been killed by a bullet through his forehead. Farmers told us that the Germans had transported the Lysander, which was only partly burnt, to their base at dawn.

After some rather fantastic adventures encountering German patrols near Boisseaux, we made it to the next field chosen for the pick-up, near Outarville. On the night of Sunday 6/7 May Alexander picked us up with no problem.

I should tell you that I was 'XP 12' and that I was a member of the Jade-Amicol Group, Deputy to Colonel Olivier and Chief of the South-West Region. The pilot whom we affectionately called "The Little Norwegian" had brought Col Olivier and his liaison agent the month before.

I smiled when I read that I had been drinking and singing all the way to England. My memory had failed me on that anecdote; but it proves that our morale was high...I am writing in french, very sorry, I have forget my english..."

On 6/7 May Flying Officer G.F.J. Alexander landed equipment at 'Pierrot's' field near Outarville on operation 'Silène'. He picked up two intelligence agents, 'XP 12' and 'Fanfouet'. They drank wine and sang songs all the way. His third passenger home was Major Walker M. ('Bud') Mahurin. Alex remembers[16] him as a successful Thunderbolt pilot with a score of something like 27 destroyed. When they landed at Tempsford, Alex told Major Mahurin that the trip would cost him a pint. He waved a cheery goodbye and that was the last that Alex has ever seen or heard of him. Perhaps this book will fall into his hands and remind him of his debt.

The second treble Lysander pick-up that ever succeeded was near Luzillé in

Touraine on 9/10 May for operation 'Mineur'. The Flight Commander, Len Ratcliff, Bob Large and Per Hysing-Dahl landed at leisurely 10 minutes intervals and transported six passengers to France and eight to England. Eight months before we had completed the other treble pick-up in nine minutes from first landing to last take-off, but there was nobody left in 161 Squadron in May 1944 who remembered that.

Bob Large told me about this operation. Their rendezvous was over Bléré, on the river Cher, where they had agreed not to wait for more than 20 minutes. They all arrived there within three minutes. They had drawn lots on the order of landing: first Len Ratcliff, the Flight Commander; second Bob and third Per Hysing-Dahl. Bob found the field and then stood off to allow Len to have it. At this point he got slightly lost and was late getting back. Per, who was impatiently "sitting up there in a Nordic sort of rage", asked why he was late. "Sorry to have been so long" said Bob, "I've been getting my hair cut." "What, in the company's time?" asked Per. Bob still wonders what the German eavesdroppers on the RT can have made of this. They probably did not know the rest of the quotation which had seemed exceptionally funny to Per when he had first heard it:

"Where have you been?"
"Getting my hair cut."
"What, in the company's time?"
"Well, it grew in the company's time."
"But not all of it grew in the company's time."
"Well, I haven't had it all cut off."

The 2/3 June was the only night that month when pick-up operations in France were mounted by 161 Squadron from the United Kingdom. No doubt the resistance networks were flat out for the remainder of the moon on their many sabotage plans for disrupting the German army's road, rail and telephone communications so that their reinforcements should be stopped or delayed on their way to the beachhead in Normandy.

The allied air forces were at this too. Just before Taylor landed near Estrées St Denis, a nearby railway station was bombed, as Robert Masson observed while waiting to be picked up. He was head of the Samson network of the French Air Force intelligence service. They had not been able to have any pick-ups for two months and they had a great accumulation of intelligence on Normandy, which was urgently needed[17]. The ORA (Army Resistance Organisation) also sent back that night a tracing giving the location of German army formations in France just before D-Day. This was carried by Commandant Verneuil, the head of TR (Travaux ruraux)[18]. His pilot must have been Flt Lt Turner.

However, it was Alexander who collected that night one of the most important people in the Allied Intelligence community of the whole war. This was Gustave Bertrand who had for many years been in French army intelligence. He had passed invaluable intelligence by wireless to London from tapped telephone lines, but it was the leading role he played with Polish Intelligence in the Enigma story which was so crucial to the history of the war. After arrest, escape and six months' hiding, he brought his wife to England by this Lysander[19].

The agent in charge of the field was Pierre Tissier. He had now received five pick-ups. This proved to be his last. On 29th June 1944 he was arrested with Philip Keun. They were both killed at Buchenwald.

No 161 Squadron was now honoured by the King's approval of a Squadron heraldic badge - an open 'fetter lock' (hand-cuff) - and motto "*Liberate*".

The RAF's double Lysander pick-up, operation 'Thicket', on a field east of Lyons was flown from Calvi in Corsica. In February 1944, Peter Vaughan-Fowler had arrived at Maison Blanche airfield, near Algiers, to establish a Lysander pick-up flight for operations from bases in the Mediterranean area. In February they had been attached as a third flight to No 148 Special Duties Squadron at Brindisi. This squadron of Halifax aircraft was engaged in parachuting men and supplies to partisans in Northern Italy, Yugoslavia, Albania and Greece. They were later to suffer heavy losses supplying the secret army in Warsaw.

Peter's flight had built up its strength in aircraft and pilots. These included Flg Off H.I. Franklin, who had a magnificent moustache and wore an immaculate silk scarf, Flg Off R.J. Manning and Flg Off N.H. Attenborrow. They had been trained on an old grass airfield at Neverano in the heel of Italy and they had completed a successful double pick-up in Greece in May. The detachment to Corsica pulled off the double on the night of 4th June. Peter and Flg Off N.H. Attenborrow landed three and picked up seven between them. One of the passengers picked up was Michel Pichard. He sent me this note:

"Actually, on June 4th or 5th I was picked up in Saône and Loire by a double Lysander. The operation officer was 'Sénateur' (Jannik Rivière); 'Charles-Henri' (Paul Rivière) was then in London. We had no idea the planes were based in Corsica - and the BBC omitted the 9 pm message. We were enjoying a big meal when someone went around midnight and saw two Lysanders circling around.

The first one landed and picked up Dr Revesz-Long, Chief Radio Co-ordinator, and two other passengers and then took off.

The second one landed and, after a brief discussion with Clouet, the pilot - who claimed that he could not "make the Alps" (that's how we found that we were going to Corsica) with four passengers - finally agreed after Clouet accepted to take "full responsibility" (sic!). So, Clouet, 'Fil' and myself got in the second plane and we did make the Alps."

Thirty-two years later, Peter commented that it was foolish of him to try to fly through the Alps in a Lysander with a full load. He had found it "very unpleasant" on his way to this pick-up. On the way back he actually flew round the Alps.

Back in England with 161 Squadron for the July moon, we find that unsuitable weather severely curtailed pick-up operations: only three Lysander sorties were authorised, of which one was a "mail pick-up" (without quite landing); but three Hudson pick-ups were laid on - the first since early May.

On 3/4 July Flight Lieutenant Affleck and his Hudson crew saw their field clearly but there was no reception for them on operation 'Baggage'. They tried again on 5/6 July and, this time, all went well with no incidents. They had eight passengers each way.

These two flights for operation 'Baggage' are fully described by Marie-Madeleine Fourcade[20]. She was returning to command 'Alliance' in the field. With her were Pierre Giraud and Raymond Pezet. For the purpose of her cover identity, she was now Madame Pezet. They flew round the battle zone, over Brittany to the Loire. They were much struck, peeping through the curtains of the Hudson, by the displays of flak, and by the numbers of Maquis reception committees they passed over, who hopefully flashed morse recognition letters at the Hudson. When they landed she was greeted by her real name: "Hello, Marie-Madeleine." Spurning a lift on one of the Reception

Committee's old lorries, she thought it safest to make off on foot, alone with her "husband" Raymond Pezet, who did not like the idea of walking through the night while they both carried the heavy luggage. After about three miles they got a lift from a farm cart with squeaky axles.

The mail pick-up was on 7/8 July with a specially fitted Lysander flown by Bill Taylor. Flight Sergeant Thomas, who is half French, was his winch-operator in the rear cockpit, though he was really an air gunner.

Per Hysing-Dahl remembered experimenting with mail pick-up training in the dark period. A 20-foot long bamboo pole, like a fishing rod, was lowered from the Lysander's tail. It carried a line with a hook on the end. On the ground two light masts were erected with a torch on the top of each and a wire loop stretched between them. This loop was connected to a mail bag lying on the field. The Lysander had to fly very low to engage the hook in the loop between the lights and then climb smartly away while the line first paid out and was then winched in. There was a cunning device to allow Tommy Thomas to hoist the mail bag inboard for the return flight.

Since the Lysanders on mail pick-up (MPU) did not actually land, I am not giving details of all the MPU operations. But there was one extraordinary incident during training flights at Tempsford which (even though a digression) must be recorded. Bob Large told me that he was practising one day with Tommy as winch-operator. Their mail bag was represented by a sack of sand in the triangle of grass between the concrete runways. When it was snatched, this sack bounced once on the edge of a runway and split open. Quite unseen by the crew, the hook flew up and engaged in the Lysander's elevators. Tommy was winching in and Bob noticed that the stick was moving back against his hand. As the Lysander started to climb uncontrollably, Bob said: "Tommy, what the hell are you doing?" Tommy had no idea what was wrong, but reversed what he was doing, ie winching in. It was only after they had landed that they discovered that the hook had whipped up over the tailplane and engaged in the elevator. If Tommy had not reacted instantly, they would certainly have stalled and crashed.

Bob Large told me another story about MPU with Tommy Thomas. On their way back from France they found radiation fog all over Southern England, ending over the coastline. They were diverted to the fighter airfield on Bolt Head, near Salcombe. After an unsuccessful attempt to make an approach through the fog, Bob realised that they had only five minutes worth of fuel left and decided that they should bale out. Not wanting to seem alarmist, he conveyed this decision to Tommy in a super-calm tone of voice and slewed the Lysander into a side-slip to make it easier for Tommy to step out. He got no reply on the intercom - only "eight cupfuls" - pause - "nine cupfuls".

While Bob was wondering what this might mean, he noticed that Bolt Head had started putting up mortar flares which burst above the top of the fog. He let down and broke through a very low cloud base right over the middle of the airstrip. A rapid, tight, low-level circuit and he landed - with virtually dry fuel tanks.

"Tommy", he asked, "Why didn't you react when I told you to bale out?"

"Oh", said Tommy, "was that what you were droning on about? I didn't pay attention. I was too busy peeing into the cup on my thermos flask."

Now, to return to the excuse for these digressions: Operation 'Toupet' on 7/8 July went smoothly. The mail was successfully snatched on the first attempt. On the return flight Bill Taylor and Tommy heard Per Hysing-Dahl on the radio transmitting for a fix. Five minutes later they heard "further remarks to the effect that he was being shot at by heavy flak over the beach-head". They heard nothing more.

Captain Hysing-Dahl and Flight Lieutenant Turner were together on a Lysander double called 'Palais' five miles ESE of Bléré on the River Cher. Because of the bridgehead they left from Tempsford and crossed the French coast at Trouville. Turner landed back at Tempsford. This must have been an operation for the 'Sussex' inter-allied intelligence missions. Each had three passengers with him and Turner delivered his three and picked up three others. Per Hysing Dahl was delayed at Tempsford by engine trouble on take-off. He took the reserve aircraft and must have been at least twenty minutes behind George Turner when he reached the Loire and went to the rendezvous. By then George Turner had already landed. Per went on to the target, but saw no lights. He returned towards the coast, heading for Trouville. He had to fly through a corridor to avoid the defences of the beach-head, but he found that he had miscalculated and was over the beach-head, off track and under fire from the coast. He thinks that it was probably American anti-aircraft guns that hit his Lysander.

One wing was hit and the aileron practically removed. The oil reservoir behind his head was punctured and he and his passengers were all covered with spurting oil. Shells were exploding all round him. One piece of shrapnel wounded him in one hand. Short of oil, the engine seized up.

He decided that it would be best to ditch in the sea, about 20 miles from the coast. He glided down at 70 mph. He had been to an air/sea rescue course a few months before and vividly remembered the drill he had been taught for ditching at night. They had said that you should line up to ditch into the moon so that you could see the surface of the water in the moon's reflection. You should disregard the direction of the wind and the waves. He prepared to do this and completed the drill: open cockpit canopy; straps very tight; remove helmet and disconnect leads; tail well down before impact. The Frenchmen had sensibly slid their rear canopy open. The Lysander's wheels caught in the water; the tail flicked over; the three passengers were catapulted out, above the sinking front cockpit. The Lysander was sinking fast, upside down. Per found himself sitting in the cockpit under water. He undid his harness, struggled out and rose to the surface. His Mae West (life jacket) would not inflate but he inflated his personal seat dinghy. His three passengers were swimming around and he eventually got two of them on to his personal dinghy. The third, who was not a strong swimmer, drowned before he could reach him.

After one and a half hours they saw a corvette about a mile and a half away but they could not attract their attention. Eventually, after another two and a half hours, they were seen by an American motor torpedo boat and were picked up at 0710 hours. On board this MTB a second passenger died of shock after several hours. He had no visible injuries. The only surviving passenger, Baudry, survived not only this ditching but the remainder of World War Two and subsequently went to Algeria.

Per Hysing-Dahl doubted if he would have survived himself if he had not been sent on that air/sea rescue course. At the end of August he was posted to HQ Royal Norwegian Air Force.

The only other pick-up that month from the UK was operation 'Tenerife' on 27/28 July, flown in a Hudson by the squadron commander, Wing Commander Alan Boxer and his crew[21]. This was the only Hudson pick-up ever flown in a non-moon period and was completed on a small grass airfield at Le Blanc, a little distance to the south-west of Châteauroux. This field had been ploughed up by the Germans about two days before the operation was completed and in the event was very rough indeed; hasty repairs completed at the last minute by the reception party saved the day and a much-needed load of medical supplies was landed. Cloud cover with a base of about 1,500 feet prolonged the search for the lights, but, once they were found, the two outward passengers and the stores were swiftly unloaded; four "evaders" boarded the aircraft and, after an alarmingly prolonged take-off run, the Hudson climbed away.

Some weeks later, after the Germans had been driven northward, an invitation to lunch was received from the townspeople of Le Blanc and the crew was entertained royally; the contrast between the culinary delights of France and the generosity of the hosts with the constrained standards of a rationed Britain was shattering[22].

Lysander pick-ups in France were also being flown from the 148 squadron detachment in Corsica during the first half of July 1944. This activity was in preparation for operation 'Anvil', the Allied landings on the French Riviera in August.

There were two double pick-ups to be done that moon from Borgo airfield south of Bastia: operation 'Tamise' on the great field called 'Spitfire' by the French, about three miles west of St Christol and north of Apt in the Vaucluse; and operation 'Thicket 2', 10 miles south of Amberieu and east of Lyon. The field for 'Thicket 2' was probably Paul Rivière's 'Figue', north of St Vulbas. In the short nights of July it would have been dangerous to attempt 'Thicket 2' from the UK and 'Tamise' was impossibly far south for a Lysander based in England.

On 8/9 July operation 'Tamise' was attempted by Flg Off R.J. Manning and Flg Off H.J. Franklin. They found the weather totally unsuitable with heavy cloud and electric storms. One of the passengers, Paul Vittori, told me that they also had to evade flak and a night fighter. Their reception's code letter was 'L' and there seemed to be many people flashing 'L's at them from different places. While waiting for the second attempt, Paul Vittori worked on the shaken morale of his fellow passengers. He found

Monument on 'Figue', unveiled in September, 1992, by Georges Libert, Président des Vieilles Tiges. Standing to the right of the monument are Hugh Verity, Paul Rivière and Peter Vaughan-Fowler, and Eddie Shine. Architect: Marius Roche.   *Audrey Verity*

this quite hard to do as he was not very keen on trying again what seemed a very unpleasant form of travel. They tried again on 10/11 July. Franklin succeeded, landing three passengers and picking up three. These included Neil Marten, who later became Minister for Overseas Development. Manning saw no signals, but on his third attempt on 11/12 July he too landed three and picked three people up. This completed operation 'Tamise'.

Soon after this, Flying Officer Manning married Diana Portman, a very attractive FANY, and they set off on their honeymoon by air from Naples where their luggage was stolen. They were both killed during take-off at Florence at the end of the leave when an American aircraft, in which they had hitched a lift, crashed, killing all on board[23].

During its annual congress in May 1976, I was a guest of the Amicale Action at an open air luncheon for 250 people on the field 'Spitfire', near a wonderful beech tree which they described as follows:

> Hêtre majestueux, témoin de nos espoirs,
> Nos amis de l'Action sont venus pour te voir,
> Lysanders, Dakota tu as vu s'envoler,
> On t'appela 'Spitfire' et ce nom t'est resté.

(Majestic beech, witness of our hopes, our Resistance friends have come to see you. You watched Lysanders and a Dakota doing pick-ups; we called you 'Spitfire' and this is still your name.)

The first attempt at operation 'Thicket 2' was on 10/11 July by two French pilots, Lt Georges Libert and Lt Bernard Cordier whose Lysanders had the cross of Lorraine painted on them. There was no reception. The following night, however, they were well received. Libert landed and his three passengers climbed out. His engine stopped and could not be restarted. Cordier landed and his three passengers got out. They decided that Libert's Lysander should be destroyed by fire. Libert returned to Corsica as Cordier's passenger. After the war Cordier was to become a monk and Libert was to reach the top of his profession as an airline captain with Air France.

Although I found no more pick-ups in France by 148 Squadron in the archives, Peter had four more trips recorded in his log-book. These were in August 1944. After two attempts when there was no reception he completed a pick-up for the American Office of Strategic Services north of St Etienne.

Peter's last pick-up in France, on 10/11 August was on the same field near Pont-de-Vaux, north of Mâcon, where he had done his first successful pick-up in October 1942. He felt it appropriate to go out where he had come in, as if he had been in a cinema. Only this time the picture was different because there was no moon. It was after the last quarter and before moonrise. As he was quietly cruising at 5,000 feet over Vienne, an enormous bombardment unexpectedly exploded beneath him on a railway target. Bomber Command were at work.

Commenting on the first edition of this book, Sir Douglas Dodds Parker wrote the following note. It refers to another previously unrecorded pick-up in this series:

"I believe the following should be in the Lizzie Book of Records. It was told me on several occasions by Willie Widmer who died 10 years ago when the *chef de cabinet* to Chaban at the Palais Bourbon. He became a General, Governor of Wurtemburg after the War. He was a Lieutenant with me in Algiers.

"The plan was to land in the South of France in August 1944; fight up the Rhône Valley; capture Lyons by October; clear the ports and supply perhaps six divisions until the spring of 1945.

"In SE France was Col 'Joseph' ie General J Zeller, later Military Governor of Paris - with Francis Cammaerts who could, Col J told me, get six times as many men into the field as he. Some days before the landings Col J was to be brought out by Lizzie from Corsica for consultations in Italy. Willie took the chance to go in on it. The field was the disused airport at Orange, N of Avignon. The two spent half an hour on the ground, discussing Col J's plan to send a column up the Route Napoleon, to turn the whole Rhône Valley. This was agreed by de Lattre. Willie stayed behind, and prepared the way. So that after 15th August a column went over the Route Napoleon, chased the Boche through Lyons, and, by October, were in the Belfort Gap, supplying 17 divisions through Marseilles (where the detonators had been removed by the Resistance).

"I will always remain convinced that, but for the availability of a Lizzie to take in and bring out key men at the vital moment, with authority and knowledge to change the original plans, the campaign might have bogged down on another 'Cassino'."

After the middle of August the South of France was liberated by the combined successes of the Allied regular forces and the Resistance networks and Maquis. No more pick-ups are recorded in France from Corsica. Peter Vaughan-Fowler's Lysander Flight of No 148 Squadron continued their work until November, landing in Greece, Yugoslavia and Northern Italy.

CHAPTER SIXTEEN

France Liberated

As the Allied forces broke out of the Normandy beach-head at the end of July 1944, landed in the South of France in mid-August and liberated Paris by the end of August, the theatre of operations for pick-ups in France shrank rapidly in size. By the end of September there was virtually no area of France left under German control in which to carry out clandestine air transport operations.

Meanwhile, before the regular forces arrived, increasing areas of France were liberated by the Maquis of the Resistance. Daylight operations became possible for parachute supplies and American Dakotas could land in these areas. Increasingly, uniformed forces of the Special Air Service, SOE's 'Jedburghs' and the American OSS Operations Groups were parachuted in to reinforce established SOE and French controlled Maquis, consisting of irregulars in plain clothes. Some SOE officers who had been with them for months could now appear, proudly, in uniform. It is against the background of this rapidly changing situation that the remaining 161 Squadron pick-ups need to be imagined.

In August 1944 the Lysanders used RAF Winkleigh, near Exeter, as a forward base. Tangmere was too close to the beach-head and the area of France already liberated. Only ten Lysander operations were carried out from the UK, of which seven were successful, but two of these were mail pick-ups. Only five actual landings in the August moon showed how the requirement was diminished. There were, nevertheless, three new pilots who went on their first Lysander operations: Flg Off J.A. Lamberton, Flg Off L.R. Newhouse and Flt Lt Peter Arkell. Peter Arkell had been with 161

Lysander over a river in 1944. *Peter Arkell*

Squadron since May, after flying Mustangs for two years.

In contrast the Hudsons, which now had four fully trained pick-up crews, completed a record number of pick-up sorties: nine, of which the Squadron Commander, Alan Boxer, did three himself.

On 4/5 August five Lysanders were out. Lamberton found no reception on operation 'Dahomey'; on his return he got the message from the field that there could be none that night. Peter Arkell was successful on his first pick-up, operation 'Pirogue', and brought back two men and a girl from St Valentin, South of Vatan. Flying Officer J.P. Alcock, also on 'Pirogue', failed to return. Peter Arkell saw him shot down in flames ahead of him on their way to the target[1]. He is buried in Messac cemetery, Ille et Vilaine.

The other two Lysanders out that night were flown by 'Lucky' Newhouse - a Canadian with thick spectacles - and 'Alex' Alexander. They were both on 'Scimitar', a double operation on a field called 'L 22' near Couture-sur-Loir[2]. Newhouse succeeded in landing three and picking up three without trouble, making this his first successful pick-up operation. One of his passengers was Paule Denise Corre (now Madame Gimpel of the famous art gallery in London). She remembers that another passenger was an evading pilot who had been sheltered by Clouet des Pesruches' father. They had been uncertain whether or not to receive the Lysanders as they could hear the German army retreating on the main road very near the field. She also remembers that there was a lot of anti-aircraft fire near them on the flight to England.

It was Alexander who had some real trouble. After being shot at by light flak, he delivered two passengers and picked up Robert Bloc-Richard and his secretary Marguerite Gianelli (now Madame-Bloc Richard) who seemed to have a broken hip. His report to his Flight Commander was as follows:

"Report to Squadron Leader Ratcliff, DSO, DFC, AFC
At approximately 0200 hours on 6th (sic) August 1944 I landed on ground L22. From the air the ground seemed excellent and the signal was well sent. My first approach was bad and I overshot. On my second attempt I touched down on stubble but on coming up level with lamps 'B' and 'C' ran into a narrow belt of standing crop. Coming out of this I ran on to stubble again, but this seemed to have obstacles in the form of stooked corn or bundles of hay. On hitting one of these I damaged my tail oleo. The field, in my estimation, was not fit at the time for pick-up operations although it would be excellent if the crop was cut and the other obstacles removed. To make sure of a safe take-off I taxied to a point about 25 to 30 yards before lamp A and with emergency boost managed to clear the obstacles.
The ground level photographs available for the field were useless and I would suggest that verticals be obtained before another pick up is laid on. It may be added that the organisation on the ground was perfect and the reception excellent."

In forwarding this report, Len Ratcliff added a footnote:
"There has been no information supplied on L22 except that brought down by a rather clueless escorting officer. There is also some doubt whether the flarepath was on the correct field."

When I met Alex in 1975 he filled in some of the details. In his encounter with the obstacles his Lysander was so badly damaged that he could not steer it normally on the ground. At normal taxying power the damaged tail-wheel made it go round in a small circle. He had to use full throttle to manoeuvre on the field. Besides that, the damage to his elevator meant that he had to fly home on the trimmer. His stick only controlled the ailerons. It could not move fore and aft. The third - and potentially most dangerous - damage was to his aerials. He had to fly home without radio to south-western England, which was covered with thick fog by the time he arrived.

In these circumstances a very lucky chance led him to RAF St Merryn in Cornwall just at the time when they were burning their fog-dispersal installation (FIDO) which consumed vast quantities of paraffin. This generated enough heat to clear the worst of the fog. Because his radio was out of action, they knew nothing of him and he did not know that a flight of four-engined Liberators were taking off one after the other. He landed in the opposite direction to the aeroplanes taking off just after the last one was airborne and just before the FIDO was turned off.

As he could not steer the Lysander round the perimeter track, he left his passengers in the back cockpit and set off on foot to find help. By this time in the war the Lysander pilots no longer bothered to cover their civilian clothes with RAF uniform. He set off through the fog in a dark grey suit, rather wondering how he would explain himself when he met somebody on duty. He walked round the perimeter track for an hour before he found the flying control tower. As he walked he thought what a remarkable aeroplane the Lysander was. Built in 1936, they were already eight years old, amazingly reliable and so tough that this one had got him home, even when very badly damaged.

Eventually he found himself explaining his arrival to the Station Commander, who made his own quarters available for the agents until they could be collected by road. Alex went back to the Lysander in the CO's car and found his two passengers entwined on the floor of their cockpit.

On 10/11 August Alan Boxer and Johnnie Affleck were both successful on their Hudson pick-ups: 'Poignard' and 'Tunisie' but Affleck had only two packages as a homeward load.

This was his last pick-up. On 2nd September he was posted to the Bomber Development Unit for a "rest" from operations. In addition to all his parachute-dropping missions Johnnie Affleck had completed six successful Hudson landings. On these he had taken to France at least 27 people and picked up 33. He was to re-enact the stickiest of his pick-ups when he took a Hudson to France in January 1945 to make a film *Now it Can be Told*.

In 1975, when the Special Forces Club thirtieth anniversary dinner was honoured by the presence of the Prince of Wales, I met Captain René O'Badia ('Pioche'), who was supporting Colonel Paul Rivière (Député de la Loire) as representatives at this reunion of the Amicale Action, the French Resistance association. 'Pioche' ('pickaxe') told me that he had been picked up, with five American aviators, from a field near Apt in the Vaucluse, in August 1944. This operation was by a Dakota borrowed from No 267 squadron based at Bari in Italy and the following account of it is taken from McCairns' unpublished memoirs. The reader will remember that Mac went to the Air Ministry to vet proposed landing strips for pick-ups, at the end of his very successful tour on 161 Squadron Lysanders, in November 1943.

When Peter Vaughan-Fowler was sent to Southern Italy with four operational Lysanders early in 1944, Mac joined him at Brindisi as Air Ministry representative and training instructor. Mac was disappointed to find that local requirements directed the Lysanders mainly to Greece and Yugoslavia which were already served by Dakotas - more or less openly - instead of operating into Northern Italy and

Southern France as originally intended. Eventually, as we have seen, they were used for Southern France in June, July and August from Borgo Bastia and Calvi in Northern Corsica.

At the beginning of August 1944, Corsica was packed with Allied aircraft and other forces preparing for the landing in the South of France which was then imminent. The Lysanders were overloaded with requests for pick-ups but the weather was bad and there was a shortage of approved fields. A week before the landing they had 14 different officers whom it was essential to fly in before it took place.

Arrangements were made to borrow a Dakota from a Transport Command squadron. The crew, captained by a South African, Flying Officer Rostron[3], had never done a clandestine pick-up and Mac got permission to fly with them as technical adviser. Although there were serious doubts about the fitness of the ground, they were told that these agents must be delivered within 48 hours even if it meant a crash landing. Operating from Cecina in Northern Italy, they set off on the night of 8th August with 14 agents, including one woman. They met violent thunderstorms and torrential rain over France at a safe height of 6,000 feet. After dropping down to 5,000 feet, they had to admit defeat.

The next day continuous rain turned their earth strip into mud-bath. The next night they just managed to unstick in 2,000 yards. When over the target there was no welcoming signal. They circled until they noticed, about five miles away, a triangle of lights and someone frantically signalling. They flew over the spot, but it looked much too undulating for a landing field, so, suspecting some sort of trap, they charged in again at low level and snapped on the small searchlight carried on the nose. In its white glare a score of maquisards scattered, thinking the Dakota was a German night fighter gunning for them. They had been waiting for a parachute drop.

As Rostron approached the field for the second time, he noticed a car tearing along the mountain road; every now and then, a light flashed from it. It was 'C' for Charlie - the code letter of the night. They circled as it approached the field and pulled in at a farmhouse. Then, by flying low, they could make out a cluster of figures leave the farm and run to the field. First of all a red lamp was laid on the boundary and then, one by one, 10 tiny dots appeared as lamps were lit for the next 1,000 yards. The line was not very straight, in fact towards the end it curved inwards, but it was good enough. The make up of the strip was puzzling as there were three different coloured patches, almost as if three fields had been joined together.

After a perfect landing just after the first light, they ran on quite smoothly until the colour of the vegetation changed and they came to a sudden halt. The searchlight revealed that the Dakota was in thick luxuriant vegetation, some 18 inches high. Muttering a curse, with full throttle on the port engine, Rostron laboriously swung round and taxied back to the crowd at 'A'.

Mac jumped down from the machine and sought out the agent in charge who was Camille Rayon.

"Hey, what the devil is the meaning of this - how much room have we?"

"1,200 yards" he answered.

"1,200 Hades - what is that stuff we landed in?"

Then, as they walked along the strip, checking the surface, he explained. There was a run of 1,200 yards, but to camouflage it from the prying eyes of the Hun, or from a chance aircraft, the constructor had planted a bed of lavender 200 yards long after a stretch of 600 yards good grassland. Then there was 400 yards of grassland and then a crop of potatoes. As Mac climbed aboard, he found 30 passengers squashed in everywhere. Some were in uniform, blue or khaki, some in smart civilian clothes, others in rags. There were eight Frenchmen and the rest were evading Americans, mostly Fortress crews.

Mac explained the distances and the lavender bed ahead. Rostron decided to attempt a take-off. With the engines developing their maximum power, he released the brakes and off they went, bumping clumsily over the rough ground but at least accelerating. They must have been nearly airborne when they reached the lavender, then their speed was checked and reduced to a standstill.

Next time they went back to the extreme edge of the field and over the red boundary light before turning into wind again. Rostron ordered the load to be cut down to 22 passengers, and Mac broke the news that eight Americans had to get out. Never had he seen better discipline; without a murmur or a question, the last eight aboard turned round, and with only a casual "Say, can you come for us tomorrow night?" jumped off and joined the waiting crowd.

Down the strip they roared a second time, anxiously watching the ground in the searchlight's glare. Mac could feel the sweat trickling down his brow and dripping on the floor. One hundred yards ahead was the lavender bed; he looked at the air speed indicator - 65, 66, 67 - they might just do it. There was a horrible lurch, the aircraft staggered as though hit and the airspeed needle dropped immediately to 45 and continued falling. They ploughed their way through 200 yards of lavender. With a speed of 30 miles per hour, they broke through and on to the firm grass beyond. Immediately the speed increased, and as they gradually accelerated, they waited for the appearance of the potato crop. There it was - black in the rays of the lamp, and, as it came nearer, they could feel the wheels occasionally leaving the ground. With 10 yards to go, Rostron heaved back on the stick, the main wheels cleared and with the tail wheel still dragging in the potatoes - in the most horrible nose-up position - they became airborne.

On the next night Rostron came back, hoping to pick up the American aircrew, but there was no reception. Camille Rayon told me in 1988 that the Germans had already burnt the isolated farm near the field 'Spitfire' and shot the inhabitants.

The September moon - the last for operational pick-ups in France - started with a maximum effort of two Hudson doubles on the night of 31st August/1st September. In the event the return loads hardly justified the name 'pick-up'. On operation 'Xylophone' Alan Boxer took eight out and there is no record of a return load. Flight Lieutenant Helfer landed six passengers and had nothing to bring back. The other double was 'Dauntsey' on which Ibbott landed three and picked up four. Sqn Ldr Wilkinson who landed only two passengers had only one letter to bring back.

Flight Lieutenant Helfer and crew (in flying overalls), with passengers and ground party. Helfer with white scarf.

On 5/6 September two more Hudson doubles are recorded. On operation 'Failsworthy' - a curious code-name - Group Captain Fielden failed, because of weather, and flew his three passengers to Brussels. Flight Lieutenant Helfer, however, succeeded. He landed nine and picked up seven people. But he did not return to base until lunchtime the next day having been away for over nine hours. This may have been when Richard Broad, Morel and six others[4] set out in a mission called 'Etoile' to work in southern Franche-Comté.

The other double Hudson pick-up undertaken on 5/6 September, operation 'Dullingham', was on the airfield at Toulouse-Francazal, which had been liberated from enemy occupation since the third week of August[5]. So, although it was conducted as a clandestine landing, it is outside the limits I have set for this book.

This completed the operational role of the Lysander pilots and Hudson crews in clandestine landings in enemy occupied France. Hardly any French territory now remained in enemy hands. The parachuting role of the rest of the special duties squadrons still continued with operations in Denmark and Norway and there were some small scale parachutings of agents into Germany itself, some of which were carried out by the Hudsons. But the main work of the Lysanders and Hudsons now became non-operational special transport services to liberated France and Belgium. In September the Hudsons made 65 sorties of this type and the Lysanders 23. Unfortunately one Lysander pilot, Flg Off Lamberton, failed to return to base on a return flight from le Bourget.

In October Squadron Leader Ratcliff was posted to Air Ministry, Directorate of Intelligence (Operations), having left Flight Lieutenant Turner in temporary charge of the Lysander Flight until it was disbanded. It was run down to a nucleus of three aircraft as the embryonic Lysander Flight for work in Burma behind the Japanese lines. There George Turner would be the pick-up flight commander in No 357 Special Duties Squadron commanded by Wing Commander L.McD. Hodges, DSO, DFC, the former squadron commander of No 161 Squadron. The nucleus of Turner's pilots for Burma were Flight Lieutenants Williams and Arkell. During the third week of November George Turner was flying at Tempsford and on the field at Somersham for the RAF Film Unit. The unit was making *School for Danger* for the Central Office of Information. Later called *Now it Can be Told*, its world premiere was not until February 1947. The Lysander used in this film, R 9125, is the one survivor now in the RAF Museum at Hendon. It has, unfortunately, been converted back to the Army Co-operation style in its exterior appearance in camouflage colours and by the removal of the torpedo-shaped petrol tank and the fixed external ladder. The rear cockpit, however, is still fitted out for pick-up passengers and their luggage. In November 1974 the Tempsford Reunion Association had a party of French Resistance friends climbing into it from step ladders.

Bill Taylor had arranged to return to Mosquitoes. Bob Large remembers that he went to specially-fitted 'Serrate' night fighters at North Luffenham. Designed for 'intruding' with our bomber stream, they had backward-looking as well as forward-looking AI (aircraft interception radar). Once an enemy night fighter was intercepting them from astern, they would swiftly orbit and shoot him down. Bill Taylor did this until he flew through the wreckage of one of his kills. This damaged one of his flaps. On his approach to land this flap did not come down and he and his radar-operator were killed.

In November the Hudson flight commander, Squadron Leader R.E. Wilkinson, and his crew[6] were shot down and killed on a parachute operation over Germany. They crashed near Aachen and were buried in Evere town cemetery, Brussels. He had taken part in three Hudson pick-ups. At the end of 1944 Group Captain Fielden, the Station Commander, RAF Tempsford, left to take over RAF Woodhall Spa as an Air Commodore. In a tribute to his leadership Greg Holdcroft, the Station Administrator, wrote to me: "Never was there a station like Tempsford. Everybody seemed to pull his or her weight and discipline was never mentioned. We were very fortunate indeed to have Group Captain Fielden as the CO. If ever he spoke of our flying personnel it was always with unstinted praise and with no adverse comment *ever*."

From 1st January 1945 the new Station Commander was Group Captain E.J. Palmer, an Australian, from the Air Ministry. Wing Commander Boxer went to HQ Bomber Command in January 1945 and the picture of senior personalities who had been involved in pick-ups was really disintegrating. Only Len Ratcliff remained. He had come back from Air Ministry to be Wing Commander Operations at Tempsford and took command of 161 Squadron in March 1945.

The Hudson crews found the night fighters operating near the front line very dangerous. (There is some doubt which side they were on.) On the night of 20/21 March three Hudsons were shot down over France on their way to drop agents in Germany. Of these, two aircraft captains, Flt Lt A.N. Ferris and Flt Lt T. Helfer, had done pick-ups. Helfer miraculously escaped, badly burned, on his parachute[7]. Most of the members of these three crews and their passengers were killed.

From May onwards the squadron was flying out supplies to liberated countries and returning former prisoners of war to the UK. During the war, including the parachute and other operations, no fewer than 140 honours and awards had been gazetted to its members. The squadron history sums up the story in Latin:

SIC PER GLORIAM IN MUNDUM TRANSIMUS.

As even the RAF archives are incomplete it may never be possible to establish final and unquestionable statistics. There does, however, seem to be convincing evidence that Royal Air Force landings moved at least the following numbers of people to and from enemy occupied France (and the unoccupied zone which, up to November 1942, was controlled by the hostile Vichy administration):

	Operational sorties	Successes	Passengers To France	From France
Lysanders	279	186	293	410
Anson	1	1	–	4
Hudsons	46	36	137	218
Dakota	3	1	15	23
Totals	329	224	445	655

Of these 224 successful landings, 125 were made in 1943 alone. In this one year of peak activity for pick-ups, about 220 passengers were landed in France and over 400 picked up. United States Dakotas based in the UK did 20 pick-up sorties to France in 1944 for SOE[8]. They took 62 people into France and brought back 108. They no doubt did many more on all-American operations for OSS (Office of Strategic Services), the forerunner of the CIA.

Turning to the losses on these operations, it is really remarkable that there were no

Hudsons lost on actual pick-ups and so few Lysanders - only 13 completely written off. Of these: two were irretrievably bogged in muddy fields; four crashed on landing in France (one pilot error, one agent's error, one engine failure and the fourth - John Nesbitt-Dufort's - was due to bad weather); three crashed in fog in the UK on return, and four were shot down over France. Seven of these thirteen pilots were recovered. Only six were killed, while actually on pick-up operations.

One of the obvious potential hazards in any penetration of enemy defences was the risk of being shot down by night fighters. We knew that this was much less serious over France than it would have been over Holland on the heavily defended approaches to Germany. It has distressed me to find reports of pick-up pilots and Hudson crews (though the latter were not on pick-up operations at the time) being shot down over France by allied fighters - British, Canadian or American - who were 'intruding' over enemy territory. They are said to have mistaken the Lysanders for Henschel light aircraft and, on one occasion, a Hudson for a Ju88. As a former night fighter pilot myself I can well appreciate how these tragedies could have happened. Aircraft recognition at night was not easy.

The whole of the effort put into pick-up operations in France throughout the war - measured by aircraft and personnel costs - was minute. In a well proportioned history of World War Two it might deserve a sentence or a footnote. And yet it is hard to imagine how the irregular forces in France could have developed to anything like the same extent without these two-way air links.

The conduct of the secret war within France demanded physical communications links to a rear base - initially Britain - for the movement of leaders, for training and for delivery of intelligence material too bulky to transmit by wireless. On a lower priority, escape and evasion for agents and aircrew was also important. Of course there were other routes - by sea, or over the Pyrenees - but these were painfully slow and uncertain and of very limited capacity.

I may be biased but it seems to me that there may be a connection between these two facts:

Firstly, France was the only occupied country in Western Europe which had an air transport service to the allied world, as well as clandestine sea communications, and, of course, parachuted people and supplies.

Secondly, France was the occupied country where clandestine networks and secret armies made the greatest physical contribution to liberation by the fully equipped regular forces of the Allies.

A useful analogy is drilling for oil. The population of an occupied country which is hostile to the occupying power represents an enormous supply of potential energy underground. This is of little value if communication links are not adequate to harness the energy and direct it. It may then be agreed that the pick-up service in France was a highly cost-effective use of very small resources.

A considerable part of the pick-up service was at the disposal of SOE, and, through SOE, of de Gaulle's resistance organisations. By D-Day all these irregular forces were under command of General Eisenhower, who wrote to General Gubbins on 31st May 1945:

"In no previous war, and in no other theatre during this war, have resistance forces been so closely harnessed to the main military effort.

While no final assessment of the operational value of resistance action has yet been completed, I consider that the disruption of enemy rail communications, the harassing of German road moves and the continual and increasing strain placed on the German war economy and internal security services throughout occupied Europe by the organised forces of resistance, played a very considerable part in our complete and final victory…"

The other supreme allied commander operating across France, Sir H. Maitland Wilson, is quoted on the subject of the value of resistance troops to the regular forces liberating Southern France:

"He unofficially estimated that the existence of this force reduced the fighting efficiency of the Wehrmacht in southern France to forty per cent at the moment of the 'Dragoon' landing operations[9]."

What of the people involved in pick-ups? The reader will have noticed what a mixed bag we were. Few of us were in the RAF before the war as regulars. A very few stayed on to make successful peacetime careers in the RAF. The level of morale and individual motivation was exceptionally high in both aircrews and ground crews, but it was the challenge to the individual pilot-navigator or very small Hudson crew, operating on one's own - not military discipline keeping a large formation together - that was our inspiration. We were all different and our greatest common factor must have been our individualism.

Looking back on it there is no doubt that we all thought the job more dangerous than it actually was. We did not realise at the time that the German counter-espionage security services were more interested in trailing our passengers than in capturing and interrogating us. Yet there are several indications that this was the case. Nevertheless, ordinary flying risks were multiplied by the nature of the task and successful achievement brought great personal satisfaction.

Imperial War Museum

Imperial War Museum, Duxford, October 1993: roll-out of facsimile of Lysander 'J', with Peter Arkell, Hugh Verity, Sir Lewis Hodges, Peter Vaughan-Fowler, Sir Alan Boxer, Len Ratcliffe and Tommy Thomas.

CHAPTER SEVENTEEN

Postscript

As a sequel to this story, the reader may be interested in a brief summary of what happened to the pilots and aircrews whose names are mentioned most frequently in earlier pages.

The pioneers of pick-ups in World War Two were: Farley, Murphy and Lockhart, who were killed on other types of operations later in the war; and Scotter and Nesbitt-Dufort, who survived the war and made careers in civil aviation, though Scotter died while in his prime and Nesbitt-Dufort in 1975.

My contemporaries in 1942/43 included: Bathgate who was shot down over France on a pick-up; Hankey and McBride who were killed in fog on return to base after pick-ups; Pickard who was later shot down in his Mosquito on the Amiens prison operation; McCairns and Bridger who were killed in flying accidents after the war; Livry-Level who died in 1960 of a heart attack; Air Vice Marshal Sir Edward Fielden, our much-loved Tempsford Station Commander, who died in 1976 at the age of 72, having been responsible for royal flights for thirty - three years from 1929. Sir Robin Hooper, who had been Ambassador to Greece, died in June 1989 aged 74. Group Captain Vaughan-Fowler, who made his career in the RAF, and had eight children, died in April, 1994, aged 71. Squadron Leader Frank 'Bunny' Rymills, who retired in 1963, became a successful pig farmer in Suffolk and manufacturer in Cambridge. He died in January 1997 aged 76. Flight Lieutenant Eddie Shine left the RAF after the war to run a country pub. His funeral in 1997 saw the large parish church at Knaresborough packed with his friends. Survivors of those days include: Air Chief Marshal Sir Lewis Hodges, whose RAF career has been outstandingly successful; Captain Affleck, a retired training captain in British Airways and Squadron Leader Wagland, who was in the RAF for the war only and was then in the City.

The 1944 vintage of pick-up pilots included: McDonald, Alcock and Whitaker, who were killed on pick-ups; Taylor and Lamberton, as well as Ferris and Wilkinson and their crews, who were subsequently killed on operations during the war; Turner, who died while gardening in 1976, had commanded the Lysander pick-up flight in Burma as a Squadron Leader and returned to the Metropolitan police after the war; and Per Hysing-Dahl, who died in April 1989 after being President of the Storting, the Norwegian Parliament.

Survivors from that period include: Air Vice-Marshal Sir Alan Boxer, who, after a successful RAF career, conducted planning enquiries; Len Ratcliff, who was running his family business; Peter Arkell, who did no fewer than 35 Lysander pick-ups behind the Japanese lines in the mountains of Burma and is now Chairman of his family brewery; Murray Anderson, who made his career as a civil airline captain in India and England; Bob Large, who was also in civil aviation and then a probation officer; 'Alex' Alexander, a director of Reckitt & Colman. Douglas Bell, who became a V-bomber Wing Commander, died in 1986.

On 28th February 1980 the first edition of this book led to a meeting of seventeen surviving pick-up aircrew with the Royal family. Sir Douglas Dodds-Parker had astonished me by suggesting that I should present copies to Her Majesty The Queen and to H.M. Queen Elizabeth, The Queen Mother.

Sir Lewis Hodges spoke first, outlining the history of Tempsford which had been commanded for most of the war by 'Mouse' Fielden, the Captain of the King's Flight. After I had presented the only two leather-bound copies of this book, we all had tea, swiftly followed by drinks. Sir Martin Gilliat told me that in twenty-five years with the Royal Family he could not remember another reception like it. It was so small and so relaxed. Nor could he remember one on that small scale where so many members of the Royal Family had wanted to come.

Ministry of Defence

Half-a-dozen pick-up pilots thirty years later. Seated: Sir Robin Hooper, Sir Lewis Hodges, Per Hysing-Dahl, Peter Vaughan-Fowler. Standing: Hugh Verity and Sir Alan Boxer.

APPENDIX A

Glossary

Abwehr

German forces security service under Admiral Canaris which competed with the *SS Sicherheitsdienst* under Himmler (See *SOE in France* pp. 115-9).

AI2C

The branch of Air Intelligence which vetted and approved requests for air operations by secret agencies. It was a part of the Directorate of Intelligence (Operations) or DOI (O).

Alliance

A French Intelligence organisation led by Marie-Madeleine Méric and Commandant Faye.

Back Bearing

Compass direction from a direction finding radio or radar station behind the aircraft.

BAT

Beam approach training.

BCRA

Bureau Central de Renseignements et d'Action. De Gaulle's secret service covering (from 1942) both intelligence and operations.

BOA

Bureau d 'Opérations Aériennes. The body set up in 1942 to organise air operations in the occupied zone.

Boost

Expressed as pounds (per square inch) in British aircraft or inches (of mercury) in American aircraft, boost was a measure of fuel pressure at the carburettor inlet and therefore of engine power.

Castor (verb)

To swivel.

Ceux de la Libération

A network in Northern France, founded by Maurice Ripoche, with air force links.

Circuit

A network of agents.

Circuit

The pattern flown round an airfield before landing.

CND

Confrérie Notre-Dame. Rémy's intelligence network.

COPA

Centre des Opérations de Parachutages et d'Atterrissages. The equivalent in the South of BOA. It was renamed SAP, *Section d'Atterrissages et de Parachutages*.

DCA

La défense contre avions. Anti-aircraft defence or 'flak'.

Dead Reckoning (DR)

The estimation of an aircraft's position from the time flown, airspeed, compass course (or heading) steered and estimated wind speed and direction, but without visual, radio or astronomical observations.

Demarcation Line

The border between the northern and western zone of France which was occupied by the Germans in 1940 and the 'unoccupied zone', which was also occupied in 1942.

Deuxième Bureau

French intelligence department.

DF Section

SOE escape section.

DREM system

A layout of airfield, circuit and approach lighting (originated at Drem in Scotland) which facilitated night flying in poor visibility.

Evade	To avoid capture in enemy held territory and make a clandestine journey back to one's own side. Escapers had escaped from captivity.They also used evasion routes and the assistance they provided.
FIDO	'Fog Investigation and Dispersal Operation'. Actually lines of paraffin burners which dispersed fog on runways.
'Firms'	Slang for the various secret organisations.
Flak protection colour	A visual identification by flares (or Very lights) of prearranged colours to stop an aircraft being shot down by its own side. Also referred to in code as 'sisters'.
Free French Committee	Strictly, *Comité Français de Libération Nationale*. In Algiers, this became the provisional government of France in June 1944.
French Forces of the Interior	
	The army of the new France that was to be formed in March 1944 by de Gaulle's decree.
F (French) Section	The SOE country section in Baker Street, London, headed by Col. Maurice Buckmaster, which ran networks in France independently of de Gaulle. Cf. RF Section.
Gee	Medium-range radar aid to navigation employing ground transmitters and airborne receiver.
Giraudist	A supporter of General Giraud who escaped from the Riviera by submarine in 1942 and was for a time a potential rival to General de Gaulle.
Group	An RAF formation of stations commanded by an Air Vice-Marshal, the Air Officer Commanding.
IFF	Identification Friend or Foe. A device in an aircraft for identifying 'friendlies' to radar stations.
Interallié	The intelligence organisation headed by Czerniawski.
Intruder	Offensive night patrols over enemy territory intended to destroy hostile aircraft and to dislocate the enemy flying organisations.
ISLD	Inter-Service Liaison Department.
Jazzing the throttle	Pumping the throttle as one might the accelerator of a car, when starting.
Lamp 'A'	The first torch in the flarepath for a pick-up landing, near which the 'reception committee', - agent and passengers - stood on the left and the aircraft touched down on the right.
Libération	A large resistance network among those under Jean Moulin's influence and hence de Gaulle's.
Line-book	A note-book in which amusing remarks, generally jocular boasting, were written. In RAF slang one 'shot a line'.
Meta fuel	Camping fuel in tablet form.
Military Delegate	*Délégués Militaires Régionals* were nominated by the French in London from 1943 as a national military command structure over resistancc in zones and regions in France.

MI9	The department concerned with escape and evasion from enemy, enemy-occupied and neutral territory (MI = Military Intelligence).
'Money' Flares	Very bright flares used to augment a flarepath during a fog.
MVO	Member of the (Royal) Victorian Order.
National Council of the Resistance	The *Conseil National de la Résistance* was the senior body inside France set up by de Gaulle in 1943 with Jean Moulin as President.
Occupied Zone	The northern and western parts of France which were occupied by the Germans from the 1940 armistice. From November 1942 the whole of France was occupied.
OCM	*Organisation Civile et Militaire*. A body run by former French army officers.
Oleo (leg or strut)	Hydraulic shock absorber in undercarriage.
ORA	Army Resistance Organisation which grew in secret after the demobilisation of the French Army in November 1942.
ORB	Operations Record Book.
OSS	Office of Strategic Services. The American secret service organisation with responsibility for both intelligence and special operations.
OTU	Operation Training Unit.
PAT	The escape and evasion line run by Lt-Cdr 'Patrick O'Leary', R.N., actually Albert Guérisse, a Belgian army doctor.
Patriotic School	The custody in which new arrivals from enemy-held Europe were held until their bona-fides were established. (The Royal Victoria Patriotic School - now 'Building' - opposite Wandsworth prison).
Pinpoint	A visual fix of position by positive identification of features on the ground.
Pitch	The angle of the blades of a propellor to the air through which it is moving. (Fine pitch for take-off and coarse pitch for cruising.)
Pitot tube (or pressure head)	The device which measured static and dynamic air pressure outside the aircraft for altimeter and airspeed instruments.
PRU	Photographic Reconnaissance Unit.
Radio loop	A rotating loop aerial for determining the direction of a transmitter by minimum signal strength.
RF Country Section	SOE's staff which worked with the Free French, headed by Jim Hutchison from August 1942 until the autumn of 1943 and, later, by L.H. Dismore. Cf. F Section.
RCAF	Royal Canadian Airforce.
R/T	Radiotelephony.
SAP	*Service d 'Atterrissages et de Parachutages*. The organisation in the southern half of France that arranged and received landings and parachute operations for the Free French. Cf BOA.
SD	Special Duties (for example, of RAF squadrons).

SD	*Sicherheitsdienst.* The German security service under Himmler's SS.
Secret Vote	The Government funds which met the costs of the secret service.
SIS	Secret Intelligence Service.
Slats	Narrow aerofoils which open and close automatically (with airspeed) along the whole leading edge of a Lysander wing. Inboard slats lower trailing edge flaps gradually as the speed decreases.
SOE	Special Operations Executive.
S-phone	An early portable microwave radio telephone developed by SOE for agents to talk to aircraft or ships.
SR	*Service de Renseignements*, French Army Intelligence.
SR Air	French Air Force Intelligence Service.
SS	*Schutzstaffel.* The SS was under Himmler. See SD and *Abwehr*.
Tail arm	A long handle to attach to the swivelling tail wheel of an aeroplane so that it can be manoeuvred by hand on the ground.
Trim, trimming tabs	An aeroplane can be trimmed to fly 'hands off', or nearly so, by adjusting the trimming tabs at the trailing edge of ailerons or elevator. The Lysander tail plane itself could be trimmed by adjusting its angle of incidence with a handwheel in the cockpit.
Vichy	Pétain's government of defeated France which more or less co-operated with the Germans.
V-Weapons	*Vergeltungswaffen.* Reprisal weapons: Vl flying bomb or 'doodle bug' and V2 long-range rocket.

APPENDIX B

Summary of RAF Pick-up Operations in France

This appendix includes the most recently available details from the author's contacts and correspondents as well as from archives in the Public Record Office opened since earlier research and from recently published books. The numbers in brackets under 'Location of field' are, of course, the *Départements*. See page 211.

Unit, Date and Aircraft	Crew	Operation and Agent	Location of field	Passengers to France	Passengers From France
419 Flight 19/20 Oct 40 Lysander	Flt Lt. W.R. Farley	? Phillip Schneidau	SSE of Fontaine- bleau, 1.5 km NNW of Montigny (77)	- -	(1) Phillip Schneidau ('Felix') -
					(Crashed near Oban, Scotland on return)
1419 Flight March 1941	Flight number changed. OC Sqn Ldr E.V. Knowles DFC. Based at RAF Stradishall in 3 Group, Bomber Command.				
11/12 Apr 41 Lysander	Flt Lt F.M.G. Scotter	CART Cartwright	6 km NNE of Châteauroux, 10 km S of Brion (36)		(1) Lt 'Cartwright'
10 May 41 Lysander	Flt Lt Scotter DFC	? Philip Schneidau	Near Fontainbleau, on edge of forest (77)	-	(1) Flg Off Philip Schneidau
22 May 41	1419 Flight moved to Newmarket Racecourse.				
25 Aug 41	No 138 Special Duties Squadron formed from 1419 Flight. CO Wg Cdr E.V. Knowles DFC.				
4/5 Sep 41 Lysander	Flt Lt John Nesbitt-Dufort	LEVEE/ FACADE Maj J. de Guélis	NE of Châteauroux, 6 km N of Neuvy Pailloux (36)	(1) Gerry Morel (Morel boarded at Ford airfield, near Littlehampton.)	(1) Jacques de Guélis
1/2 Oct 41 Lysander	Sqn Ldr J. Nesbitt-Dufort	BRICK Lt Mitchell	WNW of Compiègne, 2 km NE of Estrées St Denis (60)	-	(1) Roman Czerniawski ('Armand')
7 Nov 41 Lysander	Sqn Ldr J. Nesbitt-Dufort DFC	BRICK Lt Mitchell ('Brick')	W of Soissons, 4 km NW of Saconin (02)	(1)	(2) Lt Mitchell, Claude Lamirault ('Fitzroy')
8/9 Dec 41 '38 (SD) Sqn	Flt Lt A.M. Murphy	STOAT Capt Cassart	Belgium, near Neufchâteau	(Landed but failed. Ambushed and shot, but returned)	
18 Dec 41	138 Sqn moved to Stradishall,. Strength now 12 Whitleys, 3 Halifax and 3 Lysanders. CO Wg Cdr W.R. Farley DFC.				
28 Jan 42 Lysander	Sqn Ldr J. Nesbitt-Dufort DSO, DFC	BERYL Lt Mitchell	(1) SSE of Issoudun, 4 km WSW of Ségry (36) (2) E of Issoudun, Le Coudray, Civray (36)	(1) Simon (Picked up two passengers, Maurice Duclos and Roger Mitchell, but landed in France again because of bad weather and crashed.	
14 Feb 42	161 (SD) Squadron began forming at Newmarket Racecourse, CO Wg Cdr E. H. Fielden MVO, AFC. 7 Lysanders from 138 Sqn, 5 Whitley 5s, 2 Wellingtons and one Hudson - The King's aircraft.				
161 (SD) Sqn 21/22 Feb 42 Lysander	?	CRÈME 'Pierre'	'FAUCON' S of Vatan (36), 2.5 km W of Villeneuve	(2) (Not in RAF Operations Book)	
27/28 Feb 42 Lysander	Flt Lt A. M. Murphy DFC	BACCARAT	NNE of Rouen, 1.5 km E of St Saëns (76)	(1) 'Anatole'	(2) 'Rémy' (Gilbert Renault-Roulier), Pierre Julitte
1 Mar 42	161 Sqn moved to RAF Graveley.				

Unit, Date and Aircraft	Crew	Operation and Agent	Location of field	Passengers to France	Passengers From France
1/2 Mar 42 Lysander	Flg Off W. G. Lockhart	'CREME Jean Faillon	S of Vatan, 2 km NW of Les Lagnys	-	(2) Louis Andlauer, Stanislas Mangin
		(In 1942 Jean Faillon looked after five landings in his fields at Les Lagnys and on those lent by Monsieur Mouchet of Barillon.)			
1/2 Mar 42 Anson R3316	Sqn Ldr Alan Murphy, Plt Off Henry Cossar	BERYL II and III Lt Mitchell	ESE of Issoudun, 1.5 km NE of Ségry (36)	-	(4) J. N- Dufort, Lt Mitchell, M. F. Duclos ('St Jacques'), Gen Julius Kleeberg ('Tudor'/Zaremski')
26/27 Mar 42 Lysander	Flg Off Guy Lockhart	BACCARAT II Georges Geay, Robert Delattre ('Bob')	'ROI DE COEUR' S. of Samur, 2.5 km NW of St Léger de Mont-brillais (86)	(1) 'Rémy' (G. Renault-Roulier)	(2) Christian Pineau, François Faure
		Stuck in mud for 17 minutes, having gone into plough about 50 yards beyond Light 'B'. About seven men pushed the Lysander round. See C. Pineau, *La Simple Verité*, pp 143-151			
1/2 April 42 Lysander	Sqn Ldr Murphy	EASTER 'Trellu' (Pierre Hentic)	WNW of Gisors, 3.5 km ENE of Etrépagny (27)	(1) FFL Agent 'Claudius'	(2) Lamirault ('Fitzroy'), 'Fitzroy II' (Micheline?)
		The Pilot's report refers to a female passenger who was airsick in a thunder cloud.			
8-10 Apr	161 Squadron moved from RAF Graveley to RAF Tempsford, near Sandy, Bedfordshire.				
26/27 April 42 Lysander	Flt Lt Guy Lockhart	JELLYFISH/ GAZELLE G. Tavian ('Collin')	'FAUCON' S of Vatan (36), 2.5 km W of Villeneuve	(1) Pierre Beech	(2) Gaston Tavian, Lieut Mariotti (Rousseau)?
				The engine caught fire on the field.	
27/28 Apr 42 Lysander	Sqn Ldr Murphy	BRIDGE Robert Delattre	NNE of Rouen, 1.5 km E of St. Saëns (76)	(2) Christian Pineau, François Faure	(2) Jacques Robert, Pierre Brossolette
		An operation for Col. Rémy's CND Castile network.			
28/29 May 42 Lysander	Flt Lt Lockhart	GEAN	N of Châteauroux, 3.5 km SSW of Brion (36)	Failed. No signals seen. The agent, André Simon, was already in prison. Pierre Hentic was put into the same cell.	
28/29 May 42 Lysander	Flt Lt A. J. Mott	? Lamirault	SSE of Issoudun, 3.5 km W of Ségry (36), Le Fay	(1) Alex Nitelet of MI9	-
		The Lysander was bogged and lost. Pierred Hentic gave John Mott his papers and was arrested as 'the pilot'. John Mott was later arrested by Vichy police, but escaped.			
29/30 May 42 Lysander	Sqn Ldr Murphy	SHRIMP E. Tupet	LES LAGNYS 8 km S of Vatan (see 1 Mar 42)	(2) Gaston Tavian, Jacques Pain	(2) E. Tupet, Philippe Roques
16 Jun 42	Sqn Ldr A. M. Murphy, DFC replaced as CO of the Lysander Flight by Sqn Ldr W. G. Lockhart, DFC.				
23/24 Aug 42 Lysander	Sqn Ldr Lockhart	MERCURE Dallas and Gachet	E of Ussel, Thalamy Airfield (19)	(1) William Ugeux (now a Belgian Count)	(2) Maj Léon Faye ('Aigle')
31 Aug/1 Sep 42 Lysander	Sqn Ldr Lockhart DFC	BOREAS II 'Tarn'	'FAISAN' N of Pont de Vaux, 1.8 km NNW of Arbigny (01)	? Pierre Delaye	Lysander in ditch had to be burnt. Pilot returned 13 Sep after visiting Yves Farge in Lyons (See his 'Rebelles, Soldats, Citoyens')
31 Aug/1 Sep 42 Lysander	Flg Off R. G. McIndoe	CATFISH Pierre Julitte	N of Mâcon	Signals not seen. Stormy weather.	
23/24 Sep 42 Lysander	Flt Lt Huntley	VESTA Pierre Dallas	E of Lyons 1.5 km E of Loyettes (01)	Turned back by weather.	
25/26 Sep 42 Lysander	Plt Off J.C. Bridger	VESTA P. Dallas	Ditto	(1) Cdt L. Faye ('Aigle')	
		Aircraft bogged and dug out. Expected passengers did not arrive.			

Unit, Date and Aircraft	Crew	Operation and Agent	Location of field	Passengers to France	Passengers From France
25/26 Sep 42 Lysander	Plt Off P. E. Vaughan-Fowler	CATFISH Fassin ('Sif')	'MARGUERITE' NNE of Mâcon, 2.5 km NW of Feillens (01)	Not completed because of bad weather. Landed at Exeter.	
1 Oct 42	Wing Commander E. H. Fielden, MVO, DFC, promoted Group Captain to command RAF Tempsford. Wing Commander P. C. Pickard, DSO, to command No 161 (SD) Squadron.				
23/24 Oct 42 Lysander	Flg Off R. G. McIndoe	GIBEL-CATFISH Fassin	'COURGETTE' W of Lons-le-Saunier, I km NNE of Courlaoux (39)	Bad weather near target. Abandoned. Passengers for pick-ups on 'COURGETTE', 'LEONTINE' and 'ORION' were generally put up by three sisters, Mlles Bergerot and Mme Wurtz, 'Les Dames de Villevieux'.	
26/27 Oct 42 Lysander	Plt Off Bridger	ACHILLES Arthur-Louis Gachet	THALAMY AIRFIELD E. Of Ussel (19)	(2) Mary Lindell (MI9, Comtesse de Milleville), Ferdinand Rodriguez	-
26/27 Oct 42 Lysander	Plt Off Vaughan-Fowler	SADLER/ ELECTRICIAN 'Armand'	S of Mâcon, 4 km ENE of La Chapelle-de-Guinchay (71)	(2) J. Paimblanc, Auguste Floiras	(2) Benjamin Cowburn, Dubourdin
27/28 Oct 42 Lysander	Wg Cdr P. C. Pickard DSO	SQUID	LES LAGNYS S of Vatan (see 1/2 Mar 42)	Abandoned. Low cloud over target area.	
27/28 Oct 42 Lysander	Flg Off McIndoe	GIBEL-CATFISH	Lons-le-Saunier area	Abandoned. Bad weather.	
31 Oct/1Nov Lysander	Wg Cdr Pickard	SQUID	LES LAGNYS	Abandoned. Cloud down to ground level.	
17/18 Nov 42 Lysander	Flg Off Bridger	GIBEL-CATFISH Fassin and Paul Rivière	'COURGETTE' W of Lons-le Saunier, 1 km NNE of Courlaoux (39)	(2) Henri Frenay, E. d'Astier de la Vigerie	(2)Gen François d'Astier ('Star'), Yvon Morandat
17/18 Nov 42	Wg Cdr Pickard	?	?	Unsuccessful. No reception. In flight 6.45.	
18/19 Nov 42 Double Lysander	Sqn Ldr Lockhart, DSO, DFC, Plt Off V-Fowler	SQUID/SKATE	LES LAGNYS (See 1/2 Mar 42)	Could not locate target.	-
22/23 Nov 42 Double Lysander	Wg Cdr Pickard, Flt Lt Bridger	SKATE/SQUID Gaston Tavian	LES LAGNYS S of Vatan (see 1/2 Mar 42)	(2) Lardy and a radio operator sent to help Jean Moulin	(3) Gaston Tavian, Georges Descroizette, Philippe Serra ('Morisot')
25/26 Nov 42 Hudson	Gp Capt E. H. Fielden and crew	STEWARD	N of Toulon, near Vinon-sur-Verdon (83)	Incorrect letter flashed and no flare-path. Waited 45 minutes. (EHF's papers) Airborne 2009-0331	
25/26 Nov 42 Lysander	Plt Off J.A. McCairns, MM	PIKE/CARP/ RUFF Lt Harrow	'UNIVERS' 25 km S of Bourges, 800m N of Chavannes (18)	(2) J.F.G. Loncle	(2) Col François de Linares (Assistant to General Giraud), Lt Vellaud
25/26 Nov 42 Lysander	Plt Off Peter V-Fowler	APOLLO Dallas	THALAMY Airfield E of Ussel (19)	Packages only	(3) Piani, Rutali, Reverbel
28/29 Nov 42 Double Lysander	McCairns Vaughan-Fowler	PERRY Jacques Courtaud	'PAMPLEMOUSSE' E of Rouen, 2 km NW of Morgny (27)		(4) Max Petit, his wife and their two children
	Only McCairns found the field and landed. There was no room for Maître Simon. Accommodation provided by the pharmacist Vinay at Lyon-la-Foret and by Messieurs Regnier, Lanoy and Marnay.				
17/18 Dec 42 Lysander	Sqn Ldr Lockhart	CHUB MINOR/ STARFISH Paul Schmidt	'UNIVERS' S of Bourges (See 25 Nov 42)	(2) Louis Kerjean, Jean Simon and 18 packages	(2) Cdt Marchal
	Damaged tail while landing. Almost uncontrollable aircraft flown home.				

Unit, Date and Aircraft	Crew	Operation and Agent	Location of field	Passengers to France	Passengers From France
22 Dec 42 Lysander	Sqn Ldr Lockhart	JAGUAR J. Langlois(?)	N of Mâcon, Sermoyer (01)	Fog and thick cloud near target. Abandoned.	
22 Dec 42 Lysander	Flt Lt Bridger	AJAX	THALAMY E of Ussel	Fog over target. Abandoned.	
22 Dec 42 Lysander	Wg Cdr Pickard	LOBSTER/ CUTTLEFISH Jacques Voyer	'VAUTOUR' N of Châteauroux, 3 km WSW of Brion (36)	(2) P. Deshayes, G.E. Ledoux	(2) Pierre Queuille, Guy Chaumet
23 Dec 42 Lysander	Plt Off McCairns	AJAX	THALAMY E of Ussel	Fog over target. Abandoned.	
23 Dec 42 Lysander	Sqn Ldr H.B. Verity	JAGUAR J. Latour	NNE of Mâcon, between Saône and Sermoyer (01)	Fog over target. Abandoned.	

Sqn Ldr Verity now CO of 'A' Flight (Lysanders), 161 Squadron.

Unit, Date and Aircraft	Crew	Operation and Agent	Location of field	Passengers to France	Passengers From France
23/24 Dec 42 Hudson	Gp Capt E.H. Fielden and crew	STEWARD	11km SE of Arles, Les Chanoines (13)	No sign of reception committee. Waited one hour (EHF's papers).	
14/15 Jan 43 Lysander	Flt Lt John Bridger, DFC	AJAX	THALAMY Airfield E of Ussel (19)	(1) A Belgian spy	(3) Léon Faye, Claude Hettier de Boislambert, Henry Leopold Dor
14/15 Jan 43 Lysander	Flg Off P.E. Vaughan-Fowler	ATALA	NNE of Mâcon, near Sermoyer (01)	Heavy cloud. Abandoned.	
14/15 Jan 43 Lysander	Sqn Ldr Verity	CORINE Pierre Delaye	'LIÈVRE' 29 km E of Lyons, 3 km NE of Loyettes (01)	Only two packages Airborne 2040-0520 (*La Simple Vérité*, p. 276)	(3) C. Pineau, Boris Fourcaud, André Boyer
23/24 Jan 43 Lysander	Plt Off J.A. McCairns	MINER Peter Churchill	Périgueux Aerodrome (24)	No signal. Airfield defended.	
23/24 Jan 43 Lysander	Plt Off F.E. Rymills, DFM	ATALA (?)	Near Issoudun (36)	No signal seen. Not recorded in Squadron Operations Record Book.	
26/27 Jan 43 Lysander	Wg Cdr Pickard	ATALA	'MARABOUT' E of Issoudun, 3 km W of Le Grand Maleray, Primelles (18)	(1) Pierre Brossolette	(2) René Massigli, A. Manuel

Landed at Predannock with no fuel left. Passengers had beeen staying with the Jolivet family in Le Grand Maleray and Floquets of Maurepas. (See Rémy; 'La Ligne de Démarcation'.)

Unit, Date and Aircraft	Crew	Operation and Agent	Location of field	Passengers to France	Passengers From France
26/27 Jan 43 Double with spare Lysander	Plt Off McCairns, Flg Off Rymills, Sqn Ldr Verity Paul Rivière	PRAWN/ GURNARD/ WHITEBAIT	'COURGETTE' W of Lons-le-Saunier, 1 km NNE of Courlaoux (39)	(2) Intelligence agents McCairns was recalled.	(2) Col Manhès, Jean Fleury
13/14 Feb 43 Hudson	Wg Cdr Pickard, Plt Off Taylor (navigator), Flg Off Figg, DFM	SIRENE/ BERENICE Pierre Delaye ('Var')	W of Charolles, St Yan aerodrome (71)	(5) André Boyer, Henri Gorce, Fernand Gane, Félix Svagrovsky, Jean Fleury	Only mail
13/14 Feb 43 Double with spare Lysander	Flg Off Vaughan-Fowler, Flg Off McCairns, Sqn Ldr Verity Pierre Boutoule	PORPOISE/ PRAWN/ GURNARD	'LÉONTINE' NW of Lons-le-Saunier, 2 km SSW of Ruffey-s-Seille (39)	(3) Col F. Manhès, R. Heritier, 'Kim A'	(4) Jean Moulin, General Delestraint, + 2

A monument to commemorate this operation was unveiled at Ruffey in 1986.

Unit, Date and Aircraft	Crew	Operation and Agent	Location of field	Passengers to France	Passengers From France
19/20 Feb 43 Lysander	Flg Off Rymills	TUNDRA Michel Thoraval	NE of Montbrison, aerodrome 4.5 km SSW of Feurs (42)	(1)	(2) Michel Thoraval, Capt Bonnefous

First pick-up for Travaux Ruraux (counter-espionage) and ORA, the French Army Resistance Organisation. See '*l'ORA*' p. 177, and Navarre: *Le Service de Renseignements*, p. 264, and M Thoraval, '*Un Parmi Tant d'Autres*' pp. 12 and 13.

20/21 Feb 43 Hudson	Wg Cdr Pickard Plt Off Taylor Flg Off Figg	STEWARD	11 km SE of Arles (13), Les Chanoines	(1)	(7) André Girard, Col Malagutti, Maroselli and son, Jean Nohain ('Jaboune'), Pierre Vautrin, Sidney Jones

This field was then obstructed by the Germans who had it covered with heaps of stones, paying 10 francs per heap. Airborne 8 hours 40.

24/25 Feb 43 Hudson	Wg Cdr Pickard and same crew plus Flt Lt Putt of 138 Sqn	PAMPAS Claude Lamirault	E of Tournus, Cuisery aerodrome (71)	(?)	(7) Robert Gautier, Louis Niger, Henri Nart, C. Lamirault, Pierre Hentic, Commissaire Principal and Madame Rollin

Bogged from 0330 to 0530. Dug out by 50 local people.

24/25 Feb 43 Lysander	Sqn Ldr Verity	ECLIPSE	'MARABOUT' E of Issoudun. See 26 Jan 43	Fog over target and on return. Crash landed at Tangmere. The passenger both ways was Jean Moulin.	
26/27 Feb 43 Lysander	Sqn Ldr Verity	ECLIPSE (second try)	Ditto	Correct signal not seen. Dots flashed (danger signal).	
17/18 Mar 43 Double Lysander	Flg Off Rymills Flg Off Vaughan-Fowler	TRAINER Henri Déricourt	S of Poitiers, 4.5 km N of Marnay (86)	(4) Mme Francine Agazarian, J. Goldsmith, Pierre Lejeune, R. Dowlen	(4) Claude de Baissac, J.F.A. Antelme, R. Flower and his radio operator
19/20 Mar 43 Lysander	Sqn Ldr Verity	YOLANDE I J. Courtaud	NW of Arras, 2.5 km SW of Mont-St-Eloi (62)	(3) Lieut Duboys, Maître Simon, 'Loir' (?)	(3) Gen Beynet, Capt Bouheret, Capt Gaujour

I nearly hit a sowing machine that Monsieur Rogez of Haute Avesnes had left in his field. (Letter from Rogez to Roger Lequin, 1985)

19/20 Mar 43	Flt Lt Bridger	SIRENE II Pierre Delaye, Asssistant: Henri Morier	N of Roanne, S of Marcigny, 1.2 ENE of Melay (71)	(3) Jean Moulin, Gen Delestraint, Christian Pineau	(1) Jacques d' Alsace

A fine monument commemorating this operation was inaugurated at Melay in March 1990.

19/20 Mar 43 Lysander	Flg Off Rymills	HECTOR (or PLUTO?) Rodriguez	3.5 km NNE of Villefranche-sur-Saône (69)	Could not find the field	
20/21 Mar 43 Lysander	Wg Cdr Pickard	HECTOR (second try)	Ditto	(1) Léon Faye	(3) Dallas, Dr Zimmern, Col Delamaire
23/24 Mar 43 Lysander	Sqn Ldr Verity	JOCKEY/ PLAYWRIGHT Marsac	WNW of Compiègne, 5.5 km N of Estrées-St-Denis (60)	(2) Francis Cammaerts, E.G.J. Dubourdin	(2) Peter Churchill, Frager
13/14 April 43 Double Lysander	Sqn Ldr Verity Flg Off Rymills	HALIBUT Bruno Larat and Paul Rivière	'MARGUERITE' NNE of Mâcon, 2.5 kms NW of Feillens (01)	(2) 'Luc A'	(4) Henri Queuille, E. D'Astier, J.P. Lévy, Daniel Mayer
14/15 Apr 43 Double Lysander	Flg Off Vaughan-Fowler, DFC Flg Off McCairns, DFC, MM	SALESMAN Déricourt	'BRONCHITE' ENE of Tours, 1.5 km SSE of Pocé-s-Cisse (37)	(4) J.R.A. Dubois, H. Frager, P. Liewer, J.C.G. Chartrand	(1) Clech

McCairns' Lysander was damaged flying through a tree before landing.

Unit, Date and Aircraft	Crew	Operation and Agent	Location of field	Passengers to France	Passengers From France
15/16 Apr 43 Hudson	Wg Cdr Pickard Flg Offs Broadley and Cocker	DOGFISH Bruno Larat and Paul Rivière	'JUNOT' NNW of Pont-de-Vaux, 3 km WNW of Arbigny (01)	(2) Francis Closon, Fraval and 12 suitcases	(8) P. Laroque, H. Deschamps, G. Buisson, Martin, Fassiaux, Dr. Robert Blochet
	Wing Commanders Brooks and Lockhart also 'made the journey unofficially' both ways.				
15/16 Apr 43 Lysander	Flt Lt Bridger	ANTINEA Pierre Delaye	'LIÈVRE' E of Lyons, 3 km NE of Loyettes (01)	Four packages Airborne 2200-0545	(3) R. Wackherr, Henri Morier, Claude Pineau
	Henri Morier ('Le Grand') and Jean Delaye assisted Pierre Delaye in all pick-ups for the Phalanx network.				
15/16 Apr 43 Double Lysander	Flg Officers Vaughan-Fowler and McCairns	LIBERTÉ/ JULIETTE Jacques Courtaud	'PAMPLEMOUSSE' E of Rouen, 2 km NW of Morgny (27)	(3) Jean Cavaillès, 'Bernard', 'Parsifal'	(5) Col Passy, Pierre Brossolette, Yeo-Thomas, Capt Ryan (pilot), Jargon (W.Op)
15/16 Apr 43 Lysander	Sqn Ldr Verity	SCULPTOR Déricourt	N of Tours, 1 km ENE of La Chartre-s-le-Loir (72)	(2) Pierre Natzler, an old Belgian (?) Damaged tail-wheel on landing.	(1) Julienne Aisner
16/17 Apr 43 Lysander	Flt Lt Bridger	PÉTUNIA Michel Thoraval	SSE of Clermont-Ferrand, 1 km NE of Pardines (63)	Two packages	(2) Georges Guillaume ('Gilbert'), Col Bonoteaux
	Flew through high tension cables. One flat tyre.				
16/17 Apr 43 Lysander	Wg Cdr Pickard	SABINE	'PLANÈTE' ESE of Tours, 2.5 km WSW of Luzillé (37)	Signal not seen. Until the Gestapo raid on 11 Nov 43, hospitality for this field was provided by Jacques and Mme Nolle, farm des Fontaines, Luzillé.	
16/17 Apr 43 Lysander	Flg Off Rymills	ULYSSES Capt Henri Cormouls	3.5 km NNE of Villefranche-sur Saône (69)	(3) Pierre Dallas, H.L. Dor	(3) Cdt Cros, Pierre Berthomier, Robert Rivat
18/19 Apr 43 Hudson	Wg Cdr Pickard Flg Off Broadley Flg Off Cocker	ZINNIA Michel Thoraval ('Parrain')	S of Mende, Causse Méjean, Florac aerodrome, 4 km NNE of Hures (48)	200lb of luggage	(8) Petitjean, Koenig and son, Col Guénin, Capt Callot, Capt René Brohan, Ph. Michelin, Champion
	Brohan was to become an Aviation General. Petitjean and Koenig were Commissaires de Police (counter-espionage)				
19/20 Apr 43 Lysander	Flg Off McCairns	SABINE Félix Svagrovsky	'PLANÈTE' ESE of Tours; see 16/17 Apr 43	(2)	(4)
20/21 Apr 43 Double Lysander	Flg Off Rymills Flg Off Vaughan-Fowler	PENCILFISH Dr Lapeyre Mensignac	'SERIN' NNW of Angoulême, 1.2 km S of Ambérac (16)	-	(4) Jacques Voyer, Two Députés: Vienot and Poimboeuf, 'Israël'
	For pick-ups on 'SERIN' and 'ALBATROS' hospitality was provided by Charles Franc of Mallaville (16)				
22/23 Apr 43 Double Lysander	Sqn Ldr Verity DFC, Flt Lt Bridger	TOMY Déricourt	'TORTICOLIS' N of Tours, 2 km E of Couture-sur-Loir (41)	- Only one passenger. Bridger ordered not to land.	(1) Déricourt
13/14 May 43 Lysander	Flg Off McCairns	JEANETTE Félix Svagrovsky ('César')	'PLANÈTE' 2.5 km WSW of Luzillé (37)	(1)	(3)
14/15 May 43 Double Lysnder	Sqn Ldr Verity Flg Off Rymills, DFC, DFM	INVENTOR Déricourt	'GRIPPE' ESE of Tours, 1.5 km ENE of Azay-sur-Cher (37)	(4) Julienne Aisner, Vera Leigh, Sidney Jones, Marcel Clech, 14 packages	(2?)Francis Suttill, J.F.A. Antelme?, Mme Gouin?
15/16 May 43 Hudson	Gp Capt E.H. Fielden, CVO, AFC, Sqn Ldr Wagland, DFC, Flg Off Cocker	TULIP Michel Thoraval	S of Mende, Causse Méjean, Florac aerodrome, 4.5 km NNE of Hures (48)	Much fog in area. Not completed.	

Unit, Date and Aircraft	Crew	Operation and Agent	Location of field	Passengers to France	Passengers From France
19/20 May 43 Hudson	Ditto	TULIP (Second attempt) M. Thoraval	Ditto	(3?) Offroy, Bonnard, Lt Lheureux, Bellet? and 16 or 17 suit-cases!	(6) Gen Georges, Col Duval, Capt de Peich, M. Thoraval, Robert Masson, Capt Hugo (Later General)

To avoid day fighters on the way home, diverted to Algeria. Times: Tangmere 23.05, Plaine de Chanet 02.25-02.55, Maison Blanche 05.55.

Unit, Date and Aircraft	Crew	Operation and Agent	Location of field	Passengers to France	Passengers From France
19/20 May 43 Hudson	Sqn Ldr Verity Flt Lt Livry Sgt Shine	BLUNDERBUS Bruno Larat ('Luc')	'ORION' WNW of Lons-le-Saunier, 4 km WSW of Bletterans (39)	(1) Daniel Mayer ('Villiers') and 24 packages	(8) Valentin Abeille, Couty, Benazet, Roger and Madame Donadieu, Francis Closon, La Salle, Roger Lardy (?)

There is now a square in Bletterans called ORION after the code name of this field and a granite stele was placed on the field in May 1993.

Unit, Date and Aircraft	Crew	Operation and Agent	Location of field	Passengers to France	Passengers From France
20/21 May 43 Lysander	Flt Lt Bridger	GAUGUIN Capt Henri Cormouls	15 km E of Issoudun, 1 km NW of Le Grand Maleray, Primelles (18)	Fog over target. Passengers said later that the Lysander flew overhead.	
21/22 May 43 Lysander	Flt Lt Bridger	GAUGUIN (second attempt)	Ditto	Five packages	(2) Col René de Vitrolles, Inspector Fernand Clément? Lieut Silva?

The reception team used a car headlamp

Unit, Date and Aircraft	Crew	Operation and Agent	Location of field	Passengers to France	Passengers From France
21/22 May 43 Lysander	Flg Off Vaughan-Fowler	MADELEINE Jacques Courtaud	'PÊCHE' NW of Compiègne, 3 km NW of Gournay-sur-Aronde (60)	Abandoned after repeated returns to the field with no signal flashed. The agent, in Paris, could not hear the radio message through jamming. Passengers burned newspapers.	
11/12 Jun 43 Double Lysander	Flg Off Vaughan-Fowler Flg Off McCairns	LOUISIANE Félix Svagrovsky	'PLANETE' ESE of Tours, 2.5 km WSW of Luzillé (37)	No reception	
13/14 Jun 43 Double Lysander	Flg Off Vaughan-Fowler Flg Off McCairns	LOUISIANE (Second attempt)	Ditto	(5) Henri Morier,	(6) Achille Peretti, Cap de Vaisseau Nomy, Jacques Tayar, Jacques Robert, Cohen, a lady
15/16 Jun 43 Hudson (home 18 June)	Sqn Ldr Verity Flt Lt Philippe Livry, Sgt Eddie Shine	KNUCKLE-DUSTER B. Larat and Jannik (now Mme P. Rivière)	'MAGUERITE' NNE of Mâcon, 2.5 km NW of Feillens (01)	(2) Claude Bouchinet-Serreuilles, Peri	(8) Paul Rivière, R. Fassin, H. Frenay, Claude Marcus, Capt de Vaisseau Robert, Gen Arnault, Maurice de Cheveigné, Jean Ayral (?)

Very dark and raining. Landed on third attempt. Home via Algiers.

Unit, Date and Aircraft	Crew	Operation and Agent	Location of field	Passengers to France	Passengers From France
15/16 Jun 43 Lysander	Flg Off Rymills, DFC, DFM	DEGAS	NNW of Meaux, 3 km SSE of Nanteuil-le-Haudouin (60)	(2) Pierre Berthomier	(3) Georges Lamarque, Jean Vinzant
15/16 Jun 43 Double Lysander	Flg Off Vaughan-Fowler Flg Off McCairns	NICOLETTE Jacques Courtaud	'PÊCHE' NW of Compiègne (see 21 May 43)	(3)Henri Morier	(5) Mme Grenier, Roger Hérisse, Bernard Cordier, 'Berthier'(?), Jean Ayral(?)

Gaston and Marie Courseaux, farmers in Gournay-sur-Aronde, sheltered the passengers. Betrayed and arrested, they were deported to Germany and died there.

Unit, Date and Aircraft	Crew	Operation and Agent	Location of field	Passengers to France	Passengers From France
16/17 Jun 43 Double Lysander	Flg Off McCairns Flg Off Rymills	TEACHER Déricourt	'INDIGESTION' NNE of Angers, 3.5 km WNW of Villevêque (49)	(4) Charles Skepper, Diana Rowden, Cecily Lefort, Noor Inayat Khan	(5) Mme Pierre-Bloch, Jack and Francine Agazarian, Lejeune, Vie Gerson?, L. Rachet?

Unit, Date and Aircraft	Crew	Operation and Agent	Location of field	Passengers to France	Passengers From France
16/17 June 43 Lysander	Flg Off Vaughan-Fowler	ESTHER	N of Châteauroux, 2 km SE of Bretagne (36)	-	(2) Herbinger
20/21 June 43 Lysander	Flg Off Rymills	POLYANTHUS Pierre Hentic ('Trellu')	Pontijou N of Blois, 3 km WSW of Maves (41)	-	(1) Philip Keun ('Amiral' Deputy Chief of Jade Amicol)
		Pierre Hentic had been freed from prison illegally by Cdt Jean Feyfant (see ASTER 15 Aug 43).			
20/21 June 43 Lysander	Sqn Ldr Verity	CURATOR/ ACOLYTE Déricourt	'BRONCHITE' Pocé-sur-Cisse, 3 km NNE of Amboise (37)	Failed. No reception.	
22/23 June 43 Lysander	Ditto	Ditto (Second try)	Ditto	Generator Failed. Operation abandoned.	
23/24 June 43 Lysander	Sqn Ldr Verity	CURATOR/ ACOLYTE Déricourt	'BRONCHITE' See above	(2) Robert Lyon, Col Bonoteaux	(2) Richard Heslop, P. Taylor (evading meteorologist)
14/15 July 43 Lysander	Sqn Ldr Verity	ATHALIE 'Durham'	'UNIVERS' 25 km S of Bourges, 800 m N of Chavannes (18)		(1) Albert van Wolput? Flt Lt Stephen Hankey, a new pilot, came both ways as a passenger for operational experience.
15/16 Jul 43 Lysander	Flg Off Rymills, DFC and bar, DFM	HOWITZER Chartier	11 km SSW of Auxerre (89)	-	(2) Guy Lenfant, Rapin
15/16 Jul 43 Lysander	Sqn Ldr Verity	HEATHER P. Hentic ('Trellu')	N of Orleans, 3.5 km NNE of Baigneaux (28)	-	(1) Robert Champion 'Fanfouet' (Hentic's assistant)
15/16 Jul 43 Double Lysander	Flg Off McCairns Flg Off Vaughan-Fowler	ARROW Paul Schmidt ('Kim')	'GIDE' WSW of Tours, 2 km NNE of Rivarennes (37)	(2) Emile Laffon, Maurice Pascouet	(4) Charlot, René Vivier, Francois Delimal?
		Michel Pichard refers to passengers on Arrow and Popgun in *L'Espoir des Ténèbres*, p. 83 (ERTI PARIS) Passengers were put up by Marcel Blée of Bréhémont and his Resistance friends in Tours.			
16/17 Jul 43 Hudson T9465	Gp Capt Fielden Sqn Ldr Wagland Sgt Shine	BUCKLER Péry ('Nard') de Beaufort ('Jac')	'FIGUE' SSW of Amberieu en Bugey, 3 km NNW of St Vulbas (01)	No contact at target. E. d'Astier and J.P. Lévy flown to Algiers, where the Hudson was damaged while parked.	
17/18 Jul 43 Lysander	Flt Lt Peter Vaughan-Fowler	RENOIR Pierre Dallas	N of Meaux, 4 km ENE of Brégy (60) Betz-Bouillancy aerodrome	(3) Georges Lamarque, Pierre Bocher, Michel Gaveau	(3) Marie-Madelaine Méric ('de Villeneuve' later Mme Fourcade), Lucien Poulard, André Liess
17/18 Jul 43 Lysander	Flg Off McCairns	ATHLÈTE Déricourt	'GRIPPE' ESE of Tours, 1.5 km ENE of Azay-s-Cher (37)	No reception	
19/20 Jul 43 Lysander	Flg Off McCairns	ATHLÈTE (second try) Déricourt	'GRIPPE' (see above)	(2) Isodore Newman +1	(3) F. Antelme, Jean Savy
21/22 Jul 43 Double Lysander	Sqn Ldr Verity Flt Lt Vaughan-Fowler	FLORIDE Félix Svagrovsky	NW of Château-roux, 2 km SSW of Villers-les-Ormes (36)	(3) Cdt Peretti, Jacques Tayar ('Cazenave')	(7) Mme Jacques Robert and two children, Maurice Andlauer
22/23 Jul 43 Hudson	Wg Cdr L. McD. Hodges, DFC Flt Lts Broadley and Reed	GAMEKEEPER Déricourt	'ACHILLE' NE of Angers, 1 km SE of Soucelles (49)	(3) N. Bodington, J. Agazarian, Cdt Adelin Marissal (Belgian)	(3) 'Raoul' Latimer and two Belgians; Jean Pierre Carrez and Joseph Pans

Unit, Date and Aircraft	Crew	Operation and Agent	Location of field	Passengers to France	Passengers From France
22/23 Jul 43	Flg Off McCairns	ANTIRRHINUM André Duthilleul	'JULES' SSE of Soissons, 6 km WNW of Fère-en-Tardenois (02)	Failed. Thick low cloud all the way.	
24/25 Jul 43 Hudson (Home 27 Jul)	Sqn Ldr Verity Sqn Ldr Livry Sgt Shine	BUCKLER (second attempt) Paul Rivière	'FIGUE' See 16 Jul 43	(2) Emmanuel d'Astier de la Vigerie, J.P. Lévy	(8) F. De Menthon, Deglise-Fabre, Gérard Brault, Maurice Roschbach, Georges Libert, Victor Beaufol, Caillaux, Berthier
	Brault brought his gaoler, Roschbach, who had released him. In September 1992 a fine monument to special air operations on the Plaine de l'Ain was unveiled on this field.				
25/26 Jul 43 Lysander	Flg Off McCairns, DFC and bar, MM	ANTIRRHINUM	See above	Second attempt also failed. Low cloud and visibility 1000 yards. Shot at over Creil.	
14/15 Aug 43 Double Lysander	Flt Lt Vaughan-Fowler Flg Off McCairns	FRANCE Félix Svagrovsky	S of Bourges, 5.5 km N of Dun-sur-Auron (18)	(3)	(5)
14/15 Aug 43 Lysander	Flt Lt R.W.J. Hooper, DFC	ASTER P. Hentic	WSW of Dreux, near Laons (28)	Operation (for Jade Fitzroy) failed. Bad weather	
15/16 Aug 43 Lysander	Flt Lt Robin Hooper	ASTER (second try) P. Hentic	2 km E of Laons (via Nogent le Rotrou)	(1) Robert Champion	(2) Cdt Jean Feyfant (see 20 June 43), Paul Fortier (Fitzroy's Deputy)
15/16 Aug 43 Lysander	Flt Lt Vaughan-Fowler	DURER	N of Meaux, 4 km NNE of Brégy (60) Betz-Bouillancy aerodrome	(2) Lucien Poulard, Robert Rivat	(3) Léon Faye, Johannes Ambre, Ferdinand Rodriguez
15/16 Aug 43 Double Lysander.	Sqn Ldr Verity Flg Off McCairns	POPGUN Schmidt	'RABELAIS' N of Tours, E of Couture-s-Loir, 1 km SE of Sougé (41)	(4) Jacques Bingen?, Closon, Degliame (Closon said Védy was one of three)	(5) Henri Pergaud, Marc de Bièville, André Rousse, Delimal(?), Capt C. Four
16/17 Aug 43 Lysander	Sqn Ldr Verity	DIPLOMAT Déricourt	'TORTICOLIS' N of Tours, 2 km E of Couture-s-Loir (41)	Only one package	(3) Claude and Lise de Baissac, Maj. Bodington
19/20 Aug 43 Hudson	Wg Cdr Hodges Flt Lt Alan Broadley, Flt Lt 'Lofty' Reed	DYER Déricourt	'ACHILLE' NE of Angers, 1 km SE of Soucelles (49)	(1) 'Dyer' ('Paul' Deman of SOE/DF Section)	(10) Marie-Thérèse Le Chêne, Tony Brooks, Boiteux, Octave Simon, Marchand, Vic Gerson, Robert Benoist, F. Basin, Raymonde Mennessier, J.L. de Ganay
	Ground mist and cattle on the field.				
19/20 Aug 43 Lysander	Flt Lt Vaughan-Fowler	CHAPEAU	3.5 km NNE of Villefranche-sur Saône (69)	(1)	(2)
20/21 Aug 43 Double Lysander	Flg Off McCairns Flt Lt Hooper	ANTIRRHINUM André Duthilleul	'JEAN' ESE of Chartres, 4.5 km N of Neuvy-en-Beauce (28)	(2) Capt Joseph Schaller, Deschamps	(4) Duthilleul, R. Guattary, L. Philouze, Georges Bourguignon
20/21 Aug 43 Double Lysander	Sqn Ldr Verity Flt Lt Vaughan-Fowler	CAROLINE 'Gulliver'	'HECTOR' N of Orleans, 3 km SSW of Outarville (45)	(1) An operation for Turma-Vengeance (BCRA)	(4) Jean Viaud
22/23 Aug 43 Hudson	Sqn Ldr Verity Sqn Ldr Livry Plt Off Shine	TROJAN HORSE P. Rivière	'MARGUERITE' NNE of Mâcon, 2.5 km NW of Feillens (01)	Saw lights through fog but landing impossible	

Unit, Date and Aircraft	Crew	Operation and Agent	Location of field	Passengers to France	Passengers From France
23/24 Aug 43 Hudson	Wg Cdr Hodges Flt Lt Broadley Flt Lt Reed	Ditto	Ditto	(1) Louis Franzini	(8) Maurice Graff, Francois Maurin, Prof Vermeil, Armand Khodja, Sgt Patterson RAF
10/11 Sep 43 Lysander	Flt Lt Vaughan-Fowler, DFC and bar	LARKSPUR Pierre Hentic	'MAROT' W of Reims, 4 km NNW of Méry-Prémecy (51)		(3) P. Keun ('Amiral'), André Caffot, 'Victor' (a Polish radio operator)

Col de Dainville thought the pilot was Polish! (P. 26 of his book *L'ORA* about the French Army Resistance Organisation). The field had been an airfield in '14 -'18, used by Guynemer.

Unit, Date and Aircraft	Crew	Operation and Agent	Location of field	Passengers to France	Passengers From France
10/11 Sep 43 Double Lysander	Flt Lt Hooper Flg Off McCairns	CALIFORNIE	S of Bourges, 5.5 km N of Dun-sur-Auron (18)	Failed. Weather bad en route.	
11/12 Sep 43 Double Lysander	Flt Lt Hooper Flg Off McCairns	CALIFORNIE (Second try)	Ditto	(6)	(6) Gaston Defferre (?)

But see also SOUVENIR on 20/21 Sep 43.

Unit, Date and Aircraft	Crew	Operation and Agent	Location of field	Passengers to France	Passengers From France
12/13 Sep 43 Treble Lysander	Sqn Ldr Verity Flg Off McCairns Flt Lt Vaughan-Fowler	BATTERING RAM 'Galilée' and Paul Schmidt	'GIDE' WSW of Tours, 2 km NNE of Riva-rennes (37)	(8) Lt Col Marchal, V. Abeille, Col Rondenay, Ct Palaud, André Boulloche, Henri Kammerer, Henri D'Eyrame, J. Allard	(8) Paul Schmidt, Francoise Schmidt, Prof Rocard, G. Védy and Mme Védy, R. House, Emile Laffon, R. Heuzé

First landing to third take off: 9 minutes.

Unit, Date and Aircraft	Crew	Operation and Agent	Location of field	Passengers to France	Passengers From France
13/14 Sep 43 Lysander	Sqn Ldr Verity, DSO, DFC	BRASENOSE Cdt D. Potier(?)	WNW of Reims, S of Laon, 1 km SSE of Dhuizel (02)	Only two packages	(3) 'Grand Pierre', Survivors of two RAF bomber crews: Flt Sgt Herbert Pond, Sgt Fred Gardiner (from Belgium)

Lysander waited for one hour for reception. Haystacks too close to lights. An operation for MI 9's 'Possum'.

Unit, Date and Aircraft	Crew	Operation and Agent	Location of field	Passengers to France	Passengers From France
13/14 Sep 43 Lysander	Flt Lt Hooper	INGRES	N of Meaux, 4 km ENE of Brégy (60)	Reception not seen.	-
13/14 Sep 43 Lysander	Flt Lt S.A. Hankey	DAISY P. Hentic	ENE of Dreux, 1.5 km SSW of Goussainville (28)	-	(1) André Pierre and some boxes See STOCKS 18 Sep 43

Electrics, including R/T, failed on the way home.

Unit, Date and Aircraft	Crew	Operation and Agent	Location of field	Passengers to France	Passengers From France
14/15 Sep 43 Hudson	Wg Cdr Hodges Sqn Ldr Wagland Flt Lt Reed	TANK Paul Rivière	'ORION' WNW of Lons-le Saunier, 4 km WSW of Bletterans (39)	(8) Emile Laffon, Maj 'Vic' (British), Louis Mangin, Cambas, Bourgès-Maunoury, Gaillard, Leistenschneider, Camille Rayon	(4) Jarrot, 'Mary' Basset, Marcel Reveilloux and another maquisard. Waited ten minutes for the other passengers who missed the flight.

A small fire on board during the flight was put out by the crew.

Unit, Date and Aircraft	Crew	Operation and Agent	Location of field	Passengers to France	Passengers From France
14/15 Sep 43 Double Lysander	Flg Off J.R.G. Bathgate Flt Lt Hankey	GLADIOLA P. Hentic ('Trellu')	ESE of Chartres, 1.5 km W of Baudreville (28)	-	(3) Victor Chatenay ('Bernard'), Kopp, Fernand Kugler ('Tam Tam')

Hankey failed to find the lights. Names of passengers quoted by Roger Lequin from Chatenay's book: *Mon Journal des Temps du Malheur.*

Unit, Date and Aircraft	Crew	Operation and Agent	Location of field	Passengers to France	Passengers From France
15/16 Sep 43 Lysander	Flt Lt Hooper	INGRES	N of Meaux, 4 km ENE of Brégy (60)	(2) Léon Faye, Ferdinand Rodriguez	(2) Duke of Magenta, Philippe Koenigswerther
16/17 Sep 43 Double Lysander	Flg Off McCairns Flt Lt Vaughan-Fowler	CLAUDINE	'PÊCHE' NW of Compiègne, 3 km NW of Gournay-sur-Aronde (60)	(1)	(6) Jean Guyot, Robert Claudius, Jean Tillier ('Debesse') and his wife, Mme Lejeune, Lecointre(?)
16/17 Sep 43 Lysander	Flt Lt Stephen Hankey	DAMSON TREE	SE of Chartres, 3.5 km NNW of Viabon (28)	No reception seen	

Unit, Date and Aircraft	Crew	Operation and Agent	Location of field	Passengers to France	Passengers From France
17/18 Sep 43 Lysander	Sqn Ldr Verity	WINGS	ESE of Rouen, 2 km NNE of Vandrimare Château du Fayel (27)	-	(4) Aircrew evaders
17/18 Sep 43 Double Lysander	Wg Cdr Hodges Flg Off Bathgate	MILLINER Déricourt	'INDIGESTION' NNE of Angers, 3.5 km WNW of Villevêque (49)	(4) H. Peulevé, Yolande Beeckman, Harry Despaigne, d'Erainger	(6) Cowburn, Gold-smith, Rémy Clément, two(?) Polish agents including André Renan, Lecointre(?)
	Operation watched by *Sicherheitsdienst* (SD). Ben Cowburn remembers a young RAF air gunner who was with them.				
18/19 Sep 43 Lysander	Flt Lt Hankey	STOCKS P. Hentic	N of Orléans, 3.5 km NNE of Baigneaux (28)	(1) P. Keun ('Amiral')	(1) Félix Jonc 18 boxes (200 kg)
18/19 Sep 43 Double Lysander	Flt Lt Vaughan-Fowler Flg Off McCairns	BOMB E. Bornier/ Lapeyre-Mensignac	'SERIN' NNW of Angoulême, 1.2 km S of Ambérac (16)	(3 or 4?) Yeo-Thomas, Brossolette, André Deglise-Fabre ('Laplace')	(4) E. Bornier, J. Pain, Le Trocquer, Mercier (a Député)
19/20 Sep 43 Lysander	Flt Lt Hooper	SOUVENIR Félix Svagrovsky	(see below)	Failed. Weather bad and getting worse.	
20/21 Sep 43 Lysander	Flg Off Bathgate	SOUVENIR (second try)	NW of Châteauroux, 2 km SSW of Villers-les-Ormes (36)	-	(4) Gaston Defferre(?) (Future Minister), Boyer, a Colonel
21/22 Sep 43 Hudson	Sqn Ldr Verity Sqn Ldr Livry Plt Off Shine	PEASHOOTER P. Rivière and Pierre Rateau	'JUNOT' NNW of Pont-de-Vaux, 3 km WNW of Arbigny (01)	(4) R. Heslop ('Xavier'), J. Rosenthal, F. Michel 42 packages	(8) Marc Rucart, Dumesnil de Grammont, Charles Laurent, Capt Worthington, H. Guillermin, Roger Boisson, 'Guy' Chrysler, F. Morin
	Low cloud. Landing only possible on third approach.				
8/9 Oct 43 Hudson	Wg Cdr Hodges, Flt Off Affleck, Sqn Ldr Wagland, DFC and bar, Flg Off Bradbury	SHIELD Paul Rivière	'AIGLE' 9 km NNE of Mâcon, 3 km NNW of Manziat (01)	Much cloud and visiblity too low for landing. Lights seen.	
15/16 Oct 43 Lysander	Flt Lt Hooper	ENTRACTE	ESE of Rouen, 2 km NNE of Vandrimare (27)	Heavy haze, failed.	-
16/17 Oct 43 Lysander	Flt Lt Hooper	Ditto (second try)	Ditto	Ditto	-
16/17 Oct 43 Lysander	Flt Lt Hankey	PILOT Déricourt	'BRONCHITE' ENE of tours,1.5 km SSE of Pocé-s-Cisse (37)	(2) Rémy Clément, Arthur Watt	(3) Maurice Southgate, Dr Simond?
16/17 Oct 43 Lysander	Flg Off Bathgate	MAGDALEN Cdt Aviateur D. E. Potier	NW of Soissons, 2 km SW of Selens (02)	Given wrong back-bearing by radio. Failed.	
16/17 Oct 43 Lysander	Flg Off McCairns	MARGUERITE André Duthilleul	'ROGER' WNW of Compiègne, 2 km WNW of Estrées St Denis (60)	(2) Henri Ziegler (later a General), André Caffot (of French Special Services in Algiers)	(3) Abbé Vorage, Crouzillat, René Gervais (Head of *SRAir*)

Unit, Date and Aircraft	Crew	Operation and Agent	Location of field	Passengers to France	Passengers From France
16/17 Oct 43 Hudson	Sqn Ldr Verity Sqn Ldr Livry Plt Off Affleck Flg Off Bradbury	SHIELD (second try) P. Rivière, 'Mémé' Broyer	'AIGLE' (See above)	(5) Jacques Maillet, Armand Philippe, Michel Caillaux, Henri Deschamps + 1	(8) Gen De Lattre de Tassigny, 'Claudius' Petit, Richard Heslop, Jean Rosenthal, G. Hennebert, F. Froment, Thierry, Madame Berger and baby

Andre Gillois said that we picked up ten, including J.J. Mayoux.

Unit, Date and Aircraft	Crew	Operation and Agent	Location of field	Passengers to France	Passengers From France
17/18 Oct 43 Lysander	Flt Lt Hankey	FREDERICK	NNW of Chartres 2 km NW of Challet (28)	Failed. Ground mist.	
17/18 Oct 43 Lysander	Sqn Ldr Verity	ENTRACTE (third try)	ESE of Rouen, 2 km NNE of Vandrimare (27)	(1) Speed ('Deweer') Belgian radio op.)	(2) Madeleine Fauconnier ('Claire' a Belgian spy, later Mme Lovinfosse), Georges Coeckelbergh, Belgian radio operator

An operation for Delbo-Phénix, whose agents were sheltered by Mme Jaffré, Hotel de la Poste, Fleury-sur-Andelle. Her husband was already a prisoner and she would be arrested and deported.

Unit, Date and Aircraft	Crew	Operation and Agent	Location of field	Passengers to France	Passengers From France
17/18 Oct 43 Double Lysander	Flg Off McCairns Flg Off Bathgate	CADEAU Félix Svagrovsky	'BALEINE' E of Châtillon-s- Indre, 3.5 km NNE of Le Tranger (36)	(6) Jean Guyot, André Boyer, Gen Gentil. Gaston Defferre(?)	(6)
18/19 Oct 43 Double Hudson	Wg Cdr Hodges, DSO, DFC and bar, Sqn Ldr Wagland Flt Lt Reed Flg Off McDonald Plt Off Affleck Flying Officers Richards, Bradbury and Goldfinch	HELM Paul Rivière and Janik	'ORION' WNW of Lons-le- Saunier, 4 km WSW of Bletterans (39)	(4) Jean Rosenthal, Richard Heslop, Elizabeth Reynolds, Capt Denis Johnson USA - 'Paul')	(18) E. D'Astier, Vincent Auriol, Albert Gazier, Brunschwig, Sénateur Roger Farjon, Lecompte-Boinet, Juste Evrard, Cdt Adelin Marissal, Maurice Rossi, Paul Molinier, 'Jean-Jacques' et al.

Vincent Auriol later became President of France.

Unit, Date and Aircraft	Crew	Operation and Agent	Location of field	Passengers to France	Passengers From France
18/19 Oct 43 Lysander	Flg Off McCairns	MAGDALEN (second try)	See 16/17 Oct	No reception (confirmed by message).	
18/19 Oct 43 Lysander	Flg Off J. McBride	PRIMROSE P. Hentic ('Trellu')	ESE of Chartres, 1.5 km W of Baudreville (28)	(1) 'Victor'	(3) Capt Louis, Col Brosse, a radio chief who had been denounced, Joseph Cornwall (US aircrew)

Cornwall had escaped from the tail of a Flying Fortress, cut off by another Flying Fortress, which had been shot down by flak.

Unit, Date and Aircraft	Crew	Operation and Agent	Location of field	Passengers to France	Passengers From France
20/21 Oct 43 Hudson	Plt Off J.R. Affleck and same crew	MATE Déricourt	'ACHILLE' NE of Angers, 1 km SE of Soucelles (49)	(4) Browne-Bartroli, Marchand, Benoist, Col Zeller?	(4) H. Frager, Francis Nearne, M. Leprince, A. Lévy?, Durmont-Guillemet

An operation watched by Sicherheitsdienst.

Unit, Date and Aircraft	Crew	Operation and Agent	Location of field	Passengers to France	Passengers From France
20/21 Oct 43 Double Lysander	Flt Lt Hooper Flg Off Bathgate	WATER PISTOL	W of Angoulême 1.5 km S of Vibrac (16)	Failed. Bad visibility near target.	
20/21 Oct 43	Sqn Ldr Verity	FREDERICK (second try)	NNW of Chartres, 2 km NW of Challet (28)	(3)	(3)
21/22 Oct 43 Lysander	Flg Off McCairns	SWORD M. Pichard/ Delahayes	'BOUCHE' SSE of Provins, 1.2 km NW of Passy s. Seine (77)	(2) André Schock, José Aboulker	(3) 'Senator Azais' (M. Godet), Maurice Juillet, André Rousse

M. Juillet was arrested in January 19 44 and died in Germany.
See *L'Espoir des Ténèbres* by Michel Pichard pp. 84 and 205.

Unit, Date and Aircraft	Crew	Operation and Agent	Location of field	Passengers to France	Passengers From France
6/7 Nov 43 Lysander	Flg Off Bathgate	AMOUREUSE Marcel Bureau ('Guéridon')	'LULLI' NW of Provins, 1.5 km SE of Jouy-le-Châtel (77)	(1) Jacques Donot ('Ronsard')	(3) Maréchal, Jaqueline Gauthier, Thion de la Chaume.

The field belonged to M. Robert Pivert, Vimbré Farm, who put up passengers, as did M. and Mlle Florin.

Unit, Date and Aircraft	Crew	Operation and Agent	Location of field	Passengers to France	Passengers From France
7/8 Nov 43 Lysander	Flg Off McCairns	MAGDALEN (Third try) Cdt D.E. Potier (For 'Possum')	NW of Soissons 2 km SW of Selens (02)	(1) Count Georges d'Oultremont (a Belgian in MI9).	(4) American aircrew.
8/9 Nov 43 Double Lysander	Sqn Ldr Verity Flg Off McBride	CANADA Félix Svagrovsky	'CREVETTE' SE of Bourges, 5.5 km N of Dun-sur-Auron (18)	(6) Including Gaston Defferre?	(6)
9/10 Nov 43 Treble Lysander	Wg Cdr Hodges Flt Lt Hooper Flt Lt Hankey	ORIEL (Naval) Lieut Le Hénaff ('Fanfan')	42 km SE of Châtellerault, 3.5 km NNW of Haims (86)	Bad weather. Failed. Six passengers not landed.	-
9/10 Nov 43 Lysander	Flg Off McCairns	NATHALIE	'PÊCHE' NW of Compiègne, 3 km NW of Gournay-sur-Aronde (60)	Failed (fog).	
11/12 Nov 43 Treble Lysander	Flt Lt Hooper Flg Off Bathgate Flg Off McCairns Mud. Hooper cancelled other two landings	ORIEL (Second try) Yves Le Hénaff	'COCONUT' (see ORIEL 9 Nov)	(2) Bostangues and another French officer	(3) Cdr Ouince, Lt Cdr Saguo, Flt Lt Matthews, RAF
11/12 Nov 43 Lysander	Flg Off McBride	EXPLORER	W of Vendôme, 1.5 km E of Couture-s-Loir (41)	Enemy action stopped reception arriving.	
11/12 Nov 43 Double Lysander	Sqn Ldr Verity Flt Lt Hankey	SALVIA P. Hentic ('Trellu')	W of Reims, 1.5 km W of Rosnay (51) An operation for Jade Fitzroy.	-	(6) Paul Fortier, Capt Bertin, P. Hentic, M. and Mme Potelette, 'Simorre'
12/13 Nov 43 Double Lysander	Sqn Ldr Verity Flg Off Bathgate	GLOXINIA André Duthilleul	'ROGER' WNW of Compiègne, 2 km NNW of Estrées-St-Denis (60)	(4) Cdt René Gervais, Robert Geneix	(3) Georges Bourguignon, Henri Roth, Capt Levêque
	An operation for Service de Renseignements Air.				
15/16 Nov 43 Hudson	Wg Cdr Hodges Sqn Ldr Wagland	CONJURER Déricourt	'ACHILLE' NE of Angers, 1 km SE of Soucelles (49)	(5) +? Victor Gerson, E. Levene, J. Menesson, Paul Pardi, Maugenet, H.J. Fille-Lambie?	(10) + ? Francis Cammaerts, François Mitterrand, Pierre du Passage, Mulsant, Mme Fontaine, Barrett, Charles Rechenmann, 5? aircrew evaders
	François Mitterrand, future president of France, left for London by this flight. The pick-up was watched from a distance by Kieffer and other Germans.				
15/16 Nov 43 Lysander	Flg Off McCairns	TOMMY GUN Pierre Deshayes	'CHARENTE' W of Arras, 1 km NW of Canettemont (62)	(2) R. House, Georges Broussine ('Bourgoyne')	(3) Yeo-Thomas, Mme M. Guyot ('Mlle Virolle'), Mlle Pichard
15/16 Nov 43 Double Lysander	Flg Off Bathgate Flg Off McBride	WATER PISTOL Guy Chaumet/ Charles Franc ('le Pointu')	'ALBATROS' W of Angoulême, 1.5 km S of Vibrac (16)	(4) C. Bonnier, A Charlot, A. Desgranges, J. Nancy.	(8) L. Nautin, six British aircrew (one dying on a stretcher), and one Canadian
15/16 Nov 43 Double Lysander	Sqn Ldr Verity Flt Lt Hankey	SULTAN Félix Svagrovsky	'PLANÈTE' ESE of Tours, 2.5 km WSW of Luzillé (37)	No reception. Failed. We almost collided over the field.	
15/16 Nov 43 Lysander	Flt Lt Hooper	SCENERY Jean Depraetere	SE of Niort, 1 km WSW of Perigné (79)	After 1.5 hours of cloud down to the ground and ice forming on the aircraft, turned back.	

Unit, Date and Aircraft	Crew	Operation and Agent	Location of field	Passengers to France	Passengers From France
16/17 Nov 43 Lysander	Flt Lt Hooper	Ditto	Ditto	(2) Armand Dubois, Willy Le Quin	Aircraft bogged and burnt
16/17 Nov 43 Lysander	Flt Lt Hankey	GITANE	NNE of Châteauroux, S of Vatan. 2.5 km W of Villeneuve (36)	Cloud down to ground	Abandoned
16/17 Nov 43 Double Lysander	Sqn Ldr Verity Flg Off McCairns, DFC and bar, MM	MAGDALEN II Cdt Potier and Count Georges d'Oultremont	WNW of Soissons, 2 km SW of Selens (02) Le Champ Ste Marie	(2) Lucien Dumais, Ray Labrosse (Canadians of the Shelburne Line)	(6) Cdt Potier and five aircrew evaders. A Begian operation for MI9
	See Henri Bernard *La Résistance* p. 56 (pub. Brussels, 1969)				
10/11 Dec 43 Double Lysander	Flg Off McBride, Flg Off J.R.G. Bathgate, DFC	STEN Deshayes	'FARMAN', NE of Laon, near Vervins (02)	Killed with - Bathgate: Capt Claudius Four, 'Moreau'	Planned: Brossolette, M. Pichard, C. Longetti
	Bathgate was shot down near Juvincourt. 'Moreau' is buried next to him in the British military cemetary there. McBride abandoned in the bad weather.				
10/11 Dec 43 Lysander	Flt Lt Hankey	SNOWDROP André Duthilleul	'ROGER' WNW of Compiègne, 2 km NNW of Estrées St Denis (60)	Bad weather.	Failed
15/16 Dec 43 Lysander	Wg Cdr Hodges Sqn Ldr Wagland (navigator)	SCENERY II Flt Lt Robin Hooper	20 km NE of Parthenay, 1.5 km ESE of Assais (79)	Failed. Compass deflected by experimental 'Gee' installation.	
16/17 Dec 43 Lysander	Wg Cdr Hodges Sqn Ldr Wagland	SCENERY 2 (Second try) Flt Lt Hooper	20 km NE of Parthenay (79), 1.5 km ESE of Assais	(1) François De Kinder (Belgian)	(2) Flt Lt Hooper, Joseph Dubar ('Jean de Roubaix')
16/17 Dec 43 Double Lysander	Flt Lt Hankey Flg Off McBride	DIABLE	NE of Châteauroux, 6 km N of Neuvy Pailloux (36)	(6) Georges Charaudeau, Head of network Alibi	(4) Of which two, Albert Kohan and Jacques Tayar, were killed on return.
	Both pilots killed near base trying to land in fog. Marcel Sandeyron and a girl agent ('Atalas') survived.				
January 1944	No pick-ups attempted. Bad weather. Sqn Ldr Robin Hooper, DSO, is now CO of the Lysander flight.				
4/5 Feb 44 Hudson	Sqn Ldr L. F. Ratcliff, Flg Offs Wooldridge and Johns, Plt Off Hall	KNACKER Déricourt	NE of Angers, 1 km SE of Soucelles (49)	Morel made the round trip	(9) Robert Benoist, Philippe Liewer, Bob Maloubier, H. Borosh, Madeleine Lavigne, Col Limousin, Le Barbu, the innkeeper at Tiercé and her husband
4/5 Feb 44 Hudson	Flg Off Affleck and his crew.	BLUDGEON	'ORION' 4 km WSW of Bletterans (39)	Failed. Fog. Reception waiting at another field.	
4/5 Feb 44 Double Lysander	Flt LtWhitaker Flt Lt Anderson	ROUMAINIE F. Guilcher ('Romain')	NE of Châteauroux 6 km N of Neuvy Pailloux (36)	(5) Robert Wackherr Marcel Sandeyron An operation for Ecarlate and Azur	(3)
4/5 Feb 44 Lysander	Flg Off J.D. McDonald	CANARI	?	Failed. No reception seen.	

Unit, Date and Aircraft	Crew	Operation and Agent	Location of field	Passengers to France	Passengers From France
8/9 Feb 44 Hudson	Flg Off Affleck and his crew	BLUDGEON (Second try) Paul Rivière	'ORION' see above	(7) Lt Col Pierre Fourcaud, Louis Burdet, Jacques Lecompte-Boinet, A. Salles, 'Lesage', 'Adolphe', 'Herse'	(4?) Flt Lt J.F.Q. Brough, Raymond and Lucie Aubrac and their young son. (See her 'Ils Partiront dans L'Ivresse' Le Seuil, 1986)

Bogged for over two-and-a-half hours.
See 'La Résistance du Jura' by F. Marcet.

Unit, Date and Aircraft	Crew	Operation and Agent	Location of field	Passengers to France	Passengers From France
8/9 Feb 44 Lysander	Flt Lt. L.L. Whitaker	GROWER Déricourt/Rémy Clément	'GRIPPE' ESE of Tours, 1.5 km ENE of Azay-sur-Cher (37)	(2) Lesage, A. Beauregard Operation watched by SD.	(2) Henri and Mme Déricourt
8/9 Feb 44 Double Lysander	Flt Lt. M.C.B. Anderson, Flg Off J.D. McDonald	CANARI Robert Pivert	'LULLI' NW of Provins, 1.5 km SE of Jouy-le-Châtel (77)	(4) Éric Petite, Michel Avenier, and two radio operators	(4?) Jean Guyot, Sérandour (Député), Lafontaine, Marcel Bureau, Cdt Ely?

Sérandour was Head of the BCRA network Mabre Praxitelle.

Unit, Date and Aircraft	Crew	Operation and Agent	Location of field	Passengers to France	Passengers From France
10 Feb 44, Lysander	Flt Lt Milsted	GITANE	See below	Failed.	
10/11 Feb 44 Double Lysander	Flg Off J.D. McDonald, Flg Off D.S. Bell	SERBIE F. Svagrowsky (of Amarante)	SE of Bourges, 5 nm N of Dun-sur-Auron (18), La Chaussée	(2) Jean Lacroix, Willy Josset (Belgian)	-

McDonald landed too fast and was killed. Bell returned. Lacroix, badly burned, was looked after in hospital in Bourges by Dr Malgras until March. (Research by Roger Lequin.) See FANTÔME 3/4 March.

Unit, Date and Aircraft	Crew	Operation and Agent	Location of field	Passengers to France	Passengers From France
11/12 Feb 44 Lysander	Flt Lt Leslie Whitaker	GITANE 'Greyhound' (G. Lovinfosse)	'FAUCON' S of Vatan, 2km NW of Les Lagnys.	Abandoned. Bad weather and ice on Lysander.	
15/16 Feb 44 Hudson	Wg Cdr Hodges and crew	CORPUS	?	Bad weather. Failed.	-

MARCH 1944 NOTES

Wg Cdr A.H.C. Boxer from Air Ministry Directorate of Intelligence (Operations) succeeds Wg Cdr L. McD. Hodges, DSO, DFC, as CO of No 161 Squadron. Sqn Ldr G. De G. Sells attached to take over 'A' Flight (Lysanders) from Sqn Ldr R.W.J. Hooper, DSO, DFC, posted to Air Ministry (DOI(O). Sqn Ldr L. Ratcliff DSO, DFC, formerly CO of the 161 Sqn Halifax Flight, now commands the new Hudson Flight, mainly on parachuting and radio telephone intelligence operations.

Unit, Date and Aircraft	Crew	Operation and Agent	Location of field	Passengers to France	Passengers From France
2/3 Mar 44 Lysander	Flg Off Bell	LABURNUM Pierre Tissier	ESE of Chartres, 1.5 km W of Baudreville (28)	(2) Robert Benoist, Denise Bloch (his radio operator)	(1) A Pole

Denise Bloch, arrested in June, was shot in Ravensbrück. Benoist died in Buchenwald.

Unit, Date and Aircraft	Crew	Operation and Agent	Location of field	Passengers to France	Passengers From France
2/3 Mar 44 Lysander	Flt Lt Murray Anderson	GITANE (Third try) Georges Lovinfosse	S of Vatan, 2 km NW of Les Lagnys (36)	(2) Savy, Eileen Nearne	(2) M. Durieux, G. Lovinfosse
3/4 Mar 44 Double Lysander	Lt P. Hysing-Dahl, Flg Off Bell	FRAMBOISE 'Nazolin'	ESE of Issoudun 1.5 km NE of Ségry (36)	(2) Count Elie de Dampierre, Robert Lorilleux	(2) Two picked up, but Bell's engine trouble caused a crash landing in Normandy

Pilot and passengers were given first aid by Mme Lechevalier on her farm at Plumetot (14).

Unit, Date and Aircraft	Crew	Operation and Agent	Location of field	Passengers to France	Passengers From France
3/4 Mar 44 Double Lysander	Flt Lt Anderson Flt Lt Whitaker	FANTÔME R. Wackherr ('Bonnet') for 'Pourpre'	25 km S of Bourges, 800m NNE of Chavannes (18)	(4) Henri Gorce ('Franklin'), F. Bistos ('Frank'), Commelor	(6) Achille Peretti, Bouchinet-Serreulles, Chancel, Parizot, Jean Lacroix, General Cochet's wife (?)

Base: Catteloin family at Terlan farm near Dun-s-Auron.

Unit, Date and Aircraft	Crew	Operation and Agent	Location of field	Passengers to France	Passengers From France
6/7 Mar 44 Double Lysander	Flt Lt Anderson Flt Lt Whitaker	SNOWDROP Roger Camous	'ROGER' WNW of Compiègne, 2 km NNW of Estrées-St-Denis (60)	(2) Capt Gérard	(6) René Gervais, Jean Koenig, Maurice Rolland, Serge Meyer, François Gourion, Louis Jourdan

Unit, Date and Aircraft	Crew	Operation and Agent	Location of field	Passengers to France	Passengers From France
14/15 Mar 44 Lysander	Flt Lt Anderson	LAUTREC (or RUBENS ?) 'Raynal'	'SIGNAC' 14 km E of Angers, 2 km SSW of Corné (49)	(2)	(3?) Count Elie de Dampierre, Jean Sainteny, Flg Off Bell, Micheline Grimprel?
	See Noguères, Vol IV, p. 453 and note on RUBENS, 9/10 Apr 44.				
15 Mar 44 Lysander	Lt Hysing-Dahl	ALEXANDRE 'Dunois'	SE of Rouen, 1.5 km ESE of Amfréville-sous-les-Monts (27)	Abandoned. Cloud and haze.	-
17/18 Mar 44 Lysander	?	?	Massif Central	(2) Deman, Langard	
	An operation for SOE/DF Section VAR organisation, not in RAF archives, but see p. 398 of *Par les Nuits les Plus Longues* by Roger Huguen (Editions Breiz, 1978). My thanks to Sir Brooks Richards.				
31 Mar/1 Apr 44 Lysander	Lt Hysing-Dahl	FUREUR F. Svagrowsky ('Vector' or 'César')	ESE of Issoudun, 1 km E of Ségry (36)	(1) Stéphane Hessel Operation for the 'Nestlé' intelligence network under Henri Jacquier.	(2) Louis Marin (?)
31 Mar/1 Apr 44 Double Lysander	Flt Lt Whitaker Flt Lt Anderson	DILIGENCE F. Guilcher	'PLANÈTE' ESE of Tours, 2.5 km WSW of Luzillé (37)	(5) An operation for Réseau Écarlate, probably a 'Sussex' intelligence mission.	(5)
5/6 Apr 44 Double Lysander	Flt Lt Whitaker Flt Lt Anderson	DOMINIQUE R. Wackherr	'UNIVERS' S of Bourges 800m N of Chavannes (18)	Failed. Radio message to change the target was not received. Briefed field recognised while agents waited on another.	
5/6 Apr 44 Double Lysander (From Tempsford — landed at Tangmere)	Flt Lt W. Taylor Flt Lt G.A. Turner	UMPIRE Rémy Clément ('Rivière')	'GRIPPE' ESE of Tours, 1.5 km ENE of Azay-s-Cher (37)	(4) Lilian Rolfe, Marie-Christine and André Studler (OSS)	(6) A.P.A. Watt, J.M.L. Besnard, Julienne Aisner (who was to marry Besnard on 27 April)
	Lilian Rolfe was arrested in July and shot at Ravensbrück.				
5/6 Apr 44 Lysander	Lt Hysing-Dahl	LILAC Pierre Tissier ('Pierrot')	ESE of Chartres 1.5 km W of Baudreville (28)	-	(2) Col Olivier, Head of Jade Amicol Intelligence network and his secretary Mireille. See 11/12 April.
9/10 April 44 Lysander	Flt Lt M.C.B. Anderson	DOMINIQUE (Second try) R. Wackherr (for 'Pourpre')	'UNIVERS' S of Bourges, 800m N of Chavannes (18)	(3) A double was planned, but the other aircraft was unserviceable.	(3) Mlle Hartman, Louis Marin (?)
9/10 Apr 44 Lysander	Flt Lt R.G. Large	RUBENS 'Bertrand'	'SIGNAC' 14 km E of Angers (49)	(1) Count Elie de Dampierre	(1) Capt Jean Godet?
	The evidence about this operation and LAUTREC on 14/15 March is confusing.				
9/10 Apr 44 Lysander	Flt Lt Taylor	CHAUFFEUR Maurice Southgate, 'Régis'	'BILLIARD' NW of Château-roux, 2 km SSW of Villers-les-Ormes (36)	(3) Lise de Baissac, Philippe de Vomécourt, Arnaud de Vogüé. Diverted to Dunsfold on return.	(3) Jacqueline Nearne, Mrs Josette Southgate, M. Régis (or Savy)
11/12 Apr 44 Double Lysander	Flt Lt Turner Lt Hysing-Dahl	HOLLYHOCK Pierre Tissier	N of Orléans, 1 km N of Outarville (45)	(4) Col Olivier, Mireille, L. Philouze, Jean Sainteny?	(7) Joseph Campana, Gisèle, Guy Dath, Jeanson, Freyeisen, Jean Bougier, Fernand Kugler
	Campana was Head of the Jade Fitzroy sub-network at Marseilles. Gisèle married André Pierre in England. Dath died after deportation. Freyeison, hunted by the Gestapo, joined the SAS. Bougier was radio operator for Hentic's group 'Maho Trellu' and Jeanson had worked with him on maritime (MTB) operations in Brittany. (Many thanks to Lt Col Hentic for these details.)				

Unit, Date and Aircraft	Crew	Operation and Agent	Location of field	Passengers to France	Passengers From France
28/29 Apr 44 Double Lysander	Flt Lt Taylor Sqn Ldr Len Ratcliff	CHARBONNIER F. Guilcher	S of Vatan, 1 km SSW of Dormes Farm, St Valentin (36)	(3) Richard Landsell	Five large packages

Taylor had engine trouble and turned back. Sqn Ldr L.F. Ratcliff, CO of the Hudson flight, replaces Sqn Ldr Sells as CO of 'A' Flight (Lysanders).

Unit, Date and Aircraft	Crew	Operation and Agent	Location of field	Passengers to France	Passengers From France
30 Apr/1 May Double Lysander	Flt Lt Large Flg Off J.P. Alcock	ORGANIST Alexandre 'Shaw' (Schwatscho)	7.5 km SSE of Issoudun, now le Fay Airfield. Alcock's propeller was holed by flak	(3) Dupuis ('Pharaon')	(3) 'Staunton' (Liewer), Violette Szabo.
3/4 May 44 Hudson	Flt Lt Affleck, DSO Flg Off Ibbott Flt Lt McMillan Flg Off Jarman Flt Lt Corner	HALBERD Paul Rivière	'AIGLE' NNE of Mâcon, 3 km NNW of Manziat (01)	(8) Gen Barthélémy, Marcelle Somers, Davout d'Auerstadt	(8) Mme Fleury and her baby, M. Bourgès-Maunoury, F. Closon, Jean Rosenthal, Maj Thackthwaite, Paul Rivière
3/4 May 44 Lysander	Lt Hysing-Dahl	PIPE 'Nazolin'	'ALHAMBRA' NE of Châteauroux, 6 km NNE of Neuvy Pailloux (36) or 1 km E of Ségry (36)	(2)	(2)
3/4 May 44 Lysander	Flt Lt L.L. Whitaker DFC	FORSYTHIA Philip Keun/P. Tissier	ESE of Chartres, Near Ouarville (28)	Shot down at 0130 over Mondésir airfield, 10 km SSW of Etampes. Pilot killed and buried at Guillerval, l'Essonne (91).	
6/7 May 44 Lysander	Flg Off G.J.F. Alexander	SILENE P. Tissier	N of Orléans, near Outarville (45)	Equipment only	(3) 'XP 12' (Dr A. Perpezat), Robert Champion, Maj Mahurin (USAAF).
8/9 May 44 Lysander	Flt Lt E.A.G.C. Bruce	UTRILLO 2 'Reynal'	'SIGNAC' E of Angers, 2 km SSW of Corné (49)	(2) Joseph Dubar, Bruaux (radio operator)	?
9/10 May 44 Treble Lysander	Sqn Ldr Ratcliff Flt Lt Large Lt Hysing-Dahl	MINEUR F. Guilcher	'PLANÈTE' SE of Tours, 2.5 km WSW of Luzillé (37)	(6) J. Rosenthal, Denis Rake, Corbin? (Airborne 4 hours 15 min.)	(8) W. Savy
10/11 May 44 Lysander	Flg Off L.R. Newhouse	FORSYTHIA P. Tissier	NNE of Orléans, 1 km N of Outarville (45)	Operation failed.	
2/3 Jun 44 Lysander	Flt Lt Taylor	JAPONICA Roger Camous	'ROGER' WNW of Compiègne, 2 km NNW of Estrées St Denis (60)	(2) Foujols, Guy Jafflin	(3) Jean Rousseau-Portalis, Gérard and Robert Masson

An operation for SR Air, the French Air Force Intelligence Service, the fifth on this field.

Unit, Date and Aircraft	Crew	Operation and Agent	Location of field	Passengers to France	Passengers From France
2/3 Jun 44 Lysander	Flt Lt Turner	CAMARADERIE F. Guilcher	NW of Issoudun, NE of St Valentin, 800m WNW of Lizeray (36)	(3) (Away 6 hours 35 mins)	(1) Cdt Verneuil?
2/3 Jun 44 Lysander	Flg Off Alexander	FORSYTHIA II Pierre Tissier	N of Orléans near Outarville (45)	(1) Joseph Campana	(3) Cdt and Mme Gustave Bertrand, Hogbin ('Jesuit')

Pierre Tissier, the successor of 'Trellu' (Lt Col Pierre Hentic, MBE, MM) received five pick-up operations before he was arrested on 29th June 1944 with Philip Keun. They were both killed at Buchenwald.

Unit, Date and Aircraft	Crew	Operation and Agent	Location of field	Passengers to France	Passengers From France
3/4 Jul 44 Hudson	Flt Lt Affleck (see crew below)	BAGGAGE	See below	No reception	-

Unit, Date and Aircraft	Crew	Operation and Agent	Location of field	Passengers to France	Passengers From France
5/6 Jul 44 Hudson	Flt Lt Alffleck, Sqn Ldr Wilkinson, Flt Lt McMillan, Flg Off Saunders, Flt Lt Corner	BAGGAGE 'Barnel'	SW of Provins, 2.5 km N of Egligny (77)	(8) Marie-Madeleine Méric (later Mme Fourcade), Pierre Giraud, Raymond Pezet	(8) Airborne: 2250 - 0142 0149 - 0415
6/7 Jul 44 USAAF Dakota from Harrington	Col Heflin, Capt W. Stapel, Maj E.C. Tresemer, Maj C. Tear, Sgt A.L. Krasevac	MIXER I Hamilton	NW of Nantua, Izernore (01)	(11) Marcel Veilleux, Maj G.E. Parker (RAMC), Gordon Nornable, L. Nonni, R. Aubin, L. Miguet Col Dulac	(11) Lt Col R Heslop, 3 French trainees 7 evaders: 2 USAF, 2 RAF, 1 RCAF and 2 Indian Army

Although not an RAF operation, included for its special interest. In an area controlled by the Maquis, the aircraft was camouflaged and flown back on 9/10 July. Dr Parker was for an emergency hospital in Nantua for wounded maquisards of the Jura. See *OSS La Guerre Secrète en France* by F. Calvi, pp. 450-461. (Pub: Hachette 1990).

Unit, Date and Aircraft	Crew	Operation and Agent	Location of field	Passengers to France	Passengers From France
161 (SD) Sqn 7/8 Jul 44 Double Lysander	Flt Lt Turner Capt Hysing-Dahl	PALAIS F. Guilcher	'PLANETE' SE of Tours, 2.5 km WSW of Luzillé (37)	(3) 'Jean', 'Janello'. A Belgian	(3) Roger Hérisse, Louis Prache, Lucien Germereau

Per Hysing-Dahl was shot down near the bridgehead in Normandy and ditched in the Channel. Of his three passengers, Besnard was drowned, Leseur died after being rescued, and Baudry survived.

Unit, Date and Aircraft	Crew	Operation and Agent	Location of field	Passengers to France	Passengers From France
27/28 Jul 44 Hudson	Wg Cdr A.H.C. Boxer, Flt Lts McMillan, Reed and Johns, Flg Off Helfer.	TENERIFE F. Guilcher	WSW of Château-roux, Le Blanc aerodrome (36)	(2) The only Hudson pick-up in the dark period, with no moon. Away 7 hours 04 minutes.	(4)
4/5 Aug 44 Lysander	Flg Off J.A. Lamberton	DAHOMEY R. Wackherr ('Bonnet')	'CARPE' S of Bourges, 800 m NNE of Chavannes (18)	Bad weather. Reception not seen. Advanced base Winkleigh, Devon.	
4/5 Aug 44 Double Lysander	Flg Off L.R. Newhouse	SCIMITAR Bloc-Richard Clouet des Pesruches?	S of Le Mans La Chapelle-aux Choux (72)	(3)? Louis Gay, Pierre Vigorie	(3) Paule-Denise Corre (Now Mme Jean Gimpel), Anne-Marie Chatenay, John Oliphant (an American pilot)
-	Flg Off G.J.F. Alexander	-	-	(2)	(2) Robert Bloc-Richard, Marguerite Gianelli, who became Mme Bloc-Richard

Alexander's Lysander was damaged in landing. On return he landed in fog at St Merryn, Cornwall.

Unit, Date and Aircraft	Crew	Operation and Agent	Location of field	Passengers to France	Passengers From France
4/5 Aug 44 Double Lysander	Flg Off Peter Arkell	PIROGUE Guilcher ('Romain')	S of Vatan, 1 km SSW of Dormes farm, St Valentin (36) (?)	(2)	(3) Claude Thierry-Mieg, Léon Dupont
	Flg Off J.P. Alcock			(1) Lucien Germereau	

Arkell saw Alcock shot down. Lucien Germerau, of Réseau Ecarlate, was also killed.

Unit, Date and Aircraft	Crew	Operation and Agent	Location of field	Passengers to France	Passengers From France
5/6 Aug 44 Lysander	Flt Lt G.A. Turner	PIROGUE 2 Guilcher	Ditto ?	(1) Airborne 5 hours 15, avoiding the Bridgehead.	(3) Col. A.D. Puy-Montbrun
5/6 Aug 44 Lysander	Sqn Ldr L.F. Ratcliff DSO	DAHOMEY R. Wackherr	'CARPE' See above Away 7 hours 10.	(2)	(1) Raymond Murphy, An evading American aviator shot down near Bourges

Sent to London a quantity of documents and films on enemy works. Base: Terlan farm, Dun-s-Auron with Catteloin family.

Unit, Date and Aircraft	Crew	Operation and Agent	Location of field	Passengers to France	Passengers From France
6/7 Aug 44 Double Hudson	Wg Cdr A.H.C. Boxer and crew Flg Off H.B. Ibbott and crew	BULBASKET Lt David Surrey-Dane, SAS	'BON BON' 16 km SW of Le Blanc (36)	(6) and small arms (5) and ammunition	(10) (10)

An operation to bring home survivors of a Special Air Service detachment which had suffered heavy losses. Eight more SAS men were picked up from the same field by an American Dakota (Col Clifford J. Heflin) on 9/10 August.

Unit, Date and Aircraft	Crew	Operation and Agent	Location of field	Passengers to France	Passengers From France
7/8 Aug 44 Lysander	Flt Lt Taylor	GENISTA R. Camous	'ROGER' See 2/3 Jun 44	Failed. Bad visibility.	
7/8 Aug 44 Hudson	Sqn Ldr Wilkinson, Flt Lt Wooldridge, Flg Off Champion, Flg Off Marneweck	MACHETTE Paul Rivière	'AIGLE' 9 km NNE of Mâcon, 3 km NNW of Manziat (01)	(4) Caveçon, Galop, André Dammaw, Ribart	(13) Chaban-Delmas, Leistenschneider ('Carré'), Wolf, Blumel, Jarrot, Moreau, Flouriot, two American aircrew (Heddleson and Henderson) and three British
10/11 Aug 44 Hudson	Wg Cdr Boxer Flt Lt MacMillan Flg Off F.J. Champion Flg Off G.H. Ash	POIGNARD Henri Guillermin ('Pacha')	N of Pau, 2.5 km SSW of Garlin (64) Away 8 hrs 50 mins	(6) J.P. Roselli Eugénie Gruner?	(4) Maury, André, Jean Arhex, Paule Viatel
10/11 Aug 44 Hudson	Flt Lt Affleck Flg Off Wooldridge Flg Off Hall Flg Off Thompson	TUNISIE	3 km WNW of Pierre-de-Bresse (71)	(7) Eugénie Gruner (or by POIGNARD above)	Two packages only
31 Aug/1 Sep Hudson Double	Wg Cdr Boxer Flt Lt T. Helfer and their crews* *Boxer's crew:	XYLOPHONE Jean Triomphe (P. Rivière's assistant)	Ditto	(14) French Army officers (probably including an intelligence team from ALIBI-MAURICE of five men and two girls)	None

Flt Lt MacMillan, Flg Off Hall, Flt Lt Johns.
Helfer's: Flg Off Johnson, Flg Off Escreet, Flg Off Thompson.

Unit, Date and Aircraft	Crew	Operation and Agent	Location of field	Passengers to France	Passengers From France
31 Aug/1 Sep Hudson Double	Flg Off Ibbott Sqn Ldr Wilkinson and crews*	DAUNTSEY Paul Rivière	'JUNOT' NNW of Pont-de-Vaux, 3 km WNW of Arbigny (01) Away 6.55	(3) Charles Béraudier (2)	(4) One letter only

*Ibbott's crew: Flying Officers Barr, Kaus, Racan and Wiltshire.
Wilkinson's: Flying Officers Weddell, Champion and Ash. Plt Off Morris.

Unit, Date and Aircraft	Crew	Operation and Agent	Location of field	Passengers to France	Passengers From France
5/6 Sep 44 Hudson Double	Gp Capt E.H. Fielden, Flt Lt Helfer and crews*	FAILSWORTHY Guillermin	N of Pau, 2.5 km SSW of Garlin (64)	Failed because of weather. (9) Broad, Morel. Landing by daylight in a liberated area	(7) Col Romans-Petit, Capt Denis Johnson (USA) Flt Lt Horrex, RCAF D.H. Courtenay H.J. Fisher, RAF

*Fielden's crew: Sqn Ldr Wagland, Flt Lt Reed, Plt Off Hartman.
Helfer's crew: Flying Officers Johnson, James and Thompson.

Unit, Date and Aircraft	Crew	Operation and Agent	Location of field	Passengers to France	Passengers From France
5/6 Sep 44 Hudson Double	Wg Cdr Boxer, Flg Off A.N. Ferris and crews*	DULLINGHAM 'Jesuit' (Hogbin)	Aerodrome of Toulouse-Francazal	(3) Stores only	(1) (4)

Although carried out as a clandestine pick-up, it was in a liberated area.
*Boxer's crew included Flt Lt MacMillan. Ferris' crew: Wt Off Hutton, Flg Off A.F. Penhale, Flg Off Traill.

RAF PICK-UPS IN FRANCE FLOWN FROM CORSICA AND ITALY IN 1944

Unit, Date and Aircraft	Crew	Operation and Agent	Location of field	Passengers to France	Passengers From France
148 Sqn 4/5 Jun 44 Double Lysander Forward base Calvi	Flt Lt P.E. Vaughan-Fowler Flg Off N.H. Attenborrow	THICKET Jannik (Mme Paul Rivière)	'FIGUE' ENE of Lyon, SSW of Amberieu-en-Bugey, 4 km NNW of St-Vulbas (01)	(4) Eugéne Chavant ('Clement') Hubert Gominet, 'Soutane'.	(6) Dr Revesz-Long and his assistants Perret and Louis, Clouet des Pesruches, Toubas, Michel Pichard

Unit, Date and Aircraft	Crew	Operation and Agent	Location of field	Passengers to France	Passengers From France
8/9 Jul 44 Double Lysander Forward base Borgo	Flg Off R.J. Manning Flg Off H.J. Franklin	TAMISE Camille Rayon ('Archiduc')	'SPITFIRE' NNE of Apt, 5 km WSW of St-Christol (84)	Failed. Cloud and thunder storms.	
10/11 Jul 44 Double Lysander	Ditto	Ditto (Second try)	Ditto	(3) Paul Vittori Only Franklin was successful.	(3) Neil Marten
10/11 July 44 Double Lysander	Lt G. Libert Lt B. Cordier	THICKET 2 M. Barbachou	'FIGUE' See above	No reception	-
11/12 Jul 44 Double Lysander	Lt G. Libert Lt B. Cordier	THICKET 2 M. Barbachou (The farmer) (second try)	'FIGUE' See 4/5 June	(6) Harold Rovella, Pierre Diard, Jean le Morillon, Louis Leclerc, Gatelier, 'Rossignol'	Georges Libert, who could not restart his engine and burned his Lysander with the help of Monsieur Barbachou.
11/12 Jul 44 Lysander	Flg Off Manning	TAMISE (Third try) C. Rayon	'SPITFIRE' See 8/9 July	(3) Cdt Gonzague de Corbin-Mangoux	(3)
1/2 Aug 44 Lysander	Flt Lt Peter Vaughan-Fowler	TYLER (for OSS)	NW of St Etienne	No reception. Professor Arthur Funk's research into OSS archives says that this failure was due to cows on the field. Abbé La Pouge told me that they aborted the operation because they suspected one of the intended passengers of treachery.	
2/3 Aug 44 Lysander (?)	Ditto	Ditto	Ditto	Ditto	
2/3 Aug 44 Double Lysander	?	? Camille Rayon	'SPITFIRE' See 8/9 July	(3+) Willie Widmer and his team.	(3) Col H. Zeller and Two Americans, one with appendicitis.
6/7 Aug 44 Lysander	Flt Lt V.-Fowler	TYLER (for OSS) (Third Try)	27 km NW of St Etienne, 2 km NW of Précieux (42)	(2) General de Bénouville Capt Mangin	(3) G. La Pouge (now Abbé), Joseph Terral
	See *Le Sacrifice du Matin* by Guillain de Bénouville, pp. 534-7 (Robert Laffont 1946)				
10/11 Aug 44 Lysander	Flt Lt P.E. Vaughan-Fowler	?	'JUNOT' NNW of Pont de Vaux, 3 km WNW of Arbigny (01)	- This operation, urgent because of the imminent landings in the South of France, was carried out after the end of the moon period.	(1)
267 Sqn RAF Base: Bari 8/9 Aug 44 Dakota	Flg Off B.E.T. Rostron, Lt Gordon, Flt Lt Griffiths, Flg Off Barrett.	NUPTIAL Camille Rayon ('Archiduc')	'SPITFIRE' NNE of Apt, 5 km WSW of St Christol (84)	Impossible weather, cloud and thunder storms. Attempt abandoned. Forward base: Cecina Italy.	
10/11 Aug 44 Dakota	Ditto	Ditto	Ditto	(15) Jean Constans, Maj Crosby, Capt R. Gouvet, Charles Luizet, Francis Closon, Roger Vencell (radio operator to Col Widmer) 750 kg of freight	(23) R. O'Badia, J.G. Goldsmith, US aircrew, of whom Rayon had had to order off 8 to lighten the Dakota
	Lavender growing across the strip made it impossible to take off with 31 passengers. McCairns made the round trip as adviser				
267 Sqn 11/12 Aug 44 Dakota	Flg Off Rostron and the same crew	NUPTIAL	'SPITFIRE'	Rostron came back to pick up the eight American aircrew, who had had to disembark, but there was no reception. The isolated farm nearby had been burnt by the Germans and the inhabitants shot.	

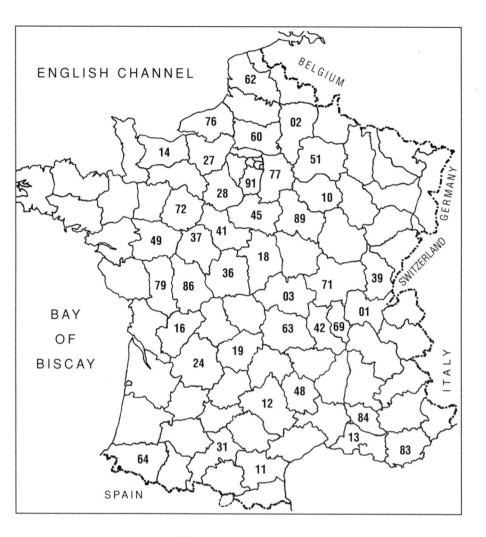

CODE NUMBERS OF DEPARTMENTS

01 Ain	28 Eure-et-Loir	62 Pas-de-Calais
02 Aisne	31 Haute-Garonne	63 Puy-de-Dôme
		64 Pyrénées-Atlantiques
03 Allier	36 Indre	69 Rhône
11 Aude	37 Indre-et-Loire	71 Saône-et-Loire
		72 Sarthe
13 Bouches-du-Rhône	39 Jura	76 Seine-Maritime
14 Calvados	41 Loir-et-Cher	77 Seine-et-Marne
16 Charente	42 Loire	79 Deux-Sèvres
		83 Var
18 Cher	45 Loiret	84 Vaucluse
19 Corrèze	48 Lozère	86 Vienne
	49 Maine-et-Loire	89 Yonne
24 Dordogne	51 Marne	91 Essonne
27 Eure	60 Oise	

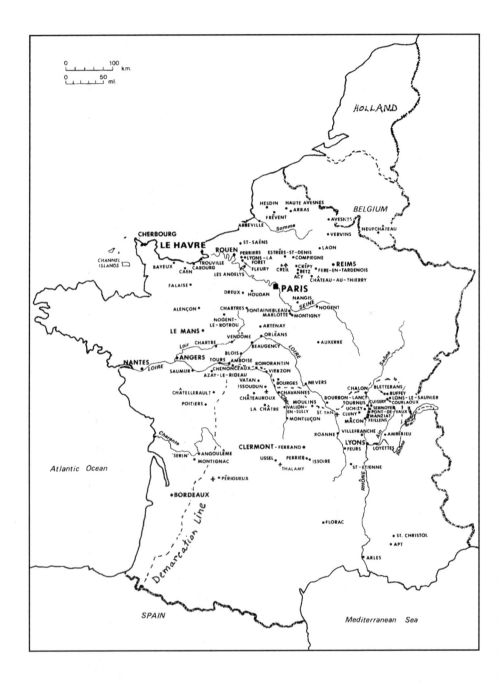

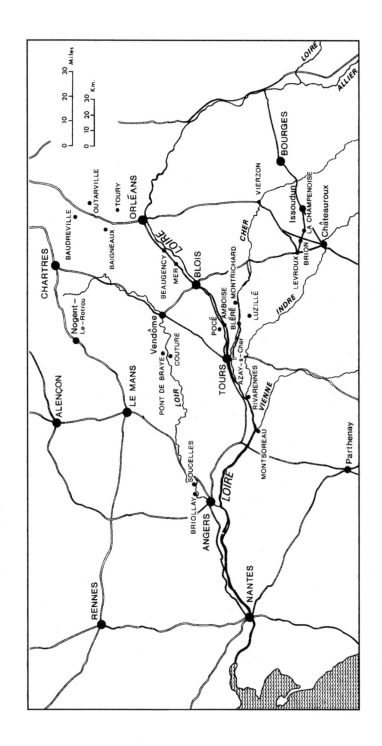

APPENDIX C

Operations Beryl II & III1

P/U BERYL II — 28.1.42

"Pilot: Squadron leader J. Nesbitt-Dufort, DSO   A/C Lysander No. T.1508

   "Airborne 1915 hours approx., set course for Trouville.

"Called up regional control and received them strength 6, with slight whistle. Intercom working satisfactorily. Climbed to 9,000ft through thin cloud, experienced slight icing. The French coast was not observed, but was able to pin-point myself well to left of track, South of the Seine. Made alteration of course, and, flying just below a thin layer of cloud, pin-pointed myself again on the Loire. Told passenger to prepare to disembark, and map read to the target, reaching it at approx. 2205 hrs. Satisfactory landing made. Passenger and luggage disembarked, and two passengers and luggage embarked.

"Take off satisfactory, course set for home via Fécamp and Beachy Head; it was now raining quite hard and after talking to passengers for about ten minutes, the intercom failed, and, as I could get no side-tone from my own mike, I rightly assumed that my radio had packed up completely. The weather deteriorated rapidly after first hour's flying, cloud being 10/10 at about 700ft, and I was reduced to hedge-hopping in heavy rain and extremely bumpy conditions (typical line-squall).

"A thin coat of glazed frost started to form on my windscreen and leading edge, so I decided to turn back and try again, after climbing above the bad weather, which had all the symptoms of a well-defined cold front. I was not very keen on doing this as I had not been able to make an accurate pin-point before losing sight of the ground owing to low cloud and rain, and had not the facilities of my radio for homing over the channel. I started to climb on my course from a D/R position of about 50 miles due South of the Seine (between Abbeville and the first loop) — course being set for Beachy Head.

"I was now flying in very thick and bumpy cloud continuously. At first, there was a slight misting of the windscreen, but at 7,000ft it started to rain and severe icing began at 8,000ft. The engine gave indications of ice in the air intake, and there three or four inches of clear ice on the leading edge of the slats. I pulled the over-ride in the hope that I might be able to clear, but at about 8,500ft I was gaining no height, and the aircraft was practically unmanageable (it must be remembered that there were two passengers and luggage in the back).

"I estimated position was between the Seine and the French coast, so throttled back my engine and shouted to my passengers to bale out! But they obviously could not hear me as they did not do so. The aircraft would not maintain height at full throttle, so I let the nose drop and tried to work her round on a reciprocal course. Speed about 240mph by the time the aircraft had turned through 180°, and at 2,500ft I started to ease the aircraft out of the dive and broke cloud at about 1,000ft. On straightening out, I found that, in spite of a certain amount of ice that still adhered, the aircraft could still be flown straight and level without much difficulty at a speed greater than 150mph. I flew west for about 40 miles and then east for another 70 miles with the hope of finding a break in the front. I had no success.

"I had now been flying for over five-and-a-half hours, most of which had been at high boost for climbing, and I had now only 40 gallons of petrol left in my main tank and about 10 gallons in the auxiliary. Having satisfied myself it was impossible to get through the front, I decided in view of the nature of my passengers and their luggage, it would be best to fly back to unoccupied France and 'force land' in the vicinity of Châteauroux.

"Setting a new course for my D/R position, I recrossed the Loire at Orléans, altered course for Issoudun, recrossing the demarcation line at Bourges. Knowing that it would not be healthy to land again at Issoudun aerodrome, I force-landed in the most likely looking field which unfortunately had a ditch running across the far end, which could not be seen in the dark. This resulted in the aircraft breaking the undercarriage, and turning up on its nose. No one was hurt, my passengers jumped out, and I tried to extract the axes, which had, however, got firmly wedged in the cock-pit. A jack knife was used to tackle the bottom of the auxiliary petrol tank, which, being self-sealing, gave some difficulty. Eventually, I managed to get petrol flowing, and, having exploded the IFF, I fired the two 'sisters' (recognition flares) and one Verey cartridge to set the aircraft on fire. Owing to a shortage of petrol, I had some difficulty in getting the aircraft to burn. After two more cartridges, however, it seemed to be well alight, and we all ran for it, as we were only about 75 yards from a house. I am afraid that when we were about two kilometres away, the fire must have gone out, as we could see no glow coming from the direction of where we left the aircraft.

"Landed at 0210 hrs, having been in the air approx. 7 hours.

"It has since been discovered that the aircraft has been totally destroyed by a locomotive at a level crossing whilst being towed away, and that a curé has been arrested in Châteauroux under the impression that he was the pilot of the aircraft!

"Having left the aircraft, two agents and myself being under the impression that we were a few miles to the left of Issoudun, proceeded to walk in an easterly direction. After three or four miles we came to St. Florent from whence, by map, a round-about route to Issoudun.

"Walking another four miles, and having been flying continuously for 7 hours, I was too fatigued to proceed any further, and against the wishes of the two agents, decided to sleep in what hiding could be found near the road. One of the agents, at considerable risk to himself, insisted on staying with me, and we hid in a three-sided shepherd's hut about 100 yards from the road. It had been raining continually all night, a strong wind was blowing, and it was very cold.

"The other agent proceeded on foot to Issoudun, arriving there about 7 o'clock in the morning, where he managed with considerable difficulty to obtain a car with a driver. He picked us up at about 2pm the following day.

"He had also managed to find somewhere for us to hide in the railway station at Issoudun, and arriving there we were given a hot meal and made most welcome.

"The agent who had stayed with me had a couple of hours sleep and proceeded south by train that evening to try and get news of our predicament through with the least delay.

"For the following 30 days I was forced to stay indoors, as I had no identity card or food tickets. I was very well looked after, and apart from lack of minor luxuries, such as cigarettes, reading material and exercise, I was extremely comfortable, if somewhat cold on occasions.

"Two days before date of departure, one of the agents was able to finish forging an identity card for me and the night before the operation I was taken for a walk through the town and shown the direction I was to take to and from the aerodrome, should we get separated.

"On the night of departure, the BBC signal came through very indistinctly through

215

jamming but a few words were just audible. This was at 6.15, and at 7 o'clock the fourth member of the party arrived from the south where he had been delayed due to illness, and at 7.45, having had a square meal, the four of us set out with a minimum of luggage, which consisted of one rather heavy suitcase carried in turn by the four of us to Issoudun. We made very good time and arrived at the aerodrome at 9.30, rested for 15 minutes, and then proceeded to lay the flarepath out, the dimensions of which I propose to adopt as standard for this type of work in future.

"By ten o'clock we were all in position lying on the ground. We were not bothered by anyone in any way, but barking of dogs gave the impression that they were uncomfortably close. We had two false alarms, and on each occasion the flarepath was lit and I signalled frantically to what later on turned out to be friendly Whitleys. They did not see me, however.

"At midnight, our ETA was up, and one of the agents approached me on the subject of waiting any longer and we decided that it was possible that we had made some mistake over the time, and we should wait until one o'clock. At 12.15, the unmistakable noise of an Anson approaching at low altitude and high speed was heard from the north. The flarepath was lit and signals sent and answered promptly. The aircraft did one circuit and made a beautiful landing without wasting unnecessary time. It was then signalled to the edge of the aerodrome and embarkation was carried out without a hitch at high speed.

"After a hasty conference with the pilot on the advisability of one member of the crew getting out again, and pushing, to assist take-off, we decided against this somewhat drastic course, and, after eight or nine anxious minutes, 'Gormless Gertie', the aircraft in question, achieved a speed corresponding to a smart trot! Having passed No 2 and No 3 lights earlier in the evening!

"On proceeding at a slightly increased but rather dangerous speed, we found, to our amazement, that we were airborne.

"The pilot informed me that if it had not been for the almost previously unheard-of, and drastic use, of 'skyhooks' this undoubtedly would not have been accomplished.

"The remainder of the trip to base was uneventful if slow. The skill of the pilot and navigator proved in this case to be exceptional, as we were only lost the majority of the way home, which only goes to prove!"

BERYL II & III, 1/2 MARCH

"Pilot: Squadron Leader A.M. Murphy, DFC   A/C Anson R 3316

Navigator: Pilot Officer Cossar

"We became airborne at Tangmere at 2100hrs, set course for Cabourg, reached at 2200 at height of 9,000ft. Course then set for Tours. Visibility remained excellent until a point was reached 40 miles north of Tours, when 10/10 cloud encountered with heavy precipitation, visibility in nature of 1,000 yards. Some time was spent in pin-pointing the Loire, and eventually course was set for Châteauroux at 2315 hrs.

"Visibility remained poor and I lost myself at 2330 hrs, but eventually reached Châteauroux at 2355 hrs. Course set for Issoudun, and lights picked up at 0010 hrs.

"Landing completed without trouble, and the four passengers embarked very rapidly. We then became airborne again at 0015 hrs and set course for Cabourg. We pin-pointed ourselves over the Loire and the Seine and crossed the French coast at Dieppe at 2200 hrs. Course was set for base and we landed at 0240 hrs.

"The above laconic report marks the completion of a very stout effort by the pilot and navigator and the Cooks tourist passenger".

Extracts from the Cottage Line Book

Sgt Booker — 21.4.43
"Someone spoke to me of bed. I had to ask him what it was. They said it was something which was kept exclusively for officers in time of war."

Henri (Déricourt), after being picked up — 23.4.43
"Give me a Comper Swift and I'll garage it in my barn and fly myself back next time."

Hugh Verity (commenting on Mac's prang in a tree on operations — 15.4.43
"It's not part of the Verity Service to collect firewood."

Bunny Rymills — April, 1943
"Oh, you are a lucky Flight Commander to have *me* coming down and smiling at you every morning."

Flg Off Rymills (commenting on the indefinite extension of his tour) — April, 1943
"In forty years time I'll tell my grandchildren that by my 300th trip I'd landed in one field so often that they had to build me concrete runways."

Flg Off Vaughan-Fowler, DFC — 23.4.43
"You feel a bit naked with just one gong."

Wg Cdr Hodges — September, 1943
"Until you've done Bomber ops you don't know what ops are."
"No. I couldn't walk into a prison camp without a tunic. They wouldn't know what rank I was."

Peter Vaughan-Fowler — 16.8.43
Subject: Swing. "It's bloody good! It keeps the mind agile."
0500 20.8.43
"This scent will come in useful when I've lost all my sex appeal."

Sqn Ldr Verity (before operating) — 20.8.43
"I suppose I'd *better* take a map…"
(Pride comes before a fall. That night I was lost for a long time. HBV 1976)

Flg Off J.A. McCairns — 22.8.43
"I beat up Pat Coghlan's place this morning." "Oh!"
"Yes, he was wearing a grey suit with herring-bone pattern. It was raining at the time and there was a 30mph wind blowing."

Flight Officer Faith Townson — 22.8.43
"I know how to say 'I love you' in Russian."

September 1943
'Group Captain' Acting Flight Lieutenant Fowler
"I never have any excitement on my ops — everything always goes perfectly."

Flt Lt Hankey
"After my BAT course, I shall be able to operate on the dirtiest nights or wear dark glasses on a good night!"

Flt Sgt Booker, when being threatened with being put on a charge, replied:
"Well, even if Sqn Ldr Verity had the energy to write it down, I should have to tell him which words to use."

Flt Lt Hooper

"It stands to reason that you won't parachute joes into a valley with peaks 10,000 high 300 yards apart…but, DAMMIT, WE'VE DONE IT!"

Flg Off McCairns

"I had a damn good look at Falaise the other night. We were shot at there once, and I was studying the form."

Stephen Hankey

"I believe in concentrating my work into 16 hours a day."

Flg Off Bathgate

"One of these days, I'm bound to be off track."

Group Captain Sofiano

"Mr. P… is really a very important man. You see, he is my opposite number in the American SIS."

Flg Off McCairns

"As I flew over the village at ten feet, I could see the shape of their helmets and the colour of their uniforms. God, it was terrifying!…Of course, it was only a dream."

Wg Cdr Hodges

"It is expecting too much of anyone to be able to talk French *and* fly by night."

Flt Lt Hankey

"If, by mistake, I work out my airspeed as my course, it doesn't matter if I know it. You just set your ETA on your compass — compensating error."

November 1943

Flt Hooper (on HBV's posting to Baker Street)
"One couldn't fail to shine in SOE."

John Hunt

"I'm going to write an ode to the death of civilisation."

Robin Hooper

"I can see it coming once again — lovely weather, lovely moon, no ops — and vice versa. Not that I'm complaining, mind you! I thrive on difficulties!"

Flt Lt Hankey

"When you have been flying as long as I have, you will probably have done about twice as many hours."

Flg Off McBride

"The only time I'll go back to Bomber ops is as Master of Ceremonies in a Mosquito: 'Move over there, 3 Group.'"

"It pays to shoot lines. I'd be an Air Commodore by now, if I'd done myself justice."

Sqn Ldr Verity

"Play rugger? Certainly not when I am engaged on operational duties. If I happened to be kicked on the head, the future history of England might be changed."

McCairns

"It was damn decent of the King to be out of the country for my investiture and let me have it with the Queen — knowing my taste for females."

Flt Lt Hankey

"If more than two members of this Flight were simultaneously bogged in France, they'd start a second front to get them out."

Somebody had stuck into the book a copy of 'Taylor's telegram after Robin Hooper's prang on 16/17 November, 1943:

"Regrette devoir annoncer avion atterri légèrement en dehors balisage est embourbé par suite des fortes pluies de la journée. Après trois heures d'effort avons dû nous résoudre à mettre le feu à l'appareil. Deux passagers et pilote sains et saufs et en sécurité. Après cet accident je ne me considère plus de votre confiance."

"Regret having to inform you aircraft landed slightly outside flarepath bogged after heavy rain during day. After three hours effort had to decide to burn aeroplane. Two passengers and pilot well and in safety. After this accident no longer think I deserve your confidence."

On his return from France, Robin added, "POOR OLD GEORGES!"

Flt Lt Anderson — 8.12.43

"I've got weak ankles — from lack of walking. I fly too much!"

Wg Cdr Hodges — 17.12.43

"I always aim to touch down at light 'A'." Five seconds later: "That IS the drill, isn't it?"

Daily Express — 11.1.44

"'F' for Freddie's Dog Reported Missing"

"Ming, sheepdog belonging to Squadron Leader (sic) P.C. Pickard, DSO, DFC, Pilot of 'F' For Freddie in the film 'Target For Tonight' is reported missing. She escaped from a car in the Marylebone Road district of London."

Daily Telegraph — 9.2.44

"Allied Planes Secret Landings in France — from our Special Correspondent, BERNE, Tuesday"

"The Germans are now reported to have ordered any stretch of land which might serve Allied planes as a landing field in the 'suspected areas' to be ditched or covered with debris.

"Allied planes landing on French soil at night are said to be carrying not only French Resistance chiefs and foreign agents to and from France, but to be laden with arms and materials for French Partisans.

"The parachuting of material for beleaguered French patriots is reported to have been discarded as too risky and wasteful."

Sqn Ldr Hooper (speaking on his return from France on the floor of a Lysander) — 14.2.44

"I was absolutely terrified — that little Jean was going to be sick all over me."

"Aeroplane" — 3.3.44

"Merciful Duty"

"Lysanders have now been taken off operational work, and honourably retired to several non-combatant duties...e.g. Air-Sea Rescue."

Flg Off Alexander — 29.11.44

"I always fly at 1,800 revs because at higher revs the noise of the engine gets on my nerves."

Author's Note: I am most grateful to 'Tommy' Thomas, who rescued the Line Book from Tangmere Cottage and gave it to me long after the war.

Movement Order—

161 Squadron, 'A' Flight

CONFIDENTIAL
Ground Crews. 'A' Flight, 161 Squadron. Tangmere Detachment — June.

Road Party — To proceed to Tangmere on 7.6.43

1166750	Sgt FIIA Sweet, L.	I/c Party.
911962	Cpl FIIE Dunstan, D.	
1010835	Cpl FIIA Niell, J.	
1032267	LAC FMA Thomas, G.	
1277815	LAC FMA Ferris, A.	
1533715	LAC FMA Curphey, F.	
1507190	LAC FME Pankhurst, E.	
1309635	LAC FME Bicknell, A.	
1544240	LAC I/Rp Taylor, J.	
1245352	LAC I/Rp Beddows	
1517858	AC2 W/M Newbold	
1452403	LAC W/M Turner, C.	
1650425	AC1 Elec. Constable, D.	
1614114	AC1 Elec. Booth, E.	

Air Party — To proceed to Tangmere on 8.6.43

			Flying in
574775	F/S FIIE Hollis, J.	I/c Detachment	J
574853	Cpl FIIA Brant, R.		G
617351	Cpl FIIE Jackson, R.		E
954491	LAC FME Seaman, S.		B
983780	LAC FMEWhite, J.		G
1252231	LAC FME Body, N.		J
1471294	AC1 FME Smith, F.		H
1451919	LAC FMA Prentice, J.		E
1446498	AC1 FMA Parsons, A.		H
1499179	LAC FMA Pears, G.		B

The *road party* are to have all their personal kit, and tool boxes, ground equipment, stores, Aircraft spares, etc., on the lorry by 10.00 hrs. 7.6.43. They are to be ready to "Move off" by *1030 hrs.*

The *air party* are to have their personal kit loaded into the A/C in which they will be flying by *1200 hrs.*, 8.6.43, and are to be in possession of parachutes. The time of "take-off" will be *1400 hrs.* approx., and all of the air party are to be ready to leave at that time. Personnel will be informed, should there be any change in plan.

J.B. HOLLIS, F/S.
1.6.43   N.C.O. i/c 'A' Flt. 161 Squadron.

Modifications to the Lysander

By Peter Procter

I was at Yeovil with Westland as a Chief Assistant Designer — there were four of us — and responsible for the Lysanders of No 161 Special Duties Squadron as well as the target-towing version. I had been detached to check on the technical problems of the Barracuda which we had built for the parent firm, Fairey, as had Blackburns and Boulton Paul. However, I still had to carry on with special duties work.

I remember the great secrecy about the question of increasing the range of the Lysander. In particular, I had to find a suitable long-range petrol tank. We found an internal 150-gallon tank coming from the Handley Page Harrow. It was mounted inside the fuselage on the left. It was a De Berg tank, riveted and ideally robust for our purpose. It was secured in the same way as on the Harrow.

Of course, we had to modify the existing oil tank to increase its capacity. This made its replacement quite a headache.

You refer to the compass error which led Pick to Cornwall instead of Tangmere. I got quite a rocket from Pick on the telephone. Furious, he charged me to check on my modification to the oil system which he had wanted to guarantee him an easy start on cold nights. This consisted of a solenoid valve which allowed petrol into the oil sump to reduce its viscosity. Pick thought that the modification had caused the compass error. I had to dash to Tempsford after advising Bill Guiseley, the squadron engineering officer, to send Pick's Lysander to the compass swinging base. I met Pick there and asked him if he was wearing the same kit as on the night in question. After checking the deviation without Pick and finding that it corresponded with the correction card, I asked Pick to climb up into the cockpit and noticed an immediate deviation of 30 degrees. I made him get down and climb up again three times, like a yo-yo. It was obvious that he had on him something that deflected the compass. I looked at his legs and noticed the handle of a bayonet emerging from the top of one of his flying boots. I advised him to take a bronze bayonet next time he flew and we had a good laugh.

I have another memory: Pick asked me to increase his radius of action even more. We found that the answer was to replace the variable pitch propeller by a constant speed propeller. I was told that the Blenheim also had Mercury XII engines and, checking with Charles Burgess of De Havilland Propellers, I concluded that there would be no problem. I asked Jimmy Bentley of Teleflex to come to meet me at Tempsford with the remote control mechanism. Then we pinched a propeller from a Blenheim that was standing at the other end of the field. I remember that there was an important football match in progress at the time. With Jimmy Bentley, Bill Guiseley and a crane driver, we carried out the modification ourselves. This modification increased Pick's radius of action by 12.5%!

At the time, modifications to the Lysander were carried out by Fairfield Aviation who had a production line at Odhams Press at Watford and ran their operation from the airfield at Aldenham. There were other modifications. The ladder was designed to make it easier to climb in or out of the rear cockpit. But the roof of the rear cockpit slid on rails with notches to allow it to be stopped in two or three positions. Plck complained that chaps who wore rings could get them caught and then jump down, minus ring and even finger. The modification took the form of an official order: "Signet rings are not to be worn"

We replaced the old radio telephone set 1133/1134 by a smaller one, the 1154/1155, and extended the floor so that four passengers could be fitted into the rear cockpit. I also remember the pilots telling the passengers to push back the automatic flaps as they left the aircraft. Teddy Petter, our technical director who had designed the aircraft, had very ingeniously designed the flaps so that they came down when the leading edge slats came out on approaching stalling speed.

The first few hundred Lysanders had beams in extruded light alloy - roughly speaking hollow tubes of six inch square section, imported from Switzerland. When our communications were cut and we had used up all our stock in the United Kingdom, we asked High Duty Alloys of Slough to extrude the upper and lower parts for us and we made the sides of steel attached with Allen bolts. The problem for the ground crew was in checking that these were tight enough. These undercarriage legs were magnificent when they were in one piece, but, made with extruded parts only at the top and bottom, they were very heavy and caused serious maintenance and corrosion problems.

Notes, Bibliography and Other Sources

The basic historical framework from the RAF side is taken from the 161 Squadron and 138 Squadron Operation Record Books, the original manuscript squadron histories which were completed each month from the pilots' reports after each trip. These give the names of the aircrew and, generally, the numbers (but never the names) of passengers. Crown copyright records in the Public Record Office are quoted by permission of the Controller of HM Stationery Office, mainly from files AIR 27/1068 and AIR 28/820. Some field locations and agents codenames became available in files released to the PRO in 1983 — since the first edition of this book. My thanks to Mr. J. B. Chamberlain, who drew to my attention to files AIR 20/8455, '69, '74, '75 and 8884. AIR 40/2352 and 2356 were also helpful. I am most grateful to the PRO staff for all their help. I am also grateful to the staff of the British Library Reading Room and to the Librarian of the Institut Français in London.

Crown Copyright photographs, which are separately identified, are fromthe Public Records Office, who have been most helpful. They are mainly from files AIR20/8492, AIR20/8884, AIR27/1068 and AIR28/820. My basic sources of information on the passengers carried were acknowledged at the beginning of the book. Most of the others are gratefully mentioned below, though some more recent sources are mentioned in Appendix B. My apologies to many brief contacts at reunion gatherings and on journeys through France whose helpful recollections have not been acknowledged in detail. They often confirmed information already available. In a few cases they turned out to be mythomaniacs. The simple facts that secret agents in the field cannot - or at least should not - keep files of archive material and that human memory is fallible have led to many variations on the detail of evidence about particular incidents. I have done my best to match what information I have discovered to the RAF's contemporary records. These were generally comprehensive and reliable. Nevertheless I have no doubt that there are still errors for which I apologise.

Chapter I

1. For the official record see pages 43-45.
2. Now Air Chief Marshal Sir Lewis Hodges, KCB, CBE, DSO and bar, DFC and bar.
3. The late Air Vice-Marshal Sir Edward Fielden, GCVO, CB, DFC, AFC. See *The Times* obituary, 9 November, 1976.
4. Operation Torch. Invasion of North Africa by the Allies.
5. A memorial tablet in the barn commemorates its wartime use. The barn is well cared for by the farmer, Mr John Button.
6. The late Group Captain P. E. Vaughan-Fowler, CVO, DSO, DFC and bar, AFC. *The Times* obituary, 30 April, 1994.
7. Arty Shaw's band was his favourite.
8. The late Group Captain Sir Douglas Bader, CBE, DSO, DFC, the famous fighter ace and legless golfer.
9. See Thetford's *Aircraft of the RAF*, p. 458.

Chapter 2

1. Some pilots preferred to fly at 7000 feet on good nights, where petrol consumption was only 25 gallons an hour.

2. Mr Dibdin's letter to the author, August 1975.

3a. Boffins working with the RAF were said to be strange birds who laid conical eggs; the more you pushed them away, the more they rolled towards you.

3b. The late John Corby told me that a Belgian pilot, Johnny Legrand, was parachuted in to steal a JU 88 night fighter from St Evere, near Brussels. The airfield no longer had night fighters, so Legrand 'walked' to Gibraltar.

4. The late J. A. McCairns unpublished memoirs, *Lysander*, kindly made available to the author by his widow, Moira McCairns.

5. Sqn Ldr A. M. Murphy, DFC. See Wg Cdr John Nesbitt-Dufort, *Black Lysander* (Jarrolds, London, 1973), pp. 112-34.

6. Christian Pineau, *La Simple Vérité*, pp. 275-277 (Editions Phalanx, Paris, 1983).

7. Henri Noguères *Histoire de la Résistance en France* Vol 3 (Robert Laffont, Paris, 1972), pp. 139-42 and 183. Letter to the author from Marie-Madeleine Fourcade.

8. Noguères, op. cit., p. 176. Gilberte Brossolette, *Il s'appelait Pierre Brossolette* (Editions Albin Michel, Paris, 1976) p.188.

9. Noguères, op. cit. pp. 101-2, 173. André Manuel was later to be assistant to Col. Passy in the BCRA.

10. André Gillois, Histoire Secrète des Français à Londres.

Chapter 3

1. The late Philip Schneidau, then called Flt Lt Philipson, told me all this in Tangmere Cottage in 1943 and reminded me in 1975. See also Gen Jean Bezy, *Le S.R. Air* (Editions France Empire, Paris, 1979), p. 114.

2. Letter to the author in 1975 from the late Gp Capt Ron Hockey, DSO, DFC. He had joined 419 Flight in November, 1940, and was later CO of No 138 SD Squadron.

3. Philip Schneidau's letter.

4. Ron Hockey found this Maryland unsuitable for SD operations.

5. For their exploits see Professor M. R. D. Foot, *SOE in France* (HMSO, 1966) and E. H. Cookridge, *Inside SOE* (Arthur Barker, 1966).

6. Nesbitt-Dufort, op. cit. pp. 103-9 and Noguères, op. cit. Vol 1, p. 114.

7. Mathilde-Lily Carré, *I was the cat* (tr. Savill, Four Square, 1961) and Gordon Young, *Cat with two faces* (Putnam, 1957).

8. Published 1961 by George Ronald.

9. Noguères, op. cit. Vol 1, p. 428 has Lt Mitchell parachuted into France on 19 June, 1941 as 'Brick'. He must have been 'Adam'.

10. Nesbitt-Dufort, op. cit. p. 110.

11. This paragraph is based on Ron Hockey's letter.

12. The German daily report from Namur on 9 Dec 1941 gives the strength of the Jagdkommando party around the airfield as one officer and 22 men. Two parties of half-a-dozen military police also converged on the Lysander. It took off when the nearest German was 30 metres away. Altogether, 100 shots were fired.

13. Nesbitt-Dufort, op. cit. pp. 112-34. He had picked up Lt Mitchell and Maurice Duclos ('St Jacques'). The latter walked into the station bar at Issoudun and shook hands with everybody there with a masonic handshake. He found that the stationmaster, Combault, was a fellow Freemason who was prepared to shelter the British pilot in spite of the police search in progress.

Chapter 4

1. Noguères, op. cit. Vol 2, p. 359.

2. Foot, op. cit., p. 25.

3. With Duclos and Mitchell, who had laid the flarepath, was Gen Julius Kleeberg. He would later represent the Polish Government in exile to the Allied supreme staff.

4. In his report Nesbitt-Dufort called the Anson 'Gormless Gertie' because it took so long to take off.

5. Noguères, Vol 2, pp. 378-9. Pineau, op. cit. pp. 143-51.

6. Noguères, Vol 2, p. 440, where the date is given as 24 April. Monsieur Gaston Tavian-Collin remembered his companion on the flight as Maurice Andlauer, but see note 19 to Chapter 8.

7. Foot, op. cit. p. 229.

8. Noguères, op. cit. Vol 2, pp. 301-402. Pineau, op. cit. pp. 219-20.

9. Gilberte Brossolette, op. cit. p. 128.

10. Lt Col J. M. Langley, MBE, MC, *Fight another day* (Collins, 1974), p. 173.

11. Foot, op. cit. p. 194. Letter to the author from the late Maurice Buckmaster, 17 September, 1976.

12. Noguères, op. cit. Vol 2, p. 592. Yves Farges, *Rebelles, Soldats, Citoyens* (Editions Grasset, Paris, 1946), pp. 10-11.

13. Marie-Madeleine Fourcade, *Noah's Ark* (George Allen & Unwin, 1973), p. 133. See also pp. 104, 124, and 129. The original book was *l'Arche de Noé* (Arthème Fayard, Paris, 1968) in two volumes.

14. Fourcade, op. cit. pp. 139-42.

15. Rémy, *Le Livre du Courage et de la Peur*, Vol 1 (Aux Trois Couleurs, Paris, 1945), pp. 116-18.

16. Ben Cowburn's letter to the author. Foot, op. cit. pp. 197,215 and 255.

17. Fourcade, op. cit. p. 155. She called it 'Mercury' on 22 October. Airey Neave, *Saturday at M.I.9* (Hodder and Stoughton, 1969. Coronet edition 1971) pp. 191-6.

18. Noguères, op. cit. Vol 3, pp. 74-5. Foot, op. cit. p. 226.

19. Noguères, op. cit. Vol 3, pp. 54-5, 76.

20. Confirmed by the late Madame Morandat in 1976. Henri Frenay, *La Nuit finira* (Laffont - Opera Mundi. Le Livre de Poche, 1973), p. 258.

21. See next chapter for Mac's story.

22. Fourcade, op. cit. p. 184 and also p. 176.

Chapter 5

1. Foot, op. cit. p. 229.

2. Langley, op. cit. pp. 192-3 and 196.

3. Noguères, op. cit. Vol 3, pp. 139-42.

Chapter 6

1. I visited this plateau above the village of Perrier in 1976. The high tension cables were too far away for John to have flown through them after a proper take-off.

2. Noguères, op. cit. Vol 3, p. 188. Laure Moulin, *Jean Moulin* (Presses de la Cité, 1982), p. 293.

3. Confirmed by Paul Rivière who added two passengers from the UK: 'Kim A' and Héritier. See also Foot, op. cit. p. 238 and for another version: Piquet-Wicks, *Quatre dans l'ombre* (Gallimard, Paris, 1957), pp. 96-100.

4. Foot, op. cit. pp. 180-2.

5. Bunny Rymills remembers my voice on the R/T telling him to take no notice. Until he saw the Dornier he could not think what I was talking about.

6. Fourcade, op. cit. pp. 218 and 223-4. Her 'Pluto' must have been our 'Hector'.
7. J. Goldsmith, *Accidental Agent* (Leo Cooper, 1971), pp. 70 and 71.
8. Noguères, op. cit. Vol 3, pp. 256-7. Col A. de Dainville, *l'ORA* (Editions Lavauzelle, 1974), pp. 177-8.
9. Foot, op. cit. pp. 259, 291.
10. Pineau, op. cit. p. 288.
11. Foot, op. cit. p. 253. E. H. Cookridge, *They come from the Sky* (Heinemann, 1965), pp. 7, 83-5.
12. Noguères, op. cit. Vol 3, p. 262.
13 Peter Churchill, *Duel of Wits* (Hodder and Stoughton, 1958), pp. 290-1. Foot, op. cit. pp. 251, 253.

Chapter 7
1. Col P. Livry-Level, Compagnon de la Libération, DFC and bar, *Missions dans la RAF* (Editions Mellottée, Paris, 1946).
2. Information on passengers (in Appendix B) from Michel Pichard and Paul Rivière's letters. Abeille was Délégué Militaire, M Region (Le Mans). He was fatally wounded trying to escape on 31 May. 1944.
3. Noguères, op. cit. Vol 3, pp. 315-17 and 361, refers to Larat taking over from Fassin and the organisation of COPA with Deshayes in the North, Pichard in the East, Schmidt in the West and Ayral in the Centre.
4. Livry-Level, op. cit.
5. Noguères, Vol 3, pp. 198 and 204.
6. Ditto, pp. 204-5.
7. Foot, op. cit. p. 217.
8. Sqn Ldr James L. W. Wagland, DFC, wrote to the author, 1975.
9. In 1988/89 I heard about operation Pampas from three of the passengers from France: Henri Nart, Pierre Hentic and Robert Gautier. I have therefore revised parts of the story in my first edition which were based on a largely fictional published narrative.
10. Bunny Rymills reminded me of the story about Scotty.
11. Noguères, op. cit. Vol 3, pp. 391-2. Bezy, op. cit. p. 118. Henri Navarre, *Le Service de Renseignements* (Plon, Paris, 1978), pp. 279-280, about Capitaine de Peich ('Laprune').
12. Wagland's letter to the author, 1975.
13. I am grateful to Sir Douglas Dodds-Parker for this story.

Chapter 8
1. Noguères, Vol 3, p. 205.
2. Col Paul Rivière's letter, June 1975. D. Veillon, *Le Franc-Tireur* (Flammarion, Paris, 1977), p. 120.
3. Gillois, op. cit. pp. 272-3. Noguères, Vol 3, pp. 328-30.
4. Foot, op. cit. p. 262. Roy MacLaren, *Canadians Behind Enemy Lines* (University of British Columbia Press, 1981), on Gabriel Chartrand.
5. Foot, p. 291.
6. Bruce Marshall, *The White Rabbit* (Evans Brothers, 1952. Quoted here:Pan Books, 1954), pp. 50-1, Brossolette, op. cit. p. 200.
7. Passy (Col A. Dewavrin), *Souvenirs III, Missions Secrètes* (Plon, 1951), p. 185.
8. Noguères, Vol 3, p. 336.

9. Fourcade, op. cit. pp. 230-1.

10. Foot, p. 292. The late Rémy Clement told the author that Mme Gouin also left France by operation 'Inventor'. For the fate of Vera Leigh and other FANYs see Hugh Popham, *F.A.N.Y.* (Leo Cooper, 1984), pp. 101-6.

11. Fourcade, op. cit. pp. 234-6.

12. Foot, pp. 256, 292, 314 and 337.

13. Noguères, Vol 3, p. 359. Foot, pp. 293 and 314.

14. The police trap was called *l'affaire Turck* after the captured agent.

15. Foot points out that Heslop was one of the relatively few agents to be awarded the DSO.

16. These paragraphs about Stephen Hankey were written for this book by the late Sir Robin Hooper and are quoted with many thanks.

17. Fourcade, op. cit. and her letter to the author.

18. Savy told Maloubier that Déricourt did not come with them.

19. My passengers on operation 'Floride' must have included Maurice Andlauer. His widow remembered that all he had told her about his pick-up was that he was in a plane with some children who threw up. (Source: his sister-in-law, Mme Louis Andlauer.)

Chapter 9

1. Frenay, op. cit. Chapter XIII. The late Maurice de Cheveigné agreed with me that Frenay's account of operation 'Knuckleduster' was inaccurate.

2. For names of passengers given in Appendix B many thanks to Paul Rivière and Gerard Brault ('Gédéon'). On J. P. Lévy, see D. Veillon, *Le Franc-Tireur* (Flammarion, Paris, 1977), p. 143.

3. Paul Rivière's letter, June 1975.

4. Noguères, Vol 3, p. 508.

5. Foot, pp. 293, 323. Letter to the author from Baron Fernand Lepage in Brussels, 25 November, 1985.

6. Foot, p. 323.

7. Foot, pp. 277, 293-1. Noguères, Vol 3, p. 580. Pierre Raynaud added Mlle Mennessier.

8. Foot, p. 325.

9. See Appendix B.

10. The passengers to France, listed in Appendix B (thanks to Paul Rivière), included: Louis Mangin, a *Chef de Zone*, Maurice Bourgès-Maunoury, *Délégué Militaire Régional (DMR)* for the Lyons region and future Prime Minister of France (*The Times* obituary 20 February, 1993); H. H. Gaillard, DMR round Bordeaux; and Paul Leistenschneider, DMR round Montpellier and Toulouse.

11. Letter to the author from Air Chief Marshal Sir Lewis Hodges, KCB, CBE, DSO*, DFC*.

12. Noguères, Vol 3, p. 621.

13. Wagland's letter to the author, 21 June, 1975.

14. Foot, p. 288.

15. Passengers names (from Paul Rivière) are in Appendix B.

Chapter 10

1. Fourcade, op. cit. p. 257.

2. Foot, p.246. Noguères, Vol 3, p. 553.

3. Foot, pp. 279, 293, 325.

4a. Fred Gardiner's letter to the author, July 1980.

4b. Hankey line remembered by McCairns.

5. Fourcade, pp. 264-8. Noguères, Vol 4, pp. 277-8.

6. Lecointre ('Guillaume'), who may have been flown to England by this operation 'Milliner' or by 'Claudine' one night earlier, is said to have brought details of the pro-Giraud movement in three areas of France. (Research by the late Michel Pichard).

7. Foot, p. 284.

8. J. Goldsmith, *Accidental Agent* (Leo Cooper, 1971), pp. 122-3.

9. Foot, p. 241. Noguères, Vol 3, pp. 602-4, and Paul Rivière's notes.

10. Bruce Marshall, op. cit.

11. Letters to the author from the late Monsieur Gaston Defferre, October and November 1979.

12. Compare Jimmy Langley's story of a pilot officer who was shot down on a Monday and brought home on the following Thursday in time for his engagement party on the Saturday. *Fight Another Day* (Collins, 1974), p. 199.

Chapter 11

1. Gen Jean Bezy, *le SR Air* (Editions France-Empire, Paris, 1979), p. 160.

2/3. The passengers (named in Appendix B from Paul Rivière's notes) were transported by Mémé Broyer, a pork butcher in Manziat, who sheltered and fed very many passengers on pick-ups in the Saône valley.

4. Librairie Plon, 1949. His enormous prestige after the war did not make de Lattre too proud to do a circuit of honour with Peter Vaughan-Fowler in a very patched and uncomfortable old Proctor, which Peter had borrowed from a communications flight to get himself to a Resistance reunion on one of our old fields near Lons-le Saunier. He had not been warned that he would be flying such a VIP. As de Lattre got out, in full uniform, the whole assembly applauded.

5. Letter to the author from McB's brother, Ian McBride, in Trinidad, January 1980.

6. The following story is based on the account written for me by Air Chief Marshal Sir Lewis Hodges, amplified by Captain John Affleck's memories, when I interviewed him in 1975, and Colonel Paul Rivière's notes.

7. Letter from Paul Rivière.

8. See Appendix B.

9. Foot, pp. 260, 294-5. A letter from Frager to Buckmaster, quoted by Pierre Raynaud, gives Dumont-Guillemet as a fellow passenger to England.

10. Foot, p. 295.

11. Foot, p. 273.

12. Bezy, op. cit. p. 164.

Chapter 12

1. In Cookridge, *They came from the Sky* (Heinemann, 1965) some details differ from the story I heard from interviews with Cammaerts and Clément.

2. Foot, p. 295, Col A. de Dainville, *l'ORA* (Editions Lavauzelle, 1974), p. 179. Langley, op. cit. p. 199, may have meant October when he said that five evaders were flown out in November.

3. Cookridge, *They came from the Sky*, pp. 66-9, but there is no RAF record of any Lysander landing which would fit this 'South of Troyes'.

4. Michel Pichard's notes on the passengers and the author's interview with Charles

Franc in Avignon, 1976.
5. Foot, pp. 246-7. Noguères, Vol 4, pp. 50, 56-61, 142.
6. McCairns' unpublished memoirs, Bruce Marshall, op. cit. p. 78 and Noguères, Vol 4, p. 142.
7. Marshall, op. cit. pp. 95-7 and Noguères, Vol 4, pp. 307-9.
8. Françoise Bruneau, *Résistance* (SEDES, Paris, 1951), p. 92. Kindly drawn to my attention by the late Michel Pichard.
9. Professor Henri Bernard, *La Résistance 1940-1945* (La Renaissance du Livre, Brussels, 1969) p. 56 and M. R. D. Foot and J. M. Langley, *M.I.9* (The Bodley Head, 1979) about Dumais and Labrosse.

Chapter 13
1. Bob Hodges had returned to Tangmere at 0130. McBride was killed at 0353. One view was that he might have taken a green signal on the railway for a green landing signal from the runway caravan. Noguères, Vol 4, p. 280, names one of Hankey's passengers who were killed as Albert Kohan ('Bertal', Head of the Nestlé intelligence network). Barbara Bertram, using code names used in the UK, said that the two killed with Hankey were 'Casenave' and 'Berthaud'.
2. Major John Golding, Intelligence Corps. Robin Hooper wrote the story so far soon after the event, originally with all the names altered. He wrote the rest in 1975.

Chapter 14
1. See Appendix B, Foot, pp. 264, 297 and Noguères, Vol 4, pp. 405-8. Déricourt sent into safety the couple who had sheltered his passengers for over three months in their inn at Tiercé.
2. Jean Overton Fuller told me this. See her *Déricourt the Chequered Spy* (Michael Russell, 1989).
3. Foot, p. 302 and Noguères, Vol 3, p. 360.
4. Foot, pp. 374 and 298.
5. Foot, p. 305 and footnote, but this was later denied by Goetz. (Letter to the author from Jean Overton Fuller, June 1985.)
6. de Dainville, op. cit. p. 204.
7. Hugo Bleicher, *Colonel Henri's Story*, edited by Ian Colvin (William Kimber Ltd, 1954), p. 129.
8. On 29 September, 1974, Jean Overton Fuller wrote to the author about Déricourt: "I would like you still to be able to think of him as a friend: certainly he regarded you as a friend. He had deep relations with the Gestapo, of which he could not possibly tell you, but he was not going behind your back in order to do you down".
9. Clément's story of the childhood of Déricourt was based on research by Jean Overton Fuller. (Her letter of 3 August, 1979.) Another point I discussed with Clément was the flying accident in northern French Indo-China in which Déricourt was reported to have been killed. Referring to Déricourt's mistress, Clément explained that this was *'un accident psychologique'*. Nevertheless, the possibility must be considered that Déricourt constructed the evidence of his death so that he could start a new life under a fresh identity.
10. Jerrard Tickell, *Moon Squadron* (Allan Wingate, 1956), pp. 125-7 and, for a more factual account, Geoffrey Norris, *Pimpernels of the Air* (RAF Flying Review, August 1977, pp. 44-5). This operation was reproduced in the film *Now it can be Told*, for which I drafted the original treatment when I was in SOE in 1944.

11. Foot, p. 240 and Noguères, Vol 4, pp. 32-3.

12. Per Hysing-Dahl, *Wings over Europe*, published in Norwegian and Danish. Extract translated into English for this book by the late Per Hysing-Dahl from page 107 of the Danish edition. Letter to the author from Roger Anthoine, February, 1980.

Chapter 15

1. Now Air Vice-Marshal Sir Alan Boxer, KCVO, CB, DSO, DFC, RAF (ret'd).

2. Many thanks to the late Sir Robin Hooper, KCMG, DSO, DFC, for his detailed notes on which much of this chapter so far is based.

3. Foot, pp. 250 and 369.

4. Hysing-Dahl, op. cit.

5. Fourcade, op. cit. (Chapter 4, note 13), pp. 298-300.

6. Fourcade, op. cit. p. 305, which does not exactly fit the other evidence.

7. Many thanks to Bob Large for these and many other stories during an excellent dinner at his club.

8. Philippe de Vomécourt, *Who Lived to see the Day* (Hutchinson, 1961), pp. 171-3.

9. Cookridge, *Inside SOE* (Arthur Barker, 1966), p. 372. After the war, Jacqueline Nearne played a leading role in the film *Now it can be Told*.

10. Foot, p. 370. The late Maurice Southgate had a letter from his wife saying that she flew to England with J. Nearne and Mr Régis.

11. The late George Turner's letter to the author.

12. Foot, p. 382.

13. Foot, p. 262.

14. Bob Maloubier, *Plonge dans l'Or Noir, Espion!* (Robert Laffont, Paris, 1986), p. 28.

15. Philip Schneidau's 1974 letter and Col Walker M. Mahurin's 1980 letter to the author.

16. W. M. ('Bud') Mahurin, *Honest John* (G. P. Putnams Sons, New York, 1962), pp. 150-1 and G. F. J. Alexander's letter to the author, June 1975.

17. Robert Masson, *Mes Missions au Clair de Lune* (Editions Pensée Moderne, Paris, 1975), pp. 215-16 and Bezy, op. cit. (Chapter 11, note 1) pp. 189-90.

18. de Dainville, op. cit. p. 248.

19. M. R. D. Foot, *Resistance* (Eyre Methuen, 1976), pp. 242-3 and Henri Navarre, *Le Service de Renseignements* (Plon, 1978), pp. 223-6. On 'Enigma' and 'Bertrand', see Appendix I to Volume One of *British Intelligence in the Second World* War by F.H. Hinsley (HMSO, 1979).

20. Fourcade, op. cit. chapter 34.

21. Flg Off Helfer, Flt Lt MacMillan, Flt Lt Reed and Flt Lt Johns.

22. Sir Alan Boxer's letter in 1975.

23. N. H. Attenborrow's letter to the author, October 1979.

Chapter 16

1. Peter Arkell's letter to the author, April 1975.

2. Mr Alexander's letter.

3. Rostron's operation report in the 267 Sqn ORB in the PRO confirms McCairns' story.

4. Foot, *SOE in France*, p. 422.

5. Yvonne Cormeau's letter to the author, July 1979.

6. Flt Lts F. J. J. Champion and G. H. Ash and Flg Off J. Weddell.

7. Wagland's letter to the author, 1975.
8. Foot, p. 89.
9. Foot, pp. 441-2 quotes the supreme commanders more fully.

Illustrations

My grateful acknowledgements are due to all who lent me photographs for reproduction in this book, including, particularly, Lady Fielden, Mrs Scotter, Mrs McCairns, Madame Rivière, Philippe Schneidau, Gérard Livry-Level, Sir Lewis Hodges, Sir Robin Hooper, Robert Large, Peter Arkell and Alex Hamilton.

For this revised edition, my thanks for extra photographs are also due to Hélène Midrie, Roger Lequin, Marius Roche and l'ACALM (Association pour la Commémoration de l'Atterrissage du Lysander à Melay).

The Public Record Office has been most helpful in supplying Crown Copyright photographs from their files: AIR20/8488, 8492 and 8493; AIR27/1068 and AIR28/820.

Photographs at Duxford are by courtesy of the Trustees of the Imperial War Museum.

Photographs of the Cottage Line Book and of George Turner's operational map were specially taken by Anthony Bugbird.

The maps were drawn by Joyce Matthews, and character sketches in the text were drawn as a student by one of the author's daughters, Charlotte Verity, now Mrs Christopher Le Brun.

INDEX

ANTIRRHINUM, operation near Fère-en-Tardenois, 99, 112, 199: near Neuvy-en-Beauce, 199

ANVIL operation: Allied landing on the Riviera, 173

APOLLO, operation at Thalamy, 54, 193

Apt. *See* St-Christol

Arbigny (01), 1.8km NNW of or 3km WNW of, NNW of Pont de Vaux: FAISAN or JUNOT fields, 51, 83, 192, 196, 201, 209, 210: Stele at, 84

Archiduc. See Rayon

Arhex, Jean, 209

Arkell, Flg Off Peter, 176, 177, 181, 185, 208

Arles (13). *See* Chanoines

Armand. See Czerniawski or Dumont-Guillemet

Arnault, Gen., 197

Arnhem, 161

Arras (62). *See* Mont-St.-Éloi, Canettemont

ARROW, operation near Rivarennes, 97, 198, 199

Artenay. *See* Baigneaux

ASCENSION operations (radio telephone intelligence), 151, 153

Ash, Flg Off G.H., 209

Assais (79), 1.5km ESE of, 20km NE of Parthenay, 204

ASTER, operation near Laons (28), 111, 198, 199

Astier de la Vignerie, Baron Emmanuel d' (*Bernard*), 54, 88, 105

Astier de la Vignerie, Gen François d', 54, 193

ATALA, operation near Sermoyer or near le Grand Maleray, 30, 32, 194

Atalas, 204

ATHALIE, operation near Chavannes, 198

ATHLETE, operation near Azay-s-Cher, 98, 198

Atkins, Vera, 94

Attenborrow, Flg Off N.H., 170, 209

Aubin, R., 208

Aubrac, Raymond, Lucie and family, 159, 205

Audrieu, Château d', 79, 80, 81

Auerstadt, Davout d', 207

Aure (08) bombed, 50

Auriol, Vincent, 126, 202

AUTHOR maquis, 115

Auxerre. *See* Éscamps (89)

Avenier, Michel, 205

AVIA air operations service, ALLIANCE network, 51, 163

Ayral, Jean (*Pal*), 197

Azaïs. See Godet

Azay-sur-Cher (37) 1.5km ENE of, ESE of Tours: operation GRIPPE, 92, 98, 196, 198, 205, 206

AZUR Intelligence network, 204

—B—

BACCARAT operations near St. Saëns and St. Léger de Montbrillais, 46, 191, 192

Badaire, Jean-Bernard, 165

Badaire, Philippe, 34

Bader, Douglas, 15, 55, 165

BAGGAGE, operation near Égligny, 170, 207, 208

Baigneaux (28), 3.5km NNE of, N of Orléans, 115, 198, 201

Baissac, Claude and Lise de, 70, 107, 112, 195, 199, 206

Baker, Flg Off, 38

Barbachou family, 105, 210

Bardet, Roger, 127, 157

Bari airfield in Italy, 178, 210

Barillon, 1.5km N of les Lagnys, 48, 192

Barnel, 208

Barr, Flg Off, 209

Barratt, Air Marshal, 34

Barrett, Flg Off D.J., 203, 210

Barthélémy, Gen., 207

Bartrum, Flt Lt Jack, 92

Basin, Francis (*Olive*), 199

Basset, Raymond (*Mary*), 200

Bathgate, Flg Off J.R.G., 111, 112, 113, 114, 117, 121, 130, 131, 133, 144, 151, 185, 200, 201, 202, 203, 204, 218

BATTERING RAM operation near Rivarennes, 113

Baudreville (28), 1.5km W of, Cottainville farm, ESE of Chartres, 114, 123, 162, 200, 202, 205, 206

Baudry, 172, 208

BBC (British Broadcasting Corporation), 6, 22, 32, 77, 89, 92, 102, 110, 127, 138, 146, 170, 215

BCRA (Bureau Central de Renseignements et d'Action), 89, 109, 127, 154, 187, 199, 205

Beamish, Victor, 37

Beaufighter aircraft, 12, 18, 103

Beaufol, Victor, 199

BOUCHE field. *See* Passy-s-Seine (77)
Bouchinet-Serreules, Claude (*Scapin, Sophie, Clovis, Pelerin*), 102, 135, 197, 205
Bougier, Jean, 206
Bouguennec, 40
bouheret, Capt, 195
Boulloche, André (*Segment*), 113, 200
Bourges. *See* Chavannes (18) and Dun-s-Auron (18)
Bourgès-Maunoury, Maurice (*Polygone*), 110, 167, 200, 207, 227
Bourgoyne. See Georges Broussine
Bourguignon, Georges, 112, 199, 203
Bouryschkine, Vladimir (*Val*), 61
Boutoule, Pierre (*Sif B*), 68, 69, 194
Boutron, Cdt Jean (*Taureau*), 52
Boxer, Wg Cdr Alan, 49, 149, 150, 161, 172, 177, 178, 180, 182, 185, 205, 208, 209, 230
Boyer, André (*Brémond*), 81, 117, 194, 201, 202
Bradbury, Flg Off, 120, 122, 124, 201, 202
BRASENOSE, operation near Dhuizel, 200
Brault, Gérard (*Gédéon, Kim W*), 105, 199, 227
Brégy (60), 4km ENE of, N of Meaux, Betz-Bouillancy aerodrome, 198, 199, 200
Bretagne (36), 2km SE of, N of Châteauroux, 198
Brick (or *Adam*). *See* Mitchell
BRICK operations, near Estrées-St-Denis and Saconin, 40, 43, 191
BRICKLAYER circuit, 71
BRIDGE operation near St-Saëns, 192
Bridger, Flt Lt John, 15, 19, 29, 49, 50, 52-54, 56, 57, 63, 71, 76, 90, 92, 185, 192-197, 231
Brimboeuf, M and Mme, 144
Brindisi, 170, 178
Brion (36), 2km SW of or 3km WSW of or 3.5km SSW of, N of Châteauroux, VAUTOUR field, 191, 192, 194
British Air Forces in France (BAFF), 34
Broad, Richard, 181, 209
Broadley, Flt Lt J.A., 83, 107, 109, 129, 151, 196, 198-200
Brohan, Capt, 84, 196
BRONCHITE field. *See* Amboise (37)Brook, Robin, 104
Brooks, Tony, 108, 199
Brooks, Wg Cdr, 84, 196
Brosse, Col, 123, 202

Brossolette, Mme (*Gilberte*), 224, 225, 226
Brossolette, Pierre (*Brumaire*), 89, 90, 116, 117, 122, 144, 145, 192, 194, 196, 201, 204, 224
Brough, Flt Lt J.F.Q., 159, 205
Broussine, Georges, 203
Brown, Anthony Cave, 158
Browne-Bartroli, Albert, 127, 202
Broyer, Aimé (*Mémé*), 202, 228
Bruaux, 207
Bruce, Flt Lt E.A.G.C., 207
Brumaire. See Brossolette
Bruneau, Françoise, 141, 229
Brunschwig, 202
Buchanan, James ('Jock'), 123
Buchenwald, German prison camp, 39, 74, 94, 169, 205, 207
BUCKLER operation near St-Vulbas, 104, 105, 106, 198, 199
Buckmaster, Col Maurice, 39, 71, 92, 94, 96, 107, 108, 115, 131, 154, 155, 157, 165, 167, 188, 225, 228
Buisson, Georges, 196
BULBASKET operation 16km SW of Le Blanc, 209
Bullet (radio telephone agent), 152
Bunker, Flt Lt, 105
Bunny. *See* Rymills
Burdet, Louis (*Circonférence*), 205
Bureau, Marcel, 202, 205
Burma, Lysander Flight in, 181, 185
Button, John, 223

—C—

Cabourg (14), 23, 24, 46, 47, 56, 59, 61, 81, 95, 102, 114, 124, 128, 135, 165, 216
CADEAU operation near Le Tranger, 202
Caen (14), 23, 24, 56, 79, 163
Caffot, André, 200, 201
Caillaux, Michel (*Max*), 199, 202
CALIFORNIE operation near Dun-s-Auron, 200
Callot, Capt, 84, 196
Call-signs, 113
Caluire, Lyons (69), 71
Calvert. See Lyon, Robert
Calvi aerodrome in Corsica, 170, 179, 209
CAMARADERIE operation near St-Valentin (or Lizeray?), 207
Cambas, Lucien (*Trapèze*), 200
Cambridge University, 73, 123
Cammaerts, Emile, 73

—H—

Halifax aircraft, 80, 92, 97, 109, 161
'B' Flight 161 Sqn, 13, 84, 151, 153, 205
138 Sqn, 46, 52, 96, 159, 191
148 Sqn, 170
Déricourt jumps from, 67
losses, 114, 129, 148, 151, 159
Hall, Flg Off, 204, 209
Hamilton, 208, 231
Hampden aircraft, 154
Hankey, Flt Lt Stephen, 96, 111-2, 114, 115,
120, 130, 141, 144, 146-148, 185, 198,
200, 201, 203, 204, 217, 227, 228, 229
Hankey, Mrs Elizabeth, 151
Harckness, 37
Harris, Flg Off, 12
Harrow, Lt, 193
Hartman, Mlle, 206
Hartman, Plt Off, 209
Haslam, Gp Capt E.B., 9
Havoc aircraft, 152
Hazells Hall, Sandy, 15
HEATHER, operation near Baigneaux, 198
Hector. See Southgate, Maurice
HECTOR, operation near Villefranche-s-
Saone, 70, 195, 199
Heddleson, 209
Heflin, Col Clifford J. USAAF, 208, 209
Helfer, Flt Lt, 180-182, 208, 209, 230
HELM, operation near Bletterans, 202
Henderson, 209
Hennebert, Gérard, 202
Henschel aircraft, 183
Hentic, Lt Col Pierre (*Trellu, Maho*), 9, 50,
95, 111, 114, 115, 123, 130, 162, 192,
195, 198, 199, 200, 201, 202, 203, 206,
208, 226
Heraldic badge for No 161 Sqn, 170
Herbinger, 198
Hérisse, Roger (*Dutertre*), 197
Héritier, R., 194, 225
Herriot, Edouard, 70
Herse, 205
Heslop, Richard (*Xavier*), 96, 110, 126, 198,
201, 202, 208, 227
Hessel, Stéphane, 206
High tension cables, flying through, 40, 63,
64, 196
Hitler, plotters, anti-, 98
Hockey, Gp Capt Ron, 37, 52, 224

Hodges, Sir Lewis ('Bob') Wg Cdr, later Air
Chief Marshal, 7-9, 13, 15, 67, 84, 93, 99,
107, 109, 110, 112, 114, 120, 124, 129,
133, 142, 145, 148, 150, 151, 154, 156,
160, 185, 198, 199-205, 217, 219, 223,
227, 228, 231
Hogbin, (*Jésuite*), 207, 209
Holdcroft, Greg, 182
Holdsworth, Flg Off, 76
Holland, Halifax drops to, 129
Hollinghurst, AVM Sir Leslie, 161, 165
Hollingsworth, Gp Capt Alan, 9
Hollis, Flt/Sgt John ('Sam'), 16, 19, 37, 43,
65, 66, 74, 118, 220
HOLLYHOCK, operation near Outarville,
165, 206
Holmes, Flt Lt, 34
Honeybourne, RAF station, 154
Hooper, Flt Lt R.J. later Sir Robin, 8, 21, 96,
111, 115, 120, 121, 130-133, 135, 141,
144-146, 148, 151, 153, 161, 185, 199,
200-205, 218, 227, 229, 231
Hooper, Lady Constance, 111
Horrex, Flt Lt, RCAF, 209
House, R., 200, 203
HOWITZER, operation near Escamps, 198
Hudson aircraft
Affleck bogged down, 158
conversion training, 13, 75-78
description, 75
Pickard bogged, 82, 83
the King's aircraft, 46, 191
Hugo, Capt, 85, 197
Huguen, Roger, 206
Hunt, Flt Lt John, 26, 218
Huntley, Flt Lt, 50, 192
Hures (48), 4-4.5km NNE of, S of Mende on
Causse Méjean, 196
Florac aerodrome, 84, 196
Hurn, RAF station near Bournemouth, 37
Hutchinson, Sir James, 230
Hutton, Wt Off, 209
Hysing-Dahl, Capt Per, 161-165, 169, 171,
185, 205-208, 230

—I—

Ibbott, Flg Off H.B., 167, 180, 207, 209
Icarus. See Lorilleux
Inayat Khan, Noor, 94, 107, 197
INDIGESTION field. *See* Villevêque
INGRES, operation near Brégy, 114, 200
INTERALLIÉ, intelligence network, 188

—L—

—X—

—Y—

—Z—